THE MEMORIES OF A RUSSIAN YESTERYEAR

Volume 1

Compiled & Presented by

TONY ABBOTT

New Angle Publishing

Copyright © Tony Abbott 2023
First Published 2023
email@tonyabbott.co.uk

INDEPENDENT PUBLISHING NETWORK
ISBN 978-1-80517-049-5
Paperback Edition

CONTENTS

CHAP		PAGE
01	PUBLIC DOMAIN BOOKS	3
02	PHOTOGRAPH OF TSAR NICHOLAS II	4
03	INTRODUCTION	5
	I Alexander Mossolov	7
	II Felix Youssoupoff	9
	III Pavel Bykov	17
04	BOOK ONE	19

AT THE COURT OF THE LAST TSAR
BEING THE MEMOIRS OF
By A. A. MOSSOLOV
Head of the Court Chancellery, 1900-1916

05	BOOK TWO	235

RASPUTIN:
HIS MALIGNANT INFLUENCE
AND HIS ASSASSINATION
By PRINCE YOUSSOUPOFF

06	BOOK THREE	387

THE LAST DAYS OF TSAR NICHOLAS
By P. M. BYKOV
Former Chairman of the Ekaterinburg Soviet

07	AFTERWORD	501
08	LIST OF ILLUSTRATIONS	505
09	REFERENCING	507
10	FURTHER READING	508
11	LIST OF NAMES	509
12	INDEX OF NAMES	519
13	OTHER BOOKS BY THIS AUTHOR	524

PUBLIC DOMAIN BOOKS

The problem with memoirs in the public domain is that they often stay hidden from the public, but due to the huge interest in Nicholas II this has not been the case. Many great works have been digitised and are freely available from online archives such as Project Gutenberg and Internet Archive. Some have been reprinted to look the same as the original but where scanning and OCR (Optical Character Recognition) software is used, this method often creates plenty of errors, and often left unchecked by the human eye.

In order to give memoirs a new life there has to be some benefit to the reader aside from simple reprinting for profit and blind reproduction that may carry the same typos and create new ones. Often it's the quality of photographs that is generally considered acceptable – neither result being intended by the original author.

In this volume, the Baskerville typeface used in Mossolov's book has been kept and used throughout. This is done to normalise the three works and present them as one book. Page numbering is accordingly adjusted and photographs have been sharpened for black and white printing; this series is only available in black and white. The original author's style is left intact so that the nuances of overly used ellipses, hyphens and colons are preserved.

Consider the original trim sizes which differ, commonly in the A5 region, where the larger font size is also preferred. In these volumes the trim size is 6.14" x 9.21" which fairly accommodates three smaller memoirs or two larger ones. Font size and line height has been chosen to afford the text adequate spacing while also accommodating far more words per page than the originals. This way, it was possible to present the best reading experience in terms of the sheer amount of material within the cover and offer a tidier collection on the shelf, without losing any of the original splendour, aside that is, from the pleasure of holding and reading a first edition.

Variances in names may be encountered which have been left as originally intended; the reader can easily distinguish, for example, that Yussoupoff from *Nicholas II - Tsar to Saint* is the same person as 'Youssupov' (Mossolov); 'Yussupov' (Bykov); and 'Youssoupoff' given by the man himself – It originates from the Russian Yusup, the equivalent for Joseph - 'Youssoupoff' means son of Joseph.

The reign of Nicholas II - 1894 to 1917

THE TSAR NICHOLAS II

Photograph courtesy from the book:
The Romance of the Romanoffs
By Joseph McCabe
Published in 1917

Cover portrait photographs : public domain
General Alexander Mossolov
Prince Felix Youssoupoff, 1914
Pavel Bykov

INTRODUCTION

The book you have begun is the perfect accompaniment to my work *Nicholas II - Tsar to Saint, the ruler that lost a dynasty*; published on 17 July 2023, that being the 105th year anniversary of the Romanov family murders at Ekaterinburg in the summer of 1918. This book in the series of supporting volumes of memoirs, Volume I, comprises of the works from three male contributors. For Volume 2 there are three female contributors; with subsequent volumes being a mix of various interesting people.

They share a commonality in that they were written some years after the reign of Tsar Nicholas II and are slightly biased depending on their personal experience of the Revolution 1917. They offer first hand insights in to the Romanov story, even though they were written some years after the events happened; as were the gospels of the four main apostles of Jesus, who didn't put down a single word for decades, the New Testament therefore written two generations later. These memoirs were discovered during my research for the main title, during which I came to realise the futility of conveying the sum of their messages in my own work; for who better is there to tell their story other than the protagonists themselves.

So much was absorbed from the memoirs of others that I was able only to use the more relevant quotes within the context of whatever was being discussed in the main title. My tutor, historian John Cannon, once told me that I would always agonise less about what to include than what to leave out. Even so, in the Introduction to the main title I felt the need to alert the reader that they were not simply holding a book of quotes and fillers. Indeed, I lamented with some certainty that they would journey through it without pause to examine the fuller work of the quoted text and would therefore never come to appreciate those wonderful chronicles. I therefore had decided pretty early on, that just as soon as the main title was published, to set about compiling and reviewing those memoirs from my research with a view to presenting the best of them to the

INTRODUCTION

avid reader. I imagined copies of the volumes lain on dusty library shelves, rediscovered decades from now by ardent researchers, what a find they would consider it, all the while searching the shelves in the hope of more.

In the selection of memoirs it was rather like the assertions of a poet, as Oscar Wilde put it, *"I have spent most of the day putting in a comma and the rest of the day taking it out."* To include Mossolov or Benkendorff; to include Youssoupoff or Witte, to include Bykov or Rodzianko - these were the musings of many a rainy afternoon.

It's not necessary to read *Nicholas II - Tsar to Saint* before the supporting volumes, as each book stand on its own merit. It might be more enjoyable though, to read them in the order they have been presented, 1) *Nicholas II - Tsar to Saint*; 2) *The Memoirs of a Russian Yesteryear Volume 1*; 3) *The Memoirs of a Russian Yesteryear Volume 2*; and so forth. Likewise, the books within this volume may share a cover, but read in the given order they first reveal life at the Imperial Court, then describe Rasputin's murder, followed by the account from a Bolshevik confirming for the first time that the murders had indeed taken place at Ekaterinburg and Alapayevsk. There is a sequential order.

— Book 1 by Alexander Mossolov
  At the Court of the Last Tsar

— Book 2 by Prince Felix Youssoupoff
  Rasputin: His malignant influence and his assassination

— Book 3 by Pavel Bykov
  The Last Days of Tsar Nicholas

In times of war, such as World War I and the ensuing Russian Civil War, the memoirs of military leaders, ambassadors and ministers are invaluable first hand sources and there are many that have given testimony to what happened in Russia. These memoirs offer more understanding than the official line of events; they are the social record of human history and as such tremendous value is placed on them, unaltered and in their original form. Revolution is the people standing up to the aristocracy. In this case the peasants, industrial workers and soldiers, against the Imperial Family and the tsarist regime. But did revolution really solve anything for the people

INTRODUCTION

and the country. The aristocracy were forced to flee Russia, but the pattern is usually that the rich get richer in times of war. In 2023, the same social divides exist; in the UK for example, aristocratic families have seen their riches double in the last decade as a result of their investment power, regardless of the state of the economy.

Nicholas II's reign was very different from others as he was not a driving force but instead was led by events brought about by his opponents. The failure to influence the outcome of two wars ten years apart and two revolutions thirteen years apart, overwhelmed the autocratic system and weakened the regime supporting it. In Russian history, the demise of Nicholas II ended the golden age of cultural achievement from Alexander Sergeyevich Pushkin to the Bolshevik Revolution (1820 - 1917). Most Russians had belonged to the Orthodox Church up until 1917, thereafter this fell to about twenty percent of the Russian population during the Soviet era. The change in Russia, socially, up to the abdication, was unparalleled.

I - ALEXANDER MOSSOLOV

This is an extraordinary book from the Head of the Court Chancellery covering the years 1900 to 1916, the majority of the reign of Nicholas II. Mossolov has a splendid knack for placing the reader in the story with the fluidity of his pen and a hidden wit is revealed at times; such as in SECTION III - THEIR MAJESTIES, when we learn that Count Benkendorff, responsible for meals and formalities at the table, was nicknamed 'the cutlet colonel.' And, that Keiser Wilhelm II, possessing a warped humour as well as a fiery temper, would purposefully call Mossolov - 'Molossov'.

The book was translated from Russian to English and a skilled penmanship is evident in the writing style, one can assume the telling of this story and the translation were in capable and competent hands. It was printed in London but geared for the wider English market as evidenced by the Americanisms; the letter 'z' used instead of the anglicised 's', for example.

It is the ideal book to begin this series of memoirs because it starts at the very beginning of Nicholas II's life, the first chapter is titled 'His Father and Mother'. It spans from Nicholas' education and his tutors, to the outbreak of World War I and up until word was received of the ex-Imperial Family's tragic end.

Mossolov paints a fair picture of what it was like from day to day,

INTRODUCTION

working directly for the Tsar; the 'habitués' being the word he uses to describe the general constitution of the Court. He tells how it was constructed around those that held 'offices' with that infrastructure supported by the liquidic wealth of the country.

Early on, he asks the question that has mystified biographers, on page 7 of his book (*p.28 this book,*) "Was he a good man?" By page 18 (*p.36 this book,*) he discusses the 'foolish dreams' from the Tsar's first speech that shocked everyone that heard it. Rasputin is first mentioned on page 40 (*p.55 this book,*). By page 50 (*p.64 this book,*) in the subsection 'THE SPIRITS', we learn of the Tsar's view of Rasputin's rise and the mystics Papus and Philippe are introduced, with their obvious link to the Tsarevich Alexei and his suffering from haemophilia.

Mossolov reveals Empress Alexandra's character in some depth describing her attitudes towards her ladies-in-waiting and the people, as well as the influence she had over the Tsar, perhaps somewhat abusive on occasions, of her husband's emperorship.

An example given on page 81 (*p.90 this book,*) describes the part Alexandra played in the banishment of Nicholas' fourth uncle the Grand Duke Paul Alexandrovitch and the confiscation of his property and wealth. This exposé on her is shared in the works of contemporaries, such as the revolutionary Leon Trotsky who wrote the following in one of his books:

> "On February 24, the tzarina wrote Nicholas at headquarters, in English as always: '*I hope that Duma man Kedrinsky (she meant Kerensky) will be hung for his horrible speeches, it is necessary (war time law) and it will be an example.*' "
> – LEON TROTSKY, The History of the Russian Revolution

In Part II from page 181 (*p.169 this book,*) Mossolov describes how the Imperial Family were supported by the wealthy individuals holding the various 'offices' at the Tsar's Court.

He talks about the Empress's Mistress of the Robes and the court balls and Sovereign State visits and we also learn more of Count Adolf Freederickz, Mossolov's boss, and other notables . . . and about interesting things like the purpose of the *Chevaliers Gardes*, the Russian Heavy Cavalry guard regiment originally founded by Catherine the Great and boasting as a member her lover the renowned statesman and nobleman Prince Grigory Potemkin.

INTRODUCTION

II - FELIX YOUSSOUPOFF

Prince Youssoupoff's friendship with Oswald Rayner was formed during their education at Oxford University. By 1910 Rayner was a solicitor at the British H.M. Treasury, with a connection to one of the richest men in the Russian Empire, who also happened to be married to Princess Irina, the niece of Emperor Nicholas II and daughter of Grand Duchess Xenia Alexandrovna.

By his own account, Youssoupoff names Rayner as his best friend, but fails to implicate him outright in the plot to kill Rasputin. Whether the relationship was a sexual one is by the by although many believe that was the basis for their close friendship. Rayner, the son of a Soho draper grew up in Staffordshire in the West Midlands county, and became part of the British Intelligence clique working for SIS (the predecessor of MI6) in Russia. Much later he worked for The Telegraph (known as The Daily Telegraph in the UK) newspaper in Sweden and Finland.

Youssoupoff implicated four conspirators in the planning of Rasputin's murder and by the time of his libel case decades later had unwittingly implied, in Rayner's appearance at court, the involvement of British Intelligence in the plot. There is no official document linking the murder to SIS, as might be expected from an intelligence service, but Rayner's connection to Youssoupoff would seem to support that theory as Rayner is known to have visited Youssoupoff's home at the Moika Palace in St Petersburg several times leading up to the murder of Rasputin and he was there on the very day of the murder.

Although Youssoupoff denied that Rayner was present at the actual murder, the British Ambassador to the Russian Empire, Sir George Buchanan, was aware of an imminent plot to do away with Rasputin that was looming, which was a highly desirable situation for British Intelligence and the Russian monarchist groups.

The memoirs of the other conspirators describe the murder of Rasputin without mention of the presence of a sixth conspirator. For example, Dr Lazovert and Duma politician Vladimir Mitrofanovich Purishkevich who published his book in Riga (Today the largest city in Latvia,) in 1924. It was Purishkevich's speech in the Duma attacking Alexandra and Rasputin that so impressed Youssoupoff to convince Purishkevich to join in the plot. At this point, Youssoupoff

INTRODUCTION

had that very close connection to Rayner and Purishkevich was on familiar terms with Samuel Hoare, the Head of SIS in Petrograd during 1916-1917, when Rasputin was murdered.

These ties alone would have given a fair bit of encouragement to set a plot in motion to kill Rasputin. Certainly, Nicholas II believed that British Intelligence were implicated in the plotting, which he challenged Buchanan about. Buchanan looked in to the matter, by which can be inferred that he asked Hoare how he should respond. Buchanan reported back to the Tsar that there had not been any such connivance – yet, a historian researcher for a UK Channel 4 programme, Andrew Cook, came across a letter confirming that Buchanan had known of the plot a week before Rasputin's murder. The researcher also uncovered a letter between two SIS operatives shortly after Rasputin's murder; from Stephen Alley to John Scale, which if one assumes they are talking about Rasputin then it takes on a significant meaning:

"Although matters here have not proceeded entirely to plan, our objective has clearly been achieved. A few awkward questions have already been asked about wider involvement. Rayner is attending to loose ends and will, no doubt, brief you." — CAPTAIN STEPHEN ALLEY to CAPTAIN JOHN SCALE, letter

Stephen Alley was second in command in Petrograd for British Intelligence at the time when the royal family were being held captive in Ekaterinburg. Andrew Cook also examined his newly discovered diary which contained a sketch of the Ipatiev House grounds and revealed that after the ex-tsar and his immediate family had been sprung from custody, they were to be rushed to the Royal Navy waiting at Murmansk and removed from Russia. A telegram dated 24 May 1918 from Alley to the War Office in Whitehall, named the six Russian-speaking officers that he wanted to carry out the rescue mission. It doesn't prove that British Intelligence had also been involved with Rasputin's murder, but it does demonstrate SIS's willingness to take active measures in Russian affairs above the diplomatic means open to them. It was because those telegrams to London were more than likely intercepted, that tighter security was put on Ipatiev House and Alley, as well as the other rescue groups, were not then able to proceed with a viable rescue attempt.

INTRODUCTION

Alley was sacked for his inaction and recalled to London. Whether British Intelligence were involved with Rasputin or Rayner acted under his own initiative to conspire with his good friend Youssoupoff, the fact remains that both entities were invariably invested in a role to some degree and the absence of evidence for this may well be because of a cover-up. In addition, Rayner's friend was none other than British Prime Minister David Lloyd George, who undoubtedly knew of the state of affairs and was in a position to draw attention away from Rayner. Through Rayner therefore, Youssoupoff's seat on HMS Marlborough had been assured when he left Russia in 1919.

A foreign Office document held at the National Archives in Kew (FO 371/2994) is a memo sent on the day after Rasputin's murder:

'*1.1.17*
'*An amazing ending to a man whose influence in modern Russian politics has still been enormous even if only half the reports about him have been true.*'

Unfortunately, Rayner disposed of his papers before his death in 1960 and the official explanation of what happened to Rasputin remains with the five conspirators, being mainly the overriding account of Youssoupoff, who managed to change his testament several times without having attracted much suspicion it would appear. Rasputin's murder and the disposal of the body took place over a two day period from when Rasputin arrived at Youssoupoff's home to when his frozen body was recovered from the River Neva. Who killed him and how he was killed has been left to Youssoupoff to enlighten the world, but his account is rather sanitised considering the severe wounds found on Rasputin's body.

Youssoupoff stated "*I realized now who Rasputin was. He was the reincarnation of Satan himself.*" Youssoupoff alone had been entrusted to carry out the actual killing. In his account he heavily relies on poisoned wine and cakes to achieve this but the body did not confirm it. The autopsy took place a few hours after the body was found, performed by one of the professors of the Judicial Department of the Military Medical Academy, Dmitry Kossorotov, at the Chesmenskii Hospice in St Petersburg. The body was found to have been brutally attacked and mutilated; the right eye was

INTRODUCTION

hanging out of its socket, the right ear was hanging off, the genitals were crushed, and the face and body had been repeatedly struck with a hard object. Rasputin had been mercilessly attacked by club and dagger, none of which is described in Youssoupoff's book. The emphasis is on the poisoning and the gun shots to finish him off.

'The truth will out,' the saying goes, but like so much from that period, we have only memoirs left to posterity. In this scenario that's remarkable – who else writes so vividly about a murder they have committed. Discussed in *Nicholas II - Tsar to Saint*, memoirs were a source of much needed income for Russian émigrés, with plenty of competition, and therefore being prone to elaborations and exaggerations to get published. If 10% of Youssoupoff's account is given to elaboration what remains is still plenty enough to understand what likely happened; death whether by poison or torture. Where did the confidence to kill come from, and the enthusiasm after his extraction from Russia to be able to write so candidly and unabashed about it, and without a shred of remorse.

His account has been heavily criticised regarding the poison and the gun shots, not least because they were not supported by the autopsy report. Perhaps it was far too obvious that he'd kept Rayner and British Intelligence out of it, whilst appearing at the same time to be approaching others around him to recruit.

On page 148, Chapter XII (*p.317 this book*), Youssoupoff tells of the *samovar* that he prepared for Rasputin, with "*various cakes and sweetmeats for which Rasputin had a great liking.*" Youssoupoff should have known, considering the number of social gatherings they attended together over several months. Yet, Rasputin's daughter stated that her father absolutely would not consume anything that was sweet, which even Youssoupoff attests to on page 160 (*p.324 this book*), in attributing the following words to Rasputin, "... *don't want 'em; they're too sweet.*"

Cyanide although bitter, with a smell of almonds that about 50% of people can detect, also tastes slightly sweet. In any case, no trace of cyanide was found nor any partly digested cake. So either; the dosage was too low; baking had killed off the active component of the cyanide; Dr Lazovert's conscience compelled him to switch the cyanide with a harmless substance; or the whole story was a fabrication to sell the book or to draw attention away from Rayner and the barbaric truth of what really happened to Rasputin.

INTRODUCTION

RASPUTIN FILM

Princess' Libel Action

Identity With Picture Role

Story of Murder in Court

LONDON, February 27.

The story of Prince Youssoupoff's assassination of the Russian monk, Rasputin, was detailed in the question of Princess Youssoupoff's identity with the film character of Princess Natasha, discussed when Princess Youssoupoff, otherwise Irina Alexandrovna, a niece of the Tsar, resumed her libel action against Metro-Goldwyn-Mayer Pictures.

Sir Patrick Hastings, for Irina, stated that Rasputin, before he was killed, boasted that he was plotting with the ex-Kaiser to induce the Tsar to abdicate after appointing the Tsarina Regent, whereon Rasputin would be supreme ruler of Russia. Sir Patrick Hastings pictured Rasputin as a sinister man of coarse appetites, whose great sway was due to convincing the Tsarina that he could cure or kill the Tsarevitch by giving or withholding certain Tibetan drugs of which he possessed the sole secret.

Prince Youssoupoff, said Sir Patrick, was aware that the police were powerless to intervene, and the Tsar was at the front, so he decided that he and his friends would rid Russia of Rasputin. Prince Youssoupoff lured Rasputin to a cellar in his great Moika Palace, and gave him cakes and wine containing enough poison to kill 20 men. He then shot him, but Rasputin recovered, and the Prince shot him again and threw the body into the river, making no secret of the occurrence. Prince and Princess Youssoupoff were eventually exiled from Russia.

IDENTITY OF CHARACTERS.

Sir Patrick Hastings contended that the character of Prince Chemodieff, who on the films kills Rasputin at Moika Palace, was based on Prince Youssoupoff, with certain alterations for the sake of love interest. Princess Natasha in the film was his cousin and niece of the Tsar, and was undoubtedly intended to portray Irina, whose chastity the film version attacked, depicting her as unfit to be the wife of the man she loved. Rasputin undoubtedly temporarily saved the life of the Tsarevitch, whose condition grew worse as Rasputin's influence waned.

The defendants, when Irina's solicitors asked them not to show the film until the action was decided, replied that it would lose them £40,000 on 1,160 contracts in July.

PRINCESS' EVIDENCE.

Having inspected the film, Irina, who is staying at Windsor with her mother, the Grand Duchess Zenia, gave evidence of her relations with the Tsar's family and her ordeal in the revolution when she and her husband lost everything. She did not doubt that Natasha, who she inferred from the film was outraged by Rasputin, was meant for herself. She sometimes wore a nurse's dress when visiting the hospitals, and so did Natasha. Witness was the only niece of the Tsar alive from 1913 to 1916. She never personally met Rasputin. The object of the present litigation was to clear her character, not to make money. She never authorised a settlement on a monetary basis, and was bringing proceedings in Austria, Germany, France, Italy, and America.

Sir William Jowitt, for the defendants, suggested that the whole manner of Irina's life made it fantastic to suppose that there were any relations between Rasputin and herself.

BRITISH INDUSTRIES

Prince of Wales at the Fair

Prime Minister Gratified

LONDON, February 27.

When the Prince of Wales flew in a private aeroplane from Windsor to the British Industries Fair at Birmingham to-day he encountered snowstorms, heavy clouds, and very bumpy conditions. He made an extensive tour of the Fair, and showed great interest in many of the displays, which principally are devoted at Birmingham to the heavy industries.

Both the London section of the Fair have been visited by Mr. Ramsay MacDonald, Prime Minister, who declared himself much impressed. "The Fair gets better every year," he said. "It cheers me to hear of the great improvement in trade that is being done."

Bones which were according to expert opinion, used as skates about 5,000 years ago, have been found during excavations in Czechoslovakia.

INTRODUCTION

Previous *Page:* The Mercury newspaper, founded in 1854
Thursday, 1 March, 1934 / Tasmania, Australia

Ten fluid ounces of alcohol was present in the stomach giving the only indication of the length of time Rasputin is known to have been alive at the Moika Palace and the level of his inebriation. Assuming all of the alcohol was consumed there, a 70cl bottle of his favourite Madeira wine at 20% ABV, which would contain around 4.70 ounces of alcohol, means that he drank a little over two bottles.

This raises the real question of who would attend a party to be ushered in to a small basement and left alone there with wine and cakes for two hours? Even if Rasputin sank the bottles in less than an hour, one might ask why he wasn't just shot as soon as he'd been lured to the basement. Youssoupoff's explanation is that he was waiting for the poison to work, but at which point Rasputin's horrific injuries were inflicted is quietly skimmed over?

As for the gun shots, Youssoupoff states on page 224 (*p.367 this book*), that there were two bullet wounds found in Rasputin's body, one in the breast and one in the neck, and reiterates this on page 226 (*p.368 this book*), signalling that there was no oversight on his part or by the publisher, "*For two hours the body was submitted to a most minute examination. apart from the two wounds caused by the shots, a number of livid bruises were discovered.*"

The true extent of the 'livid bruises' that Youssoupoff didn't mention was discussed earlier, and neither was the third bullet to the forehead which was the point of contention that Rayner had been present because of the particular gun that was used to fire that fatal shot. The first mention of Rayner is on page 203 (*p.353 this book*), thereby almost disassociating him from the whole baleful affair.

There were three bullet wounds, two were received when Rasputin was standing; one through the chest that hit his stomach and liver, and the other went through his back and hit the right kidney. The third bullet was fired when Rasputin was laying down, at close range within twenty centimetres. Professor Kossorotov revealed that the three shots were fired from different guns, each wound having been caused by a different calibre.

Youssoupoff's Browning pistol was recovered along with Purishkevich's Sauvage semi-automatic pistol. The third bullet was assessed to have come from an .455 Webley, a standard British

INTRODUCTION

armed forces service revolver issued from 1887. The gun was never found so how much weight does the assessment carry and can it really be considered conclusive. It was author Coryne Hall in her book *Rasputin's Killer and his Romanov Princess*, that suggested this revolver was Rayner's weapon of choice and that he carried it on his person at all times, albeit she acknowledged that he wasn't a bona fide assassin. She also revealed that Rayner's chauffeur (who also came from Rayner's home county Staffordshire,) had stated that Rasputin's murderer was an English lawyer, leaving no doubt that he was referring to Oswald Rayner.

A few years later, Rayner was still close enough to Youssoupoff to translate *Rasputin: His Malignant Influence and his Assassination*, from the Russian, which was published in London eleven years after Rasputin's murder. The book starts with some political ranting, perhaps intended to set the scene and he reinforces throughout, the duty he carries to arrange for the dastardly deed to be planned and carried out at the first opportunity.

Still in the Introduction, he describes the relationship between Tsarina Alexandra and Lady-in-waiting Anna Vyrubova, pointing out that she and Rasputin were each working to further their prospects at Court and that their attachment to the Tsarina had undoubtedly been sincere, but by no means disinterested, and that Anna Vyrubova had woven a net of egoistical intrigue around it — "*It must be supposed that Rasputin, relying on Vyrubova as the most convenient tool at his disposal, in his turn encouraged the empress to confide in her.*"

In chapter one, we are introduced to M. and her mother — But who actually were they? Youssoupoff acknowledges the challenges faced by Alexandra from the outset, not having been afforded any time to adjust to Russian ways. He mentions the mysticism that she introduced to the Court and by page 56 (*p.265 this book*), tells of how the Rasputin clique prised Alexandra from the sound counsel of others, Youssoupoff's mother among them.

On page 84 (*p.280 this book*), Youssoupoff confirms that Badmaev, whom he views in the lowest esteem, as being Rasputin's drug dealer for providing, what Youssoupoff terms, *Tibetan herbs*. Later, on page 249 (*p.381 this book*), he expounds on that discussion, "*She* [ALEXANDRA] *had implicit faith in the healing powers of these drugs of Badmaev which, in reality, were*

INTRODUCTION

administered to the Emperor and Tsetsarevich for purposes quite different from those she supposed." On page 142 (*p.313 this book*), Youssoupoff tells of how the opportunity arose to lure Rasputin to Moika Palace under guise to meet his wife Irina.

In the Conclusions, page 244 (*p.379 this book*), Youssoupoff says, "*If Russia had conducted the war to a successful end, she might have become the most powerful State in the world . . .*" One wonders if the many soldiers that died fighting in World War I for the Tsar, would have readily given their lives to fight for Lenin's ideology; notwithstanding that so many of them were at the front without knowing what they were actually fighting for. And he continues, "*But the Russian Empire collapsed when almost on the threshold of victory, and the Russian emperor perished at the hands of base criminals.*"

The obvious rush to print is evident in the indiscriminate use of 'am' (p.360) or 'a.m.' (e.g. p.375) and the number of typos (corrected for this book). This is down to the publisher and also explains why Rayner's translation used the universal English (e.g. letter 'z' in place of 's'), to cater for the international market.

Page 5	-	glace for glance
Page 28	-	disstisfaction for dissatisfaction
Page 38	-	sectariansim for sectarianism
Page 68	-	Tsarkoe for Tsarskoe
Page 125	-	aslyum for asylum
Page 166	-	Tsarksoe for Tsarskoe
Page 197	-	alseep for asleep
Page 240	-	whch for which
Page 247	-	the the (one too many 'the')

Youssoupoff's style has its nuances; hyphenating as many words as he possibly can and in the overuse of ellipses and colons. Still, it is Youssoupoff's mastery at story telling that makes this book a cracking good read that has stood the test of time. The mark of an aristocrat is in there with delightful words and phrases here and there like '*garrulous*' on page 207 (*p.355 this book*) and "*Some sort of paroxysm seized me.*" On page 181 (*p.336 this book*).

INTRODUCTION

III - PAVEL BYKOV

Pavel Bykov was the first Chairman of the Soviet Executive Committee (the Ispolkom) in 1917 (later Head of the REVKOM in 1919 - i.e. the Revolutionary Committee). The introduction is given by Andrew Rothstein who also did the translation from Russian to English (*see p.409 for more about him*). Rothstein was a pro-revolutionary who is blatantly biased against Nicholas and the whole autocratic ideology and contributes little other than his political opinion. Born, raised, and died in London, the son of a political refugee from Russia, he was a journalist and prominent member of the British Communist Party.

Bykov begins his account by setting out the boundary between the bourgeoise (*pronounced bourge·waa·zee*) i.e. the privileged that don't need to work, and the proletariat, i.e. those which have only their labour to make ends meet. His tone takes on a French revolution feel, at least at first. The content does not challenge the authorities but it does discuss the fate of the ex-royal family in some detail, which was the reason this book was banned in Soviet Russia for many decades.

Like Mossolov and Youssoupoff, Bykov was a believer that the country and the Tsar were under the influence of Rasputin, '*the Court Camarilla headed by Rasputin,*' as he called it. He discusses the rise of Rasputin at length and on page 19 (*p.412 this book*), there is mention of the 'dark forces', a reference to the murder of Rasputin, which he calls an 'heroic' step.

By page 24 (*p.419 this book*), the Tsar's abdication and the search for the Act of Abdication as well as the renunciation of the succession by Mikhail Alexandrovich, are discussed in some detail.

In *Nicholas II - Tsar to Saint*, I explain that Fr Alexei Vasiliev's services were stopped because he offered up a blessing for the Tsar, but Bykov, on page 48 (*p.449 this book*), provides more insight, in that for some weeks Vasiliev had also rang the church bells as the imprisoned family left his church and even arranged for a monk to distribute leaflets in the town, promoting the ex-tsar's cause. He also elaborates on Bishop Hermogenes' efforts to fund a rescue attempt.

On page 49 (*p.450 this book*), Lily Dehn (Alexandra's friend), is first mentioned, by her full name of Julia Alexandrovna Den. On page 52 (*p.453 this book*), he explains how orders from Omsk were

INTRODUCTION

largely ignored by Tobolsk and Ekaterinburg because the extent of the situation in Petrograd had not reached them for some weeks. As news arrived, fewer officials remained loyal to the Provisional Government as the districts fell gradually under Soviet control.

Bykov seems well versed on all the surreptitious plans to rescue the royal family and explains on page 58 (*p.460 this book*), how the ex-empress Alexandra, having shunned Hermogenes and others, firmly believed that all attempts other than through Anna Vyrubova, were unnecessary and that their interference was compromising the only viable hope for a rescue. Anna Vyrubova's team were the former Rasputin Circle who were now allied with the Petrograd initiative led by Markov II, and the Moscow group of Russian monarchists, to free the prisoners. Unfortunately, the various groups had plenty of funding but no cohesion to be effective enough to mount an assault on Ipatiev House and elsewhere.

Bykov reveals that funds from monarchists were misappropriated by Father Vasiliev and Lieutenant Soloviev, who were not motivated by a love for their monarch but only for greed. Bykov sarcastically remarks that these were the good Russians on whom the Romanovs pinned all their hopes of escape. In fact, he goes further in naming the enemy within, in the form of Zaslavsky, who Bykov suspected was planning to snatch the prisoners and reveals that Yakovlev had intended to ambush the train with the ex-tsar, at Kulomzino.

Synopsis taken from the original English version front matter of Bykov's book; available for one shilling net:

> *'Here is a first-hand document, by the Chairman of the body responsible, of the actual circumstances of the execution of the Royal Family — the military and political circumstances and the methods of execution.*
>
> *'In the preface A. Rothstein, using the official materials found and published by the Soviet Government, analyses the character of the Tsar and his entourage.'*

Like the other memoirs of this volume, Bykov's book has its editorial nuances, this time with the overuse of double quotation marks. But there are just a few typos, corrected here. It is highly readable and rather short considering the revelations that it contains and its historical importance.

BOOK ONE

General Alexander Alexandrovich Mossolov was Head of the Chancellery during 1900 to 1916, working under the Minister to the Imperial Court, Baron Freedericksz. Mossolov held an important role in the everyday workings of the Court and was a respected figure with the army and within the royal family. His memoirs are exceptionally well written and informative, offering a rare glimpse from the bureaucratic angle and considered to be an invaluable historical resource. He became the Minister Plenipotentiary at Bucharest after 1916.

General Alexander Mossolov with Sir George Truscott, Lord Mayor of London, at the Cowes Regatta, 1909, inspecting Fabergé Imperial gifts of Cufflinks given to Prince Edward by Nicholas II.

Original book published by Methuen & Co. Ltd., London, 1935
Measurements: 14.4 x 22 x 3.5 cm / Pages: 273

THE EMPEROR NICHOLAS II

The uniform is that of the Hussars, the regiment in which the Emperor served in his youth. This unique photograph was taken for the Empress, who ordered the negative to be destroyed, and kept the picture on her table at night

AT THE COURT OF THE LAST TSAR

BEING THE MEMOIRS OF
A. A. MOSSOLOV
Head of the Court Chancellery, 1900-1916

EDITED BY A. A. PILENCO
(*Formerly Professor in the University of Petrograd*)

AND

TRANSLATED BY E. W. DICKES

LONDON
METHUEN & CO. LTD.

This translation first published in 1935
PRINTED IN GREAT BRITAIN

CONTENTS

PART I

| CHAPTER | PAGE |

I. THE EMPEROR NICHOLAS II AND HIS FAMILY .... (3) 23
    I. THE TSAR
    II. THE EMPRESS ALEXANDRA FEODOROVNA
    III. THE CHILDREN

II. THE RELATIVES OF NICHOLAS II .... (65) 77
    I. THE DOWAGER EMPRESS
    II. THE GRAND DUKES

III. EMPEROR NICHOLAS II AND HIS ENTOURAGE .... (101) 107
    I. 'OKRUJENIE':
        A. The Minister of the Court, 'The Old Gentleman'
        B. The Head of the Chancellery
        C. The Tsar's Immediate Suite
    II. 'SREDOSTENIE'

PART II

IV. THE COURT OF NICHOLAS II .... (181) 169
    I. THE COURTIERS
    II. THE GRAND CEREMONIES:
        A. Their Majesties' 'Processions'
        B. Court Balls
        C. The Sovereigns' Visits
    III. EVERYDAY LIFE

EPILOGUE .... (255) 229
GENEALOGICAL TABLES .... (263) /
INDEX .... (267) /

PART I

CHAPTER I

THE EMPEROR NICHOLAS II AND HIS FAMILY

I. THE TSAR

HIS FATHER AND MOTHER

ALEXANDER III, son of Emperor Alexander II and of the Empress Marie Alexandrovna, Princess of Hesse-Darmstadt, was educated at home, as was the custom in his day, and did not attend any school. He had had one idea instilled into him above all others—that of the omnipotence of the Tsars of Russia, and of the consequent necessity of maintaining the prestige of the Imperial authority. On this latter point the tradition inherited from his august father and his grandfather Nicholas I was maintained in its full grandeur and integrity. The doctrine was continually impressed on the future Emperor that the Russian Tsars are the masters whom God has willed to bestow on Holy Russia in her boundless immensity. The Tsar was his country's guardian and a symbol of the national unity; he must stand forth as the last rampart of paternal benevolence and chivalrous justice.

Alexander's mother had taught him to hold in high honour the ideas of marriage and the family. She had, of course, been equally concerned that on its social side her son's education should produce a docile submission to all the rigours of etiquette and ceremonial.

In his personal sympathies he came much nearer to his grandfather, Nicholas I, than to the liberal spirit of his father, Alexander II. He considered that the evolution of the Russian people had to be slow and gradual—that too rapid a development of its political institutions would foster the subconscious tendencies towards anarchy that have always characterized the Slav race. He feared that precipitate reforms would be followed by disorders and would prejudice the true interests of the country. It is well known what masterly expression Prince Troubetzkoy, a sculptor of exceptional talent, who had been charged with the erection in St. Petersburg of the equestrian statue of the great Tsar, gave to these conservative ideas of Alexander III. With an iron hand Nicholas II's father grips the tautened rein of his massive and almost clumsy palfrey. Every time I passed this marvellous statue in the Znamenskaya Square I used to say to myself, old cavalry general that I am:

'Slacken the rein! A horse is not to be mastered by forcing him to mark time!'

The second element in the character of Alexander III on which it is necessary to say a few words was his passion for everything that was characteristically Russian. Emperor William I and certain petty German princes had exercised far too much influence at the Court of Alexander II, and the reaction in the soul of Alexander III was correspondingly violent. He grew to detest everything that was German. He tried to be Russian down to the smallest details of his personal life, and that was why his bearing seemed less aristocratic than that of his brothers: he claimed, perhaps without reasoning it out, that a true Russian should not be too highly polished in his manners, that he should have a touch of something like brutality. He yielded to the exigencies of Court etiquette, but as soon as he came into a more restricted circle of friends he threw off every artificial form: he regarded ceremony as necessary only to German princelings with no other means of sustaining their 'dying' prestige and defending their claim to existence.

Alexander's consort, the Danish princess, mother of Nicholas II, had been brought up in one of the most patriarchal courts in Europe; and she instilled into her son an unquestioning reverence for the principle of the family; she also transmitted to him a great deal of the personal charm which had made her so popular in Russia. All the Princess Dagmar's children were smaller in stature than their uncles and aunts. The majesty of bearing that distinguished the earlier generation did not descend to the last of the Romanovs. That was why Count Freedericksz, the Minister of the Imperial Court, never tired of advising Nicholas II to ride on horseback when he had to appear in public. I remember the Emperor saying once, with a laugh:

'The Count loves caracoling in front of a crowd; I'm sure that is why he insists that I should not go in a carriage.'

Count Adolf Andreas Woldemar Freedericksz, c1900
Finno-Russian General of the Cavalry: -
Life-Guards Horse Regiment and Chevalier Guard Regiment
"*The very personification of court life*" - Maurice Paléologue
"Nothing less than a knight" - Count Sergey Witte

In spite of his short stature the Tsar was an accomplished horseman; his bearing on horseback was very imposing.

Nicholas II

HIS EDUCATION

Two of my friends, General Vassilkovsky, A.D.C., and Mr. Heath, the English teacher of the heir to the throne, have given me some details of the education of the children of Alexander III. According to them, the Emperor's children were not well disciplined. One might fairly say that their manners were much like those of the children of petty provincial nobles. Even when dining with their parents, they did not deny themselves the amusement of throwing pellets of bread at one another, if they knew that they would not be caught. They all had good health and spent a great deal of time at sports, with the exception of George Alexandrovitch, the second son, who had a weak chest and died in the flower of his youth.

Special attention was given to their language studies, and the tutors devoted a great deal of care to correcting their pronunciation of foreign words. For the rest, the children all had an excellent memory, especially for names and faces. His good memory enabled Nicholas Alexandrovitch to gain a wide knowledge of history. At the time when I first met him he was certainly a well-educated man. His parents had taken no particular trouble over the education of his brothers and sisters.

The future Emperor's tutor was named Danilovitch, and had been given the title of General A.D.G. My friend Vassilkovsky never called him by any other name than 'that old dotard of a—Jesuit'. Danilovitch started his career as head of a military school, and it was there that he was endowed with that sobriquet. He was in general charge of the education of Nicholas II, and trained him to adopt an impenetrable reserve, which was an essential trait of his own character. Alexander III was ruthless even with his children, and loathed everything that savoured of 'weakness'. The children and even the Empress herself were often obliged to conceal from him not only mistakes of their own but those of persons in their entourage. Thus a spirit of dissimulation and restraint was engendered in this family; and it did not disappear after the father's death. Many a time have I heard Nicholas Alexandrovitch speak in severe terms of people who had failed to keep their promise not to divulge a secret.

When he became Tsar, Nicholas II made it a fixed rule that he was in no way bound by his position as monarch to do anything that he did not want to do. In this his natural timidity played a part. He hated to have to investigate anything, to complain of anything, to 'stand up' to anybody. Following out his fixed rule, he never worried and never grew heated, even in situations in which an outburst of temper would have been only too natural. If he found anybody seriously in the wrong, he brought the matter to the notice of the offender's immediate superior; he commented on it in the gentlest of terms; and never in any case did he show the slightest sign of disapproval to the actual offender.

The teaching of the 'Jesuit' Danilovitch had borne its fruits.

I can bear witness that the Tsar was not only courteous, but thoughtful and affable towards all around him. His attitude was always the same, whether he was with a Minister or a menial; he treated all men with respect, whatever their age or position or social status.

He could part with the greatest ease even from those who had served him for a very long time. The first word of accusation breathed in his presence against anybody, with or without evidence, was enough for him to dismiss the victim, though the charge might have been a pure fabrication. He did so without the slightest regret, and without attempting to establish the facts; that, in his view, was the business of the victim's superiors or, if necessary, of the courts. Still less would it occur to him to defend anybody, or to examine the motives of the calumniator. He was distrustful, like all weak persons.

Was he a good man?

It is very difficult to penetrate the depths of another's soul, especially when that other is an Emperor of Russia. When he visited the military hospitals during the war he showed a touching concern for the fate of the wounded. In the cemeteries, before the thousands of crosses erected on 'fraternal' (collective) graves, he prayed with a fervour that could not have been feigned.

The Emperor's heart was full of love, but it was a 'collective love', if the phrase may be permitted; so that his feelings were very different from those which plain men sum up in the single word 'love'.

He had a sincere and intense love for the Empress and his children; I shall return to this later.

Did he love his more distant relations? I doubt it. Freedericksz was personally responsible for dealing with all requests, big and little, submitted by members of the Imperial family. The Tsar rarely refused one. Yet the Count told me many times over that the Tsar bestowed honours or money or property without the slightest sign of any satisfaction in the act. It was simply a part of his duties as sovereign. It was a nuisance, and sometimes contrary to the interests of the State; but it 'had to be done'. It was out of the question to offend an uncle or a nephew. Once the grant of the favour had been authorized, it would be some little time, the Tsar hoped, before the beneficiary came back with some fresh importunity.

He had more regard for his two sisters and his brother Michael. He felt a real tenderness towards his nephew Dimitri Pavlovitch, who had grown up under his eyes and whose youth appealed to him. As for the rest, he knew how to show just as much feeling as the proprieties demanded, just as much as was required in the due performance of his duties as Tsar, as much as would stave off any unpleasantness.

INSINCERE OR TIMID?

He has been charged with insincerity. Instances are quoted of Ministers who imagined that they enjoyed his entire confidence being called on, with staggering suddenness, to resign. That is not quite just to him.

These Ministerial dismissals were peculiar events; but whatever the explanation of the Tsar's actions, it must not be sought in any lack of straightforwardness.

In the Tsar's eyes his Ministers were officials like any others in the service of the Empire. He 'loved' his Ministers in exactly the same way as he loved each one of the 150 millions of his subjects. If a Minister came to grief the Tsar regretted it, as every man of feeling would regret another man's misfortune. But Count Freedericksz was the only one who really enjoyed the Tsar's confidence.

If a Minister was in disagreement with the Tsar, if some accusation had been made against him, or if for any reason the Tsar no longer felt confidence in him, Nicholas was still perfectly able to give him a friendly reception, to thank him for his collaboration, and to shake hands warmly with him when he left—and then to send him a letter calling on him to resign.

This was certainly due to the influence of Danilovitch, the 'Jesuit'. The Ministers did not allow for the Tsar's ingrained dislike of an argument.

Almost always the same vicious circle recurred. When he had appointed a new Minister the Tsar would evince for some time the utmost satisfaction with him; he felt entirely happy with the new official. This honeymoon period might last quite a time. But then clouds would begin to appear on the horizon. They would come all the sooner if the Minister was a man of principle, a man with a definite programme. Statesmen like Witte, Stolypin, Samarin, Trepov, felt themselves on fairly solid ground when their programme had received the Tsar's approval; they imagined that their hands were then free in regard to all the details of its execution. The Tsar saw things in a different light. Frequently he would try to impose his personal views in matters of detail, such as the appointment of some subordinate official.

Confronted with this attitude on the part of their sovereign, the Ministers would act as their temperament prompted. Some, like Lamsdorff, Krivosheyin, or Sukhomlinov, temporized or compromised. Others were less compliant; they would try to get their way by some devious method, or would try persuasion. It was thoroughly dangerous for a Minister to turn to either of these expedients, but especially the former, which exasperated the Tsar.

It must never be forgotten that Nicholas II had very little of the combative spirit. He had a great capacity for grasping his interlocutor's thought halfway through its expression, of appreciating every delicate distinction in a report, of giving their true value to details which had deliberately been slurred over. But he made a point of preserving the appearance of acquiescence. He never contested the statements made by his interlocutor. He never adopted a definite and energetic attitude, an attitude which would have enabled him to break the resistance of a Minister, to bend him to his will and so to retain a useful servant in a post in which he had gained experience. The Tsar was incapable of unmasking his batteries, or of provoking his Minister to an energetic rejoinder that might have induced the sovereign to change his mind.

The Tsar's contribution to a talk was never sharp or direct, never argumentative, never hot-tempered, never made in other than even tones. The Minister would take his leave, delighted at having, to all appearance, carried his point. But he would be sadly mistaken. What he had taken for weakness was merely dissimulation. He had forgotten that the Tsar was absolutely without moral courage; that he loathed making a final decision in the presence of the person concerned. Next day the Minister would receive a letter from him—a letter of dismissal.

I repeat: the very idea of discussion was wholly alien to the nature of Nicholas II. We must not forget that he inherited from his father (whom he venerated, and whose example he followed assiduously even in small details of his everyday life) an unshakable faith in the providential nature of his high office. His mission emanated from

God. For his actions he was responsible only to his own conscience and to God. In this view the Empress supported him with intense conviction.

Responsible only to his conscience, his intuition, his instinct—to that incomprehensible thing which in our days is called the subconscious, and of which the notion did not exist in the sixteenth century, when the Tsars of Moscow forged for themselves an absolute power. Responsible to elements that are not reason and at times are contrary to reason. Responsible to imponderables; to the mysticism that steadily increased its hold over him.

The Ministers relied exclusively on considerations that were based on reason. Their arguments were addressed to the understanding. They spoke in terms of figures and statistics, of precedents, of estimates and forecasts based on the principle of the weighing of probabilities; they referred to reports from officials, to the example of other countries, and all that. The Tsar could not have argued with them, and evidently had no desire to. He preferred to write a letter announcing his Minister's 'resignation'. The Minister had ceased to give satisfaction—nobody could say how or why.

For the rest, the Tsar, like so many Russians, believed that no one can run counter to his fate. What is to happen will happen! Everything will come right in the end, for Providence is watching over us.

In other words, the Tsar took his role of God's representative with the utmost seriousness. This was particularly evidenced in the sustained attention which he gave to the consideration of petitions for the reprieve of condemned men. It was this arbitrament over life and death that approximated him most closely to the All-Powerful.

As soon as a reprieve was signed, the Tsar would unfailingly urge me to pass it on with all speed, so that the message should not arrive too late. I remember receiving an appeal for reprieve late one night, during one of the Tsar's journeys.

I had my name sent in for an audience. The Tsar was in his own compartment, and seemed astonished at my, appearance at that late hour.

'I have ventured to disturb your Majesty,' I said, 'as it is a question of a man's life.'

'You did entirely, entirely right. But how can we get Freedericksz's signature?' (Under the law the telegram conveying the Tsar's reply could only be sent out when it had been signed by the Minister of the Court, and the Tsar knew that Freedericksz had gone to bed long before.)

'I will send the message over my signature, and the Count can countersign it in the morning.'

'Excellent. Lose no time.'

Next morning the Tsar returned to the subject.

'Are you sure,' he said, 'that the telegram was sent off at once?'

'Sire, it could not fail to be.'

'Can you guarantee that these telegrams containing my orders get priority?'

'Without exception.'

The Tsar seemed satisfied.

As God's representative on earth, the Tsar conscientiously and systematically set himself standards to which the ordinary mortal could not aspire.

It is a significant detail, not, perhaps, generally known, that this Tsar of all the Russias never had a private secretary. He was so jealous of his prerogatives that he himself sealed the envelopes containing his decisions. He had to be very busy before he would entrust his valet with this relatively trivial task. And the valet had to show the sealed envelopes, so that his master could satisfy himself that the secrecy of his correspondence could not be violated.

The Tsar had no secretary. Official documents, letters not strictly of a private character, were written, of course, by third parties. Taneyev drew up the 'rescripts' to high dignitaries who were to be decorated. The Minister of the Court prepared the official letters addressed to the members of the Imperial family. The drafting of communications for foreign sovereigns would come within the province of the Minister of Foreign Affairs—and so on.

But there were other things that the private secretary to a sovereign could do—prepare reports, file papers, keep an eye on outstanding matters, receive correspondence, all sorts of things. There was enough of this work to occupy two or three confidential secretaries.

But that was the difficulty. It would have been necessary to take a third party into his confidence, and the Tsar hated to confide his ideas to anybody. There was another danger—the secretary might magnify his position, impose his own personality, try to influence his master. To influence one who was not prepared to consult anything but his own conscience. The very thought of it was enough to make Nicholas II tremble!

The Minister of the Court encouraged His Majesty in this outlook, since it would not have been pleasant to him to see an interloper come between the Sovereign and his chief servant.

The Empress had a private secretary, Count Rostovtzev; the Tsar had none!

He wanted to be alone.

Alone with his Conscience.

I recall our return from Compiegne, where we had been present at a memorable review of the French Army. We had been among soldiers, and, needless to say, many hours had been devoted during the long railway journey to the study of a problem in which all were intensely interested—'Is the French Army capable of holding in check the battalions of William II?'

The whole future of Russia's foreign policy depended on the answer at which we arrived. Some of our specialists held that the French troops were less disciplined and less stubborn in resistance than the Teuton phalanxes. Others declared that in the defence of his own soil the French peasant would fight like a lion; events proved that they were right. The disputants grew heated and excited. The Tsar spoke not a single word!

At Livadia, during the holidays that Nicholas II allowed himself from time to time, I had the honour of accompanying him on horseback on several occasions. I was a little inexperienced in those days, and supposed that it was my duty to 'amuse' my master and keep him in conversation. I began with the latest news from the papers, the big political events, the questions of the day. The Tsar replied with evident reluctance, and changed the subject to tennis, horses, the weather, mountains, and so on. Often, instead of giving any reply, he put the spurs to his horse and galloped on, making any discussion impossible.

It did not take me long to understand. The Tsar never talked of serious matters with members of his entourage, even if they belonged to the Imperial family. He disliked expressing an opinion. He was afraid that his opinion might be retailed to other people; in any case, he felt that he had enough important decisions to take already without needlessly adding to them. The Ministers were in attendance at the appointed times to receive his final decisions—that was quite enough.

It was all the easier for him to make this his rule since, whatever the occasion, he unfailingly remained outwardly imperturbable. I remember the arrival of the telegram reporting the total loss of the Russian Fleet at Tsushima. It came when I was with the Emperor on a railway journey. Freedericksz had remained a good half-hour in the Tsar's compartment; the Tsar had been utterly cast down. It was now impossible for us to win the war; the Fleet, the object of such solicitude on the part of the Emperor, was annihilated; thousands of officers whom he had met personally and had learnt to appreciate highly had been killed.

An attendant came to tell us that His Majesty was taking tea in the dining-car. We went in one by one. There was a dismal silence: no one dared to be the first to speak of the terrible news.

The Tsar broke the silence. He talked to us of the army manoeuvres then in progress, of various insignificant events. He went on talking for more than an hour. Not a word did he breathe about Tsushima.

He left us with the impression that he was entirely unconcerned at what had happened. Freedericksz undeceived us, telling us of the consternation that the Tsar had shown an hour and a half before.

'His Majesty wants to see the Minister of War, in his compartment.'

General Sakharov had a long audience. He, too, when he came back from the Imperial coach, told us that the Tsar had shown deep concern.

'His Majesty discussed the situation with me. He showed that he thoroughly realized the problems ahead of us, and he sketched a very sensible plan of action. His composure is admirable.'

Much later I discovered how seriously the disaster of Tsushima had impaired His Majesty's constitution, strong as it was.

'YOUR' PETER THE GREAT

In the whole of my seventeen years of service I only had occasion twice to talk politics with my Imperial master.

The first time was at the bi-centenary of the foundation of St.

Petersburg by Peter the Great, that reforming Titan of our country. The newspapers were full of articles devoted to the victories and the reforms of the creator of modern Russia. One day I was talking enthusiastically of Russia's first Emperor. The Tsar did not seem to want to pursue the subject. I knew how non-committal His Majesty always was in conversation, but ventured to ask him whether he agreed with me.

After a short silence he replied:

'I recognize my ancestor's great merits, but I should be lacking in sincerity if I were to echo your enthusiasm. . . . He is the ancestor who appeals to me least of all. He had too much admiration for European "culture". . . . He stamped out Russian habits, the good customs of his sires, the usages bequeathed by the nation, on too many occasions. . . . It was a period of transition. . . . Perhaps he could not have acted differently. . . . But to go on from that to say that I feel in any way drawn to him—'

As the conversation proceeded I gained the impression that the Tsar blamed Peter the Great for the 'showman' element in all that he did. I seemed to hear my august interlocutor pronounce the word 'adventurer'.

Apparently the Emperor long remembered the sympathetic interest that I had shown in Peter the Great.

One day, in the Crimea, when we were ascending to the plateau of Outchan-Sou, where a wonderful view is to be had of Yalta and its environs, the Emperor told me what a pleasure it was to him to come to the southern shores of the Crimea.

'I should have liked to be able to live here always,' he said.

'Sire, why not transfer the capital here?'

'I must admit,' the Sovereign replied, 'that the idea has often occurred to me.'

The other officers joined in the conversation. Some thought the mountains were too close to the sea, others that there was not room enough for all the public buildings.

'And,' said one, 'where shall the Duma be put?'

'On top of Ay Petri,' someone suggested.

'But Ay Petri is buried in snow in winter, and there would be no possible way of getting up there for the sessions of Parliament.'

'So much the better,' said an aide-de-camp.

Half an hour later, on the way down, the Tsar was at my side on a narrow footpath. Turning to me, he said, with a little smile of resignation:

'No, it is impossible. Besides, once we had set the capital on the flanks of these mountains, I should certainly have ceased to love them. Castles in Spain!'

Then, after a few moments' silence, he burst out laughing.

'As for your Peter the Great! If he had conceived any such plan, he would have carried it out regardless of all the political and financial difficulties. He would never have asked himself whether Russia could benefit from his pet idea!'

That was the last time we touched on the subject of the 'Reformer Tsar'.

His antipathy for that great creator of modern Russia was in keeping, in any case, with the character and mentality of Nicholas II. It will be remembered how, at the very outset of his reign, the young Tsar received a deputation from one of the provinces of Russia, and gave them a rebuff that resounded from end to end of the country. These delegates were sincerely imbued with liberal ideas, and were all sincere constitutionalists. The Tsar made a short speech in reply to their representations. It was as brusque in tone as a command, and ended with this unhappily famous phrase:

'You must give up all these foolish dreams!'

This first public speech of the young Tsar's came as a thunderbolt to the intelligentsia, who had hoped for a moment that Nicholas II would return to the path of liberal reform on which his grandfather Alexander II had entered with such success, and from which his father, Alexander III, had at once turned back.

'IMPOSSIBLE TO BE TOO PRUDENT'

My only other political conversation with Nicholas II had reference to Bulgaria. It was in 1912. The war with Turkey was approaching its end; the Bulgarian army was exhausted after a series of superhuman efforts.

General Radko Dimitriev had sent me a letter asking me to inform the Tsar that the appearance of the Russian Fleet in the neighbourhood of Constantinople would be likely to modify the situation to the advantage of the Bulgarians. I determined to speak to the Tsar on the matter.

After some remarks on the general political situation he replied, in substance:

'I am sorry for Bulgaria. But I cannot sacrifice Russian soldiers to enable her to cover herself with laurels.'

Then, after a moment's thought, he added:

'It would be best for you to send no answer at all to Dimitriev. I do not want to drive him to despair.... I am whole-heartedly on the side of the Bulgarians; I admire their brave little army.... But the slightest intervention on my part might provoke a European war. It is impossible to be too prudent in these questions.'

He took up the reins of his charger, which went on at a quicker trot. We continued on our way in silence. Then the Tsar repeated:

'A pity! There is nothing I can do for your Bulgarians.'

And he changed the subject.

A MODERATE NATIONALIST

Like his father, Nicholas II was keenly interested in all that was characteristically Russian. I recall his words to Mme Plevitskaya, a singer well known and appreciated for her singing of peasant songs. After a concert at Livadia he said to her:

'I thought it would be impossible for anybody to be more Russian than I am. Your singing proved to me that it is not. I thank you with all my heart for that revelation.'

The Tsar had a perfect knowledge of Russian. Our language is exceptionally rich in terms denoting the degrees of family relationship; it has special names for every category of relationship by birth and through marriage, not excepting the most distant, and with particularly subtle shades of distinction. One day the Tsar had a list of the terms used by the peasants brought to him. It was clear to us at once that he was thoroughly acquainted with all of them, however quaint or obsolete. None of us was able to answer the 'posers' that he set us in this improvised examination—to the great joy of the children present.

'The Russian language,' said the Tsar, after abundantly demonstrating our ignorance, 'is of such wealth that it is possible to give Russian equivalents for every expression in any foreign language; no word of non-Slav origin should be allowed to disfigure our speech.'

I remarked to His Majesty that I had made it an invariable rule that reports submitted to the Sovereign should contain no expression of foreign origin.

'I think I have succeeded,' the Tsar replied, 'in getting the other Ministries also to adopt this excellent habit. I underline in red every passage in their reports in which I find expressions of foreign origin. The Foreign Ministry is the only one on which I have been unable to make any impression.'

I ventured to point out to His Majesty a foreign word which has no equivalent in the Russian language:

'What can one say for "on principle"?'

'Really,' said the Tsar, after a few moments' thought, 'I cannot find a Russian equivalent.'

'Sire, there is a word in the Serbian language which expresses the idea. They say s*atchelno*, which means "behind the front"; this may be interpreted as "an idea behind the front"—"subconscious and preconceived".'

'Very interesting. I am going to ask the Academy to set up a special Commission to compile a dictionary of the Russian language, as is being done in France. We have no record providing an indisputable source of reference for Russian phonetics and orthography.'

There was only one field in which the Tsar admitted his nationalism to be qualified; and, in this instance, it is easy to understand it. He was very fond of music, and placed in the same rank two composers of whom only one was Russian—Wagner and Tchaikovsky. (The 'Ring' had been performed in the Imperial Theatres by the express command of the Sovereign, and repeated regularly every year.)

I may add that the nationalism of Nicholas II had not the extreme character of that of his 'monolith' father. Nicholas was far more cultivated than Alexander III, and he also lacked the energy for the outbursts that the latter had sometimes permitted himself.

Nicholas II used to wear a sort of mujik's blouse at home, and looked well in it. He had put one of his regiments, the Fusiliers of the Imperial Household, into similar garb. He had entertained an ambitious idea of abolishing all the modern uniforms of the Court dignitaries and replacing them by copies of costumes of sixteenth-century boyars. An artist had been set to work on the necessary models. But in the end the plan had been abandoned because of the expense it would have entailed. The boyars were clothed in extremely expensive furs, and wore too many diamonds and rubies and pearls.

The time had gone by (or perhaps had not yet come) for a combative nationalism to be able to take root at the Court of Nicholas II.

'WHEN THE TOMBSTONE'

In one environment only did the Tsar condescend to associate on equal terms with others—among soldiers.

After the forced march referred to below, the commanding officer of a regiment asked the favour of permission to enrol His Majesty as one of the soldiers of his first squad. The day the request reached him, the Tsar sent for the military service certificate of a soldier of the lowest rank, and himself filled it up. He entered his name as 'Nicholas Romanov'. In the place for the date of liberation from military service he wrote:

'When the tombstone lies over me.'

How significant his action looks in retrospect, and how true to character!

The famous forced march provides a convincing proof of the extreme conscientiousness and sense of duty which inspired the Tsar as head of the army.

The Minister of War was at work on an important reform, the determination of the type of clothing and equipment to be worn and carried in future by every Russian infantryman. Those who have had army service, or have even had experience of hiking, well know the importance of the smallest object added or taken off when equipment has to be carried for ten hours a day. An ounce in excess of the unavoidable minimum, when carried by each one of millions of men, may be of capital importance.

When considering the modifications proposed by the Ministry, the Tsar certainly hit on the best of all possible ways of deciding with a full knowledge of the facts. He told only the Minister of the Court and the Commander of the Palace of his intention. They had the full equipment, new model, of a soldier in a regiment camping near Livadia brought to the palace. There was no faking, no making to exact measure for the Tsar; he was in the precise position of any recruit who is put into the shirt, pants, and uniform chosen for him, and given his rifle, pouch, and cartridges. The Tsar was careful also to take the regulation supply of bread and water. Thus equipped, he went off alone, covered twenty kilometres out and back on a route chosen at random, and returned to the palace. Forty kilometres—twenty-five miles—is the full length of a forced march; rarely are troops required to do more in a single day.

The Tsar returned at dusk, after eight or nine hours of marching, rest-time included. A thorough examination showed, beyond any possibility of challenge, that there was not a blister or abrasion of any sort on his body. The boots had not hurt his feet. Next day the reform received the Sovereign's approval.

William II wrote a letter congratulating the Tsar on his enterprise. It is interesting to note that the letter had a slightly bitter undertone. Our military attaché reported later that the German Emperor had asked to be supplied with all the cuttings from the Russian newspapers concerning the march. It seems that he showed a good deal of vexation—why had not that brilliant idea occurred to him?

As for the Tsar, he said afterwards, with obvious sincerity, that he greatly regretted having authorized the publication in the newspapers of the story of his forced march. He had made it entirely on account of military considerations, and the publicity given to it was distasteful to him.

'TO GO TO THE FRONT WITH THEM'

The Tsar regarded himself as a soldier—the first professional soldier in his Empire. In this respect he would make no compromise: his duty was to do what every soldier had to do.

Indirectly, and within certain limits, that was the cause of the downfall of the dynasty and of Russia.

The reader will have guessed my meaning. I am brought now to the subject of His Majesty's assumption of the supreme command during the Great War. It is one of the most enigmatical and most tragic pages of the history of the period with which we are concerned.

Nothing is more dangerous for a great country at war than to retire a Generalissimo who is surrounded by people whom he has learnt to know and to judge according to their merits, and to give the command to another Generalissimo. This step is only permissible in the last extremity; as a rule it can only be taken at the cost of an enormous sacrifice. For Russia, the taking over of the supreme command by the Tsar himself was bound to involve not only grave difficulties in the field of strategy but incalculable political consequences. We know now that a great war may cost a throne, even in a country much less ripe for revolution than was Russia.

The loss of his throne, with all the resulting convulsions, was the penalty that a Tsar who had placed himself at the head of his troops and had been beaten must inevitably suffer. I will pass in silence over the difficulties that followed in the administration of an immense country tormented by endless complications and deprived of the immediate presence of its Sovereign. The Stavka (G.H.Q,) was too far from Petrograd; the effective power passed into other hands than the Tsar's. It was a fatal risk to run.

The Tsar had two main reasons, military and political, for his decision. Military considerations certainly played as decisive a part as the political and dynastic considerations, with which I shall deal later.

To explain the considerations arising from the Tsar's feeling of military duty, I must recall my memories of the period of the war with Japan.

Everybody knows how disastrous that war was for Russia. The troops left in successive detachments, and the astronomical distances which separated us from the theatre of operations swallowed them up like an insatiable Moloch; every day there were fresh victims. Kuropatkin, the Generalissimo, said again and again, 'Patience, patience!' But the months went by without the smallest grain of good news to give us fresh courage. Already there was talk of dissensions between the principal military leaders—a very bad sign.

The Tsar was present at the departure of the troops whenever a large detachment was leaving. He made well-phrased speeches (the more entirely improvised they were, the more effective they proved), and distributed icons to each regiment as it left. I used to note how sad and careworn he looked as he came away in silence from these leave-takings.

One day he said in my presence;

'I ought not to be bidding them farewell. It would be better to go to the front with them.'

Few of those who were present had particularly noticed what he said. Later on I realized its full significance.

It was hardly more than a colonial war—a war in China, so remote that it took twenty days' journey by rail to reach the scene of hostilities—and the Tsar thought of going to the front! His duty, as he saw it, was to be in the midst of the fighting, at the point where danger was.

He who would never accept promotion above the rank of Colonel of the Preobrajensky regiment—was fretting at his enforced inaction.

THE SUPREME COMMAND

The Great War.

The Winter Palace transformed once more into a huge factory for dressings and surgical apparatus.

The first successes.

My regiment of Horse Guards routing an enemy division. . . . My son's letters telling me of the splendid deeds of the Cossacks of the Guard, which he had joined. . . .

Then, the annihilation of Samsonov's army. . . . the general retreat . . . the inglorious surrender of some of our fortresses . . . the mass evacuations of the populations of territories abandoned to the enemy . . . the stories of espionage. . . . Public opinion began to show signs of alarm.

People set about hunting for a scapegoat. There was a tendency, especially among the entourage of the Empress, to throw the blame for all the reverses on the Generalissimo, Grand Duke Nicholas Nicolayevitch. It was said that in spite of his forcefulness he was inclined to bow in passive resignation before 'Fate'—that defect of so many Russians who accept defeat in advance at the hands of what has been 'written in the decrees of Providence'. Instances were also being quoted of undue severity towards brave Generals: some had taken their lives in consequence of extravagant censure from the Grand Duke. . . .

The Tsar said nothing. Disturbed but undecided, he let no sign of his secret feelings appear. But for all his reticence he was anxiously watching what was going on around him. Then, one day, he sent for the Minister of the Court and announced his decision: it was his duty to take over the supreme command.

Freedericksz showed the utmost hostility to the idea.

The Tsar discussed it with other persons in his entourage. He found some encouragement, especially in quarters attached to the Empress's Court. He considered that Nicholas Nicolayevitch and General Yanushkevitch had made serious mistakes. General Alexeyev was inclined to look on a battle-field as simply a chess-board; but he was an officer of exceptional intelligence, and if he were made Chief of Staff he might, the Tsar hoped, change the face of things.

The Tsar decided to go to his duty, the duty of active service.

THE SO-CALLED PLOT OF THE GRAND DUKES

From the political point of view the Tsar's decision is much more difficult to explain. What follows is no more than guesses and indications.

Nicholas Nicolayevitch, the Generalissimo, certainly had plenty of 'go'; he had a reputation for firmness and energy. The strong measures that he had taken against the civil populations of the regions that had to be evacuated were quoted in evidence of what he 'could do if he had his hands free'. The Left wing had claimed him for its own: it was constantly said that it was he who had wrung from the Tsar in 1905 the October manifesto, that first swallow of constitutional liberties; it was he who had championed Count Witte, the author of the legislation which had set up the Duma. The Allies were disturbed at the constant friction between the Government and the representatives of the nation, and it was only too natural that they should urge forward the only one of the Grand Dukes who could continue and bring to completion the work of emancipation begun in 1905.

It began to be whispered that the Empress was going to be sent to Livadia, or else to a convent. If the Tsar did not fall in with the plan, he would be deposed by a *coup d' état*. Nicholas Nicolayevitch would be made Victory Dictator, and when he had won the victory he would become Tsar.

At one time there was almost open talk in Petrograd of a coming

Palace revolution. Had Grand Duke Nicholas Nicolayevitch himself been a party to the plot? I do not believe it. I am convinced, indeed, that the plot existed only in the imagination of drawing-room chatterers. The only courts then in Petrograd were those of the Grand Duchess Marie Pavlovna and the Grand Duke Nicholas Michailovitch; and neither alone nor in association could they possibly have taken any decisive action. All the other members of the Imperial family were at the front. After the Tsar took over the supreme command, the Grand Duke Nicholas Nicolayevitch stayed in the mountains of the Caucasus and Armenia. None of those who might have acted as his agents were in Petrograd. Just before his nephew's abdication in 1917 he wrote him the famous letter begging him 'on my knees' to abdicate; but that, I think, is the only false step that can be laid to his charge.

But the State police, the *Okhrana*, were certainly aware of the rumours that were so persistently in circulation in society circles. The Tsar could not have been in ignorance of them. Did any documents come into his hands? I do not know.

In any case the idea of falling back on the *Stavka* (G.H.Q.), where it would be virtually impossible for a *coup d' état* to be carried out, might have been considered for the political reasons that I have just indicated.

But I shall always hold that for Nicholas II as I knew him it was the military considerations that counted. The Empress may have been guided by motives of a more personal character; she is said to have been jealous of the ascendancy that Nicholas Nicolayevitch might gain with the mass of the people if the troops under his high command won a decisive victory.

DISTRUSTFUL

The aloofness which the Tsar made his rule of life was all the more pernicious since he distrusted even the persons in his own suite. The only exception was Count Freedericksz.

The Tsar came to the throne at the age of 26; his character was not then definitely formed, and he had not had the experience needed to enable him to acquire the art of judging people.

His only contact with the outside world up to then had been his stay in three different regiments, for about six months each. One may be sure that life in these regiments was made as pleasant and carefree as possible for the heir to the throne: 'Everything is in order in the regiment under my command'—that sacramental formula in the daily 'report' from every regiment, battalion or squad in the Russian army—will have been the outstanding leitmotiv of the initiation into military duties of Nicholas Alexandrovitch.

He soon realized that the formula was deceptive; and that destroyed his trust in people. He could detect a lie; but he could place no trust in truth. It was his distrustfulness that rendered the task of the Emperor's immediate suite so difficult.

He strove as best he could against 'unprofitable servants' among Ministers and members of his suite. And when he left for the front he took the opportunity to delegate his powers to the Empress: he credited her with a great deal of will power and strength of character.

I admit that his final abdication was the gesture of a tired man. He had lost courage through his own hesitations. And he had assumed that he would be left in peace, that he and his son would be able to 'cultivate their gardens' at Livadia. But his supreme motive was his desire not to have to shed blood in suppressing the revolution.

A FATHER WORTHY OF ALL PRAISE

The paternal love shown by Nicholas II was worthy of all praise. He adored his children and showed special pride in them. I shall never forget how the Tsar brought me for the first time into the presence of the Cesarevitch.

The child was a few months old. The Imperial family were cruising in the Finnish fiords, and the nursery of the Cesarevitch was in a sunny spot on the *Standard's* upper deck. I came past the Tsar just as he was coming away from the nursery.

'I don't think,' he said, 'that you have yet seen my dear little Cesarevitch. Come along and I will show him to you.'

We went in. The baby was being given his daily bath. He was lustily kicking out in the water.

'It's time to take him out. Let's see if he'll be good in front of you. I hope he won't make too much noise!'

Alexis Nicolayevitch was picked up and dried, and did not show so very much resentment. The Tsar took the child out of his bath towels and put his little feet in the hollow of his hand, supporting him with the other arm. There he was, naked, chubby, rosy—a wonderful boy!

The Emperor covered him up again and gave him to me for a moment; after that we came away.

The Tsar went on talking to me of his son's strong constitution.

'Don't you think he's a beauty?'

He added, almost naively:

'His legs are in good proportion with his body. And, best of all, what lovely 'bracelets' he has on his wrists and ankles! He's well nourished.'

Next day the Tsar said to the Empress in my presence:

'Yesterday I had the Cesarevitch on parade before Mossolov.'

I had the impression that Her Majesty was not altogether pleased. Did she think her husband had been too hearty and unreserved for a sovereign?

LOVER OF HIS WIFE

Nicholas II was much more than a loving and devoted husband. He was literally the lover of his life's partner. He was a lover, and could not hide a slight feeling of jealousy of the persons who made up his wife's entourage, of her occupations and the things that belonged to her.

In every union there is one side that loves and another that lets itself be loved. Of the Imperial couple, it was the Emperor who loved with his whole heart; the Empress responded with an affection that showed her happiness in being loved by one whom she cherished and esteemed.

But she herself showed jealousy of everything that deprived her of the company of her husband. She had all the characteristic German conscientiousness, and she understood how manifold were the Tsar's duties. Not only did she never prevent him from working, but she actively encouraged him in his devotion to his duties as head of the State. She readily recognized that Nicholas II needed the long solitary walks that he took in order to be able to ponder over his decisions. But she set rather narrow limits to what she regarded as 'work'.

Any talks with people unconnected with 'the Services', any receptions not absolutely necessary for reasons of State, were, in her eyes, simply and purely a waste of time. She did all she could to reduce to a minimum the occasions when the Tsar undertook such 'duties'. She made no allowance for any exceptional circumstances or any enthusiasm, no matter for what: everything had to be planned out in conformity with the established routine.

Then there were the sacrosanct hours of reading aloud in the evening. I find it difficult to imagine any affair of State of sufficient importance to induce the Empress to forgo a single one of these fireside evenings, tête-à-tête.

Nicholas II loved to read out loud to his family.
He reads to Tatiana when she was sick with typhoid fever in 1913.

The Tsar was a master of the difficult art of reading aloud. He could read in Russian, English (the language in which their Majesties were accustomed to talk and write), French, Danish, and even German (the language with which he was least familiar). The head of his private library, Mr. Stcheglov, was expected to provide the Tsar with about twenty of the best books of the month. At Tsarskoe Selo these works were placed in a room opening out of His Majesty's private apartments. One day when I came into this room the Tsar's valet saw me approach the table on which the collection was laid out. He asked me not to touch the books. 'His Majesty,' he said, 'himself arranges these books in a particular order, and he has forbidden me once for all to disarrange them.'

It was from this collection that the Tsar chose the book of the evening for reading to the Empress. Usually his choice would fall on a Russian novel giving a general picture of one of the social classes in his Empire.

'I can assure you,' he said to me one day, 'that I am afraid to go into that room. I have so little time, and there are so many interesting books! Often half of the books have to go back to Stcheglov without even having had the pages cut.'

He added, almost apologetically:

'Sometimes an historical book or a book of memoirs has waited here for a whole year, I so much wanted to read it. But it has had to go in the end.'

These readings aloud were at all times the favourite leisure occupation of the Imperial couple, who looked forward to the quiet homely intimacy of their evenings.

* * *

II. THE EMPRESS ALEXANDRA FEODOROVNA
'MY PERSONAL BUSINESS'

Alexandra Feodorovna never understood how the affairs of her family could interest the whole country. 'It is my personal business', she would say again and again during the Tsar's illness; 'I wish people would not meddle in my affairs.' She took up the same attitude each time the sick Cesarevitch had a relapse.

That attitude was to have important political consequences.

The Tsar was staying at Livadia when he fell rather seriously ill with typhoid fever. Before typhoid had been definitely diagnosed, Freedericksz asked the Empress, through one of her maids of honour, for an audience. The Empress came down into the garden, and when she learned that the Minister wanted to see the Tsar she categorically refused to let him. He had to explain at length that under the fundamental laws of the Empire the personal intercourse between the Sovereign and the Government could not be interrupted for a moment. If the Tsar was unable to receive his Ministers a regency would have to be set up at once.

The Empress indignantly rejected this last suggestion, but promised that she would let Freedericksz but no one else—see the patient on the following morning. Freedericksz went away thoroughly embarrassed and in doubt what to do. He asked the Court surgeon, Dr. Hirsch, to convey to the Tsar at his next consultation the message that Freedericksz felt it important that he should be admitted every day without exception to the Sovereign's sick-room, even if only for a few moments. In that way the letter of the law could be considered to have been observed.

This was done. The Tsar's view of a regency was sought by an indirect reference to the question—Freedericksz asked whether he would not wish his brother Michael to be asked to come to see him. The Tsar sided with his wife:

'No, no! Mischa will get everything into a mess: he is so easily imposed on.'

In the end it was decided that Freedericksz should have a daily audience, and that all reports sent in by the other Ministers should be submitted to the Tsar through him.

It was not easy, indeed it proved impossible, to carry this out.

The Empress guarded the sick-room like a veritable Cerberus. She did not even admit people for whom the Tsar had sent. As for Freedericksz, most of his visits were reduced to a few minutes behind a screen, out of sight of the Tsar, and with no possibility of speaking a word to him. The consequence was an accumulation of urgent business. It was at this stage that the Empress began to make a practice of giving 'orders' concerning affairs of state. Until then she had only had to do with her maids of honour and the female staff in attendance on the children. Suddenly, at a day's notice, we saw her take the affairs of the State into her hands.

At that time the Empress had three maids of honour. Princess E, Obolenskaya, Princess S. Orbeliani, and Mlle A. Olenina—manifestly an insufficient number. She summoned back from Rome Princess Marie Victorovna Bariatinskaya, a former maid of honour with whom she had broken off all communications for some three years past. This lady, who had a great deal of energy and plenty of common sense, at once established herself as a sort of Chief of Staff to the Empress. She discussed with me and with Ministers the problems that the Empress wanted to settle, and 'prepared' solutions that would be satisfactory to her mistress. We saw at once that Her Majesty's 'orders' were going beyond the petty instructions to be given to 'Cutlet Colonels' (as the junior officers in subordinate posts at the Court, responsible only for matters coming within the very limited range of the affairs of the palace, were nicknamed), and were infringing the provinces of all the Ministers. The consequence was that Freedericksz found himself at times in a very delicate situation, especially as the maids of honour, in passing on the Empress's 'orders' to his subordinates, frequently asked them to 'keep these orders secret—don't tell the Minister of the Court'.

We began to realize the Empress's inadequacy to the task that she had determined to undertake.

THE GERMAN PRINCESS

She was a princess from a petty German principality, and she remained true to type throughout her life. An excellent mother, an economical housewife, 'house-proud', she had never developed the qualities that go to make a true Empress. She had not even succeeded in becoming Russian at heart or in sympathy. Right up to her tragic end she never brought herself to converse in Russian; she used that language, as is well known, only when talking to servants and to the Orthodox clergy. This was all the stranger since her own sister, the Grand Duchess Elizabeth Feodorovna, grew completely, radically 'Russified' in a very short time. Elizabeth filled all who knew her with deep love and admiration. The Empress never attempted to follow her sister's example.

I recall an incident that occurred during one of Their Majesties' visits to the Crimea. The Empress was expecting a baby. On leaving St. Petersburg she had told the Minister of the Court that she did not want to have any receptions on the journey or any watching crowds in the towns they passed through. Freedericksz informed the Minister of the Interior of this.

In spite of all the precautions of the police, as we came to one little station we saw a crowd of people in their Sunday best. At the sight of them the Empress at once had all the blinds of her car drawn.

The provincial governor was on the station platform, and urged that His Majesty should come for a moment to the window; he felt it would be a 'blunder' to make his police send away a crowd that had waited a good part of the night simply in order to catch a fleeting glimpse of their sovereign. The people there, he urged, were all filled with a feeling of veneration for their Emperor, and it was impossible to have them hustled by gendarmes.

Freedericksz went into Their Majesties' compartment and conveyed to them the governor's very reasonable representations. The Tsar made a move towards the window, but the Empress said to him at once that he had no right to encourage even indirectly 'those who were not carrying out his orders.' Freedericksz felt it necessary once more to press the matter. The Tsar gave way, and went to one of the windows. The enthusiasm of the crowd was indescribable. But the Empress would not move her curtain an inch. The children pressed their faces against the slits on either side between curtain and window frame. They too had received a strict injunction not to let themselves be seen.

Tsarina Maria Feodorovna - c1894

Marie Feodorovna, the Dowager Empress, learned, I do not know through what channel, of Freedericksz's happy intervention. Her comment was:

'If she was not there Nicky would be twice as popular. She is a regular German. She thinks the Imperial family should be "above that sort of thing." What does she mean? Above winning the people's affection? There's no need to go in for what I should call vulgar ways of seeking popularity. Nicky himself has all that is required for popular adoration; all he needs to do is to show himself to those who want to see him. How many times I have tried to make it plain to her. She won't understand; perhaps she hasn't it in her to understand. And yet, how often she complains of the public indifference towards her.'

Freedericksz himself told me at length of this conversation, immediately after an audience which Marie Feodorovna had granted him.

THE CARRIAGE PROBLEM

That was not the only occasion on which the narrowness of the Empress's outlook—a narrowness instilled into her in the petty court of Hesse and on the Rhine—was productive of difficulties.

During the visit to Compiègne Alexandra Feodorovna made terrible difficulties over the famous question of carriages.

Etiquette required that the Tsar should ride with President Loubet in the first carriage. The Empress would follow in a second carriage with the Mistress of the Robes, Mme Naryshkin, by her side.

All went well until the Tsar had to go on horseback for the manoeuvres. The existing rules of procedure require that the President of the Republic shall not appear to the troops otherwise than in a carriage. It was thus impossible for him to follow the Tsar's example. He must appear in a carriage—but in what carriage?

'Why, of course,' M. Crozier, *Chef du Protocole*, explained to us, 'in the Empress's carriage, by her side.'

The Empress would not hear of it. The Tsar of all the Russias on horseback, to all appearance 'escorting' the President! It was impossible. The President must ride in a separate carriage from hers, although that would look as if he were in the Tsar's suite.

In the end we found a solution at Compiègne which avoided wounding French susceptibilities. We had to resort to a subterfuge. This message was sent to M. Crozier:

'The Tsar will start in President Loubet's carriage. On arrival at the manoeuvres, he will leave the carriage and mount his horse. Would it be possible at that stage to bring up the second carriage, the Empress's, and to arrange for Mme Naryshkin to get out of the carriage so that the President could take the place left vacant by the Mistress of the Robes?'

'President Loubet,' our Masters of Ceremonies hinted, 'will not think of subjecting an old lady, one of the highest dignitaries of the Court, to such an affront.'

The French, gallant as always, gave way to our arguments, and President Loubet remained in his carriage.

For the ceremonial review the discussions had to begin all over again. Up to the last moment the French insisted that the President must accompany the Empress in her carriage. But she held out, and left in a carriage in which Mme Naryshkin had taken her place beside her. President Loubet had to rest content with a second carriage, in which he was joined by M. Waldeck-Rousseau, the Prime Minister.

Next year, when President Loubet returned the visit of the Russian sovereigns, the same difficulties came up again. There could be no reason why the head of an allied and friendly State should not be found room in the Empress's carriage.

This time the Empress employed another stratagem. The Tsar would go on horseback; the President would be in the Empress's carriage. But the carriage would be transformed into a sort of family charabanc: there would be two seats at the back, for the Empress and the President, and two in front, facing the horses, in which the Dowager Empress and Grand Duchess Elizabeth Feodorovna would ride.

This vehicle was constructed.

But now protests came from Marie Feodorovna. The state coaches had no coachman, being conducted by postilions; consequently the front part, in which the Dowager Empress was to sit, looked like a coachman's seat—a box seat, indeed; for, to add to her disgust, it was raised up.

But the young Empress had the final say. The whole ceremony was carried through in the way she

THE ALMANACH DE GOTHA CENSORED

The Empress had her own peculiar notion of the omnipotence of the Tsars of Russia. I recall the incident of the *Almanack de Gotha*. Her Majesty imagined that in my capacity of head of the Court censorship I was in a position to impose her will on a work of reference published abroad.

One day, on the way back from Tsarskoe Selo, Freedericksz told me that the Empress had been extremely annoyed by a headline in the *Almanach*. She wanted this annual to be forbidden to use the following description in the chapter devoted to Russia:

'DYNASTIE HOLSTEIN-GOTTORP-ROMANOV.'

The *Almanach* must be made to delete the first two names, on pain of being excluded from Russian territory.

I had had plenty of trouble over this already. Regularly every year the editorial office of the *Almanach* sent me proofs of the pages dealing with Russia. Regularly every year I entered the names of the newly appointed dignitaries, and cut out the words 'Holstein-Gottorp'. And regularly every year the editorial staff, with equal care, made every change I had indicated except this last one: they retained the words 'Holstein-Gottorp'. In the end I wrote to them, and received the reply that in their view the name of the dynasty could not be modified, since it depended on the historic fact that the Emperor Paul was the son of the Duke of Holstein-Gottorp.

To ban this annual, so well known throughout the world, would, it seemed to me, be ridiculous, and I begged Freedericksz to submit a report from me to the Tsar, so that he could rescind the Empress's order. Freedericksz preferred to submit my report to the Empress herself. She sent for me at once.

'Are you really unable to get these two words cut out?'

'I have already written,' I replied, 'to the editor, and have been met with a refusal.'

'But suppose I authorized you to say that it is my wish that these two words should be suppressed?'

'We should run the risk of being given quotations from the historic documents which exist to prove that the dynasty should bear the name Holstein-Gottorp-Romanov. They might also send a troublesome article to the Press.'

'Then there is nothing left,' she concluded, 'but to prohibit the entry of the book into Russia.'

'That, Madam, is even more impracticable. There would be a world-wide scandal. The story would go round everywhere that the most legitimist of all books, the aristocratic almanach *par excellence*, had been banned by the Russian censorship! The two words in dispute would at once be discovered, and irreparable harm would be done. As things are, the Russian public has not the least interest in this question of the dynastic title. If the decree banning the *Almanach* goes out, the one subject of conversation in every diplomat's drawing-room will be this particularly delicate problem.'

Finally I suggested that Grand Duchess Victoria Feodorovna, Princess of *Saxe-Coburg-Gotha*, might find a way of making the editor-in-chief of the calendar listen to reason.

The Empress cut the audience short, and never returned to the subject of the two offending words.

ECONOMY

Alexandra Feodorovna was habitually economical down to the smallest details. I recall the incident of the allowance proposed for Mme Vyrubova.

Mme Vyrubova was in an exceptional situation at the Empress's Court. She had not, strictly speaking, any official function, and did not seek any. Every day the Empress sent for her to the Palace; the two spent hours together at music, or talking and working at their embroidery. The Empress openly called her her 'personal friend'. It was Mme Vyrubova who was Rasputin's principal advocate with the Empress, and Alexandra Feodorovna felt that some of the authority which the Staretz[1] exercised over her descended even to the devotee of so extraordinary a man.

Freedericksz knew that the Taneyev family, to which Mme Vyrubova belonged by birth, was none too well off. Her daily visits to the Palace, and the dressing and preparation for the many journeys she made with the Empress, whom she accompanied almost everywhere, could not but be a heavy drain on her private resources.

One day, therefore, Freedericksz suggested to the Empress that a position at Court should be created for Mme Vyrubova, and asked for authority to make her a sufficient allowance to enable her to hold her own among the very rich people who made up the society at Court.

The Empress showed little interest in the idea of creating a new post:

'Am I not entitled to choose my friends where I like?'

In regard to the allowance she made no objection. Freedericksz asked what figure should be fixed. Alexandra Feodorovna replied that the amount was to be 2,000 roubles, equivalent to £200 per annum! Freedericksz pointed out the inadequacy of the allowance, but the Empress held to her decision.

She was economical even in providing for her own children. The Emperor's private office had received instructions to buy three pearls for each of the Tsar's daughters each time she had a birthday, so that they might have fine necklaces when they grew up. Prince Obolensky, the head of the private office, suggested again and again that it would be better to buy four duly assorted necklaces and to give one of them to each of the four children on her birthday; odd pearls would never make satisfactory necklaces and would cost more in the end. But the Empress insisted that the necklaces would cost too much. Obolensky, however, consulted Freedericksz, and with his approval bought the four necklaces.

Still more symptomatic was an incident that occurred at the time of the state visit of King Edward to Reval in 1908.

The number of decorations awarded on this occasion was relatively small. All the important personalities in the Tsar's suite had received presents instead of decorations, presents which the King had made a point of giving personally.

We had to follow the same procedure. Soon after the arrival of the *Victoria and Albert* I had got into touch with Ponsonby (now Lord Ponsonby), who was one of our guest's principal aides-de-camp. We agreed to go together to choose gifts suitable to the situation and the tastes of each of the intended recipients.

Ponsonby showed the most perfect tact; it had been a delicate task, but we felt that we had got through it with credit.

I sought an audience of the Tsar in order to deliver the gifts to him, and suggested that he should hand them personally to the various officials of King Edward's Court. But at this stage the Empress said she wanted to see the gifts we had chosen.

She said at once, to my dismay, that she was going to change the destination of certain cigarette-cases. All my arrangements were in danger of being thrown into confusion.

'Besides,' the Empress said to me, crushingly, 'these presents are all much too expensive. Another time, please let me see them beforehand!'

The only thing I could do was to pull out of my pocket the massive gold cigarette-case which the King of England had just presented to me. It was covered with black enamel, and had the royal monogram in diamonds. This case was of greater value than any of the objects at that moment in the Tsar's hands. The Empress herself had to admit it. I took advantage of her momentary confusion to get the Tsar to proceed to the distribution.

SHE WAS NEVER POPULAR

Alexandra Feodorovna had never succeeded in winning popularity in the country of her adoption. A whole series of unlucky events had completed the work of her morbid timidity in preventing it.

She was only seventeen when she came for the first time to St. Petersburg, to see her elder sister, Grand Duchess Elizabeth Feodorovna. She met the heir to the throne, who was later to become her husband. Nicholas Alexandrovitch was then twenty-one, and the young princess made such an impression on him that people at once began talking of a love match.

Nicholas told his father before the princess left that he wanted to marry her; but Alexander III would not hear of an engagement. He considered that Nicholas was too young to marry. As for the Empress Marie Feodorovna, she showed a strong dislike of the idea of 'a German girl'. Bismarck's annexation of Schleswig-Holstein in 1864 had, of course, brought a deep estrangement between Copenhagen and Berlin.

In a Court everybody knows everybody else's business. 'Society' in St. Petersburg was impregnated with the nationalist ideas of which the Tsar himself was full; and the occasion was seized for an exhibition of the Teutophobia so fashionable at the time. The princess from Hesse was treated with undisguised contempt; industriously mocked at behind her back, and made the subject of stories busily invented and as busily passed round.

Alix Victoria Helen Louise Beatrice of Hesse-Darmstadt was old enough already to realize what was going on on all sides, and strongly resented it.

Her marriage in 1894 took place in painful and tragic circumstances, which made an unfortunate impression on the mass of the Russian people. Alexander III had fallen seriously ill. Grand Duke Michael Nicolayevitch, the oldest member of the Imperial family, had gone to see the Tsar and had broken to him the news of the dangerous nature of his malady (acute nephritis), and of the urgent need, in consequence, for Nicholas Alexandrovitch to take a wife as soon as possible. The Tsar gave his consent. The Grand Duke learned from the Cesarevitch that he would never marry any other princess than the one he had loved since 1889. The necessary formalities took a good deal of time, and it was not until four weeks after his father's death that Nicholas II went through the religious ceremony of his marriage.

Shoulders were shrugged all over Russia.

Next spring, in Moscow, at the popular merrymaking organized on May 18th in honour of the coronation, there was a disaster which gave everybody in Russia, where everybody was superstitious, occasion for predicting that Alexandra Feodorovna would be dogged by misfortune.

There were to be great celebrations in the open air at Hodynka, near Moscow. The news that everybody was to receive a gift with the monogram of the young Imperial couple spread like wildfire. The police forces were insufficient to control the crowd; the barriers were broken down by the thousands of men, women, and children who had settled on the field of Hodynka since the evening before. Hundreds were trampled to death, and many unfortunates were pinned and suffocated, unable to escape from the pressure of the human torrent around them.

'Ill omen!' 'She is bringing us bad luck!' Such was the impression produced by Princess Alix of Hesse on the Russian masses.

As Empress, Alexandra Feodorovna failed equally to gain the allegiance of Court circles and of St. Petersburg society.

The crowd clamouring towards the gift tents at Hodynka Field, 1896

She was excessively timid; and she had no liking for society talk and no aptitude for that delicate art. She thus earned a reputation for hauteur.

Grand Duchess Marie Pavlovna, aunt of Nicholas II, set out to 'nurse' her, to guide her through the social labyrinth of petty rivalries and jealousies; she met with repeated rebuffs, the more violent since the Empress sought to conceal her timidity beneath a surface show of assurance and energy and strength of will. The Empress found herself faced in consequence with the hostility not only of the Court of the Empress Dowager, which was gradually outshone as the Court of the young Empress grew in importance, but of the still more important Court, from the social point of view, of the Grand Duchess Marie Pavlovna.

Aged and very respectable ladies ventured into the presence of Alexandra Feodorovna, full of good intentions, and ventured to offer a little sensible advice: they received sharp and stinging answers. They went away mumbling words that they had not dared to speak aloud; one is always full of bright ideas of what one might have said. What the old ladies did say subsequently, in the bitterness of their outraged dignity and *amour-propre*, drifted back in due course to the Court, garbled, taken out of its context, and deliberately accentuated in its malice. There followed open breaches; Alexandra Feodorovna found herself almost without a friend; and thereafter the personal humiliations suffered by the Empress were hailed as so many triumphs for 'society'.

'AS FOR MY HOSPITALS'

A characteristic incident remains vivid in my memory. The war was going on and on, more and more murderously. The Tsar had invited Freedericksz, who was very ill, to go for a rest to the Crimea. I went with him, for there were fears that his state might become critical. Almost immediately after we reached the Crimea we received a telegram saying that the Grand Duchess Marie Pavlovna* was coming on a visit. The question arose how to arrange for the Tsar's aunt during her stay.

There could be no question of putting her up in the Palace; Freedericksz knew that the idea would be thoroughly disagreeable to the Empress. Apart from that, the Palace was undergoing its annual renovation. We decided that it would be possible to fit up for the use of the Grand Duchess a set of rooms in the house occupied by the Imperial suite. We telegraphed to the Marshal of the Court, Count Benckendorff, to send us cooks, servants, and utensils. He replied that there was not time to do what we wanted.

Freedericksz showed utter astonishment at this cool reply; Count Benckendorff had always been equal to any task imposed on him. I realized at once that the telegram had been sent off with the Empress's knowledge, perhaps by her direct order.

I increased the number of workmen at the Palace, to make it more plainly uninhabitable; I had bits of scaffolding put up everywhere. Freedericksz lent me his own chef; we borrowed a sufficiency of silver from my sister-in-law, Countess Nirod; the necessary motorcars were lent by the Transport Department. I had the quarters of the Imperial suite decorated with flower-boxes. When the Grand Duchess arrived she expressed her delight with the arrangements made for her.

Next day we visited the hospitals at Yalta and within the precincts of Livadia, a domain which the Tsar had presented to his wife; then we went on to Gourzouf, a spot visited by all who came to the Crimea.

*Grandmother of the Duchess of Kent

As we got into the cars the Grand Duchess, to my astonishment, asked her maid of honour. Mlle Oliv, to go in the second car, and made a sign to me to sit by her side, a thing quite against the rules of Court etiquette.

We had scarcely passed through the gates of Livadia when she took a telegram out of her bag and passed it to me with a hand that trembled. The telegram was in English:

'Am astonished that you should be at Livadia without having asked the lady of the house. As for my hospitals, I know that they are in good order.

Alexandra.'

'What impertinence!' she said to me, flushed with anger. 'Anyhow, here is the answer I am sending.'

I read an endless message. Heavens! there was no mincing of words in it.

'I hope your Highness has not yet sent off this telegram?'

'No,' she answered, 'I wanted to see what you think.'

We discussed the draft, word by word, throughout the journey. I heaved a great sigh of relief when at last the Grand Duchess said to me:

'You are right—I will leave it unanswered. It would be beneath my dignity, at my age, to take any notice of a piece of tactlessness on the part of a woman, and a princess at that, who had to come to me to learn how to behave in society—'

And so on, until the moment of our arrival at Gourzouf.

THE ENPRESS'S FRIENDS

Apart from the problem of Rasputin, little happened to disturb the Empress's peace. She was completely satisfied with her family life. It would have been impossible for her to find food for jealousy; her husband devoted every free moment to her.

Any time when the Tsar was not there was taken up with the care of her children—to whom she was the tenderest of mothers—or spent in conversation with her maids of honour. There was deep affection between the Empress and Princess Orbeliani, an intelligent, graceful, elegant woman with a caustic wit.

But the time came when Princess Orbeliani was struck down by the malady which brought her, after terrible sufferings, to her grave.

One day at Spala, while we were waiting for Their Majesties to come to dinner, she fell to the ground for no apparent reason. Hirsch, the Court surgeon, told me that that was a very serious sign, the first symptom of creeping paralysis, which was hereditary in her mother's family.

The Princess was aware of the fate that awaited her; she faced it with great courage. One day, when talking to me, she pointed to four sorts of crutches standing in one of the corners of her room.

'So many years for this simple one,' she said, 'so many months for the next, more complicated one, and so on. My mother passed through it all, and I know exactly what I have to expect.'

The progress of the malady was very rapid. That did not prevent the Princess from accompanying Her Majesty wherever she went—on train journeys, to Livadia, to Spala, on board the yacht. The Empress went to see her every day, and told her the latest news. Her Majesty had to conceal from the Princess any new friendship that she formed. If ever the Princess suspected that the Empress had been unmindful of their long intimacy she made terrible scenes in her jealousy, with never-ending tears and reproaches. She lay helpless for eight years on her bed of suffering before death released her.

As the Princess's condition grew worse it became easier for the Empress to enjoy the society of her friend Madame Vyrubova. This admirer of Rasputin had discovered another sensitive chord in the enigmatic heart of the Empress through posing as a 'poor little orphan adrift in the world' and in need of petting and care. Vyrubova's tactics lay in alternating scenes of jealousy with despairing appeals for protection to one whom she looked upon as a second mother or as her big sister. The part was congenial to the Empress, who was always ready to act as guide and counsellor, if only to one of the ladies of her Court.

There remain to be mentioned the maids of honour less intimately associated with the Empress (Princess Obolenskaya, Mlle Olenina, Countess Hendrikov), the principal Lady in Waiting to the Empress, Madame Géringer, and Fraulein Schneider, whose official title was Reader to the Court; unofficially she was in charge of the children. That exhausts the list of those who gravitated around the Empress.

I do not know of a single case of an invitation being sent by the

Empress to any person outside the restricted circle of the Court and her immediate entourage. Even the Grand Duchesses only made rare visits to her, either on various anniversaries which had become regular occasions for celebration, or on actual invitation to tea or lunch. No artist, no writer, no man of learning, even of world renown, was ever admitted to the Tsarina's intimate circle. She felt that the fewer people she saw, the better!

When her husband went to G.H.Q. and she took upon herself the direction of affairs of state, the Empress proceeded by trial and error on her own initiative; instead of following steadily and intelligently along the lines indicated by her husband, she tried to co-ordinate her own ideas with those of 'our friend' (Rasputin), and made it impossible for those Ministers who took their office seriously to get anything done.

THE SPIRITS

There was a short period of close friendship with the two Montenegrin princesses, Militza and Anastasia (Stana). Sometimes the Empress would go to Dulber (the domain of Grand Duke Peter Nicolayevitch, the husband of Princess Militza), and pass long hours there; sometimes the Montenegrin ladies would come and shut themselves up with the Empress in her apartments in Livadia. This friendship, suddenly formed and abruptly broken off, was always an enigma to me. Their bringing-up had given the two Montenegrin ladies nothing in common with the descendant of a long line of German and British sovereigns. The two princesses were exceedingly dark, almost black, and were in striking contrast to one who admitted only one superior—the foremost lady of her epoch, Queen Victoria.

It has always been said that the friendship was based on the common interest of all three in spiritualism. Both at Dulber and at Strelna, the Grand Duke's winter residence, near St. Petersburg, there were table turnings and consultations of spirits; dead Tsars answered the call of the mediums. The Emperor himself was said to have taken part in the seances, which were carried on by two foreign occultists named Papus and Philippe. This seems to have been the first manifestation of this tendency to a morbid mysticism, which later on enabled Rasputin to gain a footing at Court.

Papus was soon expelled, on an order from the Tsar himself. Philippe lasted longer, but he too was got rid of in the end. A Paris detective, M. Ratchkovsky, was instructed to undertake an elaborate investigation of Philippe's antecedents; his report was so enlightening that Philippe was told to clear out. Immediately after Philippe's disappearance from the scene Ratchkovsky himself was relieved of his post—why? Nobody knows.

In any case, in this first crisis of occultism the Tsar had the energy to intervene effectually. What a pity that he did not do the same with regard to the man who took up on his own account the 'occult' methods of Papus, and forged for himself an unparalleled influence, seasoning the Papus dish with a sauce made up of elements of the *mujik*, the mystic, the sectary, and probably the blasphemer.

GÉRARD ENCAUSSE née PAPUS — French Physician *and* PHILIPPE NAZIER — French Spiritualist & Healer

I will add only a few words concerning the people whom I found Rasputin had attracted to his side when I came back from Jassy for a short stay at Petrograd in 1917. It would be too painful to dwell on what I witnessed at the time. I was concerned to discover who these persons were, in order to establish the influences that had inspired the latest appointments. 'Which of the ladies has influence with the Empress?' I asked.

Some said 'Munia' Golovina, niece of Princess Paley. Others indicated Princess Guedroytz, the head physician of Her Majesty's hospital, an entirely masculine woman. Others said to me in a tone of surprise:

'Why, don't you know Mlle So-and-so, the head sister? She dictates to the Empress who is to have every important post.'

I asked a friend who lived at Tsarskoe Selo. He knew all these people, without being 'one of them'. He told me that these ladies were sisters of charity, of good family, and were trying to make a show of possessing great influence but probably had less than they imagined.

It was an utter nightmare. I only felt safe once more when I took train again to Jassy.

HER PIETY

Alexandra Feodorovna was deeply and sincerely devout. She gained in her early youth a knowledge and love of the Orthodox service, with its wealth of symbolic ceremonial. As soon as she became engaged to our heir-apparent she was prepared for conversion to the faith of her adoption.

Sincere in all that she did, she protested vehemently against that part of the ritual of conversion to the Orthodox religion in which the neophyte had to make a theatrical renunciation of the errors of her past religion. The ritual included the act, instituted in the Middle Ages, of 'spitting thrice on the ground' in evidence of contempt for the religion formerly professed. Our clergy were asked to suppress this painful ceremony in the case of the young German princess.

On many occasions I was able to watch the Empress during the long services of the Orthodox Church, in which the congregation stands from beginning to end. She stood erect and motionless—'like a taper', as a peasant who had seen her said. Her face was completely transfigured, and it was plain that for her the prayers were no mere formality.

Father Alexander, who became her confessor and personal chaplain, read aloud a series of prayers which, under the Orthodox rubric, priests are required to read *sotto voce* before the altar. Her Majesty was fond of the service as Father Alexander conducted it, and never grew weary.

Later, when she had become weak through illness, she had a private chapel installed, from which the whole of the service in the church at Livadia could be heard. It was only with reluctance that in the end she had a small sofa placed in the chapel, so that she could lie down if she grew too tired.

At Tsarskoe Selo the Empress preferred the sombre transept of the Feodor Cathedral, which had been built in accordance with her personal indications.

Rasputin's 'preaching' fell on a soil long prepared and eager to assimilate every mystical revelation.

The Empress's activities fell into two very different categories. When she was concerned with affairs of state she submitted herself to an occult and disastrous influence, and dissipated her energies in sterile efforts.

But when she was occupied with matters within her competence she showed herself a very efficient organizer. She showed her capacity in the installation of hospital trains, convalescent homes, and hospitals. In such matters she knew how to gather round her persons of ability and energy.

It is right that her success in that field should be acknowledged. Fate dealt hardly with this woman.

The story of the heroic courage shown by the Empress in captivity is beyond the scope of this work.

Empress Alexandra Feodorovna

III. THE CHILDREN
THE CESAREVITCH: HIS PRECARIOUS HEALTH

The children were objects of Their Majesties' special solicitude. My duties left me little time for observation of the heir to the throne and the Grand Duchesses. They grew up almost without my noticing it. The maids of honour were not authorized to take any part in their education. (Princess Orbehani and the Mistress of the Robes were exceptions to this rule.) Thus few intimate details about the children's life could become generally known.

At first the Cesarevitch was a bright and lively boy. His terrible malady (haemophilia) only showed itself later. I well remember the way he used to put in his appearance at table, when dessert was being served, as a baby of three or four years. He would go to his parents and chatter a little to them, and then make the round of the guests, talking to them without the least sign of timidity. He used to slip under the table and catch hold of the ladies' shoes; if they started he would be greatly amused. Once he pulled off the slipper of one of the maids of honour and carried it away as a trophy to his father, who told him to put it back. He plunged under the table. Suddenly the maid of honour screamed. Before putting the slipper on her foot the Cesarevitch had put into it an enormous strawberry. The cold wet mush made the young lady jump out of her chair.

The child was scolded and sent back to his room, and for a considerable time he was forbidden to appear at the dinner-table, much to his grief.

Even after the first signs of his malady showed themselves, the Cesarevitch kept his high spirits; but if one watched him closely one could see his face cloud over; sometimes it would lose all its brightness and become sickly and lifeless.

Repeated efforts were made to find a boy of his own age who could be a playmate for the Cesarevitch. At first sailors' sons were tried; then the children and nephews of Derevenko, the Cesarevitch's attendant (*diadka* in Russian—'little uncle'—that is to say, guardian and confidant and nurse for the boy). In the end the attempt was abandoned.

M. Gilliard, the Cesarevitch's tutor, an incomparable teacher and a man of the highest intelligence, often told me that the boy's education presented enormous difficulties. Scarcely had a course of study begun when the Cesarevitch would fall ill; the effusions of blood brought him terrible suffering; he spent whole nights groaning and begging for help that no one could give him. His malady exhausted him and set his nerves on edge; and in that state the little sufferer came back to his lessons, with everything to begin afresh.

Could this poor little unfortunate be blamed if he proved wanting in diligence and concentration?

THE TOBOGGANS OF SOLID SILVER

Two incidents that I recall show how simple and rudimentary were the amusements of the Grand Duchesses as young children, how easily they were pleased. The first occurred while the Imperial train had stopped in the neighbourhood of Roshkovo, in Moscow county. The Tsar was inspecting the troops of the region, and his train stopped in the open country for five days.

THE FOUR GRAND DUCHESSES
On an expedition to gather mushrooms

THE CESAREVITCH AT THE AGE OF SEVEN
On one of the lakes in Tsarskoe Selo

There were long hours with nothing to do, and one day Grand Duchess Olga, the Tsar's sister, invented a new sort of sport for her nieces. The train was standing at the top of a high embankment, and advantage was taken of the slope to enable them to toboggan—in the middle of August! It would have been difficult to find sledges, but that was not allowed to stand in the way of the sport. Silver salvers were fetched from the pantry. Each of the children had her own salver; they slid down and then climbed up again with the salvers on their backs.

The children were so delighted that it was decided to go on with the tobogganing after dinner, in the presence of Their Majesties. One of the military attachés asked me, with some apprehension, whether the guests would have to engage in the new sport. I hastened to reassure him.

One of the maids of honour set off first, to act as judge at the finishing point. General Strukov, A.D.C., announced to the children that he was going to be the first to get to the bottom. When the signal was given to start he made one jump in his gala uniform, with the ribbon of Alexander Nevsky over his shoulder, his diamond-studded sword of honour (he had taken Adrianople in the 1877 campaign) in his hand; he precipitated himself down the twenty feet of the embankment, and sank up to his knees in the slipping sand. How did he manage to come unscathed out of that risky adventure?

THE LIVE SABLE

The second incident is that of the live sable which was brought straight from the depths of Siberia.

One day I had an urgent report for the Tsar to draw up, and had given orders that I would not see any one. Suddenly my senior and confidential messenger came into my office.

'What is it? Is there any need for me to be disturbed?'

'I venture to mention to Your Excellency that an old peasant and his wife have just arrived straight from Siberia. They have brought a live sable as a present for His Majesty. The man insisted that I should announce him to Your Excellency. He says he has not the means to pay for a night's lodging.'

'And you took pity on him?'

'I cannot deny it.'

'Bring him in.'

A very attractive old man came in, a woman accompanying him. He said: 'I am a hunter. One day I caught a sable alive. I have succeeded in taming it, with my wife's help. We decided to make a present of it to the Little Father Tsar. It is a wonderful sable. We got together all the money we had, and here we are.'

He produced his sable, and it jumped at once on to my desk and began sniffing at the dockets of papers concerning Court appointments. The old man gave a peculiar whistle, and the sable jumped into his arms and took refuge behind the lapel of his caftan (a sort of long frock-coat), leaving only the tip of its snout visible.

'How did you get to St. Petersburg?'

'The money we had lasted us as far as Moscow. We were just getting ready to do the rest of the journey on foot when a gentleman—may the Lord preserve him!—gave us the money for a fresh ticket. We arrived this morning and set off at once for the

Winter Palace. The officer on guard sent us on to you. We haven't a kopek left: but we *should* like to see the Little Father Tsar!'

I decided that a live sable would delight the Grand Duchesses; they were quite children then, I gave the old man a little money and left him in charge of my messenger.

I took care, of course, to find out from the old man whom he could name in Siberia that had knowledge of him, 'Before leaving,' he said, 'I went to see the governor of the province; he told me he couldn't prevent me from going, but that I had no chance at all of being received by the Tsar. He also refused to give me a letter or write anything for me.'

I had a telegram sent to the governor, to make sure that the old man was not a revolutionary. Next day I had an entirely reassuring reply. I telephoned to Princess Orbehani and told her about the sable. An hour later a message came from the Princess telling me to send the old man and woman and their sable to the palace—'as quickly as possible, for the children are wild with impatience'.

I sent the messenger with the couple, telling him to bring them back as soon as the audience was over. It was a very long one. The two old people remained over an hour with the children, in the presence of the Empress herself.

'We meant to bring the sable back with us,' the old man told me, 'and to take it back when a proper cage had been got ready for it. But the children would not part from it. Finally the Tsarina gave the order for the animal to be left with them. I said I absolutely must see the Tsar; I could not go back to Siberia without seeing the Tsar, They told me they would let me know.'

He added, thoughtfully:

'What I'm afraid of is that my sable may make too much of an upset in the Palace. It is not used to apartments like that.'

Next day I received instructions to send the two peasants to the Palace at 6 p.m. They came back about eight; the sable was once more under the lapel of the old man's caftan.

'It's as I said,' he told me, 'The sable couldn't behave properly. And as soon as I got there it made one leap to me.'

'Little Father Tsar,' he went on, dwelling on the words, 'Little Father Tsar came in. We threw ourselves at his feet. The sable looked at him as if it understood that it was the Tsar himself. We went into the children's room. The Tsar told me to let the sable go, and the children began to play with it; when I'm there, you see, it doesn't get wild. Then the Tsar told us to sit down on chairs. He began to ask me questions—what made me think of coming to see him and how I managed to get to the Empress.'

The peasant continued, with more and more animation:

'He asked me what things are like in Siberia, how we go hunting. . . . Then the Tsarina said it was time for dinner. Little Father Tsar asked me what had to be done for the sable. When I had explained he told me to send it to the Hunters' Village of Gatchino. But I said:

' "Little Father Tsar, that won't do. All the hunters will be wanting to sell the skin of my sable. They will kill it and say the animal had an accident. I know them, those hunters. They have no pity for a live animal."

'The Tsar said:

' "I would have chosen a hunter I could trust. But perhaps after all you are right. Take it back with you to Siberia. Look after it as long as it lives. That is an order you have received from me. Go to Mossolov and tell him to give you a good present. But mind, don't forget to look well after the sable; it's my sable now. God be with you!" '

Next day, before Freedericksz had begun his report, the Tsar told him of the two hours he had had with the old Siberian hunter. The old man was given a watch with the Imperial eagle; the old woman received a brooch; they were paid on a generous scale for the sable and given the money for their return journey.

The Grand Duchesses were inconsolable.

'There was no help for it,' they said. 'Papa had made up his mind.'

THEY HAD NO GOVERNESSES

The children were given a fairly comprehensive education; but it was so organized as not to bring them into the company of too many persons, whether teachers or fellow-pupils. At the time when I commenced my service at Court, the Grand Duchesses had no teacher. There were nurses to be seen in their apartments, but that was all. When the nurses had gone the children were virtually without supervision, except, of course, that of their mother. The Empress, however, remained almost always in an arm-chair, motionless, and never spoke to her daughters in the presence of a third party.

To save them from acquiring their mother's timidity, the Grand Duchesses had had lunch with their parents from a very early age; Marie Nicolayevna had done so since she was six. As young girls they were well behaved at table, although they were under no supervision—their mother was often absent from lunch, and the maids of honour let the four children alone, as they had received no special instruction to teach them good manners. I must add that after meals, when they mixed with the grown-ups, the princesses did not always behave in the way that one might fairly have expected of the daughters of the Tsar.

Ultimately a teacher was found for them, though she was not officially given that description. Her name was Catherine Adolfovna Schneider. She was a niece of Dr. Hirsch, the Court surgeon, and had been engaged as Russian teacher by Grand Duchess Elizabeth Feodorovna after her marriage with Grand Duke Serge. Subsequently she passed into the service of the Empress.

Slender, fragile, self-effacing, this young lady was active everywhere, and ready for any sacrifice. (She was shot by the Bolsheviks somewhere in Siberia.) She adored the Empress and the children. Her capacity for work was astonishing. She taught Alexandra Feodorovna Russian, and was at the same time her private secretary; she did all the shopping for Her Majesty; she accompanied the children whenever they went out. She was infinitely sweet-tempered and good-hearted. One sole shortcoming she had: the children paid not the slightest attention to anything she said.

The time came when Freedericksz, feeling that there were objections to a young girl being constantly in Their Majesties' presence without having any officially recognized function, created for her the titular position of Reader to the Court.

It was she who gave the Grand Duchesses their first lessons; at this time she was their schoolmistress for all subjects. A little later there was a division of labour; Fräulein Schneider took the children in German (the four sisters all detested the language and refused to learn it); the Empress taught them English; M. Gilliard, the tutor to the Cesarevitch, gave them lessons in French; M. Petrov, a Russian schoolmaster, was in charge of Russian literature and all remaining subjects.

I was always told that if the Grand Duchesses had been, at a public school they would all have been among the top ten in their various classes.

THEY HAD NO GIRL FRIENDS

I shall tell elsewhere how the one and only attempt to give the Grand Duchesses a governess properly so-called came to an end. Mlle Tuytcheva remained only a short time at Court.

The four girls grew up surrounded by a large number of servants, but, in spite of their mother's supervision, they were left a great deal to themselves. Not one of them ever had a real girl friend of her own age.

The seven children of Grand Duchess Xenia were the only ones who came to see the Grand Duchesses without ceremony; they would come for tennis and tea—but they were never sent all at one time. The children of the Grand Dukes George and Constantine, aged ten, twelve, and twenty, were never present at these intimate meetings. Countess Emma, the daughter of Count Freedericksz, and a few of the officers of the yacht *Standard*, were the only persons not related to the Romanovs who joined the Tsar's daughters at play now and then.

To the best of my belief, there was one solitary ball organized for the two eldest of the Grand Duchesses, at Livadia in 1911 or 1912. The Marshal of the Court had been put in charge of the arrangements for this ball, and the officers of the *Standard* had been invited to come to the dancing, together with some other lieutenants from the Crimean cavalry division. The children long regarded this ball as one of the greatest events in their lives.

Every year a lottery was organized; the Empress and her daughters sold tickets.

In normal times there was a cinema performance every Saturday. The covered riding-school at Livadia had been appropriated for the performances, which were one of the main subjects of conversation for the whole of the week that followed.

The choice of films was a troublesome business. The Empress had settled the programme, once for all, as follows: first, as news film, the record taken during the week by the Court photographer, Jaguelsky, of the firm of Hahn; then an instructional film or a series of attractive views; finally, something amusing for the children. How many times I had to send for Mme Naryshkin, Mistress of the Robes, to view the film! She was solely responsible for deciding what was suitable or not suitable for the children. She was a pitiless censor; again and again the brightest spots in a film would be condemned as indecorous, and Jaguelsky's scissors got to work at once on them.

One day there was a real disaster. I was very busy, and told Jaguelsky not to trouble to show me the news film. 'You are not a beginner, and I don't suppose you could go wrong with nothing to show but Tuesday's review before Her Majesty!' Jaguelsky confirmed that the film had nothing in it but the review. At the performance we saw the Emperor's arrival; then Count Mussin Pushkin, A.D.C., the General Commanding the troops in the Odessa region, passed in front of the Sovereign, saluted with his sword, and stood on his right like a statue. Everything was in perfect order.

Then came the catastrophe.

The film went on. It should be explained that at every thirty or forty yards there were soldiers holding little flags; as the troops defiled before the Tsar they had to 'feel' on the right with their shoulders for the imaginary line formed by the 'markers' with the flags, so as to ensure good formation.

The soldiers began to get more and more out of line with the markers. Mussin Pushkin stood impeccably at attention; but he made a sign with his left arm for the markers' line to be kept better. The soldiers were unable to obey the mute order. The Count's face grew fierce. Finally he clenched his fist and shook it at them, apparently about to tell them in the plainest language what he thought of them.

The children began to laugh. The Emperor bit his lips to keep from laughing too. I was in despair, but could not help smiling; it really was a funny spectacle.

After the performance Their Majesties made not the slightest allusion to what they had seen. I tried to get away as quickly as possible. But I felt my arm seized, and none too gently. It was Count Mussin Pushkin himself.

'My dear chap,' he said, 'what is the meaning of it? What could induce your photographer, how could he dare to show a General in

Command of a whole region—like *that*? And before Their Majesties! I never heard of such a thing!

'Besides, I tell you he is lying! D'you get me? He has some grudge and is lying. I never, never threatened with my fist.

'I take it my word is good enough, and that this damned photographer will be placed under arrest for a week at least.

'To show me in an attitude that I never struck! It's unbelievable!'

The offending section of the film was cut out at once.

THEIR LIFE WAS MONOTONOUS

So the children grew up, living simply, in a tolerable but monotonous existence. They seemed entirely satisfied with their life; it hardly occurred to them that they might agitate for other distractions.

Olga, in 1912, was already seventeen, but she still had the ways of a 'flapper'. She was a blonde; with a face typically Russian in its curve, and a charming complexion and teeth that made her very pretty. Fräulein Schneider said she was 'as good as an angel'.

Tatiana was taller, more slender, and of more distinction; she was the best-looking of all the sisters. She was very reserved and quiet, and difficult to govern.

Marie was distinguished by her muscular strength; she was bright, energetic, and determined to get her own way. She was the least studious of the sisters.

Anastasia, the youngest, had the liveliest intelligence of all four; whoever was sitting next to her had to be prepared for some unexpected question at any moment.

As they grew up, the Grand Duchesses grew more reserved; at first it had been plain that they had never been under supervision.

During the war they passed their examinations as nursing sisters, and worked with their mother in the Palace hospital. They showed a great deal of self-sacrifice and absolute devotion. In that they were but following in their mother's footsteps. The Empress easily acquired an excellent knowledge of everything connected with the organization of hospitals, hospital trains, and sanatoria. In this field she showed herself thoroughly equal to her responsibilities, which at times were very exacting; she was successful in the choice of her immediate collaborators, and gave evidence of exceptional energy.

CHAPTER II
THE RELATIVES OF NICHOLAS II

I. THE DOWAGER
'A CHARMER'

The Dowager Empress Marie Feodorovna, Princess of Denmark, was descended collaterally from a line of princes of Schleswig-Holstein. The atmosphere of Holstein was patriarchal and thoroughly 'provincial'; but she had learned there to attach no very great importance to questions of etiquette, and to show indulgence for the little failings of those around her. Marie Feodorovna considered that her chief function as Empress was to charm those who came into contact with her. She had every quality needed for doing so, and was venerated alike at Court and by the great mass of the people.

She was particularly indulgent to all her suite. I recall the incident of the coachman who had drunk so much that he fell asleep on his seat, leaving the horses to their own devices; it was only with the utmost difficulty that they were brought to a stop. Marie Feodorovna had only one concern—to treat the incident as a joke and to make sure that it did not reach her husband's ears.

She went frequently to Copenhagen, having the yacht *Pole Star* at her disposal. On these voyages her servants used to buy considerable quantities of foreign goods.

That was forbidden alike by the Customs regulations and by those of the Court, On one occasion, on the return of the yacht to Russia, Freedericksz had all the baggage searched. There were cigarettes and playing-cards and silks in profusion. But the purchasers were neither prosecuted nor even required to pay the duty on all this contraband: Marie Feodorovna, with her charming smile, declared that she wanted everything, duties and fines alike, charged to her personal account. The personal account of the Dowager Empress was in charge of Freedericksz, so that the Minister of the Court himself paid the sums due from the persons whom he had set out to catch red-handed.

Marie Feodorovna could not refuse anything to the members of her suite. And Nicholas II agreed to everything that his mother asked.

The consequence was that most of the appointments at Court were made through the channel of the Empress Dowager's Court. She had a Lady in Waiting, Mme Flotow. This lady was officially responsible for the care of her mistress's jewels and wardrobe; but she had succeeded in gaining a position of altogether extravagant influence. As soon as the name of Mme Flotow was to be found in the papers of an applicant it was a foregone conclusion that the Tsar would grant the request, even if at first he was for rejecting it.

Somehow, I do not know how, Mme Flotow would know all about the Sovereign's decisions, at times well before the writer of these pages!

LONG STAYS IN COPENHAGEN

Did the Dowager Empress intervene directly in affairs of state? As regards foreign policy, I believe that at the outset of her son's reign she gave him advice which must have influenced him, since Marie Feodorovna was the sister of Queen Alexandra. Later, I know, Nicholas II consulted his mother more and more rarely on foreign policy. In any case she was without ambition, except the ambition to be loved and admired.

In regard to home policy I can be much more definite. Even when she occupied the throne by the side of her husband, Alexander III, Marie Feodorovna never had either the occasion or the desire to delve into the delicate and complex questions of

Russian internal politics. She considered that she had no concern with that; as a royal lady she occupied herself only with what came within the province of a personage in the highest society. Agrarian problems, the Duma, the country's finances—all this simply did not interest her.

The Dowager Empress soon began to make her visits to Copenhagen longer and longer; and well before the end of her son's reign her influence over him in matters of state had been reduced to nothing.

II. THE GRAND DUKES
TWENTY-NINE MEN

When I took up my duties at Court in 1900, the Imperial family was numerous and active. At that time the Tsar had a great-uncle, four uncles, ten 'uncles of the second degree', as they are called in Russia (sons of his great-uncles), a brother, four male cousins, and nine male 'cousins of the third degree' (sons of uncles of the second degree)—in all twenty-nine men; enough to form a good bodyguard who would die, if the call came, sword in hand around the threatened head of the family. Were they not all interested in defending their privileges?

I am deliberately leaving the women members of the Imperial family out of account. My purpose in this chapter is to show how far, if at all, the members of the family played any part in politics. The Tsar never discussed politics willingly with ladies; he made an exception now and again of the Grand Duchess Marie Pavlovna, of whom I shall write later, for he knew that she was well acquainted with the intentions of Emperor William II, through her German relatives. The two Montenegrin princesses, Militza and Stana, were ready to act as advisers to the throne; they were constantly putting forward political proposals, and hot discussions were frequent in their two Courts on all the current problems. But the Tsar kept these two princesses at a distance. They were advocates of the cause of Montenegro, and that gave the principality an importance in our Balkan policy which was out of proportion to the part it was able to play. But if ever they ventured to approach the Sovereign it was most likely to be with a request, preferably by letter, for subsidies for their father, Prince Nicholas of Montenegro.

The Tsar's two sisters were entirely withdrawn from public life. Many of the Grand Duchesses had married foreign princes and lived outside Russia; they were thus entirely eliminated from the life of the Grand Court.

Of these twenty-nine men, who were bound to the head of the family by the dynastic principle and even by interest, how many rallied to the support of the Tsar at the tragic moment of his abdication? *Not one.*

In Pskov, where the abdication took place, the Tsar had no member of his family at his side. The Grand Dukes were faced with the fact of his abdication; they were not consulted either before or after the event. The Imperial family had been put in a position in which it could do nothing to alter what had been done. Nicholas II and Michael Alexandrovitch, after the Tsar's abdication, acted on their own responsibility without attempting to get into touch with their relatives, without even consulting one another. The flood of the revolution had been so sudden that it had been impossible from the first to arrange any discussion.

But on that tragic day of his abdication the Tsar was unable to consult his family not only because of practical obstacles but also for personal reasons, resulting from the relations which had gradually grown up between them. One single initialling by him cost the lives of seventeen members of his family in less than two years. (Most of the members of the Imperial family had remained in Russia for no other reason than that their flight might have aggravated the Tsar's situation.)

I shall try to explain how these relations had developed and how they stood in 1917; I shall show the personal position in which each of the Grand Dukes who come into question stood at the moment of the abdication.

Dimitri Pavlovitch had been sent to the Persian front a few weeks before as a punishment for his part in the murder of Rasputin, though he had regarded his action as a means of saving the Imperial family.

Grand Duke Cyril had gone to the revolutionary Duma at the head of the naval detachment under his command. He thought that that gesture would be sufficient to calm opinion in the capital, to restore some sort of order, and to save the dynasty. But his effort was entirely abortive.

Grand Duke Nicholas, the Tsar's representative in the Caucasus, had implored the Tsar 'on his knees', as he said in his telegram, to abdicate. Grand Duchess Marie Pavlovna, with her son Andrew, was at Kislovodsk, in the Caucasus.

The Grand Dukes at the front were passive witnesses of the revolution. And when Michael Alexandrovitch, the Tsar's brother, became Emperor through the Tsar's abdication (on his own part and on that of his son Alexis), those Grand Dukes who were in Petrograd failed to rally round him.

The people who made up 'society' in Petrograd had hastened events, and had, indeed, precipitated the abdication by their irresponsible talk. They accepted the collapse of the throne with indifference, some of them with joy. In Jassy, in my Legation, I received whole packets of enthusiastic, frenzied letters which gave me the impression that everybody in the capital had gone mad.

In the pages that follow I shall deal in turn with each of the Grand Dukes, and try to explain the personal reasons that account for their strange attitude towards the Tsar; but I must preface that analysis by some general considerations.

DISSENSIONS IN THE ROMANOV FAMILY

The first blow at the solidarity of the family of the Romanovs was struck by Tsar Alexander II.

He had contracted a morganatic marriage with the young and radiant Princess Dolgorukaya (after her marriage she became Princess Yurievskaya). This was the second morganatic marriage contracted in violation of the Statute of the Imperial family, the fundamental code of the house of Romanov; the first was the marriage of Constantine, the brother of Nicholas I. That union was indirectly the cause of the revolt of the Decabrists in 1825.

The marriage of Alexander II brought forth protests from all the members of the family; the protests were all the livelier for being made behind his back.

Two scenes remain graven on my memory. In the spring of 1877 the Emperor asked the Cesarevitch (afterwards Alexander III) to give a grand ball at Peterhof in honour of certain German princes who had come on a visit. By the Tsar's desire Princess Dolgorukaya was invited. I remember how I was struck by the majestic figure of the Emperor as he waited under the colonnade leading to the ballroom; the princess stood in her splendour a few feet away from the Sovereign. After supper a cotillion was announced. The Tsar left the room and was escorted to his carriage by the Cesarevitch. When the Cesarevitch re-entered the room—it will be remembered how headstrong, almost violent, was his character—he crossed straight through the dancers till he came below the balcony in which the band of the Preobrajensky Regiment was playing a lively air. There he shouted at the top of his voice:

'Thank you, you Preobrajensky fellows! You can go now.'

The dancers—the wife of the Cesarevitch among them—stopped abruptly. The heir to the throne left with his wife; the guests hurriedly went home.

The second scene was witnessed almost in front of the coffin of Alexander II, who had perished a few days before, a victim of Nihilist bombs. In the hall of the Saltykov entrance of the Winter Palace, at the foot of the monumental staircase, the company had assembled for attendance at a funeral mass and were waiting for Their Majesties' appearance. To the right I saw the Grand Dukes and Grand Duchesses; at the left, in a corner, stood a pitiable group. Princess Yurievskaya and her three children, two girls and a boy, all in deep mourning. On their arrival Their Majesties turned to the group on the right. Then the Tsar took a few measured, resounding steps towards Princess Yurievskaya, who had lifted her veil. The Empress also took a few steps towards her, but stopped a little way off. After a few words with the Tsar, Princess Yurievskaya turned to Marie Feodorovna. The two women remained facing one another for a few moments that seemed to me an eternity. If Marie Feodorovna had held out her hand it would have been the princess's duty to make a deep obeisance and kiss the extended hand.* But suddenly Her Majesty fell into the arms of her mother-in-law, and the two women burst into tears. The memory of the man who had adored his morganatic wife swept away the rules of etiquette.

It was not for long. Their Majesties left the building, followed by the in their corner of the hall, a small, deserted group. A funeral mass was

---

*I have witnessed this ceremony in my capacity of head of the escort of Prince Alexander of Bulgaria.

Grand Dukes. Princess Yurievskaya and her three children remained to be celebrated an hour later for those who did not belong to the Imperial family!

GRAND DUKES WHO WERE AND WERE NOT

The second blow to the Imperial family came from Alexander III. He saw that the family was growing too large, and feared for the prestige of the title of Grand Duke; accordingly he took a step which must be regarded as dictated by the circumstances, though it was not at all to the taste of the Grand Dukes.

Under the Statute of the Imperial family, each Grand Duke was entitled to an annual allowance of 280,000 roubles (£28,000 gold). This sum was paid to the holder of the title by the 'Apanages', a sort of trust administration of domains which existed purely in order to provide funds, outside the general Budget of the Empire, for the Grand Ducal pensions. The great-grandsons of an Emperor, simple princes of the blood, had the right only to a single lump sum payment, fixed once for all, of a million roubles (£100,000).

Alexander III modified the Statute by laying down that only sons and grandsons of an Emperor should benefit in future from the Apanages. It was only natural that the distant relatives of the Tsar should be aggrieved at this totally unexpected reform, the economic consequences of which were anything but negligible. But Alexander, headstrong and energetic as he was, inspired all the members of his family with veritable terror; no protest was made aloud. The resentment was none the less intense.

When Nicholas II succeeded Alexander, it was hoped that it would be possible to breathe more freely: the new Tsar was young, and his uncles ought to be able to bring pressure on him in the interest of all his relatives.

They failed, however. The family attributed their failure to the influence of the Empress. I showed above how much animosity she could entertain towards her uncles and aunts. The ideas which had been instilled into her mind in her childhood were well adopted to reinforce her inclination for stern measures. She had grown up in an Anglo-German environment in which energies were restricted by constitutional limitations and were accordingly concentrated on relatives, on the other members of each family. She was all for the application of iron discipline to all the Grand Dukes without exception.

The Grand Dukes also complained of the Tsar's attitude to decisions of the Family Council. These decisions, in accordance with the law, could only reach the Tsar through the Minister of the Court. The Tsar did not consider it necessary to confirm them all without exception, and he would not change the law, lest he should have to have personal discussions with his relatives or their representatives. The impossibility of bringing family affairs directly before the Sovereign without the intervention of Count Freedericksz wounded the *amour-propre* of the Grand Dukes and increased their resentment against the Tsar and his Ministers.

Finally, there was Rasputin the Sinister. The family inevitably divided into two camps—those in the coterie, and the rest. After the banishment of Grand Duke Dimitri for his part in the assassination of Rasputin, the Grand Dukes sent a collective letter to the Tsar. I know of no other such collective communication, and this one was mortifying for the Empress. Grand Duke Dimitri's action was described in the letter as 'dictated by his conscience'. The disintegration of the family could not have been more complete.

THE PATRIARCH OF THE FAMILY

In studying the disintegration of the Romanov family it will be best to take separately each of the three generations of Grand Dukes. The first is that of Alexander II, the grandfather of Nicholas II.

Alexander II, the Liberator as he was called, was a monarch of very liberal views. His principal acts were the freeing of a hundred million serfs, the creation of a justiciary independent of the administration, and the liberation of the Bulgars from the Mussulman yoke. He was assassinated on March 1st 1881, on the eve of the day on which he was to have signed a Constitution which had been drawn up by Count Loris-Melikov, the Prime Minister. Only one of his brothers was still active in 1900, Grand Duke Michael Nicolayevitch, great-uncle of Tsar Nicholas II.

Grand Duke Michael Nicolayevitch was not particularly gifted. He had nobility and equanimity of character and a courtesy such as is rarely to be seen in our day. He had passed most of his life in the Caucasus, where he had been sent as Viceroy. During the war of

1877 he was Commander-in-Chief of the Russian troops; he was promoted Marshal of Artillery and decorated with the Grand Cordon of the military order of St. George; and until his death he occupied the important post of President of the Imperial Council.

He played no part of any importance in politics; he was too old (born in 1832), and preferred his villa, 'Wenden', at Cannes to the palaces he possessed in St. Petersburg; he died on the Côte d'Azur, carrying into his tomb all the traditions of a past epoch. As the patriarch of the family he was venerated by all his relatives; none of them would ever have risen against the old man's authority; his tactful interventions smoothed away the petty jealousies between the Romanovs almost as soon as they broke out.

The death of Michael Nicolayevitch was an irreparable loss, for the unity of the dynasty no longer existed except in name; from 1910 onwards the rifts steadily widened.

Grand Duke Michael Nicolayevitch

IN DIRECTOIRE STYLE

Grand Duchess Alexandra Iossifovna, *née* Princess of Saxe-Altenburg, also belonged to the generation of Alexander II. She held ultra-monarchist ideas, and kept away from St. Petersburg, where the society seemed to her too modern and advanced. She preferred her manor house at Pavlovsk, a veritable museum.

This house, a little antiquated and *démodé*, formed a setting worthy of the old lady. It is the only palace in the world in which everything is, or was, decorated entirely in the Directoire style: furniture, tapestries, chandeliers, china, everything at Pavlovsk belonged to an age that is no more. There was no difficulty in keeping up, for instance, the tapestries; towards the end of the eighteenth century the Comtesse du Nord, wife of Emperor Paul I, had ordered while in Paris such quantities of precious damask that the palace still had large stores in reserve even at the time of the 1917 revolution. Not until 1910, or perhaps even later, was electricity installed in the palace, and the electric bulbs took the place not of gas or even oil but of wax candles.

Alexandra Iossifovna was like her palace of Pavlovsk: she lived entirely in the past; her own day did not interest her.

'ONE OUGHT TO KNOW ONE'S JOB'

The second generation, that of Alexander III, the nationalist, authoritarian, reactionary Tsar, was represented in 1900 by his four brothers and ten cousins.

The four brothers of Alexander III—the four uncles of Nicholas II—were Vladimir, Alexis, Serge, and Paul. Grand Duke Vladimir Alexandrovitch and his wife, Grand Duchess Marie Pavlovna, call for the most particular consideration.

Of ruddy complexion, endowed with a voice that carried to the farthest corners of his club, a great hunter, a refined gourmet (he had a collection of menus covered with his 'annotations', and signed immediately after the meal they referred to), Vladimir was the one among the Grand Dukes who profited most from his privileged situation.

He was President of the Academy of Fine Arts, and a lover of art and literature; he surrounded himself with actors, singers, and painters. He spoke as one having authority, and would not allow any contradiction except in the privacy of a tête-à-tête. His authority was respected both in the outside world and among the Grand Dukes.

Vladimir was the eldest of the uncles of Tsar Nicholas. He was entitled to exercise an unquestioned leadership, and he could have done so. He was twenty-one years older than the Tsar and might, alongside Michael Nicolayevitch, have become the leader of the family, the guardian of its unity and traditions. But it happened otherwise.

The Grand Duke's strong personality almost struck terror into Nicholas II. His uncle felt this from the beginning of the Tsar's reign, and steadily held aloof from all affairs of state.

The final rupture came in 1905, on the occasion of the marriage of the Grand Duke Cyril, Vladimir's eldest son. On October 8th 1905 Cyril, without the Tsar's consent, married abroad Grand Duchess Victoria Melita, of Saxe-Coburg-Gotha, the divorced wife of a prince of Hesse. This marriage, contrary to the existing laws, deeply grieved the Tsar.*

Some time passed; then Cyril left for St. Petersburg. His parents felt sure that the young prince would have to listen to remonstrances from the head of the family, remonstrances which he had certainly earned, but that then he would be pardoned.

He arrived about 8 p.m. and went at once to his parents' palace. At 10 p.m. he was told that Count Freedericksz had come and wanted to speak to him 'in accordance with instructions received from the Tsar'. Freedericksz conveyed to the Grand Duke his Sovereign's decisions: he must leave Russia at once, must never set foot again on the soil of his country, and must await abroad the intimation of the further penalties that would be imposed.

That same night, at midnight, the Grand Duke left St. Petersburg by train.

This rigour revolted Grand Duke Vladimir. He was outraged at his son being given such treatment, and without any prior communication with him. He went next day to the Tsar and resigned all the positions that he held in the Russian army. That was the most vigorous protest that he was in a position to make.

---

* The Russian law required the Tsar's consent to any marriage of a member of the Imperial family; and it prohibited marriages between cousins. (Cyril's father and Victoria's mother were brother and sister.

The Tsar's drastic decision was attributed to the influence of the Empress. It was whispered that she wanted to be revenged on Grand Duke Cyril for daring to marry a woman who only a little while before had abandoned her husband, the Grand Duke of Hesse, the Empress's own brother.

There were other causes of friction between the Grand Court and the court of Marie Pavlovna, Vladimir's wife. I have already related how Marie Pavlovna failed to impose herself on the young Empress as her initiator into the petty social details which in the aggregate determine the success or failure of every woman, even the wife of a Tsar. When she found herself cold-shouldered, Marie Pavlovna, overbearing and irascible by nature, gave full vent to her spleen in acid comment on everything that her niece did or did not do. The Court—her Court—followed the example set to it. It was from the immediate entourage of Marie Pavlovna that the most wounding stories about the Empress emanated. This counted all the more since that Court had none of the exclusiveness of the Grand Court; all the artists in vogue at the end of the nineteenth and beginning of the twentieth century had access to the Court of the President of the Academy of Fine Arts, a post which the Grand Duchess assumed after her husband's death. Marie Pavlovna kept up a regular correspondence with many statesmen and authors in Europe and the United States, and her views were echoed in the four quarters of the globe.

To quote only one out of a thousand instances of the Grand Duchess's capacities—Grand Duke Vladimir was sent to Bulgaria in 1907 as representative of the Emperor of Russia on the occasion of the unveiling of the monument to Alexander II at Sofia. Marie Pavlovna went with him. On the day of the grand banquet given in honour of the Russian guests, I had scarcely more than a few minutes for the necessary explanations to the Grand Duchess about the outstanding personalities in Bulgar society who would be at the banquet and at the reception that was to follow it. For three hours the Grand Duchess was the centre of animated and brilliant conversation. She was talking with persons whom she had never before met; and she did not make a single mistake.

Later in the evening I congratulated her on her diplomatic adroitness; she replied:

'One ought to know one's job. You may pass that on to the

Grand Court.'

It must be admitted that she knew her job to perfection.

Her Court entirely eclipsed the Empress's. An appointment as maid of honour to Marie Pavlovna would have carried with it the best of opportunities for becoming a Beauty Queen if beauty competitions had been organized in Russia in those days. The charity bazaars which the Grand Duchess opened at Christmas in the salons of the Nobles' Assembly in St. Petersburg were the event of the season. Snobs who would have no other chance of access to this exalted realm of society crowded round the Grand Duchess's stand, adding large sums to her fund for her charitable works. If they showed sufficiently lavish generosity they would subsequently receive a gracious invitation to a reception at the Palace. Marie Pavlovna presided in St. Petersburg over everything connected with high society, every social event. Here, too, her sayings spread all over the town. Ineradicable jealousies, constantly fed by fresh incidents, alienated the two Courts. I have already told how the Empress treated her aunt towards the end of the regime (the incident of the Livadia hospitals). In such conditions any sort of family friendliness had long become impossible between the Empress and her uncle and aunt.

GRAND DUKES ALEXIS AND SERGE

The second son of Alexander II was named Alexis Alexandrovitch. He had a fine athletic figure and gave the impression of strength, allied—that had been the special gift of some of the Romanovs of earlier generations—with infinite charm.

I recall how one day in Paris I was walking along the Grands Boulevards behind a man in civilian dress, tall and finely proportioned. Passers-by turned round and I heard some exclaim:

'What a fine man!'

Coming up with him, I recognized Grand Duke Alexis.

Alexis Alexandrovitch was the High Admiral of the Russian navy, and was one of the organizers of the circumnavigation of Africa and Asia by Rodjestvensky's armada, which ended with the attack on the Japanese fleet off Tsushima and utter disaster in a glorious but unequal combat. That enterprise destroyed the Grand Duke's career; he gave up his post and settled in Paris. He died there in 1909.

The third son, Serge, came to a tragic end: he was assassinated by a Russian terrorist in the Kremlin Square. Smart, elegant, graceful, Serge had been the Commanding Officer of the Preobrajensky regiment, and had been adored by his officers. His private life was the talk of the town, and made his wife, Grand Duchess Elizabeth Feodorovna, very unhappy. He was reactionary as few others; and he was fond of discussing political problems with the Tsar. Nicholas II listened with visible pleasure to his uncle's exposition of his Die-hard ideas; he never contradicted his uncle and brother-in-law (they had married sisters), but had too much good sense to follow the advice of this representative of the ideas of a past age. When the Grand Duke was appointed Governor-General of Moscow—a post to which he would have been well suited a century earlier—he was pursued by the terrorists, who had marked him down as their principal victim. Elizabeth Feodorovna visited the assassin in his prison, interceded for his life with the Emperor, and then took the veil.

THE MORGANATIC MARRIAGE OF GRAND DUKE PAUL

Nicholas's fourth uncle was Paul (Alexandrovitch). The relations between Grand Duke Paul and the Emperor were broken off when the Grand Duke contracted a marriage abroad with Mme von Pistohlkors, *née* Karnovitch, the divorced wife of one of the aides-de-camp of Grand Duke Vladimir. The marriage took place at Leghorn in 1902. I was a very old friend of Mme von Pistohlkors; I had, indeed, been her witness at her first marriage. How many times we discussed her plans! I advised her not to let the Grand Duke proceed to a legal ceremony, for I was sure that, the consequences would be terrible. Mme von Pistohlkors replied that the Tsar was very fond of his uncle and would not want to destroy his future for regularizing a situation which was no secret to anybody.

What happened was more painful than the worst I had feared. The Tsar gave the order for the maximum penalties provided by law to be applied against his uncle; that meant banishment for life, the loss of all his posts and functions, and the confiscation of his revenues. It was said, and it was the opinion of my friend Mme von Pistohlkors, that the Empress's influence had entirely overcome the sympathy which the Head of the House professed towards his uncle—who was scarcely eight years older than the Tsar himself.

Later the Grand Duke was pardoned, on condition that he returned to Russia unaccompanied by his wife. There followed a long-drawn-out correspondence between St. Petersburg and Paris, where the Grand Duke had settled. In the end the Countess of Hohenfelsen (this title had been granted to Paul's morganatic wife by the King of Bavaria) was given permission to cross the Russian frontier.

The problem of precedence remained still to be settled. Grand Duke Paul had formulated his claims on behalf of his morganatic wife in six paragraphs. The Empress intervened personally and had the principal paragraphs struck out. The Countess of Hohenfelsen received the rank of wife of a General A.D.G.; but she was granted the right of being presented to her new relatives, the Grand Duchesses, not through their Mistresses of the Robes but directly by her husband. She also received the right of not signing the books in the palace ante-rooms but leaving her card.

All this bargaining produced friction between uncle and nephew and especially the nephew's wife (the Empress). Ostensibly their relations had become normal; in actual fact resentment and injured dignity robbed them of all cordiality. Grand Duchess Marie Pavlovna seized her opportunity; she loaded her new sister-in-law with attentions and favours. Grand Duke Paul's Court quickly won distinction and popularity throughout St. Petersburg society. During the war the Countess of Hohenfelsen received the title of Princess Paley; her son Vladimir, a remarkable poet and a fascinating man, was one of the centres of attraction for all that was brilliant in the capital.

These were not circumstances that could allow of good relations between the Grand Court and the Court of Grand Duke Paul; the Grand Duke had no opportunity of giving advice to his nephew; and the part played by his son Dimitri in the assassination of Rasputin completely put an end to the friendship between the Tsar and his uncle.

I am bound to add that the two long talks that I had with Grand Duke Paul after his return from Paris produced rather a painful impression on me. Exile had brought him no well-thought-out political creed. It was impossible that he should be a useful counsellor for his nephew. And the coolness with which he was received in the Grand Court hurt and angered him.

'IF IT HAD ONLY MEANT LOOKING AFTER HORSES—'

Keeping still to the generation of the father of Nicholas II, let us pass now to the sons of Nicholas's great-uncles. Strictly they were second cousins; in Russia these relations were called 'uncles of the second degree'.

There were ten of them: three sons of the late Constantine Nicolayevitch; two sons of the late Nicholas Nicolayevitch (called the Elder, to distinguish him from Nicholas Nicolayevitch the Younger, his son, the Generalissimo during the world war); and five sons of Michael Nicolayevitch (to whom reference has already been made). The eldest of this group was fifty in 1900, the youngest thirty-one—one year younger than the Tsar although he was his uncle.

We will consider them one by one.

The eldest son of Constantine Nicolayevitch was named Nicholas Constantinovitch. His story may be told in very few words. A life of dissipation brought him very serious illness and he had to be put under restraint through incurable mental trouble. He passed his life at Tashkent, in Central Asia. Thus there could be no question of his influence on affairs of state.

The second son was named Constantine Constantinovitch. He was a highly cultured man and a writer of verse; his poems were highly thought of by the Russian public. He signed them with the initials K.R., a pseudonym treated with great respect by Russian reviewers. His life was peaceful and patriarchal. Towards the end of it he was promoted to the modest post of head of the military schools. There he showed some directing ability. He always held aloof from the Grand Court, where he found none who shared either his outlook or his tastes.

The third son was Dimitri Constantinovitch, a man of wide sympathies, modest, and full of good sense. I can declare without fear of contradiction that he never took any active part in affairs of state—on principle, and from conviction, a conviction based on thoroughly prudent considerations.

'The Grand Dukes,' he said to me one day, when in a confidential mood, 'should begin their apprenticeship as simple lieutenants, and incognito. If they show aptitude for the Service, they can be promoted in accordance with the rules laid down for everybody. But they should never be permitted to reach positions of command or posts of great responsibility. Any mistakes they made would at once involve the Tsar, and that might diminish the Sovereign's prestige.'

'Does your brother' (Constantine Constantinovitch, see above) 'express the same opinions?'

'He does. These principles were instilled into us by our mother; our father rarely discussed things with us. My brother would admit, however, that there have been exceptions among the Grand Dukes; some of them have shown great capacity in command. For these exceptional cases he would have laid down severe rules defining penalties for neglect of duty; penalties far heavier than for plain subjects of the Tsar.'

'What penalties did he envisage?'

'Immediate dismissal for any Grand Duke who proved unworthy of the post he occupied. It is at that point that I disagree with my brother. The necessity of dismissing a near relative might be productive of very great difficulties for the Tsar; and we are all grouped round the throne in order to facilitate the tasks of its occupier.'

One day he told me of his first entry into official life. He was a lover of horses and wanted to join a cavalry regiment. His father, High Admiral of the Russian navy, gave his decision:

'You have got to represent our family in the navy.'

He was sent with cadets of the naval college to serve for a period on a warship. He proved unable to endure the sea. His sufferings were terrible. On his return he prayed for a long time in front of his icon, and then, gathering up all his courage, went to his father. He threw himself at his feet and begged to be freed from the naval service.

'Go away, and do not let me see you again,' his father answered. 'Admiral Nelson himself suffered from sea-sickness, but that did not prevent him from becoming a famous sailor!'

His mother had to intervene; in the end he was permitted to join a regiment of Horse Guards. His elder brother had ruined his health by excessive libations; and his mother made him swear that he would never drink a single glass of wine. He was conscientious in the extreme, and never let anything induce him to break the promise he had given.

Later, when he became Commanding Officer of the Grenadier

Guards, he found that the 'dry' régime to which he was bound interfered with cordial relations with the officers of his regiment. In spite of his age and situation, he went to his mother and asked her to free him from the solemn promise he had made. Up to that moment he had never allowed himself to touch a bottle.

It may fairly be said that Dimitri Constantinovitch was the one among all the Grand Dukes who was most deeply imbued with the sense of his duty as a prince and a cousin of the Emperor. One day he turned over to me a very considerable sum for the maintenance of a little village church.

'If you make gifts everywhere on this scale,' I said, 'your revenues from the Apanages will not last out.'

'The Apanages,' he replied gravely, 'are not intended to enable us to live as sybarites; this money is put into our hands in order that we may augment the prestige of the Imperial family.'

In spite of all his qualities, this Grand Duke never played a part of any importance. His timidity was beyond imagining. When his train arrived at a station he would hide in his compartment so as not to be seen by people on the platform. But if a deputation or some officials had come to greet him, the first breath of a suggestion that it was his duty as a Grand Duke to receive them was sufficient for him to stifle his feelings and receive his visitors with the utmost amiability. Then he would go back and lower the blinds of his compartment lest he should be asked to meet anyone else.

Like so many timid people, he imposed a fixed régime on himself, a time-table to which he kept religiously; so many hours for his official duties, so many for prayer, and the rest for endless reading 'to improve his knowledge'. He even made difficulties about accepting the modest post of State Studmaster. When the post was offered to him he said to me, with touching sincerity:

'I should gladly have accepted the appointment if it had only meant looking after horses. But it means control of men as well, I think I might have been able to be of use in this field, but I am afraid I shall never get on properly with officials. In any case, I shall make one condition for my appointment: I shall reserve the right to resign the moment I feel that I am unable to be useful to my country.'

This remarkable man, educated and cultivated in the best sense of the word, never had his talents made use of in Russia. He even gave up the Studmastership, for he came to the conclusion that he ought to work at the improvement of the breeds of the equine race as a simple private individual, within the modest limits of his private stud at Dubrovka.

THE GENERALISSIMO

The two sons of Grand Duke Nicholas Nicolayevitch the Elder, Field-Marshal of the Russian army, were named Nicholas and Peter. Nicholas Nicolayevitch the Younger was probably the only one of all the Grand Dukes who tried to play any important political part. He was also the only one who might, if circumstances had aided him, have become the leader of a movement dangerous to Nicholas II, I am bound to say that my confidence in this Grand Duke was greatly shaken, especially after the events of 1905; I never felt satisfaction in his appointment as Generalissimo of the Russian army in 1914; may God pardon him for certain of his errors which we, his contemporaries, find it hard to pardon!

His mother was descended from one of the daughters of Emperor Paul (married to a prince of Oldenburg); that Emperor's mental instability was notorious. Nicholas had inherited a nervous morbidity from both his parents. Like his mother, he was very intelligent, but excitable and violent, and liable to uncontrollable fits of temper. He was an extreme mystic; his mother had left her husband well before 1880 and had gone to Kiev, where she surrounded herself with nuns and fanatical priests; in the end she took the veil.

The first impressions that I had of this Grand Duke confirmed what I knew of his unfortunate heredity. It was in 1888, during the grand manoeuvres at Rovno.

Thirty squadrons of cavalry on either side—such was the main element in these military exercises. General Strukov was the Grand Duke's 'enemy'. I had no difficulty in securing permission to watch the final battle alongside the Grand Duke.

He was visibly worried by the importance of his task, and above all by the presence of his father, the Field-Marshal. He had about ten orderly officers, and kept sending them off right and left. They had to go at a full gallop even if there was not the slightest apparent necessity for it. If the Grand Duke thought an officer was not pushing on sufficiently he shouted after him 'On! on!'—all the time striking his own charger, which was covered with lather and foam.

The exercises proceeded in accordance with all the rules of the military art, and produced a very good impression.

At nightfall the Strukov cavalry appeared on the far side of the valley separating the forces. This was the moment of the decisive attack. Our troops deployed with spirit. The Grand Duke, however, thought they were behindhand.

'An orderly officer!' he shouted.

They had all gone off on one side or the other. I approached the Grand Duke; he said to me:

'Do you see that group? They are not deploying quickly enough. Go off and tell them to go at a full gallop.'

'Might I venture to point out that an orderly officer is already on his way to that group and another officer has gone in the same direction? But I am at Your Highness's service.'

'No, quite right, there is no use in going.'

He made a grimace that betrayed his annoyance at having lost control of himself.

'Would it not be best,' I then said, 'for me to go over to join the reserves? They hardly have time to fill up the gap that is growing in the centre of our front.'

'You're right. Quick, go along!'

After the manoeuvres were over General Strukov spoke about me to the Grand Duke. He mentioned that I had fought at his side in the Russo-Turkish war (at the capture of Adrianople). His Highness said:

'Experience of active service always shows itself. Mossolov was the only one to call my attention to the problem of the reserves. It is thanks to him that I was pronounced the victor.'

LEFT—THEN RIGHT

My own confidence in the Grand Duke was particularly shaken, as I said above, during the events of 1905.

The month of October 1905 was marked by grave disorders. There were demonstrations and rioting in the streets of the capital, and the Emperor was on the point of taking one of the gravest political decisions of his lifetime. Count Witte had been received by the Tsar on October 9th, and the rumour spread that he had recommended the Sovereign to grant a Constitution and had undertaken personally to see that it was given practical effect. Some people added that Witte had told the Tsar that there were only two possible solutions—a Parliament, or a military dictatorship.

It was learned almost at the same moment that Grand Duke Nicholas (who was then hunting on his estate of Pershin, in the Tula Government) had been asked urgently to return to Peterhof, the residence of the Imperial family.

The Die-hards were exultant; they already saw a Dictator putting an end to all the disorders. Count Freedericksz had expressed the same hope, that the Grand Duke would bring the revolutionaries to heel; after that it would be possible to think about the granting of political liberties.

I was with the Minister of the Court when the Grand Duke was announced (October 15th).

I took the Grand Duke into Freedericksz's room, and withdrew to an adjoining one. Almost at once I heard raised voices; the Grand Duke was shouting. A little later he rushed out, jumped into his motor-car, and went off. Freedericksz followed, saying as he got into his car:

'I could not have believed it!'

He told me later what had happened.

He had been delighted at the Grand Duke's arrival, and had told him that it had been looked forward to in order that he might take the responsibility of setting up a dictatorship. At that the Grand Duke had suddenly and unaccountably lost all control of himself; he whipped out a revolver and shouted:

'If the Emperor does not accept the Witte programme, if he wants to force me to become Dictator, I shall kill myself in his presence with this revolver. I am going on to the Tsar; I only called here to let you know my intentions. You must support Witte at all costs! It is necessary for the good of Russia and of all of us!'

Then he went off like a madman.

Freedericksz added:

'He suffers more and more from the hereditary hysteria of the Oldenburgs.'

I was struck by this unusual behaviour on the part of the Grand Duke, and was curious to learn how he could have acquired his sudden sympathy for Witte. I made a few inquiries among the personages of the Grand Duke's Court.

It seems that on the day of his arrival in the capital he had had a long talk with an employee in the State printing works, a man named Ushakov. This man was regarded as the leader of those workers who had remained faithful to the monarchical principle. What he had to tell the Grand Duke had deeply impressed His Highness and had given him the idea of supporting Witte.

On October 17th 1905 Witte gained a complete victory; the manifesto granting a national representative body was published in accordance with the plan which he had elaborated.

The Grand Duke had been the decisive factor in the promulgation of the manifesto of October 17th; but he did not long remain a supporter of Witte and his liberal policy. The day came, I do not know how or why, when he came out as leader of the extreme Right, in diametrical opposition to everything that Witte did and to everything connected with the manifesto of 1905.

The extreme Right contended that the manifesto had been wrung from the Sovereign by force; for this capital reason it was null and void, and it must be so interpreted that it abated not a jot or tittle from the autocratic powers of the Tsar. The Duma must be reduced to the role of a consultative assembly, with no direct influence on the course of affairs of state. If necessary force must be resorted to in virtue of the supreme prerogative of the Sovereign.

Grand Duke Nicholas was temperamentally inclined to violence, and was the first to advise the Tsar to go counter to the Constitution which he had granted. If the Tsar had listened more to him, the abyss between the representatives of the people and the Sovereign would have grown yet more rapidly and the final collapse would have come yet sooner.

The Grand Duke was under the influence of his wife, Anastasia (Stana) Nicolayevna, the divorced wife of Duke George of Leuchtenberg. She was surrounded by clairvoyants, and believed herself to be destined to a glorious career. She made her husband share this outlook; filled him with aggressive ideas in foreign policy; and all but inveigled the Empress into a circle of shifty 'spirits'. It was under her direct influence that the Grand Duke plunged into what he called high policy.

The Grand Duchess's influence at the Grand Court was, of

course, only felt through the Grand Duke. I do not know whether this ambitious princess ever intended to carry any of her plans further than simply working upon her husband.

At the time of the Tsar's abdication the Grand Duke wrote him a letter which he must have bitterly regretted after the fall of the dynasty. In exile in France, Grand Duke Nicholas was unsuccessful in gathering the Russian monarchists around himself, and was unwilling to recognize the authority of Grand Duke Cyril. His attitude did much to make the group of Russian legitimists impotent through depriving them of a common centre.

GRAND DUKE PETER NICOLAYEVITCH

The younger brother of Nicholas Nicolayevitch Junior was named Peter. He was much better balanced and less like his mother. His health was very poor—he was almost consumptive; and he lived in retirement, without showing signs of any particular ambition. He had great abilities, but was never able to take the close interest in his duties as Inspector-General of Military Engineers that his elder brother took in the cavalry, in which he held an analogous post.

Grand Duke Peter was married, as I have already mentioned, to Militza Nicolayevna, Princess of Montenegro. This lady was extremely active in everything connected with politics, but never gained the ear of her husband's nephew, the Tsar.

THE FIVE SONS OF MICHAEL

We come finally to the sons of Grand Duke Michael Nicolayevitch. There had been six, but one died at an early age. The other five had no common trait of character.

The eldest was named Nicholas Michailovitch. Fairly good-looking and very intelligent, he spun intrigues wherever he went. He began his military service in the Horse Guards, but left his regiment on the ground that his military duties prevented him from devoting his whole time to historical studies, for which he had a taste and a marked aptitude. He was always criticizing, but never did anything himself. He wrote numberless letters to the Tsar; they show that he knew how to please and to make himself amusing. But one would search in vain through the letters for a single practical idea.

Nicholas Michailovitch remained in Petrograd when the Tsar went to the front. In his club, where he was always the centre of a group, his mordant criticisms, essentially destructive, did much damage to the régime; sarcasms coming from so high a quarter affected society with a morbid tendency that helped to deprive the Sovereign of all moral authority. The Empress whole-heartedly detested him. It was this Grand Duke who was one of the protagonists of the collective letter (written after the murder of Rasputin) which made the final breach between the Tsar and his relatives.

The second of the brothers, Michael Michailovitch, was unable to play any political part. In 1891, after the failure of an attempt at morganatic marriage in Russia, he went abroad and married the Countess of Merenberg, daughter of the Duke of Nassau and granddaughter of Pushkin, our great poet. She received the title of Countess of Torby, and never showed the slightest intention of returning to Russia.

The third son, George Michailovitch, was not one who carried any weight. The Tsar entrusted him with the duty of visiting the troops to hand their decorations to them. At the last moment, I have been told, George took his stand entirely on the side of his eldest brother, Nicholas.

The fourth son, Alexander Michailovitch, married Grand Duchess Xenia Alexandrovna, the sister of Nicholas II; he thus occupied a privileged situation at Court as the Tsar's brother-in-law. He was intelligent and ambitious, but not as intelligent as his eldest brother. For a short time he held office as Minister of the Merchant Marine, a post specially created for him. During the war he devoted himself to the problem of military aviation, and had successes which were not generally acknowledged. He published a book in which he advanced a bold contention —that the Tsar of Russia ought to put his nearest relatives at the head of all the important departments of government. One of our Ministers of War often spoke to me of the incredible difficulties that were created by the pressure at the head of the military air service of a man with access to the Tsar, himself accountable to nobody.

Alexander Michailovitch was always inclined to mysticism; towards the end of his life he became the apostle of a religious theory inspired by 'divine intuition', resembling the doctrines of

Count Tolstoi; this, he claimed, would serve in some occult fashion to rid Russia of the Bolsheviks. He had many women admirers. His lecture tours in the United States will be remembered.

The fifth son, Serge Michailovitch, was an enthusiastic artillery officer. The result was some serious failures in our supplies of guns and munitions. As he was at the front throughout the war he was more or less free from the disastrous influence of his brother Nicholas. He could not have been of any service to the Tsar during the critical moments of 1917, for, from what I know, His Majesty would certainly not have asked his advice.

THE THIRD GENERATION

I shall have little to say of the third generation, that of Nicholas II himself. It consisted of a brother, three cousins, sons of Grand Duke Vladimir, and another cousin, son of Grand Duke Paul, and nine sons of 'second degree uncles', 'third degree cousins' as they are called in Russia. These cousins had not the title of Grand Duke, being only great-grandsons of an Emperor (Nicholas I). The eldest of them was four years old in 1900; the youngest was born on January 4th 1900. It is only necessary here to consider, from a political point of view, the five Grand Dukes.

The Tsar's brother was named Michael (Alexandrovitch). He was ten years younger than Nicholas II. His great defects were considered to be his excessive good nature and credulity. Tsar Alexander III, his father, often said that Michael believed everything he was told, without taking the trouble to consider the reasons that his interlocutor might have for deliberately deceiving him.

Witte, who hated the Tsar, sang the praises of Grand Duke Michael's 'abilities'. He gave him instruction in political economy, and never tired of praising his straightforwardness—an indirect way of attacking the Tsar. I am entirely ready to credit his uprightness, for he was very like his sister Olga.

But he had no influence at all over his brother. During the time when the Tsar had no male descendant, Michael was the heir to the throne, as the nearest relative of the reigning sovereign. His brother had not even conferred on him the title of Cesarevitch, a purely honorary title usually given to all heirs to the throne. The Empress was too impatiently awaiting the birth of a son!*

* Grand Duke Michael was morganatically married to Natalia Sergueevna Sheremetyevskaya. Their son George was granted by the Tsar the name of Brassov, from one of His Highness's estates. Later, in emigration, the Grand Duke Cyril, in his capacity of head of the Romanov dynasty, created him Prince Brassov, and this title was recognized by the Dowager Empress Marie Feodorovna.

Prince Brassov died from injuries received in a motor-car accident, at the early age of twenty. He was a handsome and accomplished youth. He was debarred under the fundamental laws of the Empire from access to the Crown, but through his father he was one of the persons nearest to the throne of Russia.

Grand Duke Vladimir had three sons—Cyril, Boris, and Andrew. I have already told of Cyril's marriage, in explaining the causes of the final rupture between Vladimir and the Tsar.

The time came when Cyril was pardoned and allowed to return to Russia. During the Russo-Japanese war he was saved as by a miracle when the cruiser *Petropavlovsk* was torpedoed.

On his return to St. Petersburg after his escape, he presented himself to the Emperor as soon as he was able to do so.

At that time the relations between the Grand Court and the Court of Grand Duke Vladimir were rather strained, and the tension grew after Their Majesties had been informed of the intended marriage of Grand Duke Cyril with Princess Victoria Melita of Edinburgh. Ultimately the Emperor recognized the marriage, and after the appearance of Grand Duchess Victoria in St. Petersburg in 1909 relations became, thanks to Her Highness, more normal.

After the tragedy of Ekaterinburg** and the death of Grand Duke Michael, Cyril became, under the Statute of the house of the Romanovs, head of the Russian Imperial family. A few years later he assumed the title of Emperor, but did not officially notify the Powers. In the order of primogeniture Cyril and his son Vladimir (who was born after the abdication of Nicholas) are the senior representatives of the house of the Romanovs.

Grand Duke Boris held no Court, and lived a rather dissipated life in his little cottage at Tsarskoe Selo. In the course of the war he was appointed Hetman of the Cossack troops.

Grand Duke Andrew had brilliant success in the study of law,

** The Tsar, the Empress, and their five children, were murdered at Ekaterinburg on the night of July 16-17, 1918.

and became the legal adviser and counsel of the young generation of Grand Dukes: lawyers are all protesters by profession. Among the émigrés he continued to take an interest in politics; of all the Grand Dukes he is the best informed in the international sphere. He is gifted and intelligent and a hard worker.

Grand Duke Dimitri was only a little older than the Tsar's eldest daughter. The Grand Court was always open to him, and the Emperor showed marked affection for this youngest of the Grand Dukes. The part he played in the assassination of Rasputin produced a particularly painful impression on the Tsar.

To resume, the only Grand Dukes who were in a position to exercise any influence over the Tsar's decisions were his great-uncle Michael, Nicholas Nicolayevitch, his brother-in-law Alexander, and his uncle Paul Alexandrovitch.

The other members of the Imperial family saw the Sovereign no more than two or three times a year, and then in conditions that made political conversation almost impossible; this was so even in the case of the Tsar's brother, Grand Duke Michael Alexandrovitch.

THE LAST ATTEMPT AT RECONCILIATION

It remains for me to tell how I took part in the last attempt at a reconciliation between the members of the Romanov family.

On my arrival in Roumania in November 1916 as Russian Minister Plenipotentiary I had been particularly well received by the royal family. In January 1917 Queen Marie consulted me with regard to a plan for the union of her son Carol, the present King of Roumania, with one of the Grand Duchesses. After long discussions of the question with the King and Queen and Grand Duchess Victoria I asked the Tsar to authorize me to go to Petrograd in order to present a highly confidential report.

On my arrival I went, of course, to see Count Freedericksz. We had a long conversation on the general situation.

Rasputin had just been assassinated; he had been buried, in accordance with the Empress's desire, at Tsarskoe Selo, and this had been particularly resented by all the Grand Dukes. Dimitri Pavlovitch, who had been sentenced to exile for the part he had played in connexion with the murder of Rasputin, was waiting in boredom in his palace, where he was 'under arrest' by His Majesty's order.

It was a little while before my arrival in Petrograd that the Grand Dukes had drawn up and sent to the Tsar their 'collective letter', a step that plainly ran counter to all the dynastic precedents.

I have not seen the text of this letter, and can only speak of it from hearsay. It appears to have revealed deep dissatisfaction, and was capable of being interpreted as bringing a charge against the Empress. It was drawn up in the form of an intercession in favour of Grand Duke Dimitri, and contained a statement that he had acted 'in accordance with his conscience' (in being present in Youssupov's house on the evening of the assassination)

I have been told that this letter carried the signatures of Grand Duchess Marie Pavlovna, of her sons, who were not at that time at G.H.Q., and of the Grand Dukes Paul, Nicholas Michailovitch, and Alexander Michailovitch.

On receiving this extraordinary communication, the Tsar contented himself with the marginal note: 'Nobody has a right of assassination!'

The signatories took offence at the Sovereign's annotation, and broke off all non-official relations with the Tsar. The rupture was patent and dramatic. The Tsar saw the whole of the Romanovs ranged against himself and his wife.

Freedericksz told me what followed:

'On his return from the *Stavka*, the Tsar told me that he had settled all outstanding questions in agreement with the Empress. I was made personally responsible for seeing to the departure of Grand Duke Dimitri Pavlovitch for the Persian front; pending his departure he was to consider himself as "under arrest" in his palace.'

The Count added, sadly:

'Probably His Majesty did not want to go into details with me, knowing my strong objection to Rasputin. I only saw His Majesty yesterday—at Tsarskoe Selo, in the presence of the Empress. I took the opportunity to say how sorry I was to see the Imperial family completely disunited, and added that a reconciliation was essential in the interests of the dynasty and the country.

'We had a very long conversation, in which the Empress took a most active part. It was agreed that a way out must be found by hook or by crook. I ventured to say that the first thing needed was a reconciliation between Her Majesty and Grand Duchess Marie Pavlovna. The rest would be a much simpler matter and would settle itself.

'The Empress stated her conditions:

'She was quite ready to be reconciled with the Grand Duchess Marie, but the Grand Duchess must take the first step; must recognize that there had been mistakes on both sides, and must help to restore the solidarity of the Imperial family. It was too difficult a time for these family dissensions to be allowed to continue.'

The Count, who was plainly tired out (at this time he was suffering from frequent effusions of blood on the brain), continued:

'The Grand Duchess Marie is expecting me in half an hour. I am supposed to be going to see her on my own initiative, without mentioning the conversation that I have had with Their Majesties, to do my best to persuade her to accept the Empress's three conditions. But I am too ill to be able to use persuasion; I am taking the responsibility of sending you in my place; I know that you will carry out the mission better than I could.'

I was quite out of touch with everything, but in such a situation I could only agree. At the interview with the Grand Duchess I explained to her that I had found the Minister very ill and had decided to call to let her know how things stood, especially as I had to convey to her the best wishes of the Queen of Roumania and her daughter-in-law, Grand Duchess Victoria.

Marie Pavlovna received me very kindly.

'You were quite right to leave the Count at his home. An important conversation might have brought on in my presence the thing I most fear, a fresh fit of apoplexy.'

The conversation lasted more than an hour.

The Grand Duchess Marie recognized at the outset that a reconciliation was indispensable in the interests of the dynasty and of the whole country.

'But it would be necessary, Madame, for you to take the first step.'

'If that is so I am not ready even to discuss the subject with you. It is impossible.'

I insisted. In the end the Grand Duchess agreed to a compromise:

'I will go to Tsarskoe Selo, if Count Freedericksz comes to invite me in Her Majesty's name.'

That was her last word. I went to Freedericksz to let him know the result of my mission. It was decided that he should go to see the

Grand Duchess the moment he was well enough, and should tell her that Alexandra Feodorovna, he hoped, would shortly be asking her to tea at Tsarskoe Selo.

I learned later that it had been impossible for this invitation to be conveyed to the Grand Duchess.

Three weeks later the revolution broke out.

The very beautiful Grand Duchess Marie Pavlovna the Elder

Grand Duchess Marie Pavlovna the Elder of Russia was formerly Duchess Marie Mecklenburg-Schwerinskaya. In 1874 she married a brother of Emperor Alexander III, the Grand Duke Vladimir Alexandrovich, and was sometimes referred to as Marie Vladimir of Russia up until he died in 1909. She was rather below her husband in status, being the daughter of a Prussian officer, the Grand Duke Frederick Francis II of Mecklenburg-Schwerin.

At just seventeen years old when they met, she was already engaged to a 24 year old Prince George of Mecklenburg-Schwerin, but she fell in love with Grand duke Vladimir of Russia and married him instead. They were extremely happy together and their home in St Petersburg was one of the social hubs and salons where the Imperial nobility gathered, perhaps performing the role that Empress Alexandra should have been more engaged with.

CHAPTER III

THE EMPEROR NICHOLAS II AND HIS ENTOURAGE

I. 'OKRUJENIE'

A. *The Minister of the Court, 'The Old Gentleman'*

This work is not concerned with the political history of Russia. Thus I cannot enter here into the general problem of the Tsar's relations with his Ministers, the men who were primarily responsible for the national policy.

I have spoken above of certain resignations of Ministers—resignations which excited disapproval and bitter comment. In order to judge the situation in his Empire, the Tsar received reports from his Ministers. But where could he get the necessary material for judging his Ministers? It has been said over and over again that it was the Tsar's entourage (in Russian, *Okrujenie*) that furnished the Tsar with the material for forming his personal opinion. The influence of the *Okrujenie* has often been grossly exaggerated. To show the true situation, I shall follow the same plan as with the Grand Dukes, in the preceding chapter, and shall try to delineate each of the men who surrounded the Tsar.

I must begin with Count Freedericksz, Minister of the Court, 'the old gentleman', as the Imperial couple called him. They knew his devotion in the performance of his exacting duties. Some of his tasks, such as that of watching over the relations between the Tsar and the members of the Imperial family, were of a peculiarly difficult and delicate nature.

A. A. MOSSOLOV

THE APPOINTMENT OF BARON FREEDERIGKSZ

Count Freedericksz was descended from a Swedish officer who had been taken prisoner by Russian troops and interned at Archangel. One of his ancestors had won distinction as banker to Catherine II, and had been ennobled with the title of Baron. The Count's father, a soldier, went through many campaigns: he was present at the capture of Paris, and was for a long time Officer Commanding the 13th Regiment at Erivan, in the Caucasus, at the beginning of the nineteenth century. He ended his career as General A.D.C. to Alexander II.

Freedericksz—then Baron Vladimir Borisovitch Freedericksz—began his career as an officer in the Horse Guards. Alexander III appointed him first Master of the Horse and later assistant to the Minister of the Court. The Minister was then Count Vorontzov. After the disaster at Hodynka, Count Vorontzov sent in his resignation: he had been charged with making insufficient provision for the public safety. The Tsar considered the Minister entirely free from responsibility for the disaster, and asked him to remain at his post.

But Vorontzov made one great mistake. He had known Nicholas II since he was a baby, and took up a protective attitude towards him, the attitude, as it were, of an older relation. Nicholas himself regarded this as entirely natural; but the young Empress did not. She could not permit a Count Vorontzov to be on familiar terms with her husband. One day, when nothing could have been farther from the Count's mind, he was notified that his resignation, which had 'so often been offered to His Majesty', was accepted; later on he was sent as Viceroy to the Caucasus.

Freedericksz took his brother officer's place, at first as Acting Minister and afterwards as Minister. The appointment created a great sensation at the Court. Freedericksz did not belong to the highest ranks of the nobility, and none of his family had ever been in close association with the Throne, except his father, as General A.D.C. It was plain that the Tsar had known how to appreciate his simplicity, his tact, and his unsullied integrity. Freedericksz retained his post until the final catastrophe.

Count Freedericksz (he had received the title of Count from Nicholas II) was very rich, and that gave him the sense of independence that was so necessary amid the intrigues and the raging appetites that surrounded him.

Some people alleged that he was miserly. He was merely methodical in his expenditure. He certainly refused to lend money to people who were capable of making a bad use of it. But I have known him to incur expenditure, when he thought it necessary, on a scale that was out of proportion even to his nabob's fortune.

I recall the incident of Mr. E., an extremely rich man with a liking for little short-term usury deals. This gentleman had asked Count Freedericksz to admit his son into the Horse Guards as a volunteer. Freedericksz agreed, but warned Mr. E. that his son must not expect to become an officer in this very exclusive regiment. A year later young E. successfully passed his examinations for officer of the Guards. His father came again to see Count Freedericksz, and asked that his son should be admitted after all into the family of officers. Freedericksz, as Officer Commanding, refused as gently and considerately as he could. Thereupon Mr. E. announced that all the overdue bills signed by officers of the regiment and held by him would be protested next day. That meant, in default of immediate payment, the forced resignation of all the officers concerned.

Freedericksz showed Mr. E. the door. Then he sent for his officers and asked each one of them how much E. had lent him. The total, if I remember rightly, came to something like 79,000 roubles, an enormous sum at that time—about £8,000. There and then each officer received from Freedericksz's hands a cheque enabling him to free himself from his debt. Young E. went into another regiment of the Guards.

AT FREEDERICKSZ'S

I remember as well as if it were yesterday my first visit to my old fellow-officer—twenty years after I had left the regiment—in my new capacity of Head of the Chancellery.

The Count's private residence was in the Potchtamtskaya, exactly opposite the Horse Guards' barracks. These barracks occupied an enormous area in the centre of the capital, with a drill ground surrounded on three sides by yellow and white buildings.

Count Freedericksz had steadily refused to leave this house. The Countess often said that she found herself cramped for want of room, having only five small drawing-rooms for her use. She would have preferred to have a ball-room and to occupy the fine residence that the Court was supposed to place at the Minister's disposal in accordance with the law.

'Yes,' the Count would reply. 'That would have enabled us to organize grand receptions like all the other Ministers. But, on the other hand, when I am asked to resign you will not have to move out; you will go on receiving your friends in your five little salons. Don't you think it is better to have an assured future than gala receptions?' An assured future! He did not dream that his house was to be the first to be destroyed on the morrow of the revolution, and that none of his staff would have an assured future after 1917!

The moment I entered the spacious room in which the Count had installed his desk, I saw that nothing had changed, nothing had been moved. The only new thing was a large picture on the wall—the parting present from the officers of the regiment he had commanded. It represented the drill ground that could be seen from his windows, and his regiment deployed in parade formation, with shining helmets and breastplates; in the foreground was Count Freedericksz, on foot, talking to his officers.

The Count's big easy chair was in its old place of twenty years ago, near the window; facing it was another chair, for his visitor. In between was a small table at which Freedericksz worked. The desk itself had been kept unchanged, with all the presents and portraits of members of the Imperial family placed in position once for all.

I sat down in the second chair. From then on I was the Count's 'right arm'; he gave the title of 'left arm' to Count Heyden, head of the Emperor's military secretariat.

THE MINISTER'S WORKING DAY

Count Freedericksz began work every day about 10 a.m. It was my duty to be the first to go to his room. I began by opening the letters on his desk. Usually they were requests for grants. The Count wanted to know at once why this widow or that orphan needed help; often I was able to secure the passing of these applications through the regular official channels, but not without some difficulty: the Count was thoroughly humane and kind-hearted, and insisted on learning every possible detail of each case; he was very methodical.

The conversation continued unhurriedly. Sometimes the Minister would interrupt me:

'Look! There they are exercising in the square' (the Horse Guards' drill ground, as I have mentioned, was just in front of the Count's house). 'The third man from the left is tugging at the bit and irritating his horse for nothing. His fool of an N.C.O. doesn't notice anything. . . . Well, let us get back to work. I know you, too, are a keen cavalry officer.'

The Count would light his enormous morning cigar, and we went on to important matters, above all the report to be presented to His Majesty. Freedericksz had a special gift for drawing up the reports in a form which could not annoy His Majesty; I too learned this difficult art before long.

The Minister made a practice of letting me know everything His Majesty had said during the presentation of the report; this enabled me to get a good knowledge of the Sovereign's wishes. The Minister knew that he could count implicitly on my discretion. For his part, he asked me never to retail to him any of the little stories or bits of gossip current in town and at Court.

'I am as transparent as a crystal,' he said; 'you can see through me. I can never keep back anything. I am full of discretion so far as affairs of state are concerned, but little bits of scandal are always liable to slip out of my mouth; it is better for me to know nothing about them.'

Another of my tasks was to transmit the Count's criticisms to the staff; he was afraid of going too far, of saying more than he had intended. He reserved for himself the cases that called for his approval or congratulation, a task which he performed with a tact that excited my admiration.

Soon the cigar would be finished and the report completed. We went on to the signature of the papers that I had brought in. The Count considered that those of his Ministerial colleagues who scrawled almost illegible initials had no manners. For him the affixing of his signature was a ritual practice. He wrote his name with an ordinary pen, and then underlined it with a fine flourish made with a quill. Whatever carried his signature became an important document, and it was also important that future generations should be able to admire the perfection of calligraphy. On the days on which there were new appointments to be made there might be a hundred letters to sign; it was, need I say, no small trial of secretarial patience!

My morning's duty with the Count usually ended about 1 p.m. After lunch with his family the Count went to his barber, 'Pierre', in the Bolshaya Morskaya; this visit to the Figaro of Petrograd was part of the invariable programme of every day; the Count made a point of being shaved at Pierre's and nowhere else.

The rest of the day was marked out with an equally unvarying routine. At 3 p.m. the Minister saw one by one the heads of departments of the Court, and those people who had been granted interviews with him. The evenings, if there was no urgent business, were devoted to his family; if there was business Freedericksz sent for me about 10 p.m., and we worked together, sometimes late into the night, refreshed with a bottle of good Bordeaux and some biscuits. Towards the end of his life the doctors had the cruelty to forbid the Count this innocent little pleasure!

THE MINISTER AND THE TSAR

The Minister 'reported' to the Tsar twice a week. The first audience was on Saturday mornings, and lasted an hour; the second, of about half an hour, was on Thursdays.

But the Minister saw Their Majesties much more often than this. When the Emperor was at Tsarskoe Selo he would receive an invitation every two or three days, either to lunch or to be present at a reception or a review of some regiment. Freedericksz was also regularly invited to all the intimate festivals of the Imperial family, children's birthdays, Christmas trees, and so on.

As soon as he returned from the Palace, the Minister sent for me to give me all His Majesty's orders. It was touching to hear him tell of the many kindnesses which the Tsar and the Empress showered on him.

If the Minister was prevented by illness from going to Tsarskoe Selo, the Empress would send him little presents—something that she had made herself. They would be accompanied by a little note saying that Their Majesties hoped that he would soon be well again. Nobody else was made much of in this way by the Imperial couple, and I am sure that no one else would have appreciated these attentions so much as Freedericksz did.

The little gifts and notes were the subject of conversation with the friends of the family for weeks afterwards.

The Tsar was fond of a talk with his Minister of the Court. The Minister was the only man to whom the Emperor confided his difficulties in dealing with Ministers and Grand Dukes. The Count had a special flair for the discovery of a good solution which brought all concerned into agreement with one another. The Tsar, timid and reserved, also entrusted Freedericksz with the duty of conveying his dissatisfaction to those who had incurred it. That was the most trying of the Count's duties.

The Tsar knew his Minister of the Court to be a man of high character, of noble ideals, and of absolute integrity. He knew the depth of his Minister's devotion to him. He also appreciated the delicacy with which Freedericksz put the truth, even the disagreeable truth, before him. The Count had a special gift for always avoiding any injury to his master's feelings. And he never interfered in matters that were not connected with his duties as Minister, unless the Tsar expressly asked his opinion.

For myself, I always had a veneration for the Count, as a chief full of delicacy and charm. In him I have lost my best friend.

THE MINISTER'S POLITICS

With his ideals of order and discipline and his monarchist principles, Freedericksz considered that Russia ought to maintain the best possible relations with Germany. Prussia, in his view, was the last stronghold of the monarchical idea: we needed her just as she needed us. He admitted that Berlin's activities had made a Russo-French rapprochement necessary, in order to recall the Kaiser to the realities of foreign policy. But he considered that no alliance with republican France ought to entail any permanent weakening of the dynastic relations between Berlin and St. Petersburg.

'Neither France nor Britain,' he said to me one day, 'would come to the assistance of our dynasty. They would be very glad to see Russia turned into a republic. They know what happened to Samson when Delilah caused the seven locks to be shaven off his head.'

When Isvolsky was trying to induce His Majesty to go to Cowes,

Freedericksz pointed out to the Tsar that the visit might embroil us irremediably with the Kaiser and bring a war which would be equally dangerous for both dynasties. When the voyage was definitely decided on, he talked to me for a long time of the danger which might threaten Russia; he considered that Britain would never be a loyal ally, and he predicted the worst perils for our country.

'I am not a professional diplomat,' he said to me again and again. 'I have not the necessary material for combating Isvolsky's arguments. Nor is this within my province. But instinct and reason alike make me think this voyage exceedingly dangerous. Isvolsky will get himself into difficulties through his Anglomania. One day, when I am no longer alive, you will find that your old friend was right. We shall have a war, and that war will bring us face to face with Germany.'

Up to the last moment before the declaration of war Freedericksz supported the Tsar in his efforts to remain at peace with Germany and Austria. But as soon as military operations began he submitted to his monarch's will. His chivalrous character rejected any idea of a separate peace. He was the first to protest against the methods of warfare employed by our enemies when they infringed international law.

HIS MALADY

From 1913 onwards Freedericksz was subject to effusions of blood on the brain. At times he completely lost his memory, sometimes for hours, sometimes for whole days. Those who had seen him only during these attacks of haemorrhage were liable to gain an entirely mistaken idea of the mental capacity of the Minister of the Court.

He was bound, of course, to send in his resignation. He did so several times. But the Tsar was unwilling to hurt the old man by letting him resign. It must be added that the Sovereign was quite unable to find a successor worthy to take the place of Freedericksz; he had long talks on the subject with 'the old gentleman'. The Count put the matter to Prince Kotchubey, and the Prince would certainly have been given the post, but he definitely refused it.

Thus it was as a complete invalid, greatly enfeebled by repeated attacks, that Freedericksz witnessed the collapse of the dynasty. I had a long conversation with him in Petrograd at the beginning of

November 1917; he told me the part he had played during the tragic days of March 1917:

'You were not there; there was only Voyeikov to describe the situation to me, and I did not trust him. I was unable to meet Orlov' (the former head of the Tsar's military secretariat). 'I did not expect revolution to break out immediately after the abdication; like the Tsar himself, I thought the Imperial family would be allowed to leave for Livadia. But I said again and again that I was instinctively in revolt against any idea of abdication. I pointed out that abdication would bring bloodshed, bloodshed on a scale no less than would be entailed by a forcible suppression of revolution. I implored the Tsar not to abdicate.'

B. The Head of the Chancellery
'A WEALTH OF MUSICAL RHYTHM'

It was in March 1900 that I entered on my new duties as Head of the Court Chancellery. The post, I can aver, was no sinecure.

My first task was to subject the whole of my staff to a severe testing. Most of them were sons of Grand Ducal servants. It was almost a tradition that the lackey brushing the boots of his Grand Duke, and ambitious to send his son a few steps farther up the social ladder, should get him into the Chancellery. There the young man would begin as a copyist and ultimately become an official. These young fellows, destitute alike of education and social training, worked in with one another; each of them was fortified by the backing of his Grand Duke (a backing that never failed to be forthcoming at the desired moment), and they regarded themselves as virtually intangible!

It would be too long a story to tell of all the tricks of which I was made the victim by these persons. I need only say that I had to 'sack' several of them for submitting to me for signature official documents in the diametrically opposite sense of the instructions which I, their chief, had given.

There were countless malpractices in connexion with appointments as 'Purveyor to His Majesty'. This title was greatly coveted by manufacturers and sellers of luxury articles, and very large gratuities were to be had by any one who procured an appointment of this sort, perhaps for persons with very doubtful credentials. I had to keep under lock and key all correspondence concerning the Purveyors to His Majesty.

Gradually, taking my time about it, I replaced the whole of these people by young men of good family who had studied at the Law School and the Imperial Alexander School (where the future diplomats and high officials were educated). The old staff were transferred, one by one, to posts in which they could do no serious harm.

There were some outbursts of Grand Ducal irritation; in fairness I must say that they were fewer than I had expected.

My deputy was a Mr. Zlobin. For a long time he could not forgive me for my appointment; he was older than I, and at one time had regarded himself as the obvious candidate for the post of Head of the Chancellery. He was a very good fellow for all that; and a good musician, perhaps too good, as the following story will show.

One day when he was reading to me a draft reply to an important communication, he delivered the concluding passage in a sort of triumphal chant.

'But, Zlobin,' I objected, 'that sentence surely contradicts all that you said before?'

'Quite so. Your Excellency,' he replied without turning a hair, 'quite so; but did you perceive the wealth of musical rhythm in the phraseology?'

I was driven at last to the conclusion that the rhythmical phrasing of urgent papers was taking up too much of his time. Zlobin was a favourite of Freedericksz; the Count was flattered by the respect that my deputy showed him: as soon as he came into the Count's presence he seemed to be in danger of swooning, such was his awe of 'the old gentleman'! I profited by Freedericksz's interest in Zlobin to get him transferred to a most distinguished position, that of Head of the Imperial Decorations Office. He filled this post with dignity and success, convinced that he was in charge of state business of the utmost importance. When the revolution came he was the most decorated man in all the Empire.

VISITORS

The most disagreeable of my duties was the reception of visitors. Freedericksz hated to have anything to do with strangers; he did not like refusing favours —he was too good-hearted—and he did not like promising to grant them, for they might prove later on to be contrary to the law and so produce endless difficulties. Accordingly he issued a standing instruction that nobody was to be admitted to the Minister's presence without having first been received by the Head of the Chancellery, who would go into their case. This enabled me to get rid of the majority of the visitors, and to prepare the Minister as necessary whenever one of them had to be admitted to his presence.

Most of them—such is the general impression that I got after talks with thousands and thousands of applicants for favours of every sort—most of them wanted something which was not authorized by law or, still more often, was flatly against the law. To this day I can hear the constantly repeated phrase:

'If it had been permissible under the law I should not have come to trouble His Majesty.'

My day for receiving visitors was Saturday. But highly placed personages considered that I ought to receive them on days other than those fixed for the common crowd! It will easily be imagined how much useless waste of time this cost me. It should be mentioned that the Grand Dukes were not the only ones to consider themselves entitled to treatment as highly placed personages. This privilege belonged, it appeared, to all the Court dignitaries—and, God knows, there were plenty of them!—to members of the Imperial Council (our Upper Chamber), and, I am not too clear why, to the members of the Imperial Yacht Club.

These distinguished visitors never opened up at once with the object of their visit. One might have supposed that they thought it bad form to fail to waste at least twenty minutes of my time on preliminary gossip about society and the Court. The older personages had a litany of their own to recite; the same litany in every case. They told me at length of the infirmities with which they were afflicted; they recommended me their family doctor; and they described to me the methods of cure that they had had the good fortune to discover, infallible methods against troubles which fortunately I had been spared. It was useless to try to cut short these therapeutical confidences—the story would only grow longer still, and the sufferer would go away ill-humoured into the bargain. Once the litany had been completed, the visitor would suddenly remember what he had called about; he would begin to sing the praises of some relative. That was all—but what a plague in the midst of my work!

For that matter, requests for promotions and appointments dogged me wherever I went. One day, at the New Club, the Head of the Prisons Department sat down next to me, and said, for once without any beating about the bush:

'A splendid man! Young! Rich! with a fine education! Put him into Court dress and he will be an ornament of your balls. My word, he will be better than that baboon X whom you allowed into the last promotion list—that man's Court dress sits on him like a strait waistcoat on a cow.'

'Well, what is the name of your protégé?'

'Name? His name? Here, steward, what's the name of that young man who lost to me three times yesterday at billiards?'

'Prince Karageorgevitch, Your Excellency.'

'No, no. I know Prince Karageorgevitch well. Besides, the Prince beats me, and this other fellow lost three games. How can you be ignorant of the name of a member of the club?'

'My dear chap,' I said, 'send me a little note and tell me who the young man is.'

'Yes, yes. Don't forget what I've been telling you!'

THE CROWN OF THE PRINCESS OF GEORGIA

The industry that was expended at times on waylaying the Head of the Chancellery, as the officer in charge of the distribution of Imperial favours, is almost beyond belief. The story of the princess of Georgia is worth telling.

Mlle Bezobrazova had married a prince of Georgia, a subaltern in a regiment of the Guards. She attached an altogether undue importance to her husband's title. She claimed to be considered as a 'reigning' princess (her husband's great-grandfather had been King of Georgia), which would have given her the right to go in processions alongside the Imperial family.

Year after year she complained of Masters of Ceremonies who failed in her opinion to show her due reverence. An old law of sixty years before, completely forgotten, had to be unearthed in the end to dispose of her claim: descendants of reigning princes from the third degree onwards are entitled to precedence only if it is justified by the functions with which they are entrusted by the Russian Government. The prince was a subaltern; there could, then, be no question of his being placed alongside the Grand Dukes.

The princess had recourse then to another stratagem. She sent in a request that the Tsar should be godfather to her second child. Freedericksz reported; the Tsar did not refuse—he considered it his duty to show favour to large families.

To have the Tsar as godfather brought certain privileges: there was a grant for the boy's education; the mother was entitled to a present from Court funds; on attaining his majority the young man could claim a post in the Ministry of the Court, and there were certain other grants in case of need. The Georgian princess knew how to make the most of this manna, by repeatedly declaring that she was destitute.

It was the present that ultimately brought disaster to the writer of these lines.

The value of the present was determined by the lady's 'rank'. One day I said to the keeper of Imperial presents:

'Fix up something to please her; the grant is 600 roubles; you can go a bit beyond that if necessary, but not beyond 1,000.'

A few days later I was informed that the princess wanted a 'diadem'. It was impossible to get one for so small a sum.

'Explain that to her,' I said.

'I have done, but do you think she is going to give way? She says she agrees to have Ural stones in the diadem.' (Ural stones are semi-precious coloured gems.)

'If that will please her, get her a diadem with Ural stones.'

That was all she wanted.

Count Pourtalés, the German Ambassador, was giving a ball. The princess telephoned to him and pointed out that as a reigning princess she was entitled to an invitation. 'The Tsar himself has just sent me my crown.' A crown! Pourtalés was profuse in apologies, and sent the invitation demanded of him.

The princess telephoned to the Court Stables office:

'Count Pourtalés has invited me to his ball as a reigning princess. Please send me one of the Court carriages.'

The request was refused.

The princess telephoned again to Pourtalés and explained to him why the Embassy must put a car at her disposal. That made the

Ambassador suspicious. He telephoned to the Master of Ceremonies, and the cat was out of the bag.

The Tsar asked Freedericksz for explanations. The rumour was going about that I was 'distributing crowns'.

I had to have the unlucky diadem photographed and to draw up a report several pages long to explain the case of the Georgian princess.

NO SINECURE

I may end this section as I began it: my post was no sinecure. A good part of my day was taken up by conversations with the Minister; the rest of the time was largely spent in receiving visitors; and every day there was a steady flow into my office of reports from my staff. In the evenings I worked on the most important of the reports, and read the printed matter sent to the Minister in his capacity of member of the Imperial Council, in order to keep him constantly in touch with what was going on in our Upper House; the Tsar was in the habit of asking him for information on this subject. I brought my day to an end by signing papers and going through my correspondence.

It took me a good many years to master my duties. Some of the 'tricks of the trade' could only be acquired in the course of experience and professional training. Shall I give an example? The Imperial family was, let us say, expecting what the newspapers call 'a happy event'. The Chancellery had to prepare in advance the manifesto which the Tsar would sign (writing in himself, in a space left blank, the name decided on for the baby), to inform the country of what had happened.

A manifesto? Surely two, the careful reader may say: one for a boy and the other for a girl. The careful reader will still be far from the truth. Under the law Freedericksz had to be present in the next room at the happy event; and every time he went off for that purpose he took in his dispatch-case five—I say five—different manifestos: one for a boy, one for a girl, one for two boys, one for two girls, and one for a boy and a girl. This last case has not occurred, so far as I am aware, in any reigning family since the world began.

In sixteen years I scarcely had one free night. The work came in unendingly, like the water for the millwheel. If friends came to see me and I spent a few hours in their company I had to start the next day's work without having closed my eyes for one moment. My nerves stood this infernal grind fairly well.

MY DEPARTURE FROM PETROGRAD

I left my post of Head of the Court Chancellery against the will of Count Freedericksz. To satisfy him the Tsar had signed a decree sending me to Jassy as Minister Plenipotentiary while retaining me nominally in the position which I had held for more than sixteen years. In 1913 Freedericksz had expressed the desire that I should be given the rank of Deputy Minister of the Court, but another person was appointed. From that moment I knew that the Rasputin clique would end by 'downing' me. My authority progressively declined, and his illness made it impossible for Freedericksz to support me with the necessary energy.

In December 1916, when I was in Petrograd, the Empress offered me the post of Deputy Minister of the Interior. She said to me on that occasion:

'Everybody is criticizing; nobody is ready to give any help.'

I shall tell of this incident later, in the chapter dealing specially with Rasputin. At that moment my appointment might have meant one of two things: either an attempt to cover the activities of the Rasputin clique, or the offer of the opportunity to assist in righting the helm of State. If in talking to me the Empress had touched on the problem of Rasputin, and if I had had the least hope that it was not already too late to combat her mysticism (and all that it involved), I should have accepted; I should even have asked for another audience, in order to offer my services.

I did not do so. I had not the heroic quality such a step would have called for. I left for Jassy; I do not know whether history will justify me.

When I first entered on my duties at Court I had set before myself the purpose of restoring the pedestal on which the Tsar ought to stand; of assisting the Tsar in making justice and order prevail; of seeing to it that the Tsar's subjects should enjoy all the blessings that can be showered upon them from a throne. My chief collaborated with me in that purpose, himself entirely imbued with these same ideals. I was surrounded, moreover, with members of the suite who were thoroughly honourable men and ready, as I was, to worship the Tsar and to die for the dynasty. Each one of these men did his duty. But every one of us felt that we had never succeeded in inspiring in the Sovereign the confidence without which the difficulties of our task inevitably became more than mortal man can overcome.

C. *The Tsar's Immediate Suite*
IT WAS OF NO GREAT SIZE

The Tsar's immediate suite was composed of a small number of dignitaries holding definite posts.

First of all I must mention the Marshal of the Court, Count P. C. Benckendorff. He was an old officer of the Horse Guards, and had become the supreme arbiter of all that concerned the traditions of the Russian Court. Thoroughly well-up in his job, even-tempered and hard-working, he was most punctual in the execution of his rather complicated duties.

Their Majesties treated him with great respect and entirely as a personal friend. He could also boast the friendship of the Grand Dukes and of all the sovereigns who came on visits to the Russian Court. (His brother was for a long time our Ambassador in London.)

Count Benckendorff was a man of principle. He abstained from any sort of political activity and would not even discuss politics. It was a matter of tactics, and there was much to be said for it.

He did not follow the Tsar to Siberia, for at that time he was confined to his bed, seriously ill. His place was filled by his son-in-law, Prince Vassily Dolgorukov, formerly of the Horse Guards. Dolgorukov was too young and too modest to venture to offer political advice to the Tsar. He preferred to go into exile and die with his master under the fire of the Bolsheviks.

Next came the Commander of the Palace, head of the Court police. This post was held first by General Hesse, A.D.C., and later, after various changes, by General Voyeikov.

The first of these two dignitaries kept rigidly to his specific duties. The second tried to play an important part at the Tsar's side.

Voyeikov, who had married the daughter of Count Freedericksz, was friendly with Mme Vyrubova, Rasputin's great admirer. It was on her recommendation that the Empress proposed the General for the post of Commander of the Palace after the death of General Dediulin. Freedericksz felt that it would be entirely impossible for him to work in harmony with his son-in-law; their temperaments were utterly dissimilar. He begged Alexandra Feodorovna to put forward another candidate, but his resistance was broken down. Voyeikov obtained the post he had coveted. He was very ambitious, and his tactics consisted in gradually alienating from the Tsar everybody who could interfere with his (Voyeikov's) plans. There was a time when I thought that Voyeikov and I would be able to work together in entire agreement; but a thing happened that made our collaboration impossible. Voyeikov presented to Freedericksz a report addressed to the Tsar which the Tsar sent back to the Minister, because the proposals made in the report ran counter to the existing laws. Freedericksz, greatly alarmed, said that in future all reports from Voyeikov must first be passed by me; and that, naturally, was enough to make Voyeikov hate me.

At the moment of the Tsar's abdication Voyeikov, owing to a succession of unfortunate circumstances, was at the head of the Tsar's suite, which at that time included only four other persons. Admiral Nilov, Prince Dolgorukov, Count Grabbe, and Naryshkin (Freedericksz being ill). What I have here to relate suffices to show that these people were incapable of giving proper advice to the Tsar. Among the Tsar's immediate suite, Voyeikov bears the chief responsibility for what happened after the arrival of the deputies from the Duma on their baneful mission.

There is little to say of Admiral Nilov, His Majesty's Flag Captain, who represented the Imperial navy, and who accompanied the Tsar on all his journeys. The Admiral owed his appointment to the intervention of Grand Duke Alexis, whose A.D.C. he had been for many years. Nilov had habits of intemperance which made him incapable of efficient work. He was very devoted to the Tsar, and after the revolution he remained at the *Stavka* until summoned away by the Tsar's express order.

The post of Head of the Emperor's military secretariat was held successively by Count Heyden, Prince Orlov, and, finally, Naryshkin. The Count had been in a privileged situation because he had been a friend of Nicholas II in their childhood; he sacrificed his post, his wife, and his children to a transient passion.

Prince Vladimir Orlov, a former officer of the Horse Guards, and an exceedingly rich man, soon became one of the intimates of the Imperial family. He was a highly cultivated man, sarcastic, with a dry humour, and enjoyed great social prestige. In 1915 he advocated the formation of a Ministry 'that could inspire public confidence', as the phrase went at the time. His whole policy was directed primarily to enabling Russia to escape from the disaster that he could see approaching; he was able to appreciate its premonitory symptoms at their true import. With no thought whatever for his personal career, he was devoted to the Tsar and to the cause of the Russian monarchy, devoted in the highest sense in which the word can be used. He was in regular correspondence with certain leading statesmen; he was the only one among the members of the suite who had any real political ability. Unfortunately he was no admirer of the Empress, and showed his feelings towards her in the presence alike of adherents and opponents of Rasputin, and even in audiences with the Empress herself.

I shall tell later, with all necessary detail, how this remarkable man's career was broken the very day the Empress decided to get rid of him. The Tsar had to take his wife's side (probably against his will, for he had a great regard for Prince Orlov); otherwise he would have been publicly sacrificing her prestige.

Orlov's place was taken, towards the end of the régime, by Naryshkin, a son of the Mistress of the Robes. Naryshkin made no attempt to share the captivity of Their Majesties after the revolution.

Three officers were attached to the military secretariat, Drenteln, Sablin, and Count Vorontzov Dashkov. They were the only officers attached to the person of the Tsar who were constantly at the Palace; they were regarded as assistants to the Head of the military secretariat. The rest of the officers (aides-de-camp, Generals 'in the suite', and even Generals A.D.C.) could only present themselves to the Tsar after obtaining authorization from Count Freedericksz.

Drenteln was a straightforward and intelligent man with a strong personality, and a man of culture. I found him thoroughly well qualified to be in the immediate and intimate entourage of the Tsar. He was a courtier in the good sense of the word, a man of good judgment and full of tact; apart from Freedericksz he was probably the only man to whom the Tsar was attached. The Sovereign greatly appreciated his company, and in the course of time Drenteln might have been able to render very valuable service through his good judgment of character and his ability to recognize straightforward people who were honestly devoted to His Majesty: he would not have been one to try to lure them away from his master!

Then, however, came the Orlov incident. Drenteln had been Orlov's right hand, and his position was badly shaken. To fill the cup to overflowing, there came one more incident: Djunkowsky, the officer in command of the gendarmerie, felt impelled to seek out the Tsar and tell him the whole truth about Rasputin. The whole truth! He was at once relieved of his office, and fell into disgrace. But he had belonged to the same regiment as Drenteln, on whom some of his disgrace fell accordingly. Drenteln was put in command of the Preobrajensky regiment. It was a promotion; but it meant leaving the Court.

Sablin, the Empress's protégé, was not of sufficient calibre to be able to give political advice to the Tsar. He would have been unable to impose his point of view.

Count Vorontzov Dashkov played no part of any importance.

Finally, there was the commander of His Majesty's personal escort, Count Grabbe. This officer failed to arouse in the soldiers forming the escort the indispensable sentiment of fidelity to the Sovereign, and proved personally unequal to his task when the final catastrophe came.

There was one more member of the Tsar's immediate suite, his physician—first Hirsch, afterwards Botkin and Feodorov.

Botkin was notoriously cautious in the extreme. Nobody in the suite had ever been able to get him to say what was the matter with the Empress or what treatment the Cesarevitch and his mother were being given. Feodorov was a man of great intelligence. He watched particularly over the health of the Cesarevitch; at the *Stavka* he was considered to have a great deal of influence with the Tsar. It was on the strength of his final diagnosis that the Tsar abdicated the throne in his son's name as well as his own: Feodorov had said definitely that Alexis would always be an invalid.

These were the principal personages in the Tsar's immediate suite. The aides-de-camp went on duty only for twenty-four hours at a time, in rotation; they would never have dreamed of submitting memoranda on general policy to His Majesty. Freedericksz, moreover, was jealous of his own function of adviser, and would never have tolerated such an abuse of influence. And it was well known that the Tsar himself detested those who attempted to discuss matters that did not come directly within their province.

The Head of the Apanages, the Grand Masters of Ceremonies, the Head Librarian and the Director of the Imperial Theatres only presented themselves in order to report on their respective spheres of duty.

I will say little on the subject of the Tsar's entourage at the time when he was at the *Stavka*, his headquarters, as Generalissimo. Persons who were there for many months have often told me that these officers (I deliberately say nothing whatever about them in their military capacity) produced an impression of lifelessness and apathy, of people drifting and resigned in advance to whatever catastrophe might be approaching: 'petty bureaucrats in the service of a sovereign faced with an unexampled crisis'. All the new appointments seemed to have been dictated by some malignancy of fate: good men went, and their places were taken by careerists. The cleavage between the Tsar and the rest of the country continued to grow while he was at headquarters. Ministers rarely came, and when they did they showed no solidarity with their colleagues in the Cabinet. There was a total lack of unity in action and policy alike in the Cabinet and between Government and G.H.Q.: 'We were living on another planet'.

The Tsar saw only what the Empress allowed him to gather from her personal letters; and these letters were, of course, neither objective nor even informative.

The 'wall' of which I write in the next section suddenly grew and converged above the Tsar's head, turning into a cavern without air or light.

Here I will allow myself one single quotation, the only one in this work. On page 537 of the 1928 volume of the *Revue des Deux Monies* there is this passage in the article 'Mémoires du comte Benkendorf', dated March 21st 1917:

'It was on this day that our detention in the Alexander Palace began. Our company consisted of Mme Naryshkin, my wife. Baroness Buxhoewden, Countess Hendrikov, Drs. Botkin and Derevenko, Count Apraxin (who left us at the end of a week), and myself. Next day, in the Emperor's train, my son-in-law Prince

Dolgorukov arrived. We were also expecting General Naryshkin, Head of His Majesty's military secretariat; Count Alexander Grabbe, commanding the Cossack escort, and Colonel Mordvinov, A.D.C. to the Emperor; but they did not come. In addition, Mme Vyrubova, an invalid, and Mme Denn were in the Palace, but apart from the rest.'

In all, six women and five men, one of whom left on March 25th.

THE SUITE PLAYED NO POLITICAL PART

It is clear from what I have written that the Tsar's immediate suite could have had no part in determining His Majesty's policy. It was made up of specialized officials who kept to the tasks for which they were responsible.

Their principal concern was to maintain their position amid the whirlwind that surrounded them. The best policy for each one of them was to confine himself to his own restricted province, not to go beyond his orders, and on no account to embark on any political adventure, for fear of the exceedingly unpleasant results that it might bring. 'Keep out of trouble' became the general motto, 'lie low', 'do nothing on your own responsibility if you can help it'.

Moreover, these officials were quite unfitted for playing any political part. Almost all the important members of the suite owed their positions to earlier service in the Horse Guards. Count Freedericksz, a former Commanding Officer of that distinguished regiment, felt it his duty to seek candidates for any vacancy that he had from among its officers, that big family to which he belonged and which provided the indispensable guarantees of correctness, tact, and perfect training. There was a very close solidarity between all those who had worn the white and gold uniform; that solidarity also constituted an important guarantee.

But none of the ex-officers of the Horse Guards had had any sort of preparation for playing any important political part. They all belonged to the high Russian nobility, a category of Russians who had kept a little apart from the other classes; they came to the Palace with a military education acquired in the schools for pages or cadets and completed by ten years or so passed in an elegant and socially brilliant regiment. Among them there were some very well-educated men; but most of them were without the special training through which it is necessary to pass, by one means or another, before having anything to do with affairs of state.

II. 'SREDOSTENIE'
'THE WALL'

The Tsar's immediate suite was incapable of bringing him fresh ideas concerning what was going on in his country, of suggesting political ideas independently of the reports from his Ministers. But an autocrat can only exercise his sovereign functions if he has the means of personal judgment, investigation, and supervision. In order to be an autocratic sovereign, Nicholas II required independent sources of information as a check on his Ministers.

We touch here on the problem which was the origin of the great tragedy of the last of the Romanovs; it is best described by its Russian name, *Sredostenie*. Throughout the reign of Nicholas II the *Sredostenie* was the principal subject of political discussions.

Sredostenie means literally a wall. It was virtually a technical term in Russian politics. The explanation that follows will indicate the theory underlying the term.

At the head of all stands the Sovereign, the autocrat. Below him, teeming and inchoate, is the struggling mass of his subjects. In order that Russia may live in entire tranquillity and content, all that is necessary is that there shall be direct relations between the Sovereign and his subjects. The Tsar can do no wrong; he stands above classes, party politics, and personal rivalries. He desires the good of his people, and has practically unlimited means for assuring it. He seeks nothing for himself; he has a profound love of all those whom God has confided to his supreme care. There is no reason why he should not be the benefactor of each and all. *All that is wanted is that he should know exactly what his people need.*

The subjects love the Tsar, for he is the source of all their well-being. They cannot fail to love the Sovereign, for no other feeling is possible toward Beneficence personified. The subjects are not always happy, for the resources of the State are not unlimited and not everybody can be wealthy. But they have the consolation of knowing that the Sovereign does all that he can and everything that his essentially good heart dictates, in order that each one of them may have his share of well-being. Does not the idea of being constantly the object of the solicitude of an almost all-powerful being constitute the greatest possible consolation?

I repeat: in order that this idyllic picture may be complete, the sole link needed to complete the chain is this—*The Tsar must be in possession of sound information.*

Where is this information, indispensable for the proper working of any system of autocracy, to be sought?

Two political elements are interested in keeping the Tsar in more or less complete ignorance of what is passing in the minds of his subjects. The bureaucracy (including the Ministers) forms one of the sections of the 'wall' which surrounds the Sovereign. The bureaucracy is a caste with its own interests, interests that are not necessarily the same as those of the Tsar. In an empire with a hundred and fifty millions of inhabitants, an empire stretching from Warsaw in the west to Vladivostok in the east, it is impossible to do without a bureaucracy. It is essential to appoint supervising and executive agents. But these agents tend to substitute their own influence for that of the Tsar. How many times have certain Ministers represented the rigours of their administration as proceeding from the pitiless severity of the Sovereign, and any mitigation of those rigours as the fruit of pressure put upon the Tsar by themselves, the Ministers! The bureaucracy is interested, moreover, in keeping the Tsar in ignorance of what is going on: it is in this way that it makes itself more and more indispensable.

The second part of the 'wall' is formed by the fomenters of disturbances, the Intelligentsia (intellectuals), a name which the Russians borrowed from the French language and which subsequently spread back over Europe with a special connotation. The intellectuals are those who are not the bureaucracy that is at work and would like to become the bureaucracy of a different régime, a régime that can only be introduced into Russia at the cost of revolutionary convulsions.

The intellectuals are interested in attacking the bureaucracy and the Tsar whenever and wherever they can, blaming both for all the mistakes of the Ministers. The tactics of the intellectuals, the 'Third Estate' (in a slightly changed sense), are to misrepresent the relations between Beneficence personified and the mass of the people. With their newspapers, their pamphlets, their lectures, their teaching in the universities, their doubtful foreign connexions, their money, the intellectuals are tireless in weaving a fabric of venomous lies. They tell the people the opposite of what ought to be told them in order to prevent them from becoming too agitated; they declare that the Tsar has no love for his subjects and no concern for their fate. Knowing how false all this is, the Tsar detests the intellectuals, the agitators, the disturbers, the revolutionaries.

Bureaucracy—intellectuals: those who had arrived and those who wanted to take their places. Two enemies, working together in one respect—in their tendency to reduce the personal prestige of the Tsar. Brick by brick, lie by lie, between them they built up a veritable prison wall around him, confining him to his palace and preventing him from leaving it to speak directly to his good subjects and to tell them as man to man how he loved them. That wall was equally effective in concealing the extent to which the true subjects of the Tsar, those whose natural sentiments had not been perverted by propaganda, those simple subjects with open hearts ready to accept his beneficence and grateful for it, loved their Little Father Tsar.

The peasant masses loved the Tsar. The soldiers loved the Tsar. The townspeople, who crowded to see him pass and huzzaed from the moment when his motor-car came into sight, loved the Tsar. He would have been loved still more if the 'wall' had not prevented him from doing his work as autocrat.

Towards the end of his reign Nicholas II seems to have felt that he had succeeded in destroying the accursed 'wall', the *Sredostenie*. I remember a very significant conversation that I had with him on February 14th 1917, fourteen days before the end of the régime.

In discussing with the Tsar a measure that was to be adopted, I was unable to refrain from saying:

'That will do a great deal to assure the position of the dynasty!'

In spite of his reserve, the Tsar replied with heat, plainly disturbed at what I had said:

'What! You, Mossolov, are you too going to tell me of the peril that menaces the dynasty? People are continually harping on this supposed peril. Why, you have been with me and have seen how I was received by the troops and the people! Are you too, even you, panicking?'

'I have seen all that. Sire, but I also see them when they are not in Your Majesty's presence. Forgive my freedom of speech.'

The Tsar controlled himself, and went on, with a smile:

'I am not put out—far from it. Let us go in to dinner. The Empress will be waiting for us already.'

That, I repeat, was on February 14th 1917. Did the Tsar realize the danger, and was he merely trying to keep up the courage of those who were around him?

That is a possible explanation. But I think the truth is that the Tsar did not see the danger, or did not see that it was already at the Palace gates.

THE CANONIZATION OP SAINT SERAPH

What had the Tsar done to demolish the 'wall'? Two main things. It was possible to enter into relations with the mass of the people by personally appearing in the presence of the crowds, or by making use of intermediaries. The possible intermediaries were the regularly elected deputies, representatives of the nation; more or less representative delegations; and individuals in a position to tell the Tsar what their fellow-countrymen thought.

It will be observed that this list gives the sources of information in a definite order. It begins with statutorily regularized methods and ends with purely arbitrary choice, chaos.

I was a witness of one of the principal efforts associated with the first idea, that of immediate relations between the Tsar and the masses. Its setting was the neighbourhood of the monastery of Sarov; its occasion was the canonization of the Staretz Seraph.

The monastery of Sarov is in the province of Tambov, near the town of Arzamas. The Staretz Seraph passed his last years there.

The Holy Synod had made certain objections to the canonization. Pressure had been put on it by the Court, and after a great deal of discussion the canonization was decreed. The Tsar took the opportunity of this ceremony to gain strength from the mounting tide of popular enthusiasm through communion with the lowly in their prayers. The Empress intended also to take part in the journey to Sarov; she wanted to be present at the 'miraculous' healing of Princess Orbeliani, an event that was considered certain to occur.*

---

* *The princess was one of the Empress's favourite maids of honour; she*

Sarov was not on the railway, and to get there a platform was specially built near Arzamas for Their Majesties' use. Barouches drawn by four horses were brought for the Sovereigns and the suite. This mode of locomotion seemed to have been particularly relished by the Empress and the maids of honour.

Thousands and thousands of peasants had crowded along the whole length of the mail route to Sarov, well before the Imperial procession started. I have been told that five hundred thousand peasants, from all over Russia, had swarmed into the neighbourhood of the monastery. Barracks had been built to house them, but proved totally inadequate; most of the pilgrims spent the nights in the open.

It was a wonderful spectacle. The crowds, in their Sunday best, greeted the Tsar as he passed with unfeigned enthusiasm. It was a sight to see the radiant faces of the people who were selected to present salt and bread to the Sovereign at the halts, in accordance with the old Russian custom.

The Emperor seemed fully as pleased as his subjects; he replied to the acclamations with short sentences full of good nature. The Empress herself, normally so cold and distant, did her best to put some warmth into her response to the crowd.

The arrival at Sarov was invested with remarkable grandeur. The last rays of the setting sun gilded the vestments of the priests and the countless heads of the crowd, which held its breath to catch the words of the Tsar's address. The old monastery was covered with creepers. Vespers were sung by the choirs of the arch-diocese of Tambov, choirs such as existed only in Russia.

On the day of Their Majesties' departure things went less well. It had been decided that the Sovereign should go to visit the *skit* (hermitage) of St. Seraph, and the miraculous bath alongside it.

There was a mile to walk alongside a little stream flanked by the mountain on whose slope the monastery was built. The Governor of the province, Launitz (he was assassinated later by revolutionaries) had received definite orders not to prevent the crowd from watching

---

had been attacked by creeping paralysis, and had been given up by all the doctors. She had now conceived the project of being immersed in a 'miraculous bath' near St. Seraph's retreat. No miracle of any sort was effected; Princess Orbeliani died ten years later, reduced to complete immobility.

the Sovereigns as they went on their way. Troops were brought up; the soldiers held hands to keep the peasants on the slopes of the mountain; every minute there seemed a danger that the 150,000 men and women would break through the fragile barrier so formed and press on to the path.

After a mass at the *skit*, the Sovereigns started back along the path. Half-way back a short-cut goes straight up to the monastery. When he got to it the Tsar unexpectedly took this path, deliberately passing through the crowd of peasants massed on the slopes of the amphitheatre on the left.

I saw the Tsar disappear in the peasant flood; the rest of the Imperial suite was already separated from him by the crowd. 'Come!' I shouted to Launitzj,

After superhuman efforts we succeeded in rejoining the Tsar, who was slowly going forward, repeating: 'Let me through, little brothers!'

They all wanted to touch a bit of his uniform! The situation at once became alarming. We were being suffocated. Some well-intentioned people, seeing the danger the Tsar was in, began to shout:

'Don't push!'

In vain! It was scarcely possible to move one's arms. I said to His Majesty:

'Sire, they all want to see you. If you would agree just to get up on our crossed hands, Launitz's and mine—'

The Tsar would not. But a few seconds later, amid another crush, he involuntarily sat down on our crossed hands. We hoisted him on to our shoulders. There was a veritable thunder of hurrahs!

To save the Tsar we kept him on our shoulders and made for a sort of footbridge that descended the slope a little farther on, joining the monastery with the river below. With the aid of a couple of specially vigorous *mujiks* we succeeded in getting the Tsar on to this footbridge.

But there was still great danger. The peasants followed on to the shaky structure, some yards high at that point, and it collapsed just behind the Tsar; I do not know how I managed to cling to the rail that had stood firm. The Tsar hurried on and reached the side door of the monastery.

'Where is my suite?' he asked.

'It was swallowed up at once. Sire, I saw Count Freedericksz fall. I am afraid he may have got into difficulties.'

'Go and find him.'

After some searching I saw the Count go into his cell. His face was covered with blood. It seems that he had been unable to get up again and had been trodden on by the peasants; his pince-nez had been smashed by a man's heel and had cut his cheek. Fortunately his injuries were not serious; an hour later the Count was able to present himself to Their Majesties, with his face bound up by a not very efficient attendant. The Empress made him let her adjust the dressings better.

This unfortunate incident (it might easily have led to a repetition of the Hodynka disaster!—) showed the immense difficulties in the way of allowing the Tsar to yield to the very human impulses of his good heart. The desire of the crowds to show their Sovereign their love for him almost brought a tragedy.

But I shall never cease to declare that the Sarov incidents are manifest evidence that the Bolsheviks are wrong when they claim that the people never manifested any other sentiments toward the dynasty than those of envy and hatred.

THE INTERMEDIARIES BETWEEN THE TSAR AND THE MASS OF THE PEOPLE

I come now to the indirect means employed in order to keep the Sovereign in touch with the mass of his subjects. The regular statutory method of delegating representatives of the people ultimately took the form of an assembly of elected deputies.

The first idea had been to create a consultative Duma, an assembly of deputies which would have the right to discuss the proposals submitted by Ministers but would not be able to impose its decisions on the Tsar. A Bill on these lines, drafted by M. Bulyguin, was promulgated; but the public reaction to it was such that it was not proceeded with.

October 17th 1905 brought a Duma with the right to reject the measures proposed by Ministers. It was a real Parliament, but with a Ministry independent of it, something like that of Germany at the time or that of the United States at present.

The Duma was intended to serve two different purposes: to keep the Tsar informed of the main trends of public opinion in Russia; and to serve at the same time as a nursery for the gradual replenishment of a bureaucracy that had degenerated and grown effete through three centuries of unchecked power.

A NURSERY FOR MINISTERS?

It must be freely admitted that we were entirely without statesmen equal to the crushing burdens of Ministerial power.

I recall the Tsar's words after one of the visits from William II:

'The German Emperor has been advising me to do as he does: it seems that each time a new Minister is appointed he writes down on a secret document the name of the man who could take the place of the new Minister if necessary.'

The Tsar added, bitterly:

'What is the good of giving me advice like that! How many times I find it impossible to discover a single suitable man for a vacant post! After superhuman efforts, I select a candidate; but it would be utterly impossible for me to find a second. Probably there are more men in Germany who are capable of filling positions of command than among us.'

I had exactly the same impression of our penury of men one day when talking with General Vaimovsky, Minister of Education, and a former Minister of War. (I had been his personal A.D.C., and he had no secrets from me.) We were in the hall in which one waited before going into the presence of the Tsar.

The General said:

'Who are the people who whisper in His Majesty's ear all the rubbish that it takes so much trouble to prove baseless?'

'Your Excellency, the members of the suite are too well disciplined to dare to pass on to His Majesty unverified rumours '

'Then it must come from the womenfolk. And that makes the struggle still harder. I should have resigned many months ago, but have to stop on because I cannot find a successor. It is impossible to discover anybody capable of holding the portfolio of Education.'

'But I am sure that you have His Majesty's full confidence.'

'Confidence or none, he is always in a state of nerves when I am making my report to him. He shivers!'

'Shivers—?'

'Yes! Don't you remember how one day at the manoeuvres I told you to look at Nicholas Alexandrovitch?—he was then Cesarevitch. We had all been caught in drenching rain out in the field. I said to you, "Look at him shivering!" '

He added, smiling:

'Now I am the rain. I hate the part, and I should be glad to go. But where is the man to take my place?' There was a time when it had been hoped that the Duma would produce a steady succession of politicians who would be capable of filling Ministerial posts as they fell vacant.

THE DEPUTIES IN THE WINTER PALACE

Everything possible was done to smooth the way for the first meetings between the Tsar and the deputies elected by universal suffrage. There was, especially, a formal reception of the deputies at the Winter Palace. The Masters of Ceremonies excelled themselves on that occasion.

The procession left the interior apartments and made for the throne-room. In front of the Tsar went the high dignitaries of the State, carrying the emblems of supreme power—the Imperial Standard, the Seal, the Sword, the Globe, the Sceptre, and the crowns studded with diamonds. The Palace grenadiers escorted the dignitaries, carrying their rifles and wearing their enormous bearskin kalpaks.

In the throne-room the deputies were waiting on the right, with the members of the Upper Chamber in front. The left side was taken up by the members of the Imperial Council, the Ministers, and the high dignitaries of the Court.

The Emperor, the Empress, the Dowager Empress, and Grand Duchesses Olga and Tatiana, with the other members of the Imperial family, came to a stop in the centre of the great hall. The insignia were placed on either side of the throne, which was left half-covered by the Imperial mantle. An altar was brought, and a Te Deum was sung.

Then the Empresses and the members of the Imperial family defiled before the Tsar and took up their places on the left of the throne. The Tsar was left alone in the centre of the room. He went with measured steps towards the throne, and took his seat. He was given the text of the Speech from the Throne, which he read aloud, very distinctly, standing.

Immediately afterwards the procession formed again and withdrew to the interior apartments.

What was to be said of the deputies? I saw them then for the first time in my life. Their dress contrasted strangely with the magnificent uniforms of the Ministers and the high dignitaries. Some of them were in evening dress, others in grey lounge suits. There were some peasant kaftans to be seen, some uniforms of officers on the retired list, and the national costumes of the Caucasian deputies. The whole scene created a painful impression. The deputies' faces had no friendly look.

A few hours later the Minister of the Court and I were present at the opening session of the Duma in the Taurida Palace. On our way back the Count said to me:

'The deputies? They give one the impression of a gang of criminals who are only waiting for the signal to throw themselves upon the Ministers and cut their throats. What wicked faces! I will never again set foot among those people.'

I suppose the impression made on M. Goremykin, the Prime Minister, was not very different. It is said that at the tribune in the Duma, which was too high for him, Goremykin produced a poor impression; this head of the Government, his hands trembling with ill-controlled emotion, could not but be an unimposing figure, especially alongside M. Muromtsev, the President (Speaker) of the Duma, an accomplished orator.

I am convinced that the throne-room ceremony, with dignitaries covered with gold braid and decorations, merely filled the deputies with envy and hatred. It certainly did not succeed in restoring the prestige of the Sovereign as had been hoped. The deputies seemed to me to be incapable of collaborating with the Government; they produced the effect of enemies engaged in an internecine struggle with it for the upper hand.

As for the Tsar himself, the idea never entered his head that these few hundreds of men could be accepted as legitimate representatives of his people, the people who had accustomed him to the spectacle of delirious acclamations. One felt at once that His Majesty would not dream of expecting this Duma, these deputies, these drab nobodies, to be able to assist him in the accomplishment of his duties as Tsar.

The Tsar had signed a manifesto granting political liberties. But he had no sooner done so than the representatives of reaction set themselves to insinuate to him that the manifesto had been extracted by force, and, a still more effective argument, that the Tsar of Russia had not the right to renounce the autocratic power bequeathed to him by his ancestors.

That theory found zealous partisans especially in the entourage of the Empress. Even after the abdication in 1917, the Empress continually repeated that her husband might renounce his throne but could not renounce his autocratic power, for on ascending the throne he had sworn to transmit the power to his successors as he had received it, that is to say, unfettered by any constitution.

The reactionary groups who claimed autocratic power for the Tsar (subject to the proviso that the autocrat must comply with their own demands) soon had the upper hand; and they determined the fate of the first Duma.

The second Duma was even more violent than the first; and the question of receiving it in the Winter Palace was not even considered.

REVOLUTION FROM ABOVE

At the time of the dissolution of the second Duma it had become clear that there was no way out through fresh elections: they would do nothing to facilitate collaboration between deputies and Government, the purpose which had been aimed at.

Two tendencies showed themselves among the leaders. One was represented by my brother-in-law, D. Trepov. It was in favour of entirely constitutional procedure. Trepov declared that, once the experiment had been entered on, it should be pushed to its logical conclusion: a 'homogeneous' (Parliamentary) Ministry must be formed, and the attempt made through this Ministry to procure the indispensable modification of the electoral law.

The protagonist of the second tendency was Stolypin, a courageous and very popular man, but with insufficient breadth of political views. Stolypin held that the first elections had caught our administration napping. In Western countries, he said, the officials had learnt decades ago the difficult art of influencing the electorate;

here in Russia we had made no attempt to give the governors of provinces the opportunity to bring into play their moral ascendancy over voters, who had been worked upon only by 'Leftwing propaganda'. Consequently there must be a new electoral law, and it must give the administration the necessary means for countering 'propaganda'.

Stolypin considered that it would be impossible to get this law passed by the Duma. He induced the Tsar to dispense with the Duma; this was the proposed *coup d' état* from above. It was a dangerous step, one which was bound to shake the authority of the Tsar. No more than two years after the promulgation of the Constitution, one of its principal provisions was to be infringed.

The Tsar adopted the Stolypin policy. I do not know how far he realized the political results that might follow from it. Revolutions from above are apt to provoke revolutions from below.

The third Duma entirely justified Stolypin's diagnosis; it became a docile instrument in his hands.

The fourth Duma was almost exactly similar to the third. The irony of history willed it that such a body should develop into an instrument of revolution; two members of the Right wing were sent by this fourth Duma to extract an abdication from the Tsar.

By then the original theory of the purpose of the Duma had been forgotten for many years—the theory that it was to become a nursery for Ministers and a source of information for the Tsar.

THE DELEGATIONS

Since the duly elected deputies did not seem to provide the link so long sought for between the Tsar and his trusty subjects—even after the modification of the electoral law, the search was pursued elsewhere.

Delegations were the alternative expedient tried.

On the bi-centenary of Poltava* the administration arranged, at His Majesty's desire, a meeting between the Tsar and a delegation of peasants.

These *Khokhols* (the familiar term** used, rather slightingly, by

---

* Peter the Great's victory over Charles XII of Sweden at Poltava (Ukraine), in 1709.

** The word means 'top-knots', and refers to the lock of hair by which the head was carried off the battle-field where a corpse had to be left without burial.

the Great Russians for the Ukrainians) were drawn up in serried ranks in a public square. The Tsar mixed with them and chatted right and left of him; he was so keenly interested that the reception lasted more than two hours, much longer than had been proposed for this patriarchal ceremony. The delegates seemed to me to be completely spellbound by the charm of the Tsar's approach to them.

As for the Sovereign himself, he was full of the subject afterwards, and continually referred in conversation to the knowledge that he had gained from 'those splendid, sincerely devoted *Khokhols*'.

After the promulgation of the 1905 manifesto, granting political liberties, there were attempts to group into a political party those who were declared adherents of the autocratic, rigorously nationalist régime. This party took the name of 'Union of the Russian People'. Its delegates were certainly brought on several occasions into the presence of the Tsar and the Empress.

The leader of the party was a Dr. Dubrovin. His newspaper was the *Russkoye Znamya* ('Russian Standard'). Dubrovin found means, I do not know how, of presenting himself to His Majesty not through the channel of the Master of the Ceremonies but through the simple intervention of the Tsar's valet. Dubrovin secured receptions in the same way for provincial delegations of the 'Black Hundred'—as his 'Union of the Russian People' was nicknamed by the Liberals.

The Minister of the Court only learned of the arrival and reception of these delegations through the Court harbingers' journal, a secret document that recorded the whole of the Tsar's activities from hour to hour.

Freedericksz felt it his duty to point out to His Majesty more than once that unofficial visits of this sort might involve serious political dangers. But each time the Tsar replied:

'Surely I am entitled to know what the people particularly devoted to me think of affairs!'

The newspapers of the 'Black Hundred' gave me a great deal of trouble. These reactionaries denounced the liberal reforms of which Count Witte, the Prime Minister, was the great promoter, and their attacks on him grew more and more scurrilous. Dubrovin and his staff felt that they had the Sovereign's protection. In my capacity of head of the Court censorship I had to take steps against all articles that mentioned the Tsar or members of the Imperial family unless the articles had been submitted to me before publication. Dubrovin attempted on several occasions to evade compliance with the provisions of the law. In the end I sent for him and called his attention to his neglect.

A few days later the *Russkoye Znamya* again published an account of a reception granted by the Tsar to a delegation of provincial reactionaries. Some of the Sovereign's remarks were quoted in a way that could not be permitted, and I had them struck out.

Dubrovin did not accept defeat. He came to see me and began to tell me that the accounts were 'to the Tsar's liking'. I had to recall him to a sense of realities, and energetically asserted my right to censor anything relating to the Imperial family.

On that the 'Black Hundred' began a counterattack; and I was made to realize that Dubrovin had influence. Late at night the telephone at my bedside woke me up. I heard an unfamiliar voice.

'We are aware,' it said, 'of all your intrigues against the only people who are really devoted to the Tsar. . . . I am instructed to inform you that if you do not make an end of your insinuations we shall use our opportunity to tell the Empress some scandalous things about you.'

I hung up the receiver. It was not the first time that I had received anonymous attacks.

The threats were carried out. The Empress suddenly became very distant and avoided meeting me. The maids of honour informed me that most compromising stories, completely false, had been told her about my private life.

There were also official interventions. One day, after his report to the Tsar, Freedericksz told me that Dubrovin had complained of the 'revolting' lack of impartiality that I had been showing towards him. I had to get together a whole file of articles by Dubrovin that had been struck out by the censorship. Freedericksz took it to the Tsar, and told me afterwards that my intervention had been approved by the Sovereign.

I had occasion to speak personally to the Tsar about the matter, I told him that the Liberal newspapers gave me far less trouble than the organs of the people who were 'entirely devoted to His Majesty'. I showed His Majesty an article, manifestly a fabrication from beginning to end, concerned with the Cesarevitch and attributing certain statements to him. The Emperor said to me:

'Yes, that would have rendered ill service to the cause of the dynasty. You did well to stop it. Send me this paper; I will show it to the Empress.'

In his Memoirs Count Witte declares that the reactionary Press was subsidized by the Empress, and that it was she who inspired the tone of the *Russkoye Znamya* and similar papers (the *Moscow News*, the *Tocsin*, etc.). I do not think that is true, though the case of the newspaper projected by Prince Andronnikov seemed to me a little suspicious.

I can say definitely that not a kopek of the funds administered by the Minister of the Court was ever sent to the 'Black Hundred' Press. The sums of which the Tsar disposed as 'pocket money' (about £20,000 a year) served to meet the cost of the Sovereign's wardrobe and of the small presents that he gave personally. I do not think his resources would have been sufficient to enable him to subsidize newspapers. As for the Empress's expenditure, it was in charge of her secretary, Count Rostovtzev.

All the principal clubs were up in arms over rumours that the Black Press was under the special patronage of Her Majesty, and to get to the bottom of the matter Freedericksz instructed me to investigate the stories. I sent for Rostovtzev, and an hour's talk with him sufficed to establish the baselessness of the rumours.

The Tsar's meetings with the delegations of members of the Black Hundred were not arranged through official channels, and were kept rigorously secret; it may be that their true history will never be written.

UNOFFICIAL INTERVIEWS

It remains to mention the persons whom the Tsar was able to consult personally without their communications with him being sanctioned by any other authority than their own conscience.

The first place in this category belongs to Prince Vladimir Mestchersky, editor of the weekly paper *Grashdanin* ('The Citizen'). The Prince had made the acquaintance of Nicholas Alexandrovitch (elder son of Alexander II) when he was Cesarevitch;* he had managed to get permission to visit Alexander III informally at any time, and his paper received regular subsidies from secret funds.

* Nicholas Alexandrovitch died of tuberculosis at Nice

The Prince was a man of great intelligence. He knew that his paper was read by Alexander III and by Nicholas II, and made full use of the influence that the fact gave him. His articles often contained sensational revelations; the administration stood in fear of these pungent paragraphs, based on full knowledge of everything that was going on in the Government departments.

I do not remember the Prince ever meeting with a refusal from the Tsar. He wrote direct to him, without any intermediary, and I have had many of his letters in my hands, in his illegible scrawl, with the Emperor's initials and the word 'Granted' in the margin.

Some of these letters had reference to political questions. The Prince also secured two or three private audiences every year. I am unable to say in what direction he influenced the Tsar, for His Majesty never mentioned him to Freedericksz. But this reactionary prince could only have spoken in direct opposition to every liberal reform.

I may also mention the ex-Ministers Pobedonostzev and Vannovsky, who wrote to the Tsar when they wanted to see him. The Sovereign then sent them an invitation. One more name, that of General Richter, A.D.C., and the list is virtually complete of the remarkably few persons whom the Tsar was able to consult individually.

CHANCE ENCOUNTERS

Finally there come the people whom the Tsar met in casual encounters. I recall the amusing story of Alexander III told me by Mr. Heath, the English tutor to the Cesarevitch.

One day while holidaying in the Finnish fjords, Alexander III had gone out with rod and line. Seeing a Finn peacefully installed by the riverside, he sat down a little way off and cast his fly. An hour passed in unbroken silence. At last the Tsar spoke to his neighbour:

'What do you do in the world?'

A pause. Then, in a tone that betrayed his sense of dignity, the other replied:

'I am a master mariner.'

'Ah! A fine job.'

Silence fell again, perhaps for a further half-hour.

Then the sea-captain spat out his quid and said:

'And what do you do yourself?'
'I am Emperor of Russia.'
'Ah! That's a fine job too.'
There the conversation ended.

Nicholas II was always ready to catechize any plain citizens he met. The incident of the Siberian hunter with his live sable is a typical one.

Rasputin was a typical peasant in the Tsar's eyes. He filled a gap of which the Tsar had always felt conscious. Three main elements combined to smooth Rasputin's path:

(1) The Tsar's anxiety to be kept informed of 'what those who are particularly devoted to the Throne are saying';

(2) The morbid mysticism of the Empress. She was fascinated by the medieval methods of address of which the ' Staretz' made use in talking to her: he was a master of the art of mingling his miracle-worker's gibberish with passages intoned from the liturgy in the habitual peasant style;

(3) The despair of Tsar and Tsarina at the inability of the medical world to do anything for their son, and their readiness to place him in the hands of any quack. Rasputin had incontestable success in the field of healing; I have no idea how he managed it.

Rasputin's rise was of lightning rapidity. Once he had reached the presence of Their Majesties, he succeeded in establishing an unshakable ascendancy over them. He must have had an extraordinary gift of intuition, an instinctive sense of his interlocutor's thoughts and subconscious reactions; and he adapted himself to them instantly. He never ceased to play a part in the presence of Their Majesties—a part which, indeed, was not a difficult one to keep up. The thing that is surprising is the sureness of touch with which this rustic discovered the one and only means of asserting his influence.

He certainly had a large share of elementary common sense, that sound peasant sense that creates havoc when it breaks into the hothouse existence of the *habitués* of a palace. A show of good nature, its hollowness well concealed; an impudent familiarity, combined with a servility which fitted like a glove on this upstart, this man of utterly obscure origin; a few empty formulas, borrowed unconsciously from the criminal sects of the flagellants or the 'white doves' (castrated in mystical rites), or the 'torches' (the sect whose adepts went through fire in churches fitted up for this type of sacrifice)—such was his stock-in-trade. The famous 'Slav soul' was capable of plumbing depths in the realm of mystical perversion of which the outer world has no conception. The combination of these disparate elements produced a Tartuffe of a 'little brother', professing unbounded adoration of the 'Little Father Tsar', and able to discuss political questions without any discordant note ever disturbing the Sovereign. Rasputin brought Nicholas II precisely the assurances which the Tsar had sought at Sarov, at Poltava, in the deliberations of the Duma.

This part of my story is most painful, and I shall devote only a few words to the libidinous side of Rasputin's activities. There is a widely accepted theory that all the ecstasies may merge into one another—so that religious transports may find their climax in those of sexuality. Rasputin knew nothing of this or kindred theories; but he applied them. The Orthodox liturgy has, for instance, a few moments before Holy Communion, the words 'Let us love one another, that we may profess our faith in common'. A slight distortion sufficed to give this chant a blasphemous meaning. Sin? Rasputin disburdened himself of it with ease, declaring that the true saints 'turn to filth, in order that amid the filth their aureole may shine with double brightness'. He got drunk 'in order to show the full hideousness of vice'. He preached the life of purity 'not by means of empty phrases of admonition but by exhibiting, as food for thought, the abject state in which the sinner perishes'. According to the women who surrounded Rasputin, anything whatever was permitted to him, since his mission was to expose the ugliness of vice under every conceivable form. For those who rebelled against this abominable theory, he produced another precept, borrowed from monastical practice and enlisted in the service of his lubricity:

'You have too much vainglory; you must humiliate yourself'

That could mean a great deal.

But there were also around Rasputin women who needed no prompting from epistemological theories to abandon all restraint. And, unfortunately, there were poor wretches who knew that there was only one way of paying a debt contracted towards Rasputin, the dispenser of so many coveted official posts.

THE HEALER

At Spala in 1912, as he came alongside in a boat, the Cesarevitch stretched his leg out too sharply; internal haemorrhage was set up in the groin.* The unfortunate boy suffered dreadfully. The Empress passed whole nights at his bedside. It was a painful spectacle. The anxiety of his father and mother was beyond description.

The doctors called in to attend on the heir to the throne were Dr. E. S. Botkin, Court Physician, Professor Feodorov, Court Surgeon, and Dr. Rauchfuss, Court Physician for children's diseases, who had been sent for from St. Petersburg.

The Empress had forbidden the publication of bulletins concerning her son's illness; the Minister of the Court insisted, therefore, that bulletins should be drawn up in his presence, in order that they might be preserved in the archives. The doctors used to meet in the room which was reserved for me, after their visits to the patient, and they discussed the situation in my presence. None of the remedies which they prescribed sufficed to arrest the bleeding, and the young sufferer's condition seemed alarming.

One day Professor Feodorov was the last to leave my room, and said to me:

'I do not agree with my colleagues. It is most urgently necessary to apply far more drastic measures; but they involve a risk. What do you think—ought I to say so to the Empress? Or would it be better to prescribe without letting her know?'

I replied that I could not possibly give an opinion on so delicate a question. The professor had scarcely gone when I informed the Minister of the Court.

It is said that a telegram had arrived just at that moment from the Staretz** Rasputin, in which the miracle-worker declared that the heir to the throne was recovering and would soon be out of pain,

---

* The Cesarevitch suffered from haemophilia, a congenital malady transmitted only in the female line and attacking only the sons in a family. The sufferer's blood does not congeal sufficiently, and the slightest cut produces obstinate haemorrhage. Haemophilia was congenital in the ducal family of Hesse.

and that he must not be 'allowed to be martyred by the doctors'.

Next day, at 2 p.m., the doctors came in search of me; their first words were:

'The haemorrhage has stopped.'

As they went I detained Feodorov and asked him:

'Did you apply the remedy you spoke of?'

He threw up his hands and replied as he went out:

'If I had done I should not have admitted it; you can see for yourself what is going on here.'

He hurried away.

The Empress left her private apartments for dinner, for the first time since her son's illness; she was radiant in her relief from anxiety. The Cesarevitch, she said, was suffering no longer; in a week's time they would leave for St. Petersburg. The doctors, who were present, seemed in utter consternation; their advice as to the departure had not been sought.

After dinner the Empress sent for me and told me to have the road repaired, so that there should not be the slightest jolting on the way to the station.

A week later the departure took place. The Cesarevitch played peacefully in his bed, and did not seem to be feeling the slightest pain.

'It is not the first time that the Staretz has saved his life,' the Empress said to me.

Aided by the mysticism of the Empress, Rasputin had little difficulty in making his every word law. And the words of this astute peasant were fateful. In the last resort the life of Alexis Nicolayevitch, the destinies of the house of Romanov, and the whole future of Russia depended entirely on his prayers. If he died not a stone would be left standing.

Such were the whispered comments of the household staff of the Court, when they ventured to breathe confidences.

** (Prev page) *Staretz* means literally, in Russian, 'old man', 'greybeard', with an implication of deep respect. Certain monks to whom supernatural powers were attributed were called 'Staretz'. There is a legend that one day Alexander I simulated death and that he then took refuge in Siberia and there lived as a recluse, passing his days in meditation; in this legend he is described as 'Staretz'.

Most of the men called 'Staretz' were monks, but the title can be given to any venerable old man, whether he has taken vows or not. Rasputin has sometimes been called a monk or 'pope' (priest) by foreign writers, but he was neither.

A. A. MOSSOLOV

RASPUTIN'S 'NOTES'

I do not know at what stage or by what process Rasputin began to turn to account his influence with the Empress. On several occasions I had heard of 'notes' given by Rasputin to ladies who came to Him to ask for his high protection. These notes were all drawn up in the same way: a little cross at the top of the page; then one or two lines giving a recommendation from the Staretz. They opened all doors in Petrograd, almost without exception.

My turn soon came.

One day I was told that a lady insisted on being received, though it was outside the hours reserved for official visits. I disliked her the moment she came into my office.

She wore a very low-cut dress, almost a ball dress. She handed me an envelope: inside was Rasputin's calligraphy, with the erratic spelling of which it is impossible to give an idea in translation:

'My dear chap. Fix it up for her. She is all right. Gregory.'

The lady explained that what she wanted was to become a prima donna in the Imperial Opera at St. Petersburg. I did my utmost to explain to her clearly and patiently that the post did not depend in any way whatever on me. It became evident that she was trying to stop in my office and to make the most of all the personal charms she had left....

A similar letter was brought to me one day by a deacon who was also stage-struck. He tried to explain to me that it must be possible to get him on to the stage because the Staretz Gregory had himself given him the 'needful blessing'.

A TYPICAL CASE

Rasputin's influence grew continually. He made and unmade marriages, adoptions, appointments, concessions, commissions....

The Rodzianko affair, with which, by no means willingly, I found myself closely mixed up, was a fairly typical case. The story is briefly as follows.

Tamara, daughter of one of my brother officers, Novosiltzevj had married M. Rodzianko, and had gone with her husband some years later to Italy.

There he had her confined in a lunatic asylum. She succeeded in escaping, and returned to St. Petersburg to claim her children. Her husband put up strong opposition to this.

One day, at Livadia, the Mistress of the Robes asked me to write to the competent authorities to request a re-hearing of Mme Rodzianko's case. Her children's fate depended on the decision of these authorities.

The Mistress of the Robes explained to me that Tamara Rodzianko had been granted a private audience by the Empress, and that after interrogating her at length the Empress had declared that the injustice done to her ought to be remedied.

After drafting the letter to the authorities I went to see Tamara, in order to show it to her. She was so downcast that I did my best to raise her spirits. I asked her how she had managed to get the Empress to receive her. Had not Her Majesty shown some animosity towards her a few months before?

'I met Rasputin at Mlle Golovina's; she is an old friend of mine, and undertook to arrange the audience. To-morrow,' she added with a radiant smile, 'I am going over to thank him.'

Next day Tamara rang me up on the telephone, and, in a voice choked with sobs, begged me to go to see her there and then.

I found her desolate and in utter despair.

'Do you know what happened yesterday? As soon as I entered the room the Staretz was in, all the ladies around him made obsequious bows to him and hurried away; they made no secret of their intention of leaving me alone with that man. Then Rasputin literally threw himself upon me. . . . I boxed his ears and ran away.'

Two days later I met the Mistress of the Robes.

'What has happened about my letter?'

'The Empress told me not to send it—that Rodzianko woman had been telling lies: she does not deserve help from anybody.'

From then on the Empress changed completely in her attitude toward me. Unless there was anything definite to say she never spoke to me beyond the few really unavoidable words.

I learned in the end the version of the affair that had been concocted. It was this:

It was I who had been Mme Rodzianko's protector; it was I who had almost succeeded in getting the Empress to intervene in Tamara's favour; and it was Rasputin who had unmasked the affair and had warned the Empress not do to a serious injustice to Tamara's husband.

I told Count Freedericksz of this bit of scandalmongering. He said simply:

'That fellow Rasputin—what a skunk!'

MY MEETINGS WITH RASPUTIN

It was impossible in the end for me to avoid personal contact with Rasputin. He left no stone unturned in his efforts to get into touch with me: he was trying to get received by Count Freedericksz.

It was in summer. My friends, the Mdivanis, had come to Petrograd for the season. One day, knowing that I was not well enough to go out, Mme Mdivani came to see me at my house.

The moment she entered she came straight to the purpose of her visit.

'Alexander Alexandrovitch, you have many enemies.'

'Who has not, my friend?'

'Yes, but Rasputin could do you harm. I am sure he only hates you because he does not know you. He has a fixed idea that you are constantly working on Count Freedericksz in order to obstruct him. It is essential that you should see him.'

I replied with a categorical refusal.

A few days later I was rung up by Elizabeth Victorovna (Mme Mdivani):

'I have a few friends here; come along too!'

I said I had too much work to do, but she insisted.

The Mdivanis had put up at the Hotel d'Europe. I arrived about 11 p.m., and found myself in the company of Mlle Golovina and several other ladies who were well known to belong to the Rasputin clique.

'It is a trap!' I said to Mme Mdivani. 'You are expecting Rasputin.'

At that moment a bell rang. The ladies rushed excitedly towards the door. Rasputin came in, utterly drunk. He was told my name.

'Ah, Mossolov! Here you are at last! Let us be friends—do you agree?'

He was already leading me to a table loaded with bottles.

'Your old man' (Freedericksz) 'doesn't he like me? . . . I'll tell you: to-night. I'm boozed . . . boozed, dead drunk. . . . Does it upset you? I understand. . . . Don't take any notice. . . . One day, when there's more time, we'll talk more seriously. . . . But not now. Here's to your health!'

We had several glasses together. 'You must come over to see me one day . . . everybody comes to see me . . . the Ministers . . . and "Vitia" (Witte) too . . . only you and your old man make a fuss about it. That's why Mamma (the Empress) doesn't like you any longer.'

'I suppose this intrigue was your little scheme?'

'What of that? Of course it was! Love me, and Mamma will love you.'

'There now, you're the sort I like. You don't bear ill-will. Anybody who can lift it can't have any guile in him. I don't mind a bottle now and then myself.'

'Come and see me. We'll have a drink and a talk.'

'Right ho, right ho. You've got yourself into such a state that you ought to go and lie down.'

When he left he ruined my overcoat in the hall.

Some days later Mme Mdivani came again to see me. She declared that Rasputin was determined to see me at all costs.

'You will gain nothing by showing hostility to him.'

'May be, but I have no desire at all to be seen everywhere with that gentleman.'

Finally it was agreed that I should go to the house of the assistant secretary of the Holy Synod, and there I should meet Rasputin in entire secrecy.

I went to the dignitary's residence on the day fixed. He took me through many corridors and up various staircases. In his private quarters, in a room overlooking a courtyard, I found Rasputin.

This time he was sober. He spoke at length, and, I am bound to say, with a great deal of good sense. He fixed me incessantly with his bleared eyes. He spoke of 'the old chap', that is to say, Count Freedericksz. What he was after was to get on friendly terms with the Minister of the Court. He urged me to talk to the Count and to try to arrange it for him.

Next day I found myself once more in the Empress's good graces.

RASPUTIN'S INFLUENCE OVER THE GOVERNMENT

During the war Rasputin's influence over affairs of state became virtually paramount. Most of the important appointments were settled in the Empress's *salons*. A recommendation from Rasputin was all that was needed even for a Minister's portfolio.

The plans for the most important reforms, the very problem of a separate peace, seemed to depend on what the Staretz would say. I had myself to apply to him for enlightenment on a rumour that an armistice might be declared at any moment, and also to ascertain his view concerning a plan of administrative decentralization in which I was interested.

My idea was to divide the Empire into several 'States' which would be governed by Namiestniks* with the aid of local Dumas (Parliaments).

This reform was to be carried out, under my scheme, at the moment of the conclusion of a victorious peace; it would have democratized the local administration, while preserving autocratic power for the Tsar.

This had to be discussed with Rasputin, to see whether he was in favour of the plan and would give it his support when the time came.

The separate peace was the second problem to be dealt with. I suspected that the Staretz was playing a double game, advocating war to the bitter end only so long as he hesitated to unmask his real position.

Mme Mdivani was no longer in Petrograd, and I had recourse to the services of another woman friend, whose name I prefer to suppress, since she is still in Soviet Russia and the slightest indiscretion might get her into serious difficulties. Let us call her the Baroness.

The Baroness's flat was full of guests. On his arrival Rasputin embraced All the women present. When he caught sight of me he showed anything but pleasure.

He was taken into the dining-room, where he set to, without using knife or fork. The women's flatteries of this boor were sickening. When he got up the wine had made him more talkative; he said to the Baroness:

'Verotchka' (diminutive of Vera), 'take me and Mossolov into your bedroom. He has not come to see me eat.'

When we were alone, Rasputin said to me:

'What is it you want to see me about?'

* Representatives of the Emperor; a title equivalent to that of Viceroy, which was given on some occasions to the Governors General of the Caucasus and Poland.

He glared at me in his customary way.

'I am just back from the Tsar's tour of the G.H.Q., and I want to know what you think about the war.'

'You want to know whether I am working for an armistice?'
'Yes.'
'And what do you think about it yourself?'
'Before the war I thought we ought to remain friends with Germany. But now that we are at war I think it is necessary to go on until we win. Otherwise the Emperor will have his work cut out.'
'Just so.'
I felt at once that that was all I should get out of him, and that he would reveal nothing of his actual views.
'There is another thing,' I said. 'I wanted to tell you that it seems impossible to govern all Russia from Petrograd. The country must be divided into a number of "States", each with its *Namiestnik* and its Duma.'
He cut me short at once.
'Duma! There's one already, curse it, and that is one too many!'
'Wait a minute. The Tsar will have no need to take any account of these other Dumas. The *Namiestniks* will deal with them themselves, in the provinces, far from Petrograd. If there is any criticism, it will be directed entirely against the *Namiestniks* and not a bit against the Tsar, All he will have to do will be to manifest his goodwill towards everybody. His popularity will become all the greater.'
Rasputin was silent for a moment.
'Then how will the Tsar administer the country?'
'As before, autocratically. It will be he that declares war, signs treaties, and is head of the army. The peasants will gain too; they will be called on to elect the local administration.'
'It may be so; but I do not fully grasp the plan.'
A message came that the guests were restive at his absence. Prince Shakhovskoy (then Minister of Commerce) had just come.
'I must go. Your plan seems interesting. Come and see me to-morrow; we will talk more about it.'
I went next day to see Rasputin about 9 p.m., and found him asleep. I waited half an hour. At last he appeared, his face bloated, his hair unkempt. We could not start our conversation at once from the point where we broke off the night before. We rested about an hour, while I told various yarns. Rasputin poured himself out some wine. As he opened a second bottle he said:
'Well, my friend, what about yesterday's conversation? Have you

made up your mind not to breathe another word about it to Grishka?' (Grishka is a depreciatory diminutive of Gregory; like many peasants, Rasputin rarely spoke in the first person.)

He looked hard at me again:

'You ought not to treat him like that,' he said.

'I thought you had forgotten all about it,' I replied.

'Your Madeira is so good, I should have preferred to let serious matters go to-day. But as you like—'

'That's better . . . we can drink as we talk. I like you. I am at my ease with you. If you have invented something which may be useful to Papa and Mamma' (the Emperor and Empress), 'tell us all about it. Otherwise let's drink to their health.'

I set out the plan at length. At first he did not grasp my idea. Then suddenly he understood. He not only understood but rendered my idea in his own picturesque way.

'It's a pity,' he went on, 'that we cannot consult Vitia. What a devil he is. He would manipulate everything to his liking, and would so arrange that it should injure Papa. How often he has discussed plans with me that looked admirable; and then, after careful consideration, I have discovered that his idea would only have been of service to himself, to Vitia, and would have been bad for Papa.'

After the third bottle he asked me:

'Does Papa know about it?'

'He has been given a general idea of it. I don't think he had any objection to it.'

'No use, then, for me to talk to him about it?'

'When the time comes for that,' I said, 'I will let you know, so that you can talk to him about it yourself. That would help me.'

'Help you . . . help you. . . . I will tell him to let you talk to him about it, and I am sure he will. . . .

He is full of intelligence. He will work out the idea himself. . . . As for me, what can I do but give the idea my blessing?'

I pressed his hand. The wine was having its effect on him. He embraced me and began to snivel. When I left he said:

'Come again; we will have another drink, I like you.'

* * *

VYRUBOVA 'RESTORED TO LIFE' BY RASPUTIN

At the beginning of 1916 I was going through a difficult and critical time. Freedericksz was ill and unable to come, as he always did, to my defence.

The whole of the affairs of the Court rested on my shoulders. And I could feel that I had not the entire confidence of the Empress. Intrigues of every sort were being hatched in all directions, shooting up like poisonous fungi. But for my devotion to Count Freedericksz, I should have sent in my resignation.

An invitation to dinner at the Mdivanis' came just at the right moment.

There were only to be three of us—Mme Mdivani, Rasputin, and I. It was an excellent opportunity for getting the Staretz to talk. Only he could say what were the charges that had been concocted against me. I accepted the invitation.

The dinner brought no help. Scarcely had soup been served when Rasputin was summoned to the telephone. He came back almost at once, whitefaced and trembling. A catastrophe! 'Annushka' (Mme Vyrubova, the Empress's friend) had been seriously injured in a railway accident, and her life was despaired of. He must go at once to Tsarskoe Selo.

One of the hotel cars was put at his disposal.

It has been said that in spite of her condition Mme Vyrubova was resuscitated by Rasputin. According to some of the maids of honour, the Empress, on returning to the Palace, declared that he had performed a miracle.

THE TSAR AND RASPUTIN

I had kept Freedericksz informed of my contacts with Rasputin. He made no objection to them. He felt, indeed, that they gave him indications of Their Majesties' attitude.

Well before this period Freedericksz had already made one effort to enlighten the Tsar about Rasputin. The Count had long had his report in preparation; he attached great importance to it. But he only had time to speak a dozen words when the Tsar cut him short:

'My dear Count, people have spoken to me several times about Rasputin. I know beforehand everything you can tell me. Let us remain friends; and never, mind you, never touch on this subject again.'

The situation, however, became more and more untenable, and Freedericksz felt it his duty to return once more to the subject. I do not know what happened at this second conversation. My impression, however, is that the Tsar replied much more energetically and still more decisively than before.

Persons of less importance than Freedericksz were paying with the loss of their posts for the least attempt at rebellion against the growing influence of the Staretz.

I need only mention the case of Prince Vladimir Orlov.

The Prince was descended from one of the favourites of Catherine II. For many years he not only occupied an important post at Court but was virtually a personal friend of the Tsar's.

He had plenty of wit and a sharp tongue, and made some stinging hits at the Staretz in talking about him. There are malicious persons at all times in every Court, and the Prince's witticisms quickly reached the Empress's ears.

That was enough. One day the Emperor and Empress were going on board the Standard, the Tsar's favourite yacht. Orlov had already gone down to the cabin reserved for him. The Empress sent for Freedericksz and said to him:

'Tell Prince Orlov to go ashore. I do not want to see him here.'

The order was so astonishing that Freedericksz went to the Tsar to ask his decision about it. Nicholas II took his wife's side, as always. Orlov was asked to go ashore on some pretext that I can no longer recall. A little later he lost his post at Court.

Another incident, of which several versions exist, produced the abrupt dismissal of Mlle S. I. Tuytcheva, the Grand Duchesses' governess.

When she was chosen for this important post, Mlle Tuytcheva was about thirty years old. She was a woman of exceptional personality and character, highly cultivated, belonging to an aristocratic Moscow family, and she had made an excellent impression on us all. As soon as she arrived at Livadia we noted how salutary was her influence over the children; their manners at once showed a great improvement.

I cannot say exactly how long the governess had held sway over her little empire when one day the news spread like wildfire that the Empress and Mlle Tuytcheva had 'had words'. I was not myself a witness of the event. I know that Freedericksz went to see the

Empress, and told her that the sudden departure of Mlle Tuytcheva would create a bad impression in Moscow. He was told in reply that Mlle Tuytcheva had meddled in things that did not concern her, and had tried to give lessons to Her Majesty on what children could and what they could not be permitted to do. Her Majesty seems to have replied that a mother was the best qualified to know what was proper for children. On that Mlle Tuytcheva had said she wanted to leave and had been told that she might. It would have been impossible to retain her as a maid of honour in these circumstances.

My own belief is that the Empress regarded the Staretz as a saint and was ready to let him go into the bedrooms to give his blessing. Mlle Tuytcheva's opinion was that the unsavoury *mujik* could not be allowed at night among the children.

THE 'CLIQUE'

I knew that a swarm of adventurers had joined the women admirers of the Staretz, and had succeeded in getting into the peasant's good graces. They turned his influence to account in putting pressure for their evil and criminal purposes on all the Ministries; thanks to Rasputin they were also said to be obtaining information of value to our enemies during the war, but I do not think that is likely to have been true.

It would be impossible for me to give the names and the particular departments to which one or another of them had access; I can only give an indication of the methods which these acolytes of Rasputin employed.

Prince Andronnikov was the one among them whom I met most frequently; he was, perhaps, less dangerous than the others. He was of very good family, but was not himself in good repute; he had no regular employment. I avoided him as much as I could. One day he sat next to me at a dinner given by friends of mine. A quarter of an hour's talk sufficed to show me that he was very well informed about all the proposed Court appointments. I showed my surprise; he bent his head in modesty and said;

'You know I have no official post. I might call myself the A.D.C. to the Almighty. In that capacity I have to know everything that is going on in St. Petersburg; that is my only way of showing my love of my country. I ask no other function; I follow Him who makes justice reign or, where necessary, restores its reign.'

A little while later he came into my office. He had come to tell me that he was supporting the candidature of two persons who were proposed for certain Court posts. Both were in the list of officially recommended candidates. I felt able to tell him that I would transmit his recommendation to the Minister of the Court.

But his intervention did not end there. He wanted to let me know that two other persons who were also in the official list were entirely unworthy of the honour which it was proposed to confer on them. He began to retail to me some vague gossip to their disadvantage.

'Have you any documents to prove your statements?'

'I never offer documentary evidence.'

I rose and brought the conversation abruptly to its end.

A few days passed; then I received an enormous fish, caught in the Volga; the Prince wrote that he had been given a number of these fish and felt he ought to get me to try one.

I returned his present, without a card or a word. It seems that about the same time Freedericksz had unknowingly partaken of a fish from the same quarter; his chef had found it excellent and had sent some up to the Count's table. Not until a fortnight later was the sender's name discovered.

It was too late then; the subject could hardly have been raked up.

The Prince showed no ill-feeling against me over my ruction of his present. He called to bring me a memorandum concerning a political problem, and asked me to arrange an audience for him with Count Freedericksz. The memorandum was fairly well drafted; it had many flattering remarks about the Count and the writer of these lines, but ended with a rather crude attack on one of our Ministers.

I did everything possible to prevent the Prince from seeing the Count, Reports came in from him incessantly; I passed them on to my Chief; and, to be honest, it must be admitted that Freedericksz read them with some interest, even with pleasure.

Two years later Their Majesties had gone abroad, to Wolfsgarten; their suite was housed in Frankfort. Andronnikov turned up there. He told me that he had been sent as special correspondent of one of the Russian newspapers, and in that capacity I had to receive him on various occasions in the same way as the other representatives of the Press. He wanted at all costs to be presented to Freedericksz; I found various pretexts for failing to arrange an interview.

One day I said to him:

'It is impossible. The Minister is leaving Frankfort to go with his wife to Cologne; she is taking the North Express for St. Petersburg.'

It was child's play, of course, to calculate the time of the Count's return to Frankfort after seeing his wife off.

When we came into the station at 5 a.m., Freedericksz told me afterwards, 'I saw a gentleman waiting outside my compartment, with his top hat in his hands. I assumed that he was one of the railway inspectors, and went up to him to thank him briefly for the company's attentiveness. He answered: "I am not a railway employee; I am a Russian prince, and am here to express my admiration for a chevalier".

' "A chevalier?"

' "Have you not just done something worthy of the traditions of chivalry?"

' "But—excuse me, what do you mean?"

' "Taking Madame la Comtesse back to Cologne!" '

After that Andronnikov went with Count Freedericksz, who was pretty annoyed, as far as the hotel at which he was putting up; there, in spite of the Count's protests, Andronnikov took possession of his bag and carried it up to his room, continuing all the time with a string of praises that savoured of the lowest toadyism.

An introduction of that sort, Freedericksz added, would not serve to establish social relations. As to that, he was greatly mistaken; next day the Prince called on Freedericksz, had himself announced as 'a friend of the Count's', and succeeded in getting more than half an hour's conversation with him.

From then on. Countess Freedericksz received flowers and boxes of sweets at regular intervals from the Prince.

There were a few more 'memoranda'; but they were addressed direct to the Count. He passed them on to me; they had nothing to do with the Minister of the Court. I let them accumulate in my files.

One day Andronnikov came to see me.

'I am going to be the editor of a newspaper; its policy will be to foster the loyalty of the Russian masses to Their Majesties and their children. The Empress's order is that the paper shall be exempt from the Court censorship.'

'Only the Emperor himself can give that order,' I replied. 'What is more, orders of this sort can only be transmitted to me verbally by one of the Generals A.D.C. to His Majesty. If I remember rightly, you are only A.D.C. to the Almighty; you will understand, then, that it is impossible for me to comply with this order.'

I never saw Prince Andronnikov again.

I tried with the help of friends to find out what lay behind this little incident.

I never succeeded in getting any precise information; it can only be supposed that the Prince was not telling the truth when he said that he was bringing an order from Her Majesty herself.

I think I have said enough to indicate the character of this gentleman. Rasputin was constantly to be seen at the Prince's flat, and frequently made use of it for appointments which he could not arrange at his own home.

RASPUTIN AS MAKER OF MINISTERS

I come now to the most significant incident in my relations with Rasputin. It shows the extent to which Ministerial portfolios depended on the favour of this degraded man.

Trepov had just been appointed Prime Minister. The appointment had been expected. When attending Cabinet meetings as deputy for Freedericksz, I had had frequent occasion to note that the policy suggested by my brother-in-law was almost always adopted by the other Ministers; his authority was steadily growing.

I went to see Trepov the day before he left for G.H.Q., where he was to present a report to the Tsar. He confided to me that his report would be of capital importance, since it proposed four dismissals of Ministers. If the Tsar would agree to these four dismissals, it would be possible to constitute a Ministry; if not, Trepov would be compelled to resign. He asked me how his appointment had been received at Court. I told him all that I knew, and added that he would have to take account of Rasputin. With that he agreed.

'Do not forget that I shall never be able to have any sort of personal or friendly relations with him, whatever happens.'

After his return from the *Stavka* (G.H.Q.), he told me that things had gone 'fairly well'; he had three dismissals in his portfolio; the fourth had been signed by the Tsar, but had ultimately been deferred; this was the decree relating to Protopopov.* At the last moment the Tsar had said:

'Leave me this report; I will send it back to you to-night or to-morrow morning.'

If he had his way with these four Ministries, Trepov hoped that he would be able to form a Cabinet 'of public confidence', as the phrase went at the time. It would not be a Parliamentary Cabinet in the full sense of the word, but it would include several members of the Duma. This was a supreme concession in face of the rising tempest of public opinion. But the presence of Protopopov in the Cabinet would make the attempt hopeless; no leading member of the Duma would be able to co-operate with Rasputin's man.

'Can you go at once,' Trepov asked me, 'to see Rasputin?'

'Yes, but it disgusts me.'

'So it does me. And it may be very serious for me. But I am ready to take the risk. I must get Protopopov's resignation.'

'What shall I suggest to the man?'

'Offer him a house in Petrograd, with all his household and living expenses paid; bodyguards, which are indispensable for him; and 200,000 roubles (£20,000) down as soon as Protopopov has been dismissed. In consideration of this, I want him to refrain from meddling further in appointments of Ministers and high Government officials. As for the clergy, I leave him a free hand if he wants it. No personal interviews with me; if he wants to say anything to me he must do it through you. You know the man. Try to make him listen to reason.'

'You know that if he does not accept he will telegraph at once to the Tsar and tell him that you have been trying to bribe him? It may all come to grief.'

'If it must it must. I will risk it. In any case I am quite prepared to go. The Tsar will say nothing to me about Rasputin, but he will find a pretext that will do to get rid of me. I am putting all my stakes on this one card. So long as Protopopov is Minister of the Interior it

* Protopopov, a member of the Duma, was Minister of the Interior. He owed his appointment to the influence of Rasputin. He was implicated in a mysterious attempt at a separate peace with Germany. Protopopov suffered from a grave nervous malady.

will be impossible for me to carry on the Government.'

'And what about me?' I asked Trepov. 'What sort of a situation shall I be in if Grishka refuses? And we are almost certain to get a categorical refusal.'

'Do the best you can for yourself In any event your appointment to Roumania is practically a certainty. You will be better off there than here. Go along and come back as soon as you can.'

I took a car to the Gorokhovaya, the street in which Rasputin was living. On the way I said to myself again and again that I had made a great mistake in having anything to do with a question in which Rasputin was involved.

'Gregory Efimovitch,' I began, 'you know my friend and brother-in-law Trepov has just been made Prime Minister. I should be so glad if I could see you two on the best of terms. There is no reason why you should not be. He has nothing against you. But he does ask you not to put a spoke in his wheels; he is in a very delicate position. In return he will do nothing to interfere with you.'

'That's all right; by all means let him go ahead on these lines. But on one more condition,' Rasputin added, 'he must let my friends alone.'

'That is what I am telling you. You can have what you want for living expenses for yourself and those who depend on you. You will have a bodyguard; you cannot do without one. Take what you like and do what you like, but don't interfere in appointments of Ministers and heads of departments. You will have a free hand with ecclesiastical appointments; any one you recommend will be specially looked after.'

I did not get to the end of my offer. His eyes flamed: they showed almost nothing but the white, the iris disappearing and the pupil closing to a pinpoint.

'If that's it,' he shouted, 'I'll pack my bags and go; I see I'm no longer wanted here.'

I was not prepared for so violent a counter-move, and was greatly taken aback.

'Keep calm, Gregory Efimovitch. I am talking to you as a friend. Come now, keep calm; do you suppose you can govern all Russia unaided? If Trepov goes there will be someone else in his place, and who can say what he will have to offer? Perhaps nothing at all.'

His eyes flamed yet more angrily.

'You're a simple chap, you are! Do you think Papa and Mamma

will let you do what you like? I don't need money: the poorest of shopkeepers will keep me supplied with enough to give to the needy.

Bodyguards? You pack of fools, none of your bodyguards for me and be damned to you!'

He stopped short, as if he had just realized something startling.

'Ah! It's Protopopov he wants to get rid of.' (He gave Protopopov some nickname, as he always did, but I no longer remember it.)

I was cool again now. I had picked up my hat to go, but threw it down on a chair and said to Rasputin:

'Don't be an ass! Come along and give me a glass of Madeira— let's talk as friends, as we are.'

For almost a minute we did not speak another word. Then he smiled. The Staretz had nearly forgotten his anger.

'Come along, Sasha' (a diminutive of Alexander). We had two or three glasses each, in unbroken silence. Then I felt that we could go on with our discussion.

'Listen, Gregory Efimovitch. After all, you don't really want Trepov to come to consult you about the Ministers to be chosen? Get it into your head that that is out of the question. Are you set on Protopopov remaining in the Ministry? He can have Shakhovskoy's portfolio (Ministry of Commerce); Shakhovskoy is a good friend of yours, and he can take over Protopopov's office. Why are you singing out like that before you know what it's all about?'

'Why does he want to dismiss him? He will never get another man so devoted to Papa.'

'Devotion is not everything! It is necessary also to be able to conduct business—'

'Business, business—there is only one business, to love Papa sincerely. Vitia was cleverer than any of the others, but he did not love Papa. He was an impossible Minister.'

We talked on for more than an hour. Our two bottles had not had the effect on him that I had been hoping for: he was still master of himself. At last I got from him a promise that he would send 'Papa' a telegram asking him to dismiss Protopopov.

He refused to draft it while I was there.

'He'll telegraph not to dismiss him,' I said to myself. But I pretended to believe him—and I realized at once that he knew I was insincere.

Rasputin had a supreme gift of reading the thoughts of his

interlocutor. I have known many people to have the gift, but none in so astonishing a degree.

As I left he said:

'Let us remain friends. I will not attack your Trepov, if he will leave my friends alone. If he doesn't, I shall go back at once to Pokrovskoye' (Rasputin's native village in Siberia). 'Mamma will beg me to come back, and Trepov will have to go. One more glass. In spite of everything, I like you.'

After this fiasco I went back to Trepov. He realized that he was done for.

Everything happened as I had expected. The Emperor kept back the decree which he had signed and Protopopov remained at his post. Trepov had to make way for Prince N. D. Golitzin.

It was the beginning of the end.

ALEXANDER DIMITRIEVICH PROTOPOPOV and ALEXANDER FYODOROVICH TREPOV
Minister of Internal Affairs　　　　　Prime Minister
(September 1916 to February 1917)　(23 November 1916 to 9 January 1917)

THE 'PROTÉGÉ'

The Empress had held on to Protopopov because he was Rasputin's protégé. I realized it at the time of my last talk but one with Her Majesty.

I had been appointed Minister Plenipotentiary in Roumania. One day when I had returned from Jassy I learned from one of the ladies of the Rasputin coterie that the Empress insisted that I should make the acquaintance of Protopopov before the audience which she was going to grant me.

I telephoned to the Minister to ask for an appointment, and he replied:

'Come along at once.'

Protopopov kept me more than three hours. He wanted to explain his 'programme' to me; but he did so in an extraordinary manner, jumping from one project to another, and making me read whole pages of various files of papers that he put in front of me. I could see plainly that I had to deal with a lunatic.

Next day I was received by the Empress. She told me at once how glad she was to learn that I had met Protopopov.

'What do you think of him?'

I replied, in Russian:

'*Sumburnyi tchelovek*' ('A muddle-headed person'). I added, in German:

'I cannot find a word to express it in German.'

I made a few attempts to explain the sense of my Russian phrase.

'That is perfectly true,' she said; 'he does not always, perhaps, pursue his idea to the end. But his ideas are good. And, besides, he is so devoted to us! He is unable to discipline his ideas. He is not always able to carry them out, for they pursue one another in his brain. He ought to have a deputy who would be responsible for sifting out what is reasonable in his plans; in a word, a deputy who is not so erratic, and who has the energy to carry Protopopov's schemes to a successful conclusion when he has launched them.'

'I listened attentively to him yesterday for three hours, but I did not notice a single practical suggestion.'

'Quite so,' the Empress replied, 'he is extremely nervous and easily loses his thread.'

The Empress was silent for a moment; then, without any transition, she said:

'Would you not act as his deputy? If that post is not of sufficient standing for you, you could be given the right of reporting personally to His Majesty!'

I replied, in entire sincerity:

'Madame, I would accept the most insignificant of

posts if I felt that I could be useful to my country in doing so. I am obliged to say that I cannot possibly work with a man whose ideas have no coherence. Apart from that, there seem to be very grave objections to the idea of letting two persons report for the same Ministry.'

'Very well—whom would you suggest as deputy for Protopopov?'

'It must be somebody well acquainted with affairs of state.'

'Yes, that is why I suggested you for the post; have you not been all these years in charge of the Court Chancellery?'

'But that,' I objected, 'has nothing to do with the Ministry of the Interior. I have not the slightest knowledge of police administration.'

We went on to other questions that I had to put before Her Majesty, On taking leave of her I said:

'Will you excuse me, Madame, if I was rather uncompromising in regard to Protopopov?'

She smiled a little dolefully:

'Not at all. I was very glad that you spoke straight out. We so rarely hear the truth from anybody! As to Protopopov, I do not feel that a man of devoted loyalty ought to be judged harshly; it would have been better to help him.'

There the audience ended; it was the last but one that I had.

I may add that Rasputin took no revenge for my intervention against Protopopov; he made no further effort to injure me with the Empress. In view of the Rodzianko incident I had had every reason to fear the worst.

This made Rasputin a more enigmatic figure to me than ever.

RASPUTIN AND THE DUMA

To end this melancholy section of my story, it remains for me to describe how Rasputin helped to make final the breach which had come between the Tsar and the body that represented the nation—the Duma. It was, of course, this breach that brought the downfall of the dynasty.

The last Duma was not of the revolutionary character of the first two. Many of its members were animated by the purest patriotism; they were genuine monarchists, and were concerned before all else to preserve Russia from revolutionary convulsions.

At this period we had Count Kokovtzov as Prime Minister; the Count considered that the country's future depended on close and whole-hearted collaboration between the Duma and the Tsar's

Ministers. In accordance with this conviction he had made a change in the Cabinet over which he presided. Three of the appointments brought new men into crucial posts, men who could not be out of sympathy with the members of the Duma.

The first months of Kokovtzov's premiership, his Parliamentary honeymoon, gave reason for hope that he would succeed in his plan for rallying the Duma to the Tsar's side. The Count sincerely believed that he would be able to dispel the animosity that the Sovereigns had felt towards the first two Dumas.

But his illusions were soon dissipated.

The Press began to be full of references to Rasputin as a sinister adventurer and an indescribable curse to the country. It was continually being said that Rasputin controlled all the important appointments in the Orthodox Church; it was whispered that he had the ear of the Empress.

It is by no means easy to explain the view that Their Majesties took of the problem of the Press. They recognized freedom of speech, but not of publication. The newspapers were no more than 'tolerated' in their view, and it was never possible to get the Empress to understand that a misstatement published by the Press could not be visited there and then with penalties inflicted by administrative action—that is to say, not by the courts but by the police.

The Tsar would not understand that his will might be insufficient to prevent the appearance of 'lying' articles; and it seemed to him absurd that his Ministers should be obliged to apply to the courts for remedy, especially when it was a question of his wife's honour —as, indeed, it often was.

The censorship of all articles relating to the Court was my responsibility. What could I do? I rigorously suppressed all issues of newspapers in which Rasputin's name appeared in connexion with that of anybody belonging to the Imperial family. But articles in which no member of the Imperial family was mentioned by name were, under the very precise text of the law, not liable to be submitted at all to the censorship of the Court. That made me completely helpless.

The Empress incessantly complained that the competent authorities were neglecting to carry out His Majesty's strict orders.

News sometimes of a tendencious nature and often exaggerated by the Press circulated in Parliamentary quarters. The lobbies were full of talk that was an outrage on the Imperial family; some of it was reflected in statements made in the full publicity of the Parliamentary debates.

The Tsar sent for the Minister of the Interior, and told him that he required that discussions affecting the Empress's honour should cease both in the lobbies and in debate. Makarov could only reply that he was entirely unable to guarantee that His Majesty's order could be carried out.

The Tsar then turned to the Prime Minister, who brought all his legal knowledge to the demonstration that the law gave the Government no means of control of the Duma and its members in this particular field.

The Tsar and the Empress took great offence at this. From then on, all the declarations from Count Kokovtzov of success in maintaining cordial relations between Parliament and the Government were received merely with smiles of angry scepticism.

To the Tsar the Duma had become a rebel organization.

Vladimir Kokovtzov, Prime Minister 1911-1914

PART II

CHAPTER IV
THE COURT OF NICHOLAS II

I. THE COURTIERS
'THE OFFICES'

THE principal function of a sovereign's Court is to heighten his prestige. The Court is also responsible for looking after the details of the monarch's everyday life.

The Russian Court was certainly the most opulent in Europe. Great wealth had been accumulating during three hundred years in the hands of those responsible for its safe keeping. In its splendour the Russian Court came nearest to those of Louis XIV and Louis XV. In its etiquette it resembled the Court of Austria.

The credits required to meet the needs of the Court came from three main sources (apart from the personal fortunes of the Grand Dukes, which were by no means negligible):

(1) The general budget of the country, which supplied the 'civil list'; that is to say, the credits necessary for the maintenance of the Courts of Their Majesties and that of the heir to the throne.

(2) The Apanages, a fund (it would now be called 'Self-governing') created by Emperor Paul I and intended to yield for each of the Grand Dukes and Grand Duchesses, from the day of

their birth, an annual income of 280,000 roubles (about £28,000 gold). The purpose of the Apanages was to relieve the general budget of the burden of the expenditure necessary for the maintenance of the Imperial family. Their prime source of revenue was a gift of real estate made by Emperor Paul; this estate had been managed with great prudence by its successive administrators, and a little before the Revolution it constituted the greatest domain in all Russia, covering many millions of acres, and had a liquid reserve of some 60,000,000 roubles.

(3) His Majesty's private fortune, the properties belonging personally to the Tsar. It included the mining districts of Nertchinsk and Altai, rich in gold and precious stones.

Under Count Freedericksz as its head, the Russian Court consisted of persons holding 'offices'.

These 'offices' were purely titular, and were divided into two classes. The first included (in 1908) fifteen officials, with the titles of Grand Chamberlain, Grand Marshal, Master of the Imperial Hunt, and Grand Cup-bearer. In the second class came 134 offices entailing actual services and 86 'honorary' offices: the two Grand Masters of Ceremonies, the Grand Esquire Trenchant, the Huntsmen, the Marshals, the Director of the Imperial Theatres, the Director of the Hermitage Museum, and the Masters of Ceremonies (14 active and 14 honorary). This list should be completed by 287 Chamberlains, 309 Gentlemen in Waiting, no persons 'attached' to Their Majesties and to the members of the Imperial family; 22 ecclesiastics, 38 medical officers, 3 harbingers, 18 valets de chambre to Their Majesties, and 150 officers in the suite (Generals A.D.C., Generals in the suite, and aides-de-camp). The grand total, with the 240 ladies of various ranks and the 66 ladies of the Order of St. Catherine, came to the imposing figure of 1,543 persons.

The titles borne by the ladies of the Court were as follows: the Empress's Mistress of the Robes, the Mistresses of the Imperial Court and of the Grand Ducal Courts; the Dames a portrait; the maids of honour 'of the chamber', 'of the suite', and 'of the city'. Ranked with them were the Dames of the Order of the Cross (grand and lesser) of St. Catherine, and the maids of honour who had been presented to Their Majesties on marriage. None of the members of the Court personnel could marry without having obtained the permission of the Tsar himself.

Each office carried a uniform, with appropriate changes for various circumstances, full dress, gala dress, ordinary dress, and travelling dress. The gold embroidery grew, of course, with the person's rank. When one had become Grand Chamberlain one no longer had a strip of clothing without its covering of garlands of gold!

We may note that the appellations conferred on the high dignitaries retained a certain practical significance: when the Tsar was seated on his throne at the Coronation banquet, the dishes presented to him were escorted by the Grand Esquire Trenchant, at whose side two officers of the *Chevaliers Garde** marched with naked swords. The Grand Cup-bearer passed the golden goblet to the Tsar at this banquet and announced in a loud voice that 'His Majesty deigns to drink'. The Master of the Hunt was present at the Imperial hunting expeditions. The Equerry assisted the Tsar and the Empress when they were entering the stage coach; the Master of the Horse escorted the coach on horseback.

THE GRAND MASTER OF CEREMONIES

Everything concerned with etiquette and ceremonial came under the Grand Master of Ceremonies and the Empress's Mistress of the Robes.

The post of Grand Master of Ceremonies was held by Count B. A. Hendrikov; the second Grand Master was Baron Korff.

The Count, a man of fine presence and of extreme elegance, had a very strong sense of the importance of his duties; this, of course, facilitated matters, for a Master of Ceremonies cannot carry out his duties effectively unless he takes them seriously.

This Hendrikov certainly did. At the time of the reception that he had to organize for the members of the first Duma, he considered it necessary to set up a regular committee, composed of the best specialists on his staff, together with persons in a position to give him information concerning the future deputies, and a certain

---

* There were two regiments of cavalry charged with the protection of the Tsar's person, the Horse Guards and the *Chevaliers Gardes*. Both regiments had the same privileges, and they disputed the honour of military precedence. In point of fact, it was the *Chevaliers Gardes* who formed the last barrier around the person of the Sovereign; hence the particular distinction which attached to being a courtier with the privilege of 'going past the *Chevaliers Gardes*'.

number of 'experts', that is to say, officials who had had experience of similar processions in other countries.

Count Hendrikov went at the head of this committee from one room to another of the Palace; he personally marked out in chalk the positions to be reserved for the dignitaries and the representatives of the people. There were long discussions to settle whether this or the other body of State officials or group of senators should be placed on left or right, in front, or behind. Count Hendrikov grew thoroughly agitated at the idea that the deputies, unaccustomed as they were to Court ceremonial, might get out of alignment during the ceremony.

I had good reason to remember the anxieties of Count Hendrikov at the time of the arrival of the Landgrave of Hesse, a relative of the Empress. The Minister of the Court had transmitted to the Tsar a list of dignitaries from which to choose one to be attached to the person of the Landgrave. His Majesty selected Prince Ourussov for the honour.

The Landgrave was to arrive next morning at eleven o'clock. At 11 p.m. I was rung up by Count Hendrikov; he was completely panic-stricken.

'There has been a catastrophe!'

'I'll bet it's the Winter Palace on fire.'

'No, really. Jules Ourussov has fallen ill; he can't go to welcome the Landgrave. Whatever can I do?'

'Select somebody else,' I answered, trying hard not to laugh.

'I can't. You told me yourself that Ourussov had been appointed by His Majesty's ukase.* Telephone to Freedericksz and ask him to get another ukase.'

'Right you are,' I said, and hung up the 'phone.

Five minutes later I 'phoned him to let him know that the Minister of the Court took the whole responsibility; another officer could be designated by an order from the Master of Ceremonies. 'You see, we can't disturb His Majesty at this late hour.'

Needless to say I had not spoken a word to the Minister of the Court. But Hendrikov kept me a full hour longer, suggesting every conceivable candidate. At last we agreed on an appointment. It was to be Gourko.

* Order given by the Tsar, which could only be modified by a further similar document.

An hour later the 'phone rang again.

'Gourko is impossible! His full-dress uniform is at the dyer's, being cleaned, and it seems that it's all bright, as it must be for such an important meeting, down one side, but not down the other. My God, whatever can I do? It's sending me off my head.'

It was already 1 a.m., and the situation was getting a little complicated.

'See if you can telephone to the "Aquarium"' (a *café-concert* then in the height of fashion). 'You'll be sure to find Prince Mestchersky there.'

At 3 a.m. Hendrikov considered it worth while to ring me up once more to say:

'It's all right—Prince Mestchersky's going.'

Next morning I told Count Freedericksz of the tribulations of Count Hendrikov, and we had a hearty laugh over them.

I ought to mention, in this connexion, that Nicholas II, like his father Alexander III, was completely indifferent to all questions of ceremonial.

I can imagine the anguish of the Masters of Ceremonies during the reign of Alexander II, who was rigorous in exacting every punctilio of the rules of behaviour at Court.

Hendrikov was never able to understand how anybody could, as so many did, agitate persistently for a Court appointment, and then, having got it, show complete indifference to a courtier's duties. There were frequent masses, for instance, for the souls of dead Grand Dukes, and the attendance of the Tsar's suite at these services was never anything like complete.

Hendrikov discovered in the archives of the Court a ukase of Catherine II. That Empress had had a sense of humour. She had 'presumed' that all the absent courtiers must be ill; 'they are therefore,' she commanded, 'to be required each to pay severally the sum of 25 roubles, in order that the said sum may be paid to a priest who shall be charged with the saying of a mass for the recovery of the health of the absent courtier.'

THE EMPRESS'S MISTRESS OF THE ROBES

The duty of preserving the traditions of Court life among the ladies admitted to the Court fell on the Mistress of the Robes, Princess Galitzin, *née* Pashkova.

I do not think it would have been possible to discover a lady better fitted than was Princess Galitzin to live up to the full importance attached to the high office of Mistress of the Robes. Of perfect breeding, very sure of all her movements, she had the authority needed for fending off anything that was not strictly in accordance with etiquette. She regularly dressed in 'the fashion of the year before last', and, according to a quip which went the rounds of the Court, her hats were apparently 'built at the Imperial coachworks'.

She had tactics all her own for the maintenance of discipline. If she had noticed anything that called for comment she never spoke about it to the young girls who had recently come to Court; she only attacked the ladies of maturer age, of whom the maids of honour stood in desperate fear.

On Their Majesties' way to Kiev there was a boat journey down the Dnieper. Sitting opposite the Empress was Her Most Serene Highness Princess Lopukhina-Demidova; and the princess had had the coolness to light a cigarette. The Mistress of the Robes sailed up to her, seized her cigarette, and threw it overboard, saying aloud for all to hear:

'My dear, you are forgetting that there is no smoking in Her Majesty's presence.'

The princess was furious, full of injured dignity, but said not a word. Later the Mistress of the Robes explained to her:

'You know I smoke myself like a corporal. What I said to you will be a lesson to the young ones. I don't want to have to pull them up.'

There was a similar scene later, after my appointment as Head of the Court Chancellery. I was talking to Princess Galitzin, and suddenly saw Countess Vorontzova coming up to us. The Countess hated Count Freedericksz and all his staff. I bowed low to this influential lady. She did not deign to make the slightest sign of recognition.

The Mistress of the Robes turned at once to her:

'This is Mossolov, the new Head of the Chancellery.'

'I have known him a long time.'

'Then why on earth did you cut him? You can behave as you like at home, but at Court you must have manners'

I got away as quickly as I could, and I cannot say how that conversation continued.

II. THE GRAND CEREMONIES

A. *Their Majesties' 'Processions'*

Their Majesties' 'processions' took place on the most important anniversaries.

The processions were divided into grand and minor. All the Court staff had to attend a grand procession. A special invitation was required for participation in a minor one.

The processions were so called because Their Majesties left their private apartments and went in great pomp to church. After divine service Their Majesties returned to their private apartments amid the same ceremonies.

Half an hour before the procession, the members of the Imperial family assembled in the Malachite Room, where no one was admitted but the relatives of the Tsar. Court 'Arabs', in resplendent uniforms, guarded the entrance to this room. The courtiers gathered in other rooms of the palace, where they got ready for the procession. They were controlled by the Ceremonies Service; this might be described as the most important manifestation of its existence.

As soon as the procession had been duly formed, the Minister of the Court went into the Malachite Room and reported to His Majesty. At once the Grand Dukes, who knew exactly their degrees of proximity to the Throne, ranged themselves behind Their Majesties; the Grand Duchesses took their places in the procession according to the rank of their fathers or husbands.

The first couple in the procession was made up by the Tsar and the Dowager Empress, Alexandra Feodorovna was one of the second couple. The Minister of the Court kept on the right of the Tsar, a few steps behind the Sovereign. He was followed by the officers 'on duty'—a General A.D.C., a General in the suite, and an A.D.C, These officers were the only persons who did not go two by two.

The Sovereign regularly wore the uniform of the regiment which was celebrating its anniversary that day or which had been chosen to provide the sentinels within the Palace. Very often the Tsar changed this uniform for that of the Preobrajensky Regiment or of the Hussars, with whom he had gone through his military apprenticeship.

The officers in waiting had to be present at the processions dressed in the uniform of the Tsar's suite, and not in their regimental uniforms. The ladies of the Court were only admitted in 'Russian' dress with trains,

A 'Russian' dress is described in detail in the *Court Calendar*. It had to be of white silk, reaching only to the shoulders, weighed down with a long train of red velvet embroidered in gold (the colours were different for the Grand Ducal Courts). Each lady wore on her head a *kokoshnik*, a sort of diadem, borrowed from the usage of the Muscovite Courts; this also was of red velvet, embroidered in gold.

The ladies 'with access to the Court' might have dresses in other colours, as they liked.

The *kokoshnik* and the dress could, of course, be ornamented with jewels according to the fortune of the wearer. In this respect some families established records which it would not be easy to beat. I remember seeing Madame Zinoviev, wife of the Marshal of the Nobility of St. Petersburg, wearing nine or ten emeralds as buttons, each bigger than a pigeon's egg. The most remarkable diamonds ornamented the dresses of Countess Shouvalova, Countess Vorontzova Dashkova, Countess Sheremetyevskaya, Princess Kotchubey, and Princess Youssupova, among others.

As they came from the Malachite Room into the Concert Room, Their Majesties stopped and replied to the reverences from persons grouped in this second room, that is to say, the courtiers who had the right to 'go past the *Chevaliers Gardes*'. That expression was derived from a picket of *Chevaliers Gardes* placed at the entrance to the Concert Room. It was a special privilege to be entitled to pass this picket of honour. Hence came the two categories of people: those who went past the *Chevaliers Gardes*, and those who did not go past them.

After the Tsar's entry into the Concert Room, the procession began to form. The principal dignitaries of the Court remained facing Their Majesties until the Masters of Ceremonies indicated to them that they had to lead the procession, in the order of their 'proximity' to the Tsar.

The Sovereigns followed immediately after the principal dignitaries of the Court. They were followed by the members of the Imperial family. Then came the ladies of the Court, the other high dignitaries, the Ministers, the Senators, and the military suite.

They went into the Nicholas Room, where the officers of the guard stood in picturesque groups. Finally the procession went through the other rooms passing in front of the *dii minores*—'merchants with great names', and even 'newspaper correspondents' (who in most cases were admitted to galleries above these rooms).

The Sovereigns went into the church followed by the Grand Dukes, the high dignitaries, and the Mistresses of the Robes to the Courts. The rest of the procession remained in order in the adjoining rooms. This was the most delicate moment for the Masters of Ceremonies, for they were supposed to repress every attempt to speak aloud or to smoke. The greater ones among the *habitués* of the Palace knew where they could find certain back staircases, which made improvised smoking-rooms during divine service; these were frequented especially by Grand Dukes who had quietly slipped out of church. It was, by the way, a well-established tradition that the talk on the staircases should never touch on business or official matters. The Masters of Ceremonies took care not to go near these 'smoking-rooms' or the main conservatory of the Palace, where the old Generals obstinately went to smoke in spite of all orders.

On their way back from church Their Majesties stopped in the Concert Room, and there the newly appointed maids of honour and other ladies entitled to the distinction were presented.

I have a vivid personal memory of the complications entailed for the young officers by service as 'inside' sentinels in the Palace. On great occasions like a procession or a ball, they had to wear full-dress uniform. This uniform comprised in addition to the regulation jacket a 'super-vest' (a glorified waistcoat); Wellingtons; and elk-skin breeches. The 'superjacket' took the place of the cuirass worn on outdoor duty; for the Horse Guards it was of scarlet with large metallic eagles on front and back. The *Chevaliers Gardes* wore a large star of St. Andrew.

It was essential that the breeches should not have the slightest crease. To attain this result they were damped, smeared with soap, and put on—after taking off the pants, if I may venture to say so. The operation called for the services of a couple of vigorous soldiers, I hope my readers will pardon me for descending to a slightly vulgar detail: there is no other way of giving an exact idea of the function performed by the two soldiers. Have you ever watched a miller trying to get the flour to settle in an insufficiently filled sack? He 'punches' the sack. That is just what the two soldiers had to do. They 'punched' the elk-skin breeches, and in due course the officer settled down into them.

An officer on duty as inside sentinel remained at his post for twenty-four hours on end. He had an arm-chair for his use; if all was quiet around him he had the right to undo the chain of his helmet and to take off one glove.

B. *Court Balls*

Of Still greater importance were the ceremonies on the occasion of Court balls.

As a rule the first ball of the season was arranged in the Nicholas Room, which could hold 3,000 guests. There followed a few weeks later the 'Concert' balls and the 'Hermitage' balls, with 700 and 200 guests; they were named from the rooms reserved to dancers, the Concert Room and the Hermitage Room.

Only one ball a year was organized in the Nicholas Room. In order to attend this ball it was necessary to belong to one of the first four 'classes' (of the fourteen classes into which the Russian officers and officials were divided); all the foreign diplomats and their families were also invited, the senior officers of the regiments of the guard (with their wives and daughters), certain young officers recognized by their chiefs as dancers, and, finally, persons invited individually by Their Majesties. The sons of personages admitted to the Court balls could not be invited with their fathers; they had to merit the favour through their own position.

The Court staffs could not know the names of all the personages present in the capital. The first thing to be done was therefore to call on the Marshal of the Court and sign a special register. Ladies who had not already been presented to the Empress had to sign the register of the Mistress of the Robes. This lady had the right to refuse admission to the ball in certain cases. The invitations were sent out a fortnight before the ball.

A ball in the Nicholas Room was thus not by any means reserved to the 'high life' of St. Petersburg. A practised eye could distinguish the men or women who did not belong to real 'society': their clothes might, for instance, be too new. Yes! too new. The persons in the authentic high society did not wear the latest Paris models for the Nicholas Room; the great crush made it impossible adequately to display all the magnificence of the dresses. There was also the way of wearing a uniform or a ball dress, and that indefinable something that gives to the well-born the air of being 'at home everywhere'.

The time for arrival was about 8.30, not later. Everybody knew his proper entrance to the Palace. The Grand Dukes went in by the Saltykov entrance; the members of the Court had 'Their Majesties'' entrance reserved to them; civil officials came by the 'Jurdan' entrance; officers had the privilege of using the 'Commander's' entrance.

The scene was fairy-like.

January. Intense cold. The whole of the three vast blocks of the Winter Palace inundated with light. Braziers burning around the immense Alexander Column, a granite monolith with an archangel on top of it. Carriages arriving in an unbroken line. Open sledges bringing those officers who did not fear the cold; the horses' harness covered with blue netting, to prevent accumulations of snow from being blown into the passengers' faces.

Motor-cars were regarded then as a capricious and undependable toy.

Feminine silhouettes were to be seen hurrying feverishly across the few steps that separated the arriving carriage from the entrance; some of them radiant and graceful, some bowed down with age. Furs—heavens! they were Russian furs, and that's that: sable, silver fox, arctic fox. No shawls over the heads, because of the diadems of the married ladies and the flowers worn by the girls. Police officers watched over the movement of the carriages and told the coachmen where to park.

None of the ladies had the right to bring their own footmen into the Palace, to look after their things, as was done even at the Grand Dukes'. Cloaks had to be given to the Court men-servants. Each cloak or wrap (they could not be worn in Their Majesties' presence) had to have the owner's visiting card sewn inside. The attendant (in white stockings, patent leather pumps, and a uniform bedizened with Imperial eagles in *passementerie*) indicated in a low voice the room in which it would be found after the ball. The men were well schooled in their duties! As they moved over the parquet floor their steps were inaudible.

The guests went up the grand staircases of white marble, on the soft and velvety carpets. White and scarlet uniforms; spreadeagle helmets in gold and silver; countless epaulettes; the marvellous national costumes of the Hungarian guests; the gold-embroidered *kuntusk** of Marquis Veliepolski, Marquis of Gonzago-Myszkowsky; the *beshmets*¹ of the Caucasian nobles, shod in *tchuviaks* (a sort of moccasin, with supple soles, so that in dancing these mountain warriors made not the slightest sound); white dolmans bordered with precious beaver fur; finally, the Court uniforms, heavy with gold embroidery and completed by short breeches and white silk stockings——

Yes! A perfect courtier had to have legs that were neither too fat nor too bony; he had to look well in short breeches. Shall I tell? Sometimes a 'calf' would have strange fancies of its own, and one might see the courtier bend down to seize it and restore it to the normal position from which it never should have wandered—an operation performed not without embarrassment.

It may have been on account of incidents of this sort that Prince Repnin, Grand Master of the Court, a very old man and particularly troubled with gout, asked permission to attend Court balls in white trousers, though they were not authorized by the regulations. Could the Tsar be troubled with such a detail? Could permission be given without the Monarch's approval? Freedericksz was very perplexed. Finally he mentioned the matter to the Tsar apart from his weekly 'report', unofficially, as it were.

'Oh, certainly! Answer just as you think best.'

Then, on second thought:

'No, perhaps better not. These old people would be hurt to feel that the Sovereign had not himself gone into their request. You had better report to me that So-and-so still goes about but is troubled with arthritis. I should be very interested to hear that, say, the venerable Marshal of the Nobility of Kiev, in spite of his advanced age, wants to come to a Court ball. A report on those lines, in any case, will not Take up much time.'

The flood of guests would grow visibly. Everybody in the elegant society of the capital would be going up those wide marble staircases.

* Polish and Caucasian national dress.

All the ladies wore 'Court' dresses, cut very low, with the shoulders bare, and with a long train. At that time ladies were more delicate about questions

of 'modesty' than nowadays, and one had to attend a Palace ball in order to admire the full effect of their necks and shoulders. At that time, too, there were none with the ambition to display backs bronzed by the sun; skins that should be white were white as Carrara marble.

On the left of the bodice the guests wore, according to their rank, a 'monogram' (the Imperial monogram ornamented with diamonds, distinctive mark of the maids of honour) or a 'portrait' framed in diamonds (a high distinction granted to ladies of special merit: they were given the title of Dames of the Portrait).

Here was a General 'in the suite', with his wife; she was already in the forties, but still slim, and her spangled dress displayed her figure wonderfully. Her light, almost chestnut hair was decorated with a diadem set with two rows of diamonds. A *ferronniére* with a single diamond of two square centimetres crossed her forehead. A diamond necklace; the neck of her dress bordered with diamonds, with a flower at the back entirely of diamonds set flat; two diamond chains leading, like enormous threads of fire, first to the front of the bodice and then to the buckle at the waist; rings and bracelets covered with diamonds. Nowadays when I see, in some sensational film, the 'ostentation' of the Russian Court as reproduced in the studios of Hollywood, I could weep—or laugh aloud—in irritation.

The long procession moved on between two lines of Cossacks of the Guard, in scarlet uniforms, and Court 'Arabs', gigantic turbaned negroes. They were 'Arabs' only by tradition; actually they were Christian Abyssinians.

The Masters of Ceremonies, grave and gracious, moved about quietly everywhere, to assist the flow of the arrivals. As they were on duty, each of them had his baton, a sort of long ebony wand surmounted by an ivory ball and a two-headed eagle, with a bow of bright blue ribbon (the St. Andrew's knot).

I will devote a page to the officers invited to the Court balls. I had the honour to be present at balls in three successive reigns, so that I am not writing without knowledge.

Officers rarely received a personal invitation. The regiment was simply informed that so many officers were to attend such and such a ball. For the Horse Guards in my time the number was fifteen. The Officer Commanding the regiment named those who were to take on the duty. The winners in this lottery had to present themselves to the senior Colonel on the eve of the ball, and he gave his orders:

'It is not an amusement. . . . You must not think about having a good time. . . . You are detached on duty, and you will be busily occupied with your duties. . . . You have got to dance with the ladies and do your best to keep them amused. . . . You are strictly forbidden to keep in a compact group. . . . Scatter . . . scatter. . . . Do you understand?'

At that time our O.C.'s aunt was Mistress of the Robes. Throughout the evening she devoted herself entirely to watching over the newly arrived officers. If one was 'approved', one received a personal invitation to the Concert or Hermitage ball. If one was 'highly approved', one received the supreme honour of invitation to the private balls organized by the Mistress of the Robes in her own house. There one was royally bored.

Personally I had the good fortune to please her. I was at once enrolled on the list of officers for duty on ceremonial occasions, and thereafter personal invitations were sent to the writer of these lines as his due.

Not everybody had the same good luck. One of my friends, a very young lieutenant, got into serious trouble over Princess Dolgorukaya, who later became the morganatic wife of Alexander II. The princess was divinely beautiful, and before my unfortunate friend had realized it he had spent the whole evening at the side of the belle of the ball.

This is how he was told of his offence:

'You were presented to Princess Dolgorukaya. . . . You were at liberty to invite her, and it was your duty to invite her, to a waltz. . . . Instead of that you stuck to her right through the evening. . . . It is incredible! . . . Don't you know her position at Court? . . . Your conduct has given offence, it has dishonoured the regiment. . . . You may go, but remember what you have been told.'

It will be understood with what a sinking heart I went to my first ball.

But let us get back to the 'Nicholas' ball.

The great moment was approaching. Their Majesties were

coming, in full procession of state, from the Malachite Room.

The orchestra plunged into a polonaise. The Masters of Ceremonies gave three taps with their wands; the 'Arabs' opened the doors of the room. Everybody turned toward the procession.

At that time Empress Alexandra Feodorovna was about thirty years old. She was in the full glory of her blonde beauty: tall, and imposing in the deliberation and unconcern of her movements. She was particularly fond of fine pearls; one of her necklaces went down to her knees.

Her sister Grand Duchess Elizabeth was still better looking, and more slender, although eight years older. She decorated her golden hair with a diadem in the centre of which was a tallow-drop emerald nearly an inch and a quarter in diameter.

Each of the other Grand Duchesses wore family jewellery, with rubies or sapphires. The precious stones were chosen, of course, to go with the colour of the dress; pearls and diamonds or rubies and diamonds with pink material; sapphires and diamonds or pearls with blue.

The Court 'polonaise' was a regular affair of state. The Tsar began by giving his arm to the wife of the doyen of the diplomatic corps. The Grand Dukes similarly invited the wives of the other members of the diplomatic corps, while the Ambassadors went with the Grand Duchesses; The Grand Marshal, surrounded by Masters of Ceremonies, all armed with their wands, preceded the Tsar, with an air of clearing a way for him through the crowd of guests. After once going round the room there was a change of lady partners, with strict observance of their 'seniority'. The number of turns round the hall depended on the number of ladies whom His Majesty considered it necessary to take as partner in this way. None of the guests, save those whom I have just enumerated, were entitled to the high honour of taking part in this dance.

Immediately after the polonaise a waltz was started. It was not danced in the modern fashion; that was called a two-step. One of the best dancers in the Guards opened the ball with a young lady designated in advance. The room was immense, but there were a great number of guests, and such was their desire to see Their Majesties that the space free for dancers gradually closed in. During the reign of Alexander II Baron Meyendorf, of the Horse Guards, was responsible for 'directing' the ball; he took me as his assistant.

made a practice of telling me to 'open out' the space reserved for dancers. In order to do this elegantly I took Mlle Mary Vasiltchikova, a maid of honour not without *embonpoint*, and she was very helpful in making the spectators retreat. There was also Mlle Gourko, a great adept in this particular sport. The wallflowers were pushed back toward the frescoes.

I must mention that if a Grand Duchess wanted to dance she sent her 'Court Cavalier' to fetch the dancer whom she had chosen. But the Grand Duchesses rarely joined in the 'light' dances. There was only one exception, the lovely and gracious Hélene Vladimirovna,* daughter of Grand Duke Vladimir, a passionate waltzer; officers were permitted to invite her to dance instead of waiting for her to send for some particular one. I am sure they were all desperately in love with this princess.

All the time lackeys went up and down with dishes of sweets, refreshments, and ices. In the adjoining rooms enormous blocks of ice were to be seen, shaped to hold tubs filled with champagne. It would be impossible to give any idea of the magnificence of the array of cakes and *petits fours*, fruits and other delicacies, which the Court pastrycooks had spread over buffets decorated with palms and flowers.

At a Concert or Hermitage ball certain rooms in the Winter Palace would be left empty. The time would come to offer one's arm to a lady and lead her far from the dancers, through countless suites of rooms. Suddenly one would find oneself far from the musicians, the society chatter, the hothouse temperature.... These endless, half-lit rooms seemed more homely and inviting. Here and there were to be seen sentinels and orderly officers. It was possible to stroll about in this way for a good half-hour. Outside, seen through windows as high as those of a cathedral, the Neva scintillated from every floe. One felt an element of mystery in this fairy-tale come true. How many more times, one asked oneself, shall we see it?**

During the mazurka the Empress would stand beneath the portrait of Nicholas I and talk with her partner, one of the senior officers of the Guard, not too old; and when it was over the Sover-

---

* Mother of the Duchess of Kent.
** The description of the Nicholas ball has been written in part by Princess Lobanova Rostovskaya, to whom the author owes grateful acknowledgment.

eigns went toward the supper-room. Masters of Ceremonies preceded them in the regular way.

For the supper the Sovereigns' table was placed on a slightly raised platform; the company at this table were ranged along one side only of the table, against the wall. Thus the guests in passing along the room could glance from one to another of the distinguished persons at the table. The doyen of the diplomatic corps sat on the right of the Empress, and the Grand Duke Michael, heir presumptive to the throne, on her left. The rest of the Grand Dukes and Grand Duchesses took their seats in order of rank, with the Ambassadors and some of the high dignitaries of the Court, the army, and the civil service next to them. It was necessary, of course, to have the ribbon of St. Andrew in order to be able to lay claim to the honour of a seat at this table.

A number of round tables, decorated* with palms and flowers, were placed in the Sovereigns' room. Twelve persons, designated in advance, took their seats at each of these round tables. In the other rooms the guests had to find a place where they could.

The Tsar did not take part in the supper. He went from one to another of the guests, and sat down from time to time to talk to the person whom he wanted so to honour. That, of course, was settled in advance. It was impossible to let the Tsar remain standing by the table, and equally impossible for all the guests at supper to rise and stand at attention throughout the conversation. The procedure was as follows:

A seat remained free at all the tables at which the Tsar intended to 'have a little chat'. A *skorokhod* stood by this seat to show its purpose. (The *skorokhod*, literally 'runner', was a Court domestic who, in the sixteenth century, ran ahead of the sovereign's coach and made way for it in the tortuous streets.) The Tsar sat down in the seat so reserved, making a sign to the guests not to trouble to rise. The members of the suite accompanying the Sovereign retired to a respectful distance, and the conversation began. As soon as it was over the *skorokhod* made a sign to the suite, who returned to the Sovereign's side.

The Tsar had a surprisingly good memory for faces. If he asked the name of the young lady on some officer's right, one might be

---

* They had a hole in the centre, through which came a palm-tree, the table being placed over the cask containing the palm.

almost certain that she was a debutante, and that the Masters of Ceremonies would have the utmost difficulty in saying who she was, seeing her themselves for the first time.

Toward the end of the supper the Tsar would go over to the Empress and take her back to the Nicholas Room, where a cotillion would be started at once. The august hosts chose that moment to retire to their inner apartments, unobserved by their guests. At the entrance to the Malachite Room Their Majesties would take leave of their suite.

Not until then did the Minister of the Court, the suite, the Masters of Ceremonies, and the Marshal of the Court go up to the next floor, where their supper awaited them.

The great Court ball was over.

C. The Sovereigns' Visits

It is not intended in this work to give a list of the visits made by the Russian sovereigns or to describe in detail everything that went on during the meetings between Their Majesties and their 'cousins' in the various countries of Europe. I shall confine myself here, as everywhere else, to saying something of the 'human' side of those meetings at which I was present.

I shall carefully avoid all reference to any political conversations that may have taken place during the visits; others than I will concern themselves—or have done already—with the exposition of the political ends pursued in these meetings, the results they achieved, or the setbacks they met with.

THE GERMAN EMPEROR

The visits most frequently made were those to William II, and he was Their Majesties' most frequent visitor.

The Kaiser was highly excitable—he gave me the impression of a sufferer from hysteria—and he had a special gift of upsetting everybody who came near him. I remember how once at Wolfsgarten he held Nicholas II 'captive' for over two hours. After the conversation the Tsar showed plain signs of the trial that it had been to him. But every interview that he had with the German Emperor unmistakably got on his nerves.

We were thoroughly used to that. Here is one example out of a hundred. It will be remembered how, after one of these interviews, William II had his signal made from the *Hohenzollern*:

'The Grand Admiral of the Atlantic salutes the Grand Admiral of the Pacific.'

On the express order of Nicholas II, Admiral Nilov signalled this curt reply:

'Pleasant voyage!'

But to the best of my belief nobody has so far revealed the Tsar's muttered comment when the Admiral gave him the decoded German signal. His actual words were:

'He's raving mad!'

As for the Empress, she had an innate aversion to her cousin. She could not even hide her antipathy; every time she was due to lunch or dine in his company she pretended to have a bad head. I believe she only once went on board the Kaiser's yacht. She could scarcely maintain ordinary civility at their personal meetings; she confined herself to the barest compliance with good form.

When William II was joking with the children or took the heir to the throne in his arms, nobody with the slightest acquaintance with Alexandra Feodorovna could fail to see that she was literally undergoing torture.

For members of the suite, interviews with the German Emperor were a thorough martyrdom. All the time one had to be on one's guard; William II was sure to burst out with some astonishing and particularly embarrassing question. When he was in a good humour it was worse still. He permitted himself to play schoolboy tricks with the most aged and venerable of his Generals A.D.C. I myself saw him give friendly smacks to Generals like Schlieffen, on the back—and elsewhere.

One day, at lunch during a hunting expedition, William II had me placed next to him: he explained that he wanted to ask me about the Imperial ballets. But I had only time to reply to one or two questions; William II suddenly took charge and set to work to teach me the whole art of choreography. At the end of the lunch he said solemnly to me that he would have further questions to ask me later on. I am still awaiting them.

Then there was the sermon that he gave us on board the *Hohenzollern*! The Tsar had been invited to lunch; his suite had been convened an hour earlier, and found themselves in front of an altar, with William II as the officiating priest. The Kaiser had thrown over his uniform a Protestant pastor's surplice, and kept us standing for an hour while he expounded to us from every point of view a Biblical text which he had chosen for our edification.

Freedericksz, for all his experience and his even temper, admitted that every interview he had with the German Emperor left him a complete wreck.

The members of the Kaiser's suite seemed to have got used to their master's eccentricities. At Swinemunde, replying to a toast from the Tsar, William II made a fiery speech which the stenographers were able to take down word for word. What was my astonishment when I received from the Germans a text of the speech that differed vastly from the imprudent harangue which their Emperor had delivered. Chancellor von Bulow asked Isvolsky to give Reuter the text which he had prepared, as this was what William II 'was to have said' if he had not allowed himself to be carried away. Isvolsky demurred, but gave way in the end:

'The speech that the German Emperor actually made was finer, but this is more discreet; let us rest content with the official version—for the Press.'

I shall never forget the reception that William II gave to Count Lamsdorff, our Minister of Foreign Affairs, at the time of the Danzig interview. Count Lamsdorff had never left the Pevtchesky Most, our Foreign Ministry. He was a highly cultivated man, ambitious, but very timid, a defect often found in persons who have passed their whole life in offices shut off from the outer world. To make the best of his short stature the Count wore heels high enough for the most elegant of ladies, and in addition a hat of unwonted elevation. All this was ill-suited to the swell that greeted us in the Danzig roads.

I have no idea of the reason, but the Emperor William took a manifest dislike to our Minister from the moment they met. Did he want to show his contempt for a 'landlubber' who was visibly upset by the pitching of the yacht? In any case, all through the lunch Lamsdorff was chosen as the one and only butt for the stream of sarcasms that the German Emperor was pleased to pour out. Prince von Büllow sat gloomily through it all, uneasily watching this ill-treatment of his colleague, but unable to do anything to restrain his master's tasteless exuberance.

The departure brought fresh torture for the Count. The picket-boat that was to take us ashore was dancing like a cork alongside the accommodation steps. Boarding the boat was, of course, child's play for a seaman used to such exercises, but for Lamsdorff it was a desperate problem. Twice running he missed his chance to jump; at the third lurch of the yacht he was half pushed by the people behind him and half caught in mid-air by the boat's crew. At that moment a roar of laughter was heard from above: it came from William II, who shouted down in a voice half-choked with amusement:

'You haven't found your sea legs yet, Herr Minister!'

A few hours later a decoration was brought to Lamsdorff. It was not the Black Eagle to which he considered himself entitled, but the ribbon of some unknown order that William II had just created. Prince von Büllow had to go himself to console his colleague.

There was no discoverable rhyme or reason about all these idiosyncrasies; the explanation lay simply in the fact that the German Emperor had his own peculiar ways of enjoying himself.

On one occasion I had personally to endure this irritating chaff. William II suddenly took a fancy to calling me 'Molossov'. There was no getting him to pronounce my name correctly, though it offers no special difficulty to a foreigner. Finally he sent me his portrait, with its dedication correctly spelt; but the envelope containing the present bore in large letters in His Majesty's writing the words: 'General *Molossov.*'

What was the point of this jest?

I think I know the particular moment at which the ruler of Germany forgot my exact name.

It is rather a curious story. The Viborg regiment, of which William II was honorary Colonel, was carrying out landing manoeuvres on the island of Carlos, in the Finnish fjords. The Kaiser expressed the desire to put himself at the head of a detachment and to lead it to the 'attack' on the imaginary enemy. The Tsar felt that this manifestation of the German Emperor's warlike tastes was thoroughly out of place, but he had to give way before his 'cousin's' persistence.

Thus we were presented with the strange spectacle of Russian soldiers led by the German Emperor.

The manoeuvres on Carlos Island were being photographed by General Nesvetevitch, a fine old officer who had gone on pension after the war of 1877, and had since become a successful photographer for the Russian newspapers. He continued to wear military uniform, and that enabled him to work with his camera in places where his pressmen colleagues were not admitted on any terms.

In order to get a good photograph of the German Emperor, General Nesvetevitch rushed off ahead of him—and lost one of his galoshes. Galoshes were, it need hardly be said, not permitted articles of military dress.

As ill-luck would have it, William II came right on the heels of the photographer. He stuck his sword through the *corpus delicti*, and bore it off in triumph to the Tsar. General Nesvetevitch was not the man to miss so good an opportunity for a snapshot.

The horror of the general staff may be imagined. Who was the soldier or officer who had dared to put on galoshes? Finally, some one mentioned the photographer Nesvetevitch. He was hurriedly sent for and came up wearing only one galosh. William II deliberately kept up a long and very friendly conversation with the photographer, and told him that he particularly wanted to have the photographs of the attack—and of the galosh.

That same evening I was instructed by the Minister of the Court to ask the General to destroy the ridiculous photo at once. The artist was disconsolate, but the loyal subject of the Tsar could only obey His Majesty's express order—protesting all the time that it was just this photo that he had promised the Kaiser. We sent to Berlin another photo, a decent one.

William II knew how to show his annoyance even to persons in very high places. I will only mention here the incidents at the entrance to the Kiel Canal after the Cowes interview, which had been very unwelcome to Germany.

We proceeded slowly along this strategic artery of modern Germany. The Kaiser had not deigned to announce beforehand his intention to pay a visit to the *Standard*. At one of the last of the locks he appeared as though by chance. He came on board the Imperial yacht, saluted Their Majesties with the most frigid formality, and asked the Tsar when he intended to proceed on his voyage. Nicholas II replied that he would be leaving Kiel very soon, having to be back in St. Petersburg for an official ceremony. After a few minutes' talk, the Kaiser took his leave, and went ashore. Their

Majesties did nothing on their side to impart to this strange interview the slightest element of cordiality.

Scarcely had we anchored at Kiel when the Tsar received a message from the Kaiser, scrawled on a scrap of paper torn out of a note-book. It asked the Tsar to delay his departure from Kiel until 8 a.m., so that on leaving he might pass through the German Fleet assembled in the roads. Nicholas II replied with one or two friendly words: he wrote, in English, that he would be pleased to admire his cousin's fine fleet.

A few hours later, for no apparent reason, there came a message cancelling the arrangement: there was to be no review. What made it worse (the Tsar himself spoke of it afterwards) was that the message contained not the slightest indication of the reason for the Kaiser's fresh decision. The review would not take place. That was all. We steamed out, needless to say, at 5 a.m.

For all that, some of the officers of the suite got up to catch a glimpse, even if only an unofficial one, of the famous German units. A thick fog spoilt the morning for them.

At lunch the Tsar chaffed them for their keenness. He told them that their indiscretion had been punished.

'William II was not going to let us compare the German and British ships, and had his fleet dressed in a fog to measure.'

The painful impression produced by these incidents was more or less obliterated at our last visit to Berlin, on the occasion of the marriage of the daughter of William II with Duke Ernest of Brunswick-Luneburg. With a much larger number of courtiers around him, the Kaiser seemed to adapt himself better to the atmosphere which should surround a monarch.

I will end my recollections of the reigning house of Germany with an incident that occurred at Spala. It goes to show that Their Majesties' relations with their German relatives were always tinged with a measure of latent and almost instinctive animosity.

Prince Henry of Prussia had arrived at Spala with his wife, Princess Irene, our Empress's sister. (These visits occurred regularly and were apparently meant to keep William II informed concerning the views of the Tsar and of governing circles.)

On the day of the Prince's arrival, the Tsar suggested a ride on horseback. We rode a dozen miles or so through a wood of magical loveliness. On the way back the Prince said to the Tsar:

'It has been an interesting ride, but surely this was not the *Distanzritt* (a test of endurance) 'of which you wrote in your letter?'

'This was only by way of preparation,' the Tsar replied; 'tomorrow I will show you some forests farther off.'

The Tsar came over to my side, and said in a low voice:

'Prince Henry wants us to take him on a *Distanzntt*. Send the cook to the place we spoke about a few days ago. I will make him do fifty miles to begin the day with. On the way back he will not boast so much of his military training.'

He added, with a significant smile:

'Tell them to saddle my "zain".'

The Tsar's zain was a cross between an English thoroughbred and a Russian trotter; it had so long a trot that the suite had continually to change from gallop to trot and from trot to gallop. That, of course, is particularly fatiguing. The whole suite was accustomed to this form of exercise. The Prince, however, seemed tired after twenty-five miles, and began to complain of his horse. On the way back he was offered whichever of the horses of the suite he fancied. He made his choice, but was hardly able to get back. His legs were covered with blood, and he was unable to get into the saddle for five days.

The Tsar consoled him by telling him that he would get used to it, but added aside, whispering in my ear:

'He will sing a little more softly now; he won't want another *Distanzritt*. It's a funny thing, but all sailors think themselves finished horsemen.'

THE KING OF ENGLAND

What a contrast there was between the visits of William II and the reception of the King and Queen of England at Reval! How entirely at ease everybody was in their company!

On a lovely June morning, sunny and fresh, the yacht *Victoria and Albert* made her appearance in the open sea beyond the roads. Our whole squadron, preceded by the Imperial yacht, went out to meet the British Sovereigns. After the usual ceremonies, King Edward, Queen Alexandra, and their daughter Princess Victoria went on board the yacht *Pole Star*, in which the Dowager Empress had come; the state lunch began at once. The Tsar received the

King of England in the uniform of the Scots Greys, with the famous bearskin busby. Nicholas II was forthwith appointed Admiral of the Fleet, and at once put on his new uniform.

After visiting H.M.S. *Minotaur*, one of the cruisers of the British escort, the Tsar asked me whether I had in my trunks any suitable present for the officers' mess. I happened to have a big *zhban* (large bowl) of chased silver, in pure Russian style. It was at once sent over to the *Minotaur* as the first present from the new 'Admiral' of the British Navy. The *zhban* had travelled with me for many years, waiting for the appropriate moment for its appearance.

Everything was done perfectly quietly and with much dignity. The etiquette of the English Court was very different from ours. Our princes were accustomed from their earliest childhood to standing for hours and hours; after meals they formed a 'circle', dead-tired. On board the *Victoria and Albert* things were done differently. After dinner the King and his august guests sat down in comfortable armchairs; cigars and liqueurs were served; an arm-chair was left vacant alongside each person of high rank, and the officers with whom the King wanted to talk were invited to sit down in one of these chairs; after a fairly long conversation the King would nod and his interlocutor would retire for somebody else to take his place.

The whole of the two suites stayed in the room. There was no need at all to remain standing; those who preferred could sit down whenever they chose. Except when on duty, no account was taken of rank or social position.

I recall how Sir John Fisher (as he was then) marched up and down the room and asked me some question each time he came near me. I felt it my duty to rise each time to answer him. At last he said:

'I can't sit down—I have been fifty years going to and fro on deck; but that is no reason why people who have not my habits should be put out. We are not on duty; this is a sitting-room.'

At tea-time the band struck up, to the great pleasure of our ladies, young and old. Sir John was one of the first to carry one of the Grand Duchesses off to the dance.

The whole of the Imperial family retained the pleasantest memories of this visit, during which every sort of constraint or nervousness was dispelled by the tact and good feeling of our guests.

* * *

THE FRENCH

The visits made by our allies also left a very pleasant impression. I shall never forget the success that attended the meeting with President Falliéres and the hearty way we all greeted his son, not unmeaningly, as 'Dauphin'.

It is only in my capacity of historian of everyday trifles that I shall mention certain little happenings of the sort that stick in one's memory; there is a place for humorous anecdote, even about friends. Will it be credited if I say that it is the most idiotic story among my memories that jumps to my mind the most readily?

When the French sailors came to St. Petersburg a grand gala performance was organized in their honour in the immense People's Hall, a building that might have been specially erected for such monster entertainments. It was my part, of course, to inform the foreign correspondents of what had been going on. Had one of these gentlemen of the Press been, perhaps, a little inattentive? His newspaper, at all events, had as one of its big cross-heads:

'RECEPTION IN THE PUBLIC HOUSE
IN ST. PETERSBURG'

and the French 'public house' is not an establishment of the innocent respectability of the British. This inventive gentleman can certainly have had no idea of the chaffing that I had to endure on account of his slip of the pen, which I suppose must have been involuntary. It was the joke of the day in every club in the capital! Countess Freedericksz rebuked me sharply for not 'censoring' the foreign newspapers.

Here is another detail, now so insignificant, which kept us amused for many weeks.

On our way back from the review at Compiégne the Empress (who had at her side the Mistress of the Robes, Mme Naryshkin) found her carriage surrounded by an enormous crowd; it was almost impossible to move. Shouts of 'Vive l'Empereur!' 'Vive l'Emperatrice!' surged round the procession like the waves of a choppy sea. Suddenly a little man just in front of Mme Naryshkin who evidently wanted to please everybody gave a shout that carried over all the noise of the crowd:

'Three cheers for the lady on the left!'

He drew a round of applause, and thereafter Mme Naryshkin was known at Court as 'the lady on the left'.

The arrival of a foreign Court often sets pitfalls in etiquette which it is impossible to avoid with the best of good intentions. Shall I give an example?

At Vitry, during the French Army manoeuvres, the Tsar mounted a horse from his own stables, as was his habit (and also that of William II). The members of the suite had, of course, to content themselves with horses provided on the spot. Just as I was getting into the saddle an officer belonging to the President's suite came up to me and was kind enough to say:

'Your Excellency, we know you are an accomplished rider, and we have reserved a thoroughbred for you.'

So long as we were going at walking pace all was well. But the moment arrived when an echelon came into view at a distance, and the Tsar set off at a gallop. The suite did the same. Then my tribulations began. There was no holding the animal back; its paces were worthy of a Derby winner. I could see that I was going to be carried ahead of the Tsar, the worst thing possible, so I made my mount turn outwards. But the turn had no sooner been completed than it had to be begun again, for my courser took his duties with the utmost seriousness. Shall I confess it? The whole of that run was made in successive, progressively widening circles.

As I dismounted I said to the officer in the President's suite who had been so kind;

'This animal has come from a racing stable?'

'Yes, your Excellency. She has just carried off a number of prizes at Longchamps.'

'I can believe it. It was all I could do not to beat the Tsar by five hundred lengths.'

It was during the same visit that the incident occurred of the christening of a grandson of the Marquis de Montebello, French Ambassador in St. Petersburg. Some time before the Tsar's departure, the Marquis had asked the Sovereign to be godfather at the christening. The Tsar had seen no reason to refuse this favour to the Ambassador. It happened that we had arrived at Compiégne at the time when the struggle between the Waldeck-Rousseau Cabinet and the Clericals was at its height. There were long discussions with our ceremonial staff; the French Ministry wanted at all costs to prevent the Tsar from going to the chapel in which the ceremony was to take place. Nicholas II insisted that a promise given by the Tsar of Russia must be kept. I believe that this cost the Marquis de Montebello his post; shortly afterwards he was recalled from St. Petersburg.

Both sides were right.

During our visit to Compiégne some little incidents happened which I think were due to the very praiseworthy desire to place us all in an atmosphere recalling the memories of this fine old chateau.

Here is an example. To reach Compiégne we had been put into a train which had belonged to Napoleon III. The coaches were full of gilded furniture, and of every sort of decoration in the style of the Second Empire. It looked very fine, but what uncomfortable coaches they were! How huddled up we were! To crown our misfortunes, they had forgotten to change the springs: Second Empire springs were ill able to stand the speeds to which we are used in the twentieth century. The Empress was afflicted with nausea, and the strongest of us left these cages dead tired and aching all over.

The chateau itself is marvellous—for a picnic. When I reached the room reserved for me I found that there was no water, that razors and bottles of eau-de-Cologne had to be placed on little tables about the room, and that certain 'amenities' indispensable to the traveller's comfort were a hundred miles from my bedroom. In short, this chateau was all too thoroughly in Empire style!

For the state banquet the French ladies, full of anxiety to show every attention to the Russian Sovereigns, all dressed with one accord in Empire dresses (were these not shown in the pictures of the chateau that illustrated the memoirs of Napoleon I and Napoleon III?), and powdered themselves with a very dark lilac powder. The result was curious, but our maids of honour were none the less distracted at having neither dresses with exceedingly high waists nor this famous powder of—purplish blue.

It is undeniable that when two different mentalities come into contact the result is often a series of awkward misunderstandings. What a desperate problem, for instance, was that of decorations! The list given me in France was three times the length of the one that had been drawn up in St. Petersburg in agreement with the Ambassador and the military attaché. When I asked what part this or the other person mentioned in the new list had played during the Tsar's visit, I was unfailingly told:

'He wasn't there, but he has a great deal of influence.'

Long discussions had to follow to determine the decoration that should be given to this influential citizen. For some reason, I cannot say what, the French were anxious at all costs to escape from getting the order of St. Stanislas. They even refused the star of St. Stanislas.

'No, not Stanislas; say Anne, even if it ranks lower.'

Yet it was obviously impossible to give everybody the same decoration.

I will end the tale of these small trials—of which, after all, the importance must not be exaggerated—with the incident that occurred at the moment of our departure from Compiégne. I recognize that both sides were right from their own standpoint.

Everybody had gone off to attend the review, but I wanted to supervise the final preparations for our departure, and had remained in the chateau. I might have saved myself the trouble; I discovered almost at once that everybody, the commanding officer, the servants, the civil officials, the officers, had rushed off to see the manoeuvres, leaving the Tsar's luggage lying about the floor, abandoned to its fate.

I had to go in search of the Commandant of the town gendarmerie. He told me that it was nothing to do with him.

'But,' I protested, 'it will be an unheard-of scandal! Just think what it would mean if the train had to bring the Tsar back to Compiégne because the luggage had been left behind!'

Finally the Commandant put at my disposal an officer and a squad of soldiers. But I soon found that the mentality of the French Tommies was a whole world apart from that of our infantrymen:

'Sorry,' they said, 'but we are not the Tsar's porters!'

Once more, both sides were right.

I had all the trouble in the world to get them to see reason, and by the time I had got the last piece of the Imperial luggage loaded on to the lorry, the Tsar was on his way to the train.

EMPEROR FRANCIS JOSEPH

The visit to Vienna and Mürzsteg has remained vividly in my memory through a conversation that I had with Emperor Francis Joseph.

We had gone off to a hunting-box high up in the Alps, near Karlsgraben. I had been posted in a sort of eyrie at the top of the debris of an enormous moraine. I had the good luck to kill three chamois; one was hit in full flight as it jumped from one crag to another. As I descended the moraine to take possession of my quarry, I was astonished to find standing close to it the Emperor Francis Joseph.

'That was a fine shot of yours (*Das war ein Meisterschuss*),' he said very kindly.

I wanted to apologize, and to explain that I did not know that the chamois had been going towards the Sovereign.

Francis Joseph put me at my ease by telling me that in any case he 'could not possibly' kill more than three chamois that day. Otherwise he would have reached a total of three thousand chamois fallen to his gun, and that would have brought him ovations from the huntsmen which he was anxious to avoid in the presence of the Tsar of Russia.

The Emperor made me sit down on a folding chair; his attendant had gone to fetch his horse, and we had a few minutes together.

In spite of his great age, the Emperor seemed to have an excellent memory.

'Was it not you,' he said suddenly, 'who were presented to me at the time of "Sandro" Battenberg's visit to Vienna?'

I said that it was.

'I think,' the Emperor went on, 'you were one of the few of your compatriots who remained faithful to Sandro. Did I not hear that you had to give an explanation on your return to Russia? Tell me all about it. I had such a liking for Sandro.'

I told the Emperor in a few words what had happened, mentioning that Tsar Alexander III saved me from the disgrace with which I was threatened; he remembered in the nick of time that his father, Alexander II, had told me to 'serve Sandro as though he were the Tsar himself'.

Francis Joseph replied:

'The time came when the Tsar was sorry for what had been done to Sandro. Sandro's enforced departure from Bulgaria ran counter to the aims that Russia had been pursuing in the Principality. The Generals and diplomats then in Sofia had been badly chosen.'

He added that in his view Sandro was a very capable man;

'perhaps better able to lead soldiers to the attack than to reign in so young a State as Bulgaria was then'.

Many years had passed since this conversation when I found myself once more in Vienna, having been selected to accompany Grand Duke Andrew Vladimirovitch on a mission to Bulgaria. After the dinner in honour of His Highness, the Emperor came to me and said:

'Now you are in Vienna, don't forget to call on Sandro's widow. I am very fond of her.'

PRINCE FERDINAND OF BULGARIA

It would be easy to fill many pages with my conversations with the Bulgarians.

As one of those who fought in the Bulgarian war of liberation, I have been present at many Russo-Bulgarian demonstrations, some of which were of great magnificence. I may have occasion later on to devote a special work to these fine pages of Russo-Bulgarian history. Here I am confined to sketches with no sort of political character, and I shall be very brief.

As a former A.D.C. to Prince Alexander of Battenberg, it seemed impossible that I should be persona grata with Prince Ferdinand, his successor. It was for that reason that I declined the honour of being attached to his person during his first visit to St. Petersburg. Subsequent events proved, however, that I was mistaken; Prince Ferdinand showed me the greatest friendship, and invited me to Sofia as his personal guest after the Shipka ceremonies.*

It was during this visit that the Prince honoured me by taking me round the zoological garden which he had installed in Sofia, and of which he was particularly proud. He told me that he had there the most complete collection of the serpents that are to be found in Bulgaria.

' Would you like to see them?'

I have an innate and instinctive aversion from every sort of reptile. But politeness demanded the answer 'Yes'.

He took me over to some glass cases filled with these repulsive creatures. Suddenly, to my horror, I saw him put on a sort of green

---

* The commemoration of the battle of the Shipka Pass, fought in 1877.

glove and pull out the serpents one by one; they twisted and reared and coiled round his arm. Finally he brought one of the abominable creatures close to me, and told me I might caress it. With all the surface imperturbability of a Spartan, I went through the necessary performance. Needless to say I was thoroughly relieved when we were able to get away from this home of horrors and go to see the greenhouses, where the Prince Stopped before the most interesting of the plants and told me their Latin names. Savants have their manias, even when they are princes.

The visit to the garden and the palace lasted so long that the Orient Express which was to carry me away had to delay its departure, by the Prince's command, for more than an hour.

THE SHAH OF PERSIA

The visits of the Shah of Persia have left only two anecdotes in my memory. I think they are worth telling.

The first relates to a reception at Court. A long Court procession filed before the Oriental Sovereign. After being greeted by one of the ladies he said aloud, in his broken French:

'Why—old? ugly? naked?'

It must be inferred that the etiquette of his Court was not as that of the Courts of other sovereigns.

During the manoeuvres at Kursk the Shah had seen an imposing number of soldiers paraded in front of the pavilion in which he was seated. He had been told that 100,000 men had taken part in the march past. At one moment the Shah made a sign to one of his aides-de-camp and whispered something in his ear. My brother officer Bellegarde, a former instructor of the Persian cavalry, noticed that the officer stopped near the entrance to the pavilion in obvious perplexity. He went up to him. It seems that the Shah had told his A.D.C. to go and see for himself that the same battalions were not being brought back somewhere in order to march past a second time. The poor Persian officer was at a loss to acquit himself of his delicate mission.

Bellegarde took him to the place where the battalions dispersed. He was able to verify that our generals were playing no tricks.

* * *

III. EVERYDAY LIFE
MEALS

We come now to Their Majesties' daily life. I shall write first of the daily bread.

It was the Marshal of the Court, Count Benckendorff, who ruled over everything that had to do with meals and with formalities at table. He was assisted by Colonels Prince Putiatin and von Bode, the two 'Cutlet Colonels', as they were always called.

Count Benckendorff considered himself absolute lord over everything that concerned his department; he kept watch over it with jealous care, and nobody interfered in the great problems that came under his supervision. He had, of course, to keep within his budget; but he disposed of the money entirely at his own discretion. And, supreme honour, he had the right to make oral and written 'reports' himself; which means, in plain language, that he received his orders directly from the Tsar. He referred to the Minister of the Court only in exceptional cases.

Meals at the Russian Court were divided into three categories or classes:

(1) The service of Their Majesties and their immediate suite, known as the Sovereigns' table;

(2) The Marshal's service, for the remaining members of the suite, and for dignitaries invited to Court;

(3) The domestics' service, in two subdivisions, according to rank.

The first service was reserved to persons whom Their Majesties had deigned to invite to join them. If the guest, after being presented to the Sovereigns, had not received a personal invitation, he sat at the Marshal's table.

Breakfast was served in the guest's own room. Tea, coffee, or chocolate could be had as preferred, and bread and butter were brought—household bread, rolls, and sweetened bread. Ham, eggs, and bacon could also be called for.

Then came the '*kalatch*'. The *kalatch* was an agelong tradition, kept up the more rigorously because the Empress was very fond of this sort of Muscovite bread. It is rather difficult to explain to foreigners what a *kalatch* was. Outwardly, it was a little white loaf, made with hardly any yeast, and it looked for all the world like a lady's oval handbag, with the flap turned back half-way up, and on top of it a semicircular strip; a hundred years ago the *kalatchy* used to be hung on sticks by these strips for convenience of transport. The *kalatch* was an essentially Muscovite product, and the bakers had created a legend that it was impossible to make the dough for it without the water of the Moscow River. Consequently a service from Moscow had to be organized. Tanks filled with this miracle-working water were sent to the Court, wherever it might be. The *kalatch* was served with special ceremony. It was supposed to be eaten very hot, and was brought in a warm napkin.

Such was the breakfast. It would have been interesting to discover how this food figured in the budget of the Court (though this was a delicate subject which would have had to be approached with prudence). I will content myself with one anecdote; it may serve to illustrate a matter that went beyond my ken.

Tsar Alexander III had appointed one of his aides-de-camp to the post of Marshal of the Court.

'They are spending too much money on my meals,' he said; 'try to get a little order into the buying.'

The young Marshal of the Court set to work, full of enthusiasm. The first detail that came to his notice made him jump. Five pounds of Gruyere cheese was bought every day 'for His Majesty's personal table'. He made inquiries: how much Gruyere did the Tsar take for breakfast? A few days of discreet observation showed the quantity to be two or three tiny pieces.

He sent for the steward concerned:

'This five pounds of Gruyere has got to stop.'

'As you wish, your Excellency.'

A few days later the Tsar took an opportunity to say to him:

'Is it you who gave the order to serve me with three little bits of cheese? Why are they shrivelled up and oily, and quite uneatable?'

There was a further interview with the steward:

'Put on the table a big piece of Gruyere; but I think it ought to last several days.'

'As you wish, your Excellency.'

After the second day the big piece of cheese had such a look about it that the Tsar sent it away in disgust. The end of it was that the Marshal gave way. He also sent in his resignation.

I might mention an incident that occurred at the Hofburg, in Vienna, during one of our visits to Francis Joseph. It was not an incident of any great importance, but it was significant.

During dinner I had noticed some sweets wrapped up very artistically in covers which had on them photographs of members of the Imperial family. It occurred to me to take away a few in order to show them to our Marshal of the Court, but I did not have time to arrange for it. What was my astonishment when, on leaving, I was handed a box of these very sweets.

I suggested to Count Benckendorff that we might be able to do something of the sort ourselves, but he replied that it was out of the question. It was a tradition of our Court that all the sweets put out for guests and not consumed at table became the property of the domestics.

'It is quite impossible to depart from the tradition. There would be too much discontent, and in the end the guests would not get what had been prepared for them.'

Such was the confession of one of the strictest of Marshals of the Court, a Marshal in whom the Tsar had implicit confidence.

Lunch was served at noon. At Livadia and in the hunting-boxes the whole suite had the right to sit down to meals at the Sovereigns' table. Every one had to be in the dining-room five minutes before lunch time. The Emperor came in, greeted his guests, and went to the *zakusky* table, at which everybody helped himself. The *zakusky* (hors-d'oeuvre) would be caviare, smoked fish, pickled herrings, of course, and tiny snacks on fried bread. Two or three dishes of hot *zakusky* were also served: sausages in tomato *purée*, hot knuckle of ham, *gruau á la Dragomiroff*, and so on. The Emperor would take two glasses of vodka and very small portions of *zakusky*. The Empress considered this way of eating before sitting down to table to be unhealthy, and did not go near the hors-d'oeuvre table. This preliminary lasted about a quarter of an hour; meanwhile the maids of honour came up in turn to the Empress, who said a few words to each of them.

After the *zakusky* we took the seats assigned to us. It would not have done to be hunting for our seats in Their Majesties' presence, so that everybody made a point of finding where his seat was before they had come in.

At ordinary lunches the Empress sat by the side of the Tsar, on his right; the Minister of the Court sat facing Their Majesties. If there were guests, they sat by the side of the Sovereigns or of the Minister of the Court; otherwise the members of the suite arranged themselves according to rank and seniority. There was only one exception: the seat on the Empress's right was taken in turn by each of the members of the suite without exception, even by the youngest invited.

Before leaving the subject of *zakusky*, I should mention the picturesque ceremony of the *présent*. The Russian language has several words for 'present'; the ceremony that I am about to describe was a tradition dating from the eighteenth century, and the gift bore the French name of present.

This *présent* was a gift that the Ural Cossacks brought every spring to their Sovereign, and was made up of the finest fish caught in the first and most important haul of the year, and with it several barrels of fresh caviare.

The *présent* had been introduced as a spontaneous manifestation of filial reverence to the Tsar; subsequently it was regulated by laws duly promulgated. The *gramota* (decree) of the Sovereign which reserved to the Ural Cossacks the exclusive right of fishing in the waters of the Ural River and its tributaries, laid down that the whole product of the first catch, hereafter called the Tsar's haul, belonged to the Imperial house.

The Tsar's haul was no small matter. The fishing began at a time when the river was still covered by a thick layer of ice, and its technique had, if I may say so, a character of its own. Holes were cut in the ice, and suitable nets were dropped through them.

The Governor-General himself attended the Tsar's haul. The authorities were all there to a man. A Te Deum was sung, and the priests walked past the ice-holes, sprinkling them with holy water.

The caviare and the fish were prepared on the spot and sent off the same day in waggons that went direct to St. Petersburg. A deputation of bearded Cossacks, conscious of the honour done to them by the voters who had chosen them for the duty, left for the capital at the same time as the consignment. I want to emphasize the detail that the Cossacks had been chosen by their electors. The Cossacks have never ceased to live under a thoroughly democratic regime, with a *Krug* (an electoral assembly like the Agora in Athens) for each regiment. The *Krug* made its choice, entirely, of course, from among men of high repute who had at least a St. George's cross, a decoration which could only be obtained on the field of battle.

The delegation was received by the Tsar in the great dining-room of the Palace. The Cossacks came in with specimens of their fish and of caviare 'of pearl grey turning to amber'. The *présent* was placed near the *zakusky* table, and the Tsar and the Empress tasted the 'flower' of the Ural fishing. A glass of vodka was then drunk to the prosperity of the Ural Cossacks, and watches with the Tsar's monogram were given as presents to the delegation.

Thereafter the Cossacks went on to the Minister of the Court, the writer of these lines, the Grand Dukes, and the high dignitaries of the Court. The Tsar's haul must have been abundant. My share of it amounted to close on forty pounds of superb caviar and five or six fish, each a yard long. Did the Ural ultimately become less well stocked, or did the Cossacks' zeal abate? Whatever the explanation, the fact remained that in the end the *présent* diminished greatly, to about half.

For all that, there was caviare enough even for certain foreign Courts.

At lunch there were two courses, one of eggs or fish, and one of white or red meat. Those who had good appetites had time to attack four different dishes. The second course included vegetables; these, in order not to encumber the tables, were put on smaller plates, crescent-shaped. Lunch ended with a compote of fruit, and cheese.

The servant who carried the dish had to place the guest's portion on his plate; this made it unnecessary for the men guests to serve their lady neighbours. The Emperor was the only one who served himself. Ultimately his example was followed and the old custom fell into disuse.

When there were no guests, coffee was served at the dining-table. The Tsar lit a cigarette, saying that the Empress had given permission. If there were guests the company rose from the table after dessert; Their Majesties replied to the obeisances of the guests and went into another room or into the garden; coffee was then taken standing, the Sovereigns conversing with their entourage. Smoking was allowed as soon as the Tsar had lit his cigarette.

Five o'clock tea was served in our rooms. Sometimes we would go for tea to the room of the nearest maid of honour, according to the 'geography' of the Palace. Tea was only taken with Their Majesties on a personal invitation.

Dinner was at eight. Their Majesties greeted those persons whom they had not seen during the day; I always wondered what device they could employ to make sure, as they did, of never making a mistake. At Livadia there were no *zakusky* for dinner; on days spent in hunting they were served twice.

Dinner began with a thick or clear soup, *vol-au-vent*, *pirozhky* (little Russian cakes), or cheese on hot rusks. The *vol-au-vent* were served with the soup and not after it as abroad. Then came fish, roast (fowl or game), vegetables and a sweet, followed by fruit. Coffee was taken in the dining-room. At ceremonial dinners the number of courses was, of course, increased, as everywhere on the Continent and in America.

The wines were: Madeira and white and red wine at lunch; beer for those who asked for it. At dinners, a series of wines in accordance with the general custom; liqueurs with the coffee.

Each meal had to last fifty minutes, not one more and not one less. The Marshal of the Court saw to the rigid observance of this tradition. Why? I am quite unable to say. But I do know that we all paid dearly for Count Benckendorff's obstinacy; the Tsar's guests benefited little from the efforts of all the master cooks in the Imperial kitchens.

The tradition dated from the reign of Alexander II. This Tsar liked to change the room used as dining-room from time to time, and there were times when he made use of a room at a great distance from the kitchens. He insisted, at the same time, that the courses should be served one after another without interruption; as soon as he had finished the fish he expected the roast to be brought in, at once. The Marshal was reduced to sacrificing gastronomy to speed. Enormous heaters were invented, using boiling water; the course was brought up twenty minutes in advance, on a silver dish; this dish had a silver cover, and was placed on the heater until the moment came for serving. Thanks to this subterfuge. Count Benckendorff was able to maintain the fifty-minute meals. True gourmets will agree with me that no sauce could retain its full flavour in such conditions.

Freedericksz protested all his life against this system of massacring good dishes, but his authority was not sufficient to make an end of this gastronomic scandal, as we called it. He made a gallant attempt to quash it at Livadia. He sent for the engineers and asked them to construct a railway and a lift: the railway was to carry the dishes to a point just below the pantry, and the lift would do the rest; the dish would arrive at its destination in all its succulence. But the Minister had neither consulted nor even told the cooks about the plan, and they were full of wrath over the installation, which robbed of their employment the young novices who carried the dishes from kitchen to pantry. It was claimed in the circles of these successors of Brillat-Savarin that the electric train did not move smoothly enough for the sauces and the chicken croquettes; nothing but the feline tread of a cook's apprentice could save them from being shaken up. Freedericksz insisted; the cooks went on a ca'canny strike; they sent the electric carriages along in a slow motion that reduced everything to an uneatable condition. Ultimately Freedericksz gave way, and the railway functioned no more. The battery of boiling water heaters made its reappearance in triumph in the pantry, and remained there to the end.

As for the Empress, she was always on a diet prescribed by her doctors, and had her food prepared in the pantry itself, on oil stoves of a well-known Swedish make.

The only place in which we really fed well was the Imperial train. The kitchen-car was next to the dining-car, which would not accommodate more than sixteen persons. Consequently it was possible to bring in the dishes as soon as they came out of the oven. I noticed that the train was the only place in which the Tsar regularly sent for the chef to congratulate him on a particularly successful dish.

The Marshal's table differed little from that of the Sovereigns. There was perhaps not quite so much of the cream of the early vegetables, and not quite such an abundance of fruit. The meals at this table were served to the Marshal himself, to the Minister of the Court when he was at Peterhof, to the Mistress of the Robes, and to the maids of honour in the suite. Generals A.D.C. and officers commanding the detachment on guard at the palace were also entitled to feed at the Marshal's table, and I have already mentioned that persons presenting themselves to Their Majesties who had not been invited to the Sovereigns' table lunched at the Marshal's; he made a point of presiding over it himself.

The domestics' table must have been particularly well loaded, if I may judge by my own servant, who was continually obliged to change his belt for an ampler one.

When the Tsar became Commander-in-Chief of the Russian armies, he completely broke with all the customs of the Court, and had dishes of the utmost simplicity served up. He said to me one day:

'Thanks to the war, I have learnt that simple dishes are infinitely nicer and healthier than all the Marshal's spiced cookery.'

As to the wines—at lunch the Emperor drank nothing but Madeira: a large glass of a specially chosen vintage. A bottle of this wine was placed in front of his plate. He hated to have the wine poured out by a servant, who 'always made too much of a business of it'; he served himself. The guests' glasses were filled by servants; they had Madeira or white or red wine as in other countries. At dinner the wines were a little more varied.

All these wines were excellent, but they did not belong to the famous cellar which contained the real 'jewels'. This cellar—we all sighed for its contents—was guarded by Count Benckendorff.

In order to get anything out of it, it was necessary to have recourse to a regular stratagem. Nobody but the Minister of the Court could put forward any suggestion concerning this cellar. And it was necessary that he should have sufficient ground. We searched the saints' calendar accordingly for patrons and patronesses to be honoured; as soon as a suitable name was discovered we went in search of Count Freedericksz and put the position to him. Usually he would send for Benckendorff and say:

'I have a family festival to-day. You must let us have a glass of old wine all round.'

'But you know perfectly well that these wines are reserved for very great occasions, state banquets '

The case would be pressed, and at length the Count would have glasses laid for the vintage that had been chosen. When the Emperor saw them he would smile:

'Have you another niece coming of age to-day? I wonder who remembered it! I'll bet it was Nilov or Troubetzkoy. . . .'

Freedericksz was fond above all of a certain Chateau Yquem, which had been nicknamed Nectar. It was no good hoping for a glass of Nectar if the Empress was going to be at dinner.

The 'jewels' were destroyed on the day of the October revolution. The immense cellars of the Winter Palace were sacked by the revolutionaries. The wine that was not drunk was poured over the Palace square; it is said that in the evening the square looked for all the world like a field of battle; the people lying about it dead drunk would have made a good subject for a photographer in search of a picture showing how the assailants had despised death.

But, after all, wine had ceased to play in the Russian Court the part which it played among our ancestors. Only one custom remained inviolable; cynics seized on it to draw certain amusing deductions.

It was the tradition of the 'golden Coronation goblet'. At one point in the course of the state banquet given after the Tsar's coronation, the Grand Cup-bearer of the Court presented a golden goblet filled with wine, and proclaimed in a loud voice so that all should hear:

'His Majesty deigns to drink.'

At that cry the 'foreign guests' (not excluding the diplomats) had to leave the Granovitaya Palata ('bevelled room'). At the last coronation this curious toast was not heralded; but the Masters of Ceremonies invited the 'foreigners' to go into another room where tables had been laid. Only the trusty subjects of the Tsar could join in the feast in the Granovitaya Palata.

The reader will have guessed the reasons that may have led the Machiavellis of the Muscovite Court of the sixteenth century to introduce this precautionary measure.

During the reign of Alexander II, only foreign wines were served. Alexander III gave a decision which made history in Russian vinegrowing: foreign wines were in future only to be served when foreign sovereigns or diplomats were present. At other times Russian wines must be made to do. All the regiments of the guards followed suit. I remember that there were many officers who considered that this vinicultural nationalism was being carried too far; they abandoned their messes and went to the big restaurants, in order to get the wines they preferred. At that time it needed some resolution to rest content with the produce of the Crimea.

But that did not last long. Under the capable management of Prince Kotchubey, the Apanages brought their output of wine to an astonishing degree of perfection. Soon those people who laid in stocks of foreign wine did so only in pure snobbishness. It was impossible to distinguish champagnes from the domain of Abrau from those of the Rheims vineyards. Dessert wines became the speciality of the domain of Massandra; unfortunately its production was very limited. Specialists claimed that it was in no way inferior to the best foreign vintages.

The pioneer in this advance of Russian vine-growing was Prince Leo Galitzin. He was considered one of the best tasters in the world. He was elected president of the wine jury in the International Exhibition of 1900. He declared that he would never accept any official position: he was content to be 'a Russian vine-grower'.

His vineyards were about twenty miles from Yalta; in the Crimea. The domain was called the 'New World'. Alexander III was interested in this great enterprise, and offered Galitzin the post of director of Massandra. The Prince made difficulties; he stated his conditions:

'Never to have to put on a uniform; never to receive honours or official posts; to be free to do whatever he thought fit at Massandra.'

The Tsar was astonished, but agreed. For some time Galitzin administered Massandra with great success. Then he fell out with the Head of the Apanages; the Tsar sent for him; the Prince refused to give way, and resigned.

He returned to his domain and devoted himself exclusively to its development. Towards the end of the reign of Nicholas II, Gahtzin offered his property to the Tsar as a present. Knowing the Prince's eccentricities, the Tsar asked him to state in writing the conditions of this gift. The conditions were decidedly onerous: the State must undertake to create an 'Academy of Viticulture' at the 'New World', with Galitzin as its permanent president, and he must have the right to spend the rest of his life there. Calculations were made, and it was found that the Academy would cost the Apanages much more than the whole revenue of the domain. But the Prince was a man of forceful personality. The Tsar was overborne by his eloquence, and disregarded the question of economy as a minor consideration.

I recall the visit Their Majesties made one day to the 'New World'.

The cellars were nearly two miles long. At junctions of their passages the Prince had arranged circular spaces for tasting. One of these spaces was named 'Library of Wines'; it contained, in addition to endless samples of wine, an enormous collection of old cut glass, suitable for every imaginable vintage. While we tasted the most famous 'years' the Prince went on talking incessantly.

'I should like to know,' the Empress said to me, as we returned to Livadia, 'how many hours he has been chattering without a stop.'

DAILY LIFE AT LIVADIA

As to the way Their Majesties spent the day, I can only speak of what went on during their stays in the Crimea, at Livadia, where I was constantly in touch with the Sovereigns.

The Tsar devoted the mornings to work, beginning immediately after a short walk.

His Majesty received people standing in front of his desk. As he sat down he pointed his visitor to an armchair; the visitor could arrange his papers on an extension of the desk. During the conversation the Tsar would smoke, and often he would invite his interlocutor to smoke.

The Tsar greatly appreciated those persons who were able to explain to him in the course of conversation even matters of a very complicated nature. Before listening to what the Minister bringing a report had to say, the Tsar would take the report, glance through the first few lines to discover its subject, and then carefully read its final passages, in which the Minister would have stated the conclusion at which he had arrived. If the conclusion was not sufficiently clear to him, he would read the intervening pages. The Sovereign was quick in grasping the central idea of a report. He got irritated if the papers were burdened with what he considered an excessive amount of argument. General Sukhomlinov, Minister of War, had a special gift of holding the Tsar in suspense right up to the last minute, even if his audience lasted a couple of hours.

As soon as the report was dealt with, the Tsar would go over to the window and make some remark on any subject, to bring the audience to an end.

Reports were often presented in the evening, from 4 to 6.30.

The Tsar never stayed away from a religious service, however good a pretext he could have put forward in order to escape from it.

The service would not begin until after His Majesty's arrival; it would last about an hour.

The Tsar only saw his family at meals, at tea-time, and on those evenings on which he was not called to his office by urgent duties.

Before lunch was quite finished, the Empress would make a little sign to the children and they would rush into the garden, followed by Baron Meyendorf, the head of the Tsar's escort. This was a sort of special favour, and the Baron knew how to make the most of it; one could hear at once the laughing and the shouts of joy outside. Meyendorf was a past master of the art of amusing the Tsar's children.

As a 'director' of the Court balls the Baron had made himself popular with the two Empresses by his gaiety and charm. As he became older he lost nothing of his joviality, and won the close affection of the young generation.

He was an amusing figure, this poor Baron Meyendorf, whom everybody liked and nobody took seriously. But he was heavily handicapped in the presence of his wife, 'Auntie Vera', an ambitious, blundering, rather ridiculous woman.

Auntie Vera was president of the Society for the Protection of Animals; the energy with which she carried out her duties was the source of a good deal of trouble to the whole of the Crimean administration.

One day she demanded that fowls should not be carried to market with their heads down, lest they should faint. The Governor of the Crimea had to issue an order to that effect. A few days later she called on him and complained.

'Surely,' he said, 'my order has not been disregarded?'

'No, it isn't disregarded so long as these wretched peasants are going past my villa. But I have been following them to keep an eye on them. No sooner do they get round the corner of the street than the poor fowls are turned upside down again.'

There is a story of a poodle that made Auntie Vera celebrated. As ill-luck had it, this poodle ran right into her just at the moment when she was leaving her villa; and it was painted bright red!

The Baroness tried to get hold of it; a crowd of dogs of every breed, who had run up from all directions, got in her way; they went in pursuit of the scarlet bitch, and Auntie Vera ran at the tail of the procession, crying out:

'Stop him! Stop the red dog!'

A policeman succeeded in getting hold of the animal at the far end of the quay. The Baroness told him to take it at once to the Governor. The avenging woman followed close on the heels of the policeman and the red bitch. The Governor had no option but to receive her, abandoning the work he had in hand.

'What sort of an administration is this? It's a shame! The poor animal is being martyred. I hope you will have the guilty persons severely punished.'

'But, really. Baroness—where does the martyrdom come in? Ladies dye their hair, and everybody admires them!'

'But what about the poor dog's *amour-propre*?'

'Heavens, the dogs were all following her like a lady whose dress is too conspicuous.'

'I tell you that a whole rabble was in pursuit of him. You could see he was suffering, poor thing!'

'But how can you tell? It may have been flattered at attracting the attention of all the young sparks in the town.'

But Auntie Vera insisted that there should be an investigation. It turned out that the little event had been organized by one of her husband's officers. The Tsar was told all about it, and asked the Governor to inform the Baroness that it had been impossible to trace the delinquent.

. . . . .

At the end of lunch the Tsar would tell the company, with the utmost kindness and simplicity:

'I'm going for a ride at such and such a time. Any one who would like to go too might have his horse got ready.'

Little animals accustomed to climbing the abrupt slopes were brought along. The lovers of this very special sort of sport were not many in number. In the end I found myself the only one who still accompanied the Sovereign, except, of course, the A.D.C. on duty, who had no choice.

One day, near Massandra, in heavy rain, Nicholas II went off at a fast trot, without holding in the bit, as was his custom. The horse slipped on the wet clay; the Tsar fell and hurt his side. He was able to get back into the saddle and return to Livadia, but there his strength gave out and he only just managed to go up the few steps that led to the house.

The Empress was so terrified that she begged her husband never to ride again. Motor-cars made their appearance soon after; it became more amusing to go off to some little-known place and there to climb straight up some particularly steep escarpment. Soon Drenteln, the A.D.C., was the only one of the whole suite who was able to keep up with Nicholas II on the forced marches that he so enjoyed. The Tsar was a very vigorous man; outside his study he rarely sat down for long, and I never saw him lean on anything for support. His endurance was surprising.

The Tsar's excursions were inevitably a source of anxiety to those who were responsible for his personal safety. It was impossible to avoid placing a number of detectives along the road that the Sovereign was going to take, especially when he meant to go through remote villages. But the Tsar hated the sight of these men—these 'lovers of the country' or 'botanizers', as he called them, for they affected to be interested in everything in the world except the august person of the Sovereign. Nothing gave him so much pleasure as to give them the slip.

Sometimes it was painful to witness the despair of the Chief of Police of the Palace. To help him a little in his work, I undertook to let him know of any changes of route that the Tsar might propose in the course of a journey. To this end I would send one of the orderlies who followed us to telephone to the police headquarters; this would enable the 'botanizers' to be re-posted. They would bring their lounging to an abrupt end and run helter-skelter for some unexpected short cut.

One day after one of these reshufflings of the detective force, the Tsar caught the Chief of Police in the act of plunging head first into a *saklia* (Tartar hut) in a little village that we had just reached. The Tsar sent for him and began to catechize him.

'I changed my mind after leaving the Palace; how have you been able to find that out and get right on to my path?'

The poor Commandant, to avoid giving me away, began a long story of premonitions and intuitions. It was all he could do.

One more formal order was then issued—as unavailingly as ever—for lovers of the country not to linger by the side of roads that His Majesty might be taking.

At tea-time the Tsar often had a game of tennis. He was a good player, but his opponents, officers of the suite or maids of honour, were not good enough players for him. Hearing that the Youssupovs had their nephew, Count Nicholas Sumarokov-Elston, champion of Russia, staying with them, His Majesty had him invited to Livadia.

I have been told that Sumarokov, who was a brilliant left-handed player, won every set. After tea The Tsar asked for a revenge. After a few strokes Sumarokov had the misfortune to hit the Tsar on his ankle with a particularly hard ball. The Tsar fell down, and had to stop in bed for three or four days. The unfortunate champion was in despair, though nobody could fairly blame him. The Youssupovs, for all that, hauled him well over the coals.

As soon as the Emperor got up, he had Sumarokov invited to Livadia. The champion played some more sets with His Majesty, but his form was not what it had been.

COUNT NICHOLAS SUMAROKOV-ELSTON and NICHOLAS II

Few persons outside the immediate suite of Their Majesties took tea with them. Even the Grand Duchesses only came to see the

Empress if they were specially invited. Neither the Tsar nor the Empress had any desire to enlarge the circle of the persons admitted to their presence.

During the whole period of my service at Court, not a single person was ever invited to go to see Their Majesties after dinner. For their part, Their Majesties never went to see anybody, except the Dowager Empress and Grand Duchess Xenia. (There was one other exception, the visits to the Montenegrin princesses—see the section on the 'Spirits'.)

The evenings thus passed very quietly. At first the Empress remained in the drawing-room while the Tsar played dominoes or bezique; she would sing a couple of songs. As her health grew worse, she came down more and more rarely even for dinner. She dined alone or with the Tsar, 'alone together', as the formula ran in the famous Court harbingers' journal.

The suite broke up into bridge parties. But the play did not last long, for the Empress would get up very soon. As I had a great deal to do, I was in the habit of discreetly escaping from the drawing-room, leaving someone to be responsible for letting me know when hands were being kissed for 'Good night'.

On getting that message I edged discreetly into the room, and flattered myself that nobody had noticed my stratagem. One day, however, when I happened to be the last to kiss Her Majesty's hand, I heard her remark:

'You get back very cleverly at the time to say good-bye.'

'Madame, I had a great deal of urgent work—'

'As always,' she replied.

'Madame, I could not have gone without kissing your hand.'

'I quite understand,' she said kindly.

RAILWAY JOURNEYS

Railway journeys involved a mass of complications. I had scarcely been appointed Head of the Court Chancellery when preparations had to be made for departure for the Crimea, stopping at Beloviezha for a bison (*zubr*) hunt.

What instructions there were to draw up! Palace police, for protection on the way. Railway battalion: guard of bridges and tunnels along the route. Ministry of War: sentinels on the line.

Ministry of the Interior: personages to be presented to His Majesty. Marshal's office: residences to be got ready and made comfortable. Inspection of Imperial trains: route and times. Tsar's private office: presents to be taken. There was no telling who might become the recipient of an Imperial present, or when, or in what shape. I had regularly to take with me thirty-two chests filled with portraits, cups, goblets, cigarette-cases, and watches, of every sort of precious metal and of every conceivable value.

The preparations were made particularly difficult by the secrecy which surrounded Their Majesties' movements. The Tsar and the Empress hated replying to such questions as 'Where are we going? When do we start? Whom are we going to see?' Sometimes I did not know our destination at noon when we were due to leave at three. I had to get on 'friendly' terms with all the servants—messengers, footmen, court harbingers, chambermaids. They caught snatches of conversation in the passages or listened at doors and then went to the telephone to tell me what the Tsar or the Empress had said about the coming journey. Needless to say, these services had their drawbacks: the least of the lackeys had it in his power to betray me or to put me into an inextricable situation.

The Tsar's journeys were made in two trains. Externally the trains were identical: eight coaches, painted blue, with coats of arms and monograms. The Sovereigns travelled in one train, while the other served, as we have learnt to say since the war, as camouflage; it went off empty either before or after the real Imperial train. Not even the heads of the passenger department were in a position to know which was the train containing the Imperial family.

The first coach in the train conveyed the escort; the moment the train stopped, sentinels ran to take up position at the doors of Their Majesties' coach. The second coach contained the kitchen and some compartments for the chief steward and the cooks. The third, panelled in mahogany, served as dining-car: one-third of this coach was taken up by a drawing-room, heavily curtained and with furniture upholstered in damask velour. There was a piano in this compartment. The dining compartment had room for laying sixteen places.

The fourth coach, with a corridor along one side, was reserved to Their Majesties. The first compartment, a little bigger than the rest, formed the Tsar's study: it contained a desk, a couple of arm-chairs, and a small bookcase. Next came a bathroom. Then Their Majesties' bedroom, of the size of three ordinary compartments. I am unable to give a description of this room, for I never entered it. Last came the Empress's sitting-room, again about the size of three ordinary compartments; it was upholstered in grey and lilac. If the Empress was not travelling, this room was locked.

The fifth coach contained the nursery; it was upholstered in bright cretonne, with white painted furniture. The maids of honour travelled in this coach.

The sixth was reserved to the Tsar's suite. It was divided into nine compartments, the centre one, for the Minister of the Court, being a double compartment. Our compartments were much larger than those of the International Sleeping Car Company. They were thoroughly comfortable. On the door was a place for the owner's visiting card. One compartment was always kept free for persons presenting themselves to Their Majesties in the course of the journey.

Finally there came a seventh coach for the luggage and an eighth for the Inspector of Imperial Trains, the Commandant of the train, the domestics in the suite, the physician and the dispensary. The Chancellery staff and the military secretariat were accommodated in the luggage coach.

The first day that I passed in the train will always remain in my memory.

On the day before we were to start, the servants came to collect our clothes and the things we wanted on the journey and to arrange them in our respective compartments. Everything not actually wanted during the journey was put into the luggage coach, which was kept open day and night.

We assembled at the Imperial station half an hour before Their Majesties' arrival. They came with their children a few minutes before the train was due to leave. It started off the moment the Tsar had got in.

At five o'clock a 'Court runner' came down the corridors to tell us that Their Majesties invited us to tea. We gathered in the drawing-room. The Empress came up and said a few words to me, plainly in order to give courage to the new arrival. Then we all went into the dining compartment, where we sat down in order of seniority. The Tsar and the Empress were at the centre of the table, facing one another. My rank was then only that of Colonel, and I had to content myself with a seat at the very end of the table. The two eldest among the maids of honour sat on the right and left of the Tsar. The Empress had next to her Count Freedericksz and General Hesse, A.D.C. When the Empress was not there, the seat opposite the Tsar belonged to the Minister of the Court. General conversation began at once among the persons around Their Majesties. The rest of the company talked to one another in subdued tones.

I soon discovered that the presence of the Empress created an atmosphere of constraint; we were all much more lively and talkative when she was not there.

The most picturesque of the persons present was certainly the Court Surgeon, Doctor Hirsch. At the time of my appointment he was at least eighty years old; he had begun his service in the reign of Alexander II and held his post during three reigns. His medical knowledge could not have been very up to date, and the suite did not treat him with exaggerated deference; but the Empress thought very highly of him, so that Hirsch seemed like one of the Imperial family. He was even consulted on questions of the children's education. He was forgiven all his eccentricities.

For instance, he was never without a cigar; when one was getting towards the end he lit another from it. But the Empress could not endure the smell of a cigar. There were continual little altercations on the subject between the Empress and her doctor, but it was old Hirsch who emerged from them as victor. One day I heard the Empress say to Hirsch:

'Get away from me a bit, I'm suffocating.'

'But Madame, I've only been smoking quite a little cigar to-day.'

'I should like to have seen your quite little cigar. The smoke was coming out under the door of your compartment like a tobacco store on fire.'

Sometimes Hirsch was asked:

'Is nicotine a poison?'

His answer was:

'Nicotine is a poison, but only a slow poison. I have been taking it in for fifty years and it hasn't killed me yet.'

The servants brought tea. The table was covered with cakes and fruit. There was no alcohol, except when Nilov, 'His Majesty's Flag

Captain', was present; he could not do without rum or brandy and asked the servant for it.

Tea lasted about an hour. Often the Tsar would bring in the latest telegrams, if he had not had time to read them. After running through them he would pass them to his neighbours, leaving out the maids of honour, who manifested the utmost indifference to these bits of paper.

After tea we returned to our own coaches; there we talked in the corridors or read a novel.

Dinner was served at eight and lasted sixty minutes. At the end of it the Tsar got up and the rest of us saluted him with a low obeisance.

The Tsar rarely came out for the evening cup of tea, and the Empress never. We could go to the dining compartment when we pleased for this cup of tea; that is to say, there was no definite time for it as for breakfast. If we preferred, we could have it served in our compartments.

On my first morning in the train I went to my corner of the table for breakfast exactly at eight. Almost at once the Tsar came in. He told me to sit next to him, and said:

'Are you in the habit of getting up so early?'

'Sire,' I replied, 'if I got up later I should be working under pressure all day long.'

'You are quite right. I too get up in good time. Your chief is the man who doesn't. He has never finished dressing until the moment comes for going in to lunch.'

I mentioned that in St. Petersburg I regularly reported to the Count at half-past ten.

'I don't mind it a bit,' the Tsar replied. 'He is a splendid man. It will be a real pleasure for you to work with him.'

He added, after a pause:

'Were you not in the same regiment as the Count? They say that he shows too marked favour to the Horse Guards. . . . I can understand it; it is pleasanter to be surrounded with people whom one knows and can trust.'

The train stopped at the principal stations. The Minister of the Court told the Tsar beforehand who were the personages who were being admitted to the platform. The Tsar would get out on to the platform, surrounded by his suite, and enter into conversation with the members of the local administration. The provincial governors were invited to come into the train and to travel as far as the frontier of their province. This honour was often granted also to certain officers, who made their reports to the Tsar in the train; they then passed the night in the compartment reserved for visitors.

The Tsar worked in his study throughout the journey. If he took his evening cup of tea in the dining compartment, he would sometimes remain with his suite; he would then play dominoes, and if he lost he would send his servant to get the money. The Tsar never had money in his pocket. He hardly knew, indeed, the value of money. I recall the incident of his *troika* at Skernevitzy. The horses took fright, and were only brought to a stop through the presence of mind of a Cossack in the escort, who jumped on to the middle horse and seized the bridle, at the risk of his life; he did not succeed in stopping it until he had been dragged a considerable distance along the ground. The Tsar told me to reward the Cossack:

'Give him a gold watch, or twenty-five roubles, whichever he prefers.'

I gave the good fellow a gold watch, and reported to the Tsar that I had done so, mentioning at the same time that twenty-five roubles (£2 10s.) was scarcely an equivalent of the value of the gift.

'It is one of the big gaps in my education,' the Tsar said to me, smiling; 'I don't know the price of things; I have never had occasion to pay for anything myself.'

THE TSAR'S YACHT

The Tsar's favourite yacht was the *Standard*. She was built in Denmark, and was considered the most perfect ship of her type in the world. Her displacement was 4,500 tons; she was painted black, with bowsprit and stern gilded; she was a splendid seagoing ship, and fitted up with every possible comfort. When we went to Cowes, King Edward asked for plans of the yacht, for his constructors to study in case a new one should be built for him.

The yacht was commanded by Rear-Admiral Lomen, the Tsar's 'Flag Captain'.* The whole of the naval administration stood in mortal

---

* His Majesty's 'Flag Captain' was responsible for the Sovereign's safety from the moment when the Monarch set foot in any vessel, whether a yacht, a Dreadnought, or a launch. In this last case, the Flag Captain himself took the helm.

fear of the Admiral. It is true that he asked a great deal, and if he was annoyed he could be extremely rude. He claimed that on board the yacht the Tsar himself was under his orders. Off duty he was pleasant and sociable.

The actual Commanding Officer of the *Standard* was Captain Tchaguin, and the second in command Commander Sablin. Both had the satisfaction of being thought very highly of by Their Majesties. In the letters which she wrote to the Tsar when he was at G.H.Q., the Empress frequently mentioned Sablin.

Tchaguin came to a tragic end. He committed suicide; one version given of the reason is that he had as mistress a lady who belonged to the terrorist group of the Russian Social Revolutionaries. I am unable to confirm this; Tchaguin died a bachelor.

When the Imperial family went on board the *Standard*, each of the children was assigned a *diadka*, a sailor charged to watch over the child's personal safety. The children played with these *diadkas*, played tricks on them and teased them. Gradually the younger officers of the *Standard* joined in the children's games. As the Grand Duchesses grew older, the games changed into a series of flirtations, all very innocent. I do not, of course, use the word 'flirtation' quite in the ordinary sense of the term; the young officers could better be compared with the pages or squires of dames of the Middle Ages. Many a time the whole of the young people dashed past me, but I never heard the slightest word suggestive of the modern flirtation. Moreover, the whole of these officers were polished to perfection by one of their superiors, who was regarded as the Empress's squire of dames. As for the Grand Duchesses, even when the two eldest had grown up into real young women one might hear them talking like little girls of ten or twelve.

The Empress herself grew gay and communicative on board the *Standard*. She joined in the children's games, and had long talks with the officers.

The officers were certainly in an exceptional situation. Every day a group were invited to meals. In return the Imperial family accepted invitations to tea with the mess.

Had the officers of the *Standard* become too much of mere society men? That charge was often levelled against them, especially in naval quarters (but was this simple jealousy?), after the unfortunate incident known as the wreck of the *Standard*.

On a fine day in the Finnish fjords the *Standard* was shaken by a tragic jolt at a moment when there was not the slightest reason for expecting anything of the sort. Immediately afterwards the yacht heeled over. It was impossible to tell what might be coming next. The Empress rushed over to her children. She found them all except the Cesarevitch, who was nowhere to be seen. The anguish of the two parents may be imagined; they were both beside themselves. It proved impossible to move the yacht. Motor-boats started off towards her from every direction.

The Emperor hurried up and down the yacht, and gave the order for everybody to go in search of the Cesarevitch. It was only after some time that he was discovered safe and sound. At the first alarm his *diadka*, Derevenko, had taken him in his arms and very sensibly rushed to the hawse-pipes, as offering the best chance of saving the boy if the vessel should be a total loss.

The panic subsided, and all on board descended into the boats.

An inquiry followed. The whole responsibility fell on the pilot, an old Finnish sea-dog, who was in charge of the navigation of the vessel at the moment of the disaster, Charts were hurriedly consulted and showed beyond any possible question that the rock on which the yacht had grounded was entirely uncharted.

There remained His Majesty's Flag Captain, who was responsible in principle for the safety of the Imperial family. At the time the post was held by Admiral Nilov, the only master, under God, of the fate of the yacht.

He was in such a state of mind after the disaster that the Tsar felt bound to go to him in his cabin. Entering without knocking, the Tsar saw the Admiral bending over a chart, with a revolver in his hand. The Emperor tried to calm him. He reminded the Admiral that under the naval regulations he would have to go before a court of inquiry; but, the Tsar added, there could not be a shadow of doubt that he would be acquitted, for the disaster had been entirely unforeseeable. His Majesty carried away the Admiral's revolver.

All who took part in this drama are now dead. Why should I not record that the incident of the revolver created a touching friendship between the Tsar and the Admiral, a friendship that was an enigma to all who were unfamiliar with the details of this tragedy, since the character, education, and culture of the Tsar and the Admiral were so dissimilar.

There was an immediate conspiracy of silence at Court about the wreck of the *Standard*. Everybody knew that the slightest criticism of the officers of the yacht would have brought down punishment on the head of any one who ventured to utter it.

The officers were chosen for their social gifts; their task was to create on board the atmosphere of a fairytale, a charming idyll. It may be that in technical knowledge they were not absolutely up to date.

THE TSAR'S MOTOR-CARS

The first motor-cars, Serpollets, made their appearance in St. Petersburg in 1901 or 1902; one was bought by Count Freedericksz and the other by Grand Duke Dimitri Constantinovitch. (This first adept of the new sport was, it may be mentioned, a great breeder of horses.) But motor-cars were not then perfected; breakdowns were constantly occurring.

One day the Count asked the Tsar's permission to take his car to Spala, for the hunt. We had no sooner started than we had to get out and push the car out of the way between us; it had stopped dead, in the middle of the road, barring the way for the Tsar himself. Thus the whole Court passed by us, and jeers were fired at us from all sides. In the end the Count sent for another mechanic, and we were able to make two further trips without any great trouble. The Count then proposed to the Tsar—it was one Sunday, after lunch—to take him for a run in the car. His Majesty agreed, without enthusiasm. We had no sooner started than the car broke down. We had to send for horses to remove the unlucky vehicle. Under a rain of chaff from the suite, the Count definitely abandoned his efforts.

Next year an ex-officer of the Horse Guards, Kvitko-Osnovianenko, brought to Yalta another car, in much better running order. The police forbade him to use it, as it frightened the horses, and that might have produced tragedies on the mountain roads of the Crimea, M. Kvitko applied to Count Freedericksz to get the prohibition lifted. He pointed out that the roads were free for drivers of cars all over Europe, even in Tyrol. The matter had to be submitted to the Tsar. His Majesty probably had not forgotten the Spala experience. His reply was brief and decisive:

'My dear Count, so long as I live at Livadia, no car shall be allowed in the Crimea.'

In the following year the Tsar had the opportunity to take several rides in a car put at his disposal at Darmstadt by the Grand Duke. The Empress was also persuaded to have a ride in this terrifying machine, which resembled an omnibus without horses. After braving these risks, it seems that the Tsar changed his opinion.

On our return to Tsarskoe Selo, we were surprised to see a car come up, a Delaunay-Belleville, driven by Prince Vladimir Orlov. After lunch His Majesty asked the Prince whether he would not give him a ride in his motor vehicle. They went round the park, and at the end of the run the Tsar at once asked the Empress to come with him for another 'excursion'.

Prince Orlov pressed the services of his car on the Sovereigns; their rides became almost a daily event, especially when the Prince brought to his garage a new car of a still more perfected type. From then on the Prince never left the driver's seat. He took Their Majesties on short journeys in every direction; but for fear of an attack on the car, or any oversight, he did not allow his chauffeur to take his place.

About six months later, Freedericksz asked the Tsar whether he would not like to become the owner of a car. The Tsar started:

'Yes, you are right. It has been too bad of us to abuse Orlov's kindness. Give an order for two or three cars, and entrust Orlov with the purchase; he knows all about it better than a professional.'

By the end of the year the Imperial garage was well stocked. It contained ten cars, and later twenty, with a school of chauffeurs. Orlov continued to drive for the Tsar and the Empress. Only when the works sent a chauffeur especially recommended by his firm (he was a Frenchman) did the Prince agree to entrust the precious lives of the Sovereigns to his care. Even with this chauffeur he took every precaution, sitting next to him for more than a month.

A few years later the Tsar's park of cars was one of the finest in Europe.

THE TSAR'S HUNTS

The Tsar's principal hunting-ground was at Beloviezha, a forest reserve of more than a quarter of a million acres in the Government of Grodno. It was at Beloviezha that the kings of Poland had hunted for centuries. In 1888 the forest was made the private property of the Tsars.

This forest was known for the variety of the trees in it. And in this forest was the only herd of bison remaining in Europe (*zubr*—very similar to the American bison). This herd, numbering about 800, was carefully preserved. Even when taking part in an Imperial hunt it was only permissible to shoot at a bison detached from the herd; these solitary beasts were particularly vicious and would attack the rest of the herd.

The hunting at Beloviezha was a great attraction for all the crowned heads of Europe. William II was dying to be allowed to fire a few shots there, but the Tsar would never offer his cousin an opportunity to join in this royal hunt. Frequently after the two had met the Tsar would say to Freedericksz:

'He has been trying again to get invited to Beloviezha; but I turned a deaf ear to him.'

During the war, when Beloviezha was occupied by German troops, a German soldier who was captured was found to be in possession of orders concerning this forest. The orders included a prohibition of all slaughter of bison or other big game, on pain of death.*

At half-past seven one morning all the huntsmen assembled in hunting dress in front of the Tsar's palace. The Tsar came out, accompanied by the Empress and two maids of honour.

We took our places in *troikas*, two by two, followed by keepers. When we reached the forest we had to keep to the long straight *layons*—avenues specially maintained to enable the huntsmen to move about the forest. I may mention that wood-cutting was strictly prohibited throughout Beloviezha; the underwood had become almost impenetrable. As the wind could not pass through anywhere, the oak and beech trees grew as straight as candles. The grass underfoot along the *layons* was so well kept that we moved along as smoothly as over a carpet.

On our arrival at the shooting stands, we were received by the master of the hunt, who made us draw lots. This little lottery was a point of honour with the Tsar; he submitted with a good grace to the

---

* Unfortunately the herd was almost exterminated during the revolution.

chance of the throw on equal terms with all his guests. In some countries it is a familiar thing for the sovereigns to receive the best stands as a matter of course, so that persons of lower rank run the risk of not catching sight of a single animal.

There were twelve of us, and twelve stands had been prepared in advance. We took up our places in accordance with the numbers that we had drawn.

At each stand the huntsman was protected up to his chest. Behind him stood a keeper, whose duty it was to reload the guns. The Tsar had the assistance of two keepers; they were furnished with great forks for holding off the wounded animal if the necessity should arise. The Empress shared her husband's stand. She showed astonishing coolness. It was impossible to say as much for the maids of honour who were placed in the stands of less important members of the suite; they gave little inopportune cries, which baulked the game.

I had one of these ladies in my company, but that did not prevent me from killing a very large bison. My first shot wounded it in the shoulder. It stopped short, and then charged. The second shot brought it down at once; it was then scarcely twenty paces from my stand.

It weighed 525 kilogrammes, over half a ton; a fine specimen of this almost extinct species.

In the evening, after dinner, everybody went out on to the great terrace. Below were set out the whole of the day's trophies; the keepers lit up the picture with their torches. The hunting-horns sounded a clarion in honour of the Tsar, and the head keeper unsheathed his poniard in order to point to the animals killed by the Sovereign. After that the successes of the other huntsmen were similarly saluted in order of merit.

One day Grand Duke Nicholas Nicolayevitch and Prince Kotchubey simultaneously shot and killed a fine stag with antlers of thirty-two tines. Both of the huntsmen laid claim to these exceptional antlers. They began to quarrel. The Tsar intervened and said:

'I am master here. I shall take the antlers myself.'

He had two exact copies of these antlers, the finest in the whole of the Beloviezha collection, made abroad and these copies were sent to the two rivals.

The Tsar was himself a very good shot. But he only fired when he was sure of his quarry. He was sensitive about his reputation and hated missing.

At the end of the hunting, each of the guests received a printed list of his personal exploits, as well as his trophies, specially mounted, with the date and place of shooting recorded.

Nicholas II out with his hunting team at Beloviezha, the hunting grounds on the Poland Belorussia border.

Beloviezha (aka Belovezhskaya Pushcha) became the property of Alexander III in 1888, acquired in exchange for lands in the Oryol and Simbirsk oblasts (i.e. provinces); territories 650 miles apart, to the south of old Moscow state. Once fortress defences of the Russian empire; Oryel being the southern border and Simbirsk protecting the eastern border.

Catherine the Great in 1780 decreed their Viceroyalty and they were lands perhaps considered a fair trade off for the lush hunting forests of the Polish territory; Oryel being a hilly plain crossed by steep river banks and ravines, and Simbirsk (renamed Ulyanovsk in 1924,) on both banks of the Volga River where it reaches its maximum width. They were perhaps considered a fair trade off.

Alexander III built the Belovezhsky Palace on the Spala complex which today sits just inside the Polish border with the Pushcha forests extending into present day Belarus. Nicholas II continued the tradition of a yearly autumn retreat there.

EPILOGUE
JULY 1914

After the departure of the President of the French Republic, we thought that the political clouds would gradually pass away. On returning from one of his audiences with His Majesty, Freedericksz told me that the Tsar had no fears in regard to the Serajevo assassination, and had given him the impression that 'everything would be settled all right'. The Minister of War, whom I saw on the same day, held the opposite view. In his opinion, and, indeed, I agreed with him, the very cordiality of the Kronstadt meeting would itself lead William II to give his support to Austria if she formulated inacceptable conditions.

My son was on leave in Switzerland, and I telegraphed to him to return to Russia.

In the evening Freedericksz was again with the Tsar. This time His Majesty showed great anxiety. William II had just sent a telegram to say that any intervention on the part of a third Power in the Austro-Serbian conflict would endanger peace. His Majesty had replied that while he wanted peace he had been obliged to instruct the Minister of War to take certain preparatory measures in case a mobilization should prove necessary. These measures could be stopped if direct negotiations with Austria should become possible.

Next day the Austrian ultimatum to Serbia was published. The Tsar went with Freedericksz to Krasnoye Selo, where a Cabinet meeting was held.

In the evening I put before Freedericksz a plan for the partial mobilization of the office of the Marshal of the Court in the event of the Tsar proceeding to the front. The Count replied:

'No, no. I cannot ask His Majesty to give these orders; he feels sure that there will be no war.'

On July 30th Sazonov came to Peterhof and had a very long audience with His Majesty. On leaving he went to see the Minister of the Court, and told him that he had transmitted the order for mobilization to the Chief of Staff. Later I learned that General Yanushkevitch lifted the receiver off his telephone as soon as he had received the order, lest a later message should countermand it. He considered that it would be impossible to stop the mobilization once it had begun.

Next day I went to St. Petersburg on urgent business. On getting into the train on my way back I saw Count Pourtalés, the German Ambassador, enter the Court coach, followed by one of his secretaries. As soon as the train started I went into the Count's compartment. He stood up at once, took both my hands, and exclaimed:

'It must be stopped, stopped at all costs, this mobilization. Otherwise it means war.'

I replied:

'It is impossible. The mobilization is pursuing its normal course. You can't suddenly stop a car that is going at sixty miles an hour. It would inevitably capsize.'

The Count said:

'I have asked for an audience with the Emperor; I have got to ask him to stop the mobilization. It was only placarded this morning.'

The Ambassador was in a remarkable state of agitation. I did my best to tranquillize him, asking him to go to see Count Freedericksz immediately after the audience. I felt sure that my Minister would be able to persuade the Tsar to telegraph to William II to explain to him that mobilization did not in the least mean war, and that demobilization would be ordered as soon as direct negotiations had been begun.

'Above all,' I said, 'don't ask the Emperor for what is impossible.'

'No, no,' the Count exclaimed, 'if he does not demobilize at once there is no preventing war!'

I noticed the young secretary trying to catch the Count's eye in order to stop him from saying this; the Ambassador gave the impression of having lost his balance.

I went straight to Freedericksz to tell him what the Ambassador had said. Pourtalés arrived half an hour later, looking very dejected. He begged the Minister to go to the Tsar and suggest to him some telegram to William II—anything to explain the reasons for the mobilization. Freedericksz set out for the Palace.

On his return he told me that the Emperor had drawn up an excellent telegram, which had been sent off at once. He added:

'You will see—this telegram will make sure of peace.'

He had hardly finished speaking when the telephone rang. I took up the receiver. It was Sazonov speaking. I handed the receiver to Freedericksz.

I saw him grow pale. He replied:

'Yes, yes, I will arrange it.'

Sazonov had just told Freedericksz that Pourtalés had transmitted to him the declaration of war. Sazonov asked for an audience with His Majesty.

The reply to the Tsar's last telegram had been received at the moment when the movement of troops had already begun—on both sides of the frontier. The telegram from William II remained on His Majesty's desk, and it was not possible to publish it with the other documents concerning the declaration of war. I only learned of it through the revelations made later by M. Paléologue.

Next day the officers of the garrison of St. Petersburg were received in the Winter Palace. After a Te Deum the Tsar formally took the oath not to conclude peace so long as an enemy remained on Russian soil. After this there were ovations for M. Paléologue, the Ambassador of our chivalrous ally.

My son had succeeded in reaching the frontier by the last train from Berlin. Noticing that the Russian officers were being arrested, he jumped out of the train and crossed the frontier on foot, under fire from the German sentinels.

A few weeks later he was at the front; there, in 1915, he met the death of a brave man, falling during an attack near Marienburg.

Maurice Paléologue, French ambassador to Russia, (1914-1917).

A. A. MOSSOLOV

THE LAST AUDIENCES

In August 1916, at Mohilev, the Emperor sent for me to come to his study and told me that he intended to appoint me Minister Plenipotentiary at Bucarest. This appointment would coincide with the entry of our troops into Roumania.

Seeing my astonishment the Tsar explained why he was making the appointment.

He had received information, he said, to the effect that the Queen of Roumania, his cousin, was very, disturbed about the possible relations between the Russian army command, the King of Roumania, and the population of the kingdom. The Emperor's own view was that the army leaders do not give sufficient attention to the suggestions made to them by diplomats who are not themselves soldiers. It was necessary, therefore, to appoint to Bucarest somebody of sufficient weight for effective collaboration with the commander of the Russian troops. After the many years I had spent in the Sovereign's suite, I should be well qualified for imposing my will on whoever was to direct military operations in Roumania.

All I could do after these explanations was to say how sorry I should be to be no longer in the immediate entourage of my Sovereign. The Tsar added that he did not want to upset Count Freedericksz, with whom I had worked on such friendly terms. He was not to be told, therefore, of my appointment, and the Tsar would himself undertake to explain to him that my departure would only be on 'a temporary mission'. The ukase appointing me Minister Plenipotentiary would mention that I still held my post of Head of the Court Chancellery.

Shortly after my arrival in Roumania, the Queen asked me whether I thought the Tsar would consent to a marriage between the heir to the throne, Prince Carol, and one of the Russian Grand Duchesses, the daughters of Nicholas II. I left for Petrograd to present a very confidential report on this subject.

After my statement, the Tsar said to me:

'I agree with your view of the proposal, but I do not know what the Empress will think of it.'

'When might I present myself again, to learn the answer that I am to make to the Queen?'

'I shall not say anything to the Empress. Ask for an audience with her; give her the Queen's compliments, and make your report to her.'

'I will do so. Sire.'

'Why, you seem frightened! Have I not made you a diplomat? This is your business both as Minister Plenipotentiary and as an officer of the Court. So, make your report to the Empress.'

The audience took place at four o'clock on the following afternoon, at Tsarskoe Selo. On leaving Her Majesty I was told by a servant that the Emperor was in the garden and wanted to see me.

I gave a full account of the audience. The Empress intended to invite Queen Marie and Prince Carol to stay over Easter at Tsarskoe Selo. Then we should see whether the marriage could be considered.

'Of course,' I added, 'that is if Your Majesty approves the plan.'

'I did not think you would be so successful in your mission. You have the art of persuasion.'

In spite of this praise, I had the feeling that the Emperor would have been better pleased to learn that the Empress had replied with a refusal. That would not have faced him with the prospect of separation from his daughter.

A few days later I left for Roumania. That was the last time that I saw Their Majesties.

THE ATTEMPT TO SAVE THE IMPERIAL FAMILY

In 1918 I was at Kiev, in the Ukraine. The country was under German occupation, with a Hetman (Skoropadsky) at the head of a shadow government.

At Kiev I met Prince Kotchubey, my colleague in the Ministry of the Court, and Duke George of Leuchtenberg, a former brother officer in the Horse Guards.

Our one and only thought was for the rescue of the Emperor and his family from their prison in Ekaterinburg.

The Duke of Leuchtenberg undertook to speak on our behalf to the German authorities; he was a cousin of the heir to the Bavarian throne, and that fact secured him access to General Eichhorn, the Commander-in-Chief of the army of occupation, and to General Groener, his Chief of Staff.

The Germans came to our aid with the utmost readiness. They opened credits for us and promised to supply us with machine-guns, rifles, and motorcars. Our plan was to freight two vessels, which would be sent with officers in our confidence to steam up the Volga and the Kama, its tributary. They were to stop about forty miles from Ekaterinburg, where further instructions would be given.

We sent two officers into the town as scouts; one belonged to the detective staff formerly in attendance on the Tsar, and the other to the Horse Guards. They were to get into touch with German agents then secretly in the town, whose help would be of the utmost value to us.

I knew that the Tsar would not consent to exchange his captivity under the Bolsheviks for captivity in Germany. To make the position clear, I wrote a letter to William II, and entrusted it to Count von Alvensleben, who was attached to the person of the Hetman. The Count was to leave that day for the German G.H.Q.

In this letter I asked the German Emperor to place in my charge a letter addressed personally to the Tsar, guaranteeing that he would be enabled to reside in the Crimea, without having to submit to captivity in Germany.

It may be imagined with what feverish impatience we awaited the return of Count von Alvensleben.

On his return to Kiev he gave no sign of life. Next day I went to see him. He seemed very embarrassed. According to him, the Kaiser was unable to reply without consulting his Government. Alvensleben advised me to see Count von Mumm, the diplomatic representative of Germany with the Hetman.

Count von Mumm categorically refused to help me. He told me he was astonished to learn that the German military authorities had promised to give us their assistance. From now on I must no longer count on the Germans.

I made desperate efforts for more than two hours to get Mumm to listen to reason. I explained to him that in Germany's own interest he must save the Tsar of Russia.

I had no success.

Shortly afterwards we learned the news of the tragedy at Ekaterinburg.

END OF BOOK ONE

BOOK TWO

In 1921 Herbert Jonathan Cape (and Wren Howard) founded the London publishing house Jonathan Cape. Just a year later they purchased English publishing house A. C. Fifield, thereby acquiring Ian Fleming's James Bond series as well as other prominent publishing contracts such as Ernest Hemingway and T. E. Lawrence.

After Cape's death in 1960 the publisher went through several take-overs and mergers finally coming under the ownership of Penguin Books from 2013; where they have remained on stipulation that the Jonathan Cape branding is maintained.

The Edition presented here is a first printing in 1934 of book No. 65, in the Florin books series of 103 titles, that were released for publication between May 1932 to 1938.

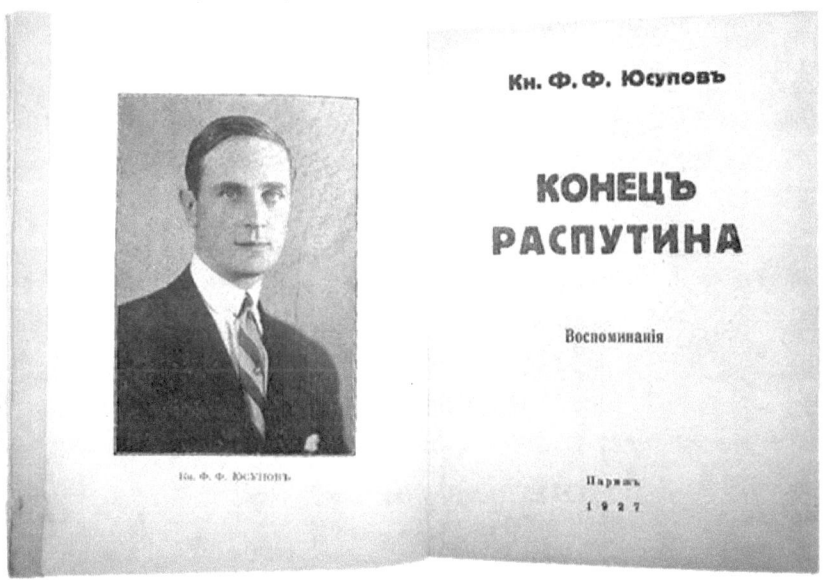

Russian Edition published 1927

The original book published in Russia in 1927. Later translated and published in Paris.
The English edition was published by Jonathan Cape, London, 1934.
Pages: 256

PRINCE FÉLIX YOUSSOUPOFF
(Photo Hay Wrightson)

"HOW I KILLED RASPUTIN."

THE DIARY OF ONE OF THE ASSASSINS

PUBLISHED IN PARIS.

THE MONK'S AMAZING VITALITY.

[It will be remembered that Rasputin, the evil genius of the Empress of Russia and of Russia itself from the time of his introduction to the Imperial Court in 1907, was murdered

RASPUTIN:

HIS MALIGNANT INFLUENCE
AND HIS ASSASSINATION

By
PRINCE YOUSSOUPOFF

Translated from the Russian by
Oswald Rayner, M.A., BARRISTER-AT-LAW

LONDON
JONATHAN CAPE 30 BEDFORM SQUARE

FIRST PUBLISHED IN MCMXXVII
Printed in Guernsey C.I., by the Star and Gazette Co , Ltd

CONTENTS

Preface	(7) 240
Introduction	(9) 241
— Rasputin and the Russian Revolution	
— Russia before and during the War	
— The State of Mind of Society	
— The Emperor Nicholas II	
— The Empress Alexandra Feodorovna	
— Life at Tsarskoe Selo	
— The Influence of Vyrubova and of Rasputin	
— Rasputin's Origin	
— From Siberia to St. Petersburg	
— A Vagabond in Power	
— Rasputinism and Bolshevism	

CHAPTER

I	HOW I MADE RASPUTIN'S ACQUAINTANCE	(47) 261
II	ANXIETY AMONG LOYAL SUBJECTS OF THE THRONE	(55) 265
III	RASPUTIN REVEALED TO ME	(59) 267
IV	THE RESOLVE TO DO AWAY WITH THE *Starets*	(71) 273
V	MY INQUIRIES	(74) 275
VI	RASPUTIN AMONG HIS FEMALE ADMIRERS	(81) 279
VII	A VISIT TO THE *Starets*	(95) 287
VIII	A HYPNOTIC *séance*	(110) 295
IX	HOW WE DECIDED TO ACT	(129) 305
X	RASPUTIN ACCEPTS MY INVITATION	(138) 311
XI	THE CELLARS AT NO. 94 MOIKA	(144) 315
XII	THE LAST VISIT TO GOROKHOVAYA STREET	(148) 317

CONTENTS

XIII	THE NIGHT OF THE 16TH DECEMBER	(158) 323
XIV	DEATH WHICH WAS NO DEATH	(171) 331
XV	WHY A DOG WA8 KILLED	(183) 341
XVI	ENTHUSIASM AT ST. PETERSBURG	(186) 343
XVII	INTERROGATORIES AND DEPOSITIONS	(199) 351
XVIII	AT THE PALACE OF THE GRAND DUKE DMITRI PAVLOVICH	(210) 359
XIX	THE BODY RECOVERED	(216) 363
XX	DISAPPOINTMENT	(227) 369
XXI	BANISHMENT	(238) 375

CONCLUSION (241) 377

APPENDIX: (252) 383

THE MANIFESTO ANNOUNCING THE ABDICATION OF THE EMPEROR NICHOLAS II, AND THE EMPEROR'S FAREWELL MESSAGE TO THE TROOPS   384 & 385

ILLUSTRATIONS

PRINCE YOUSSOUPOFF	(Frontispiece)	236
RASPUTIN	(Facing page 46)	260
ALEXEI AND HIS TUTORS		278
TRIPTYCH OF RASPUTIN'S ASSASSINS		309
GRAND DUKE NIKOLAI NIKOLAIVICH		314
RASPUTIN WITH ARM AT MIDRIFF		322
PRINT OF RASPUTIN BEING SHOT		329
NEWSPAPER PORTRAIT OF DR LAZOVERT		337
PORTRAIT OF ALEXANDER MIKHAILOVICH		342
PORTRAIT OF THEODORE ALEXANDROVICH		342
PORTRAIT OF ANNA VYRUBOVA		349
GRAND DUKE DMITRI PAVLOVICH WITH CAR		356
PORTRAIT OF OSWALD RAYNER		357
PORTRAIT OF FELIX AND IRINA YOUSSOUPOFF		386

PREFACE

I HAVE hitherto hesitated to publish my recollections of Rasputin. I have been anxious to avoid making untimely reference to events which were fatefully connected with the reign of the martyred Emperor Nicholas II.

Certain sections of the press, however, continue to publish misleading and calumnious articles on this subject; and too often even Russians, alas, gratify the morbid curiosity of the crowd with versions which are no less inexact.

Malicious scoffing at the expense of those who have atoned with their blood for all their involuntary errors is inadmissible, Yet in respect of our recent past there is another extreme - an exaggerated idealisation of the last reign, with all its unhealthy features.

These two extremes hinder in equal degree a sober and objective analysis of the past. They exert a particularly harmful influence on our younger generation, who are now growing up far away from the fatherland, but are destined sooner or later to take part in the building up of a new Russia.

We have no right to fill our children's minds with vague legends. These will not suffice to imbue them with a real love of the fatherland and a sense of duty towards it.

It is important, moreover, that we should recognise errors committed in the past. We may thus avoid many a pitfall, and provide against many a disappointment in the future.

Such are the motives which impel me, as an eye-witness of some of those tragic events which occurred round the throne, to give a true account of all that I saw and heard; and I have resolved to overcome that heaviness of heart which possesses me whenever I touch upon the past - especially when I dwell upon the terrible sequel in the cellar of Ipatievski House at Ekaterinburg.

INTRODUCTION

THE whole country was seething with indignation while Rasputin, like a dark shadow, stood near the throne. The best representatives of the clergy raised their voices in defence of the Church and of Russia against the intrigues of this criminal upstart. Persons most closely associated with the Royal Family implored the Emperor and the Empress to dismiss him.

But all was in vain. His influence grew stronger and stronger; and, as it grew, the feeling of discontent in the country increased, spreading even to the remotest districts, where the simple peasantry, with true instinct, felt that there was something wrong at the fountain-head of power. And so, when Rasputin was killed, his death was acclaimed with general rejoicing.

Since then, however, a change of opinion has perhaps taken place. Stunned by the horrors of the revolution, harassed by the hardships of exile, Russians have forgotten much of the past. The Soviet Government has turned our country into such an inferno that any other political and social regime seems a paradise in comparison. The domination of the Third International has revealed to the whole world the lengths to which crime may go.

Everything pales beside the Soviet torture chambers, in which all the technique of the twentieth century has been applied in the infliction of the most excruciating physical and mental agonies.

Oppressed by this nightmare, the Russian refugee is sometimes apt to make an unwarrantable comparison between communist Russia and pre-revolutionary Russia; and he concludes that a score of Rasputin's would have been preferable to the destruction of the old order of things.

It seems to him now that opposition to Rasputin and to his influence was in itself a revolutionary movement; that his assassination was the first shot, the signal and incentive for a *coup d'état*; and that if people had only reconciled themselves to him and had left him alone, the terrible upheaval which has laid waste the whole country would have been averted.

Such childish reasoning can only be explained by the reaction which has set in. Reaction can be just as blind and intolerant as revolution.

The revolution was not the result of Rasputin's death. Its causes were to be found at a much earlier date. They lay in Rasputin himself, in his unscrupulous and cynical betrayal of Russia; in Rasputinism, that tangle of dark intrigue, egoistic self-seeking, hysterical madness, and vainglorious pursuit of power, which wrapped the throne in an impenetrable web and isolated the monarch from his people.

Among those who openly took their stand against this baneful influence were the Grand Duchess Elizabeth Feodorovna, sister of the young Empress, the Metropolitan Anthony of St. Petersburg and Ladoga, the Metropolitan Vladimir, M. Samarin—the Head of the Holy Synod, M. Stolypin—the former Prime Minister, and M. Rodzianko—President of the Duma.

Can any tongue be found to condemn these as traitors and enemies of their country?

Yet they were convinced opponents of Rasputin. They resisted him in the name of their 'Faith, Tsar and Fatherland' in order to save Russia from revolution.

Deprived of all possibility of knowing what was happening in Russia, the Emperor could not distinguish between friend and foe. All unsuspecting, he trusted those who were driving both the Throne and Russia to their doom, and refused the aid of those who could have helped him to save the country and the dynasty.

There is no doubt that the Emperor Nicholas II was called upon to reign during a period beset with anxieties. For many decades Russia had been undermined by the destructive work of hidden revolutionary organisations, directed and amply financed from abroad.

The revolutionary movement waxed and waned, but never for a moment ceased. The Government were forced to take up a defensive position. To maintain that position without exciting and provoking public opinion was very difficult, indeed almost impossible. The public resented the so-called 'repressions,' and felt it their duty to support the most extreme tendencies, not realising the danger thereby incurred.

After the firm rule of the Emperor Alexander III, who had

suppressed revolutionary manifestations, it was hoped that his successor would allow the public to take a greater share in State affairs. At the beginning of his reign the Emperor Nicholas II declined to make any concessions whatever. But his self-appointed task of preserving intact the foundations of autocracy was incompatible with his personal characteristics. The people are always willing to submit to one in whom they feel strength and firmness. All Russia instinctively divined the young Emperor's deficiency in these qualities. The revolutionary organisations seized the first opportunity to assert themselves, and the unfavourable issue of the unpopular Russo-Japanese war induced still wider circles to advocate open action.

. . . .

The first revolutionary storm broke out over Russia in 1905. It was successfully quelled. Outwardly peace was restored but revolutionary propaganda continued slowly to undermine the authority of the Tsar.

Among the peasants, the agrarian disturbances of 1905 and the revolutionary slogan, 'Land and Freedom,' awakened dark instincts of anarchy and a thirst for possession. Workmen, especially in the big industrial centres, could not forget the appeal against capital.

As regards the educated classes, those who were inclined towards the Left began to dream of a democratic republic tinged with socialism, while more moderate elements were attracted towards an extreme form of parliamentary government. The wealthy *bourgeoisie* strove after power and political influence in the country. The vast majority of the younger members of the *intelligentsia*, especially the students, raved about revolution, often converting the university lecture rooms into places for political meetings. Young and old alike looked upon revolution as a supreme blessing, and the sole means of restoring social justice and general prosperity in Russia.

This naive and visionary idealism on the part of the Russian *intelligentsia* transformed revolution into something very like a religion, an inspiration for deeds of heroism and self-sacrifice. It had its own 'saints.' Political criminals exiled to Siberia, or in hiding abroad — especially assassins of the terrorist type — were looked upon as heroes, worthy of the greatest reverence.

The Russian educated public of that time was affected by some kind of mental derangement which was reflected both in literature and in journalism. Highly cultivated and respected people often showed themselves quite incapable of understanding the basis of the political life of the country. They subjected the whole of the existing order of things to the most bitter and one-sided criticism; and, with a lack of insight which was almost infantile, they practically ignored the incontestable services rendered to Russia by her Tsars, who, in the course of centuries, had built up a mighty empire. Hence, a quite erroneous idea of monarchical Russia was formed in foreign countries also.

Yet at the outbreak of the great war Russia presented a spectacle of amazing prosperity. Her finances were in brilliant order; industry and agriculture were developing with fabulous speed; new railways were under construction; the scope of national education was being widened; a number of State departments could be considered as models of their kind.

But at that time the *intelligentsia* — who influenced public opinion by means of the press and of the Duma — were not disposed to reckon with practical facts; they placed abstract political theories before everything else. They held it to be their primary duty to sap the bulwarks of autocracy, losing no opportunity of holding up its defects before the public.

Whenever disaster looms ahead, circumstances seem to unfold themselves in such a way as to precipitate it.

At that time, certain events were happening in the Imperial *entourage* which provided abundant grounds for the most distressing misunderstandings of every kind, and roused a feeling of discontent throughout the country.

The private life of the Tsar's family was fatefully interwoven with the course of political events. The personal characteristics of the Emperor Nicholas II and of the Empress Alexandra Feodorovna might not, perhaps, under other conditions, have exercised any noticeable influence on their reign; but these characteristics did, as a fact, play a tragic part in the fate of Russia and of the whole dynasty.

The Emperor Nicholas II, as heir to the throne, received an excellent education; but he did not have time to prepare himself for the difficult and many-sided duties of a monarch. The Emperor

Alexander III, who had held the reins of power firmly in his own strong hands, died in the flower of life, and the burden of autocracy fell upon the youthful and inexperienced Tsetsarevich.

When the young Emperor brought his bride, the Princess Alice (*sic — Alix*) of Hesse, to St. Petersburg, it was to follow his father's coffin; and the Princess, draped in mourning from the moment of her arrival in Russia, was deprived of the possibility of making preliminary acquaintance with her new country, its society, traditions and customs. Other Russian Empresses, as Tsetsarevni* had gradually familiarised themselves with Russian conditions, and had made the acquaintance of their future subjects in more simple surroundings; but the wife of the Emperor Nicholas II stepped straight into the Imperial *rôle*, to occupy that exalted position which demands wide experience of the people governed, yet offers few facilities for gaining it.

Society and the nation as a whole had their eyes fixed on the unknown young Empress, with an interest that could not but be embarrassing to her. Nervous and sensitive, she withdrew into herself. She gave an impression of reserve, coldness — occasionally even of discourtesy. Her popularity was thus prejudiced at the outset, especially as she was constantly being compared with the Dowager Empress Marie Feodorovna, who was beloved by everyone in Russia.

Nor was the early married life of the Imperial couple bathed in that care-free happiness which their position under different circumstances would have ensured. The Emperor Nicholas II was called upon to bear the twin load of his beloved father's loss, and all the anxieties and responsibilities of the Russian Crown. The Empress Alexandra Feodorovna sincerely desired to share his burden; she offered him advice, which, owing to her very limited knowledge of Russia, may not always have been sound. She thus acquired, from the very first, the habit of exercising an influence in State affairs. This did not meet with public approval; it drew forth comments on the Emperor's weakness of will, while the Empress was censured for her love of power.

The young Empress soon realised that she had failed to gain real sympathy in her new country — in any case among the higher ranks

---

* Tsetsarevna: wife of the heir-apparent.

of St. Petersburg society. She became more and more sensitive and nervous, and retired still further into private life, feeling that her good intentions were neither understood nor appreciated.

She was sometimes inclined to attribute her unpopularity in the country to the fact that four daughters in succession were born to her, instead of the long awaited son and heir.

Misfortunes such as the Japanese War, the outbreaks of terrorism, and the events of 1905, exercised a profound influence on her state of mind.

After she had embraced the Orthodox faith, she began, with the zeal and exaltation of a novice, to perform all its outward ceremonies; but she failed to penetrate into its deep and intricate spiritual meaning. Deeply religious by nature, as time went on she became more and more steeped in mysticism. She soon became attracted by the dark mysteries of occult forces, by spiritualism, and by every form of magic. She showed an interest in fanatics, soothsayers, clairvoyants. When a French occultist, a certain Doctor Philippe, made his appearance in St. Petersburg (he was reputed to have been sent to the Russian Court as a secret emissary of masonic organisations), the Empress believed in his superhuman powers. He arrived at the Court just before the birth of the heir-apparent, and the Empress placed all her maternal hopes in his supernatural aid. He left a short time afterwards, his unexpected departure giving rise to the rumour that those who had sent him to Russia were dissatisfied with their envoy, and had recalled him.

Shortly after the departure of Philippe a new 'prophet' appeared in St. Petersburg, this time of purely Russian origin, — Grigori Rasputin, a Siberian peasant who had assumed the guise of a pious Russian pilgrim. He made a very deep impression on the Empress. Those whose patronage had enabled him to gain a standing in St. Petersburg subsequently detected his true character, and tried to secure his removal from the Court. But it was already too late; Rasputin had installed himself too firmly to be dislodged.

Rasputin's influence over the Empress was primarily due to the intervention of Anna Vyrubova, who occupied a quite exceptional position at the Court of Tsarskoe Selo.

Vyrubova's proximity to the Empress, and the influence which she acquired in the Imperial Family, was just as tragic a fatality as Rasputin's appearance at the Court.

The circumstances which brought together the Empress and Anna Vyrubova are very characteristic of both. Vyrubova — at that time Mlle. Taneieva, daughter of the Chief of His Imperial Majesty's Personal Chancery — lay dangerously ill with typhoid fever. She dreamt that the Empress Alexandra Feodorovna entered her room and took her by the hand. This was the turning point of her illness; recovery set in, and she simply lived for the moment when she might be able to meet her illustrious protectress.

The Empress, who had been told of this vision, and with her natural kindness wanted to please the sick girl, went to see her; and from this moment Vyrubova's adoration knew no bounds.

Of limited and undeveloped intelligence, but cunning, servile, and of hysterical temperament, Vyrubova was inclined to exaggerate her feelings; but the Empress believed in her sincerity, and, touched by such exceptional devotion, after her recovery, brought her into close personal contact with herself.

Vyrubova's unhappy marriage and subsequent breach with her husband inspired the Empress with sincere pity for 'poor Annie,' and strengthened her attachment to this trivial woman. The closest of friendships was formed between them.

In all her subsequent actions Vyrubova was guided by her instinct. In spite of her intimacy with the Empress, her psychology was rather that of a clever maid seeking by every possible means to gain the exclusive confidence of her mistress.

While impressing the Empress with the certitude of her boundless devotion and blind and unchanging adoration, Vyrubova at the same time instilled into her a feeling of ill-will towards all others who surrounded her. She would sorrowfully and indignantly assure her mistress that not only society, but even the members of the Imperial Family were unaware of the Empress' merits. She alone, Anna Vyrubova, worshipped her, and could appreciate Her Majesty at her real value.

In spite of her lack of intelligence, Vyrubova was not slow to realise that the more she was able to isolate the Empress the greater would her own influence be, as her one true friend.

Her attachment to the Empress was undoubtedly sincere; but it was by no means disinterested, and she eventually wove a whole net of egoistical intrigue around it.

A more suitable person could not have been found to bring

Rasputin and the Empress together. It was easy for the astute *starets** to make this hysterical woman believe in his saintliness, so that she in her turn might influence the Empress with his suggestions.

But it was after Rasputin had acquired authority in the Imperial Family and the Empress had come to believe in him as a just and godly man, that Vyrubova scented the possibilities which lay before her. This insignificant person began to feel the lowest kind of craving for power. Her friendship with the Empress had already given her an exceptional position; but with the advent of Rasputin her importance was increased. She became the Empress' most trusted confidante, the only intermediary between Her Majesty and Rasputin.

It must be supposed that Rasputin, relying on Vyrubova as the most convenient tool at his disposal, in his turn encouraged the Empress to confide in her. It is difficult to believe that Anna Vyrubova, having become the centre of Rasputin's influence and of his constant interference in State affairs, cherished any political designs of her own. Her intelligence was too limited for sustained thought. But she was intoxicated with playing the *rôle* of 'an influential person.' The weaving of incessant intrigues, now giving support to one person, now withdrawing it from that, — this juggling with power completely obsessed her.

But Rasputin's influence in State affairs, through the agency of Vyrubova, did not immediately make itself felt. It was only after the Emperor had elected to change his permanent place of residence from St. Petersburg to Tsarskoe Selo that the restricted circles to which the Imperial Family was thereby confined made it possible for the *starets* to exercise his power.

The Emperor Nicholas II was shy by nature. He avoided public appearances whenever possible, and preferred a quiet life within his family circle.

---

* Foreigners persistently style Rasputin either monk or priest. He was neither. The term *starets* was applied to him by his female admirers. In Russian monasteries it is usually applied to monks who are held in special reverence on account of their holy lives. The faithful look to them for spiritual guidance, turn to them for advice in difficult moments and supplicate them in prayer. Such *startsi* were, and are, rarely found, and in but few monasteries throughout Russia. They lead an ascetic life, practising all forms of privation. Rasputin had nothing in common with them.

He became accustomed to this existence from his early youth; for the Emperor Alexander III had spent comparatively few years of his reign in St. Petersburg, and had lived chiefly at Gachina.

But the prevailing conditions during the two reigns were far from similar; stormy years had set in, and the Emperor's withdrawal from the capital had the most dire results.

The Emperor Nicholas II did not seek wide intercourse with his subjects. His most frequent appearances were among his regiments of the Guard; he was chiefly acquainted with military circles. He carried on his duties as a monarch almost exclusively at Tsarskoe Selo, where his ministers reported to him. He worked hard and with great perseverance; but he did not see his country at close quarters, and his country did not know him. Only those who had access to the Palace came face to face with a monarch who was extraordinarily fascinating, charming in the kindly simplicity of his ways, and full of an ardent love for Russia.

The Empress Alexandra Feodorovna greatly encouraged him in this life of retirement. As time went on, she shunned not only St. Petersburg society, but even the members of the Imperial Family. In the solitary surroundings of Tsarskoe Selo the Emperor shared his leisure hours with the Empress, intelligent, delicate in feeling, and exceedingly good-natured, gradually and unconsciously he became accustomed in certain matters to subject his will to the firm, tenacious personality of his wife. She became his only friend, filling his life so completely that there was no room left for the influence of others.

The Empress suffered from a malady of the nervous system, and from a serious neurosis of the heart. This affected her mental outlook and often clouded the atmosphere at Tsarskoe Selo. Her state of health alarmed and distressed the Emperor, and still more confined his attention to family cares.

But their greatest trial was the incurable illness of the long-expected and only son, the Tsetsarevich Alexis. He was afflicted with *haemophilia*, a hereditary disease, passed to male members of a family through the female line.

The Empress, who was a tender and loving mother, suffered doubly; she was tortured by her constant fear for the life of the Tsetsarevich, and by the knowledge that she herself had handed down the illness to him.

Efforts were made to keep his illness secret. But secrecy could not be indefinitely preserved; it only encouraged the rumours of all kinds which were spread in society, thanks to the solitary life of the Emperor.

A veil of mystery was thrown over the Imperial Family. Curiosity was aroused, ill will was engendered, and no one was led to imagine how deeply the parents suffered over their child, and in what constant anguish they spent their life. Such conditions offered a wide field of action to Rasputin.

The Empress blindly believed in his supernatural powers; and she tried to convince the Emperor of them.

She believed that only a miracle could save her son. Rasputin managed to imbue her with the idea that he alone could perform this miracle; and that while he remained in close contact with the Imperial Family the Tsetsarevich would remain alive and well.

Later she became convinced that Rasputin alone could save Russia and that he was endowed with a higher wisdom, with an instinctive knowledge of character, and with the gift of foresight.

An atmosphere of unhealthy mysticism and lack of equilibrium pervaded the Imperial Family. This atmosphere grew more intense as time went on, and the Emperor, at the side of the sick Empress, with Anna Vyrubova and Rasputin in close attendance, found his daily life and routine completely enveloped in it. At times he tried to resist the influence surrounding him. He went so far as to dismiss Rasputin; but he lacked the strength to fight to the end against forces which now appeared to have become a part of his life.

The outbreak of the war seemed to disperse these clouds. A wave of patriotism swept over the whole country. Party differences were set aside, and all dissatisfaction with the Supreme Power was forgotten. The Tsar and his people were at one.

But this national unity was of short duration.

As the struggle dragged on, the clouds gathered again*, and Rasputin reappeared like an evil genius at Tsarskoe Selo.

---

* The public frowned at the news of military reverses; and here and there the terrible word 'treason' was heard. Public opinion, exasperated by German propaganda, attributed to the little-loved Empress the most monstrous crimes. The vilest rumours were spread in Russia by German agents and by revolutionary organisations working in concert with them, and drawing money from the same source. One of their ruses was to lay special emphasis on the Empress' German

origin, and on her unchanging love for the land of her birth. This was a particularly obnoxious form of propaganda, as she disliked Prussia, and detested the Kaiser Wilhelm.

Nor was the emperor immune from calumny. He was alleged to be contemplating the signature of a separate peace, at the instigation of his wife. Yet not only did he when still on the throne repudiate any such suggestion, but after his abdication, in his farewell order to the Army (which was unfortunately not made public by the express interdiction of the Provisional Government), he called upon Russia to fight the enemy to the end, in full co-operation with the Allies. What is more, he refused to accept any conditional help from the Kaiser Wilhelm at the time when the whole Imperial Family were in the hands of the Bolsheviks at Ekaterinburg, where they were living under the most terrible conditions, on the very verge of destruction.

It was imperative that every cause for suspicion or slander should be eliminated by the most vigorous measures. But the Emperor had taken over the supreme command and was established at G.H.Q. His reserves of energy were undermined, and, under the weight of overpowering moral fatigue, he had almost ceded his power to the Empress.

·　·　·　·　·　·　·

Straggling along the high, bare banks of the river Tura lies the village of Pokrovskoe. From the hill in the heart of it, where the church stands, the roads stretch away in all directions; they are laid out straight, and are bordered with roomy peasant cottages.

Everything seems to breathe prosperity. The streets are full of fowl. The farmyards abound with cows, sheep and pigs, and sturdy little horses of local breed that look as if they are cast in steel. The cottage interiors are spotlessly clean. The wide window-sills are bright with flowers.

If you leave the village to stand for a moment on the banks of the Tura, you are confronted with the spaciousness of Siberia, a spaciousness the like of which is probably not to be found the whole world over. Meadows and steppes dotted with birch groves stretch away into the distance, and beyond them lies the *urman*, an endless forest of fir and pine.

In summertime the *urman* is strewn with berries of all sorts, raspberries, currants red and black, and bramble-berries. The forest-clearings are carpeted with strawberries.

The woods abound with game; the grasses and flowers grow almost to the height of man.

No village can be seen for miles around.

In Siberia villages are few and far between; they are often

separated by hundreds of *versts*. Towns are still more rare. The railway that runs through the municipality of Tyumen passes very wide of Pokrovskoe.

In the winter, communication is maintained by road only.

Wrapped in a heavy fur coat, and a dogskin cape as well — the best protection of all from the Siberian frost — the traveller is whirled along in a light sledge over the glistening snow-covered road which stretches out like a silver ribbon before him. The swift horses do not know fatigue, and the passenger drowses, lulled by the monotonous tinkling of the sledge bells.

The white plains flash by. The forests close in. Siberian cedars and fir-trees tower above in gigantic columns, shaking down snow from their heavily laden branches.

In the daytime the bright sunlight on the snow is blinding. At night there is the moon, or the distant stars; and sometimes the bluish-green aurora of the northern lights will flash out across the sky — and all around seems fairyland.

In the summer, boats ply along the Tura from Pokrovskoe to Tyumen. To the north, down-stream, the Tura runs into the Tobol, and the steamer carries you to Tobolsk, a small dreary township far removed from any railway, but the administrative centre of an immense province occupying the north-west region of Siberia.

It was along the rivers Tura and Tobol, from Tyumen to Tobolsk, that the Emperor Nicholas II and his family were taken into captivity in the summer of 1917.

The steamboat passed by Pokrovskoe, and the Empress (as was told afterwards by one of those who voluntarily accompanied the Imperial Family) watched the shore from the deck, and followed with fixed and melancholy gaze the slowly receding roofs of the peasants' cottages, and the tall white church-tower.

It was in the village of Pokrovskoe that Grigori Rasputin was born and spent his youth. He left it to take up those wanderings which eventually brought him to St. Petersburg.

The Siberians are a people of mixed origin. Chance brought their fathers and grandfathers into this rich and fertile country, just as a river's current will carry down pebbles and sand.

In Western Siberia live many Old Believers. They are of various persuasions, and they are settled in the forests and other inaccessible places. Their ancestors came here long ago, to escape the persecution of the Government. They strictly observe their ancient customs, and lead godly and austere lives, zealously guarding the memory of their past, and the books of Divine Service in their cumbrous bindings.

But there are other inhabitants of Siberia, the descendants of fugitive and banished convicts; these try not to speak or think of the past. Whose business is it if the forefathers of some of them passed through the whole of Siberia in shackles?

They are well off and independent. They have grown up in full freedom, out of the reach of all authority, and have not been accustomed to bow down to anyone.

The Siberians are a bold people, rough, but usually very honest. They strongly disapprove of theft, and often take the law into their own hands to punish it.

The only person whom they ever reproach with his past is the thief, particularly the horse-stealer. There is a special Siberian term, *varnak*, which means 'vagabond' 'run-away thief' and they can use no worse insult.

This was the very nickname by which, from his early youth, Grigori Rasputin was notorious in his village.

The blood of his forbears showed itself in him from his birth; the son of a horse-stealer, he continued in the same profession. This shameful and dangerous pursuit gave him scope for the exercise of his dexterity, his cunning and rapacious instincts.

More than once he was caught red-handed, and thrashed within an inch of his life. at least one occasion the police arrived on the scene only just in time to tear his bleeding and mutilated frame from the heavy hands of the infuriated muzhiks.

Another man would not have survived such thrashings, but it was as if a blacksmith's hammer were beating on an anvil. Rasputin bore everything, and only grew stronger from such treatment.

The settled, industrious life of a peasant could offer no attractions to his thievish nature. His instinct was to wander. He would often visit places distant from Pokrovskoe, sometimes disappearing for long intervals. During one of these prolonged absences it was rumoured that he had been converted, and was living a strictly ascetic life in some remote retreat, or in one of the distant monasteries.

It is possible that somewhere in his restless soul vague searchings had been awakened, and that for a time he had been genuinely drawn towards religion. But the pure teaching of the Orthodox Church was completely foreign to his nature; what really was likely to attract him was the obscure mysticism of the most perverted sects.

No exact information can be found concerning the places which he visited in his wanderings, or the people he met. All that is definitely established is that he often visited a certain Orthodox monastery occupied by sectarians* who had been sent thither for 'correction and reform.'

The Siberian monasteries resembled large and prosperous estates rather than the cloisters of devout ascetics. The monks themselves, few in number, were engrossed in their everyday duties, and did not pay much attention to the sectarians domiciled among them. Rasputin could, therefore, speak very freely with these dissenters. He could penetrate all their secrets, while outwardly remaining a pious, zealous and humble pilgrim.

The immense dynamic force with which nature had endowed him could not fail to attract special attention. Like an Indian fakir, he could go without food or sleep; and in order to develop his will-power, he trained himself to such a pitch of asceticism by means of these ostensibly religious practices that at times his companions might have looked upon him as a 'saint' — whereas in reality his soul was filled with an inscrutable darkness that was purely of the devil.

The sectarians looked upon him as a discovery, and in their own way greatly appreciated him.

The Orthodox clergy also became interested in him, not suspecting that this fasting and pious supplicant was playing a double game. From the very outset, he had kept his sectarian leanings dark; and for his own private designs he was careful to preserve an outward connection with representatives of the Church.

He succeeded in acquiring, by rote, a smattering of the Holy Scriptures, and in absorbing a number of spiritual and moral precepts; and he trained himself to assume the guise of a 'man of God' of a *starets* endowed with wisdom and spiritual insight.

His marvellous memory, combined with exceptional powers of observation and assimilation, aided him in this respect. He could not, at this time, have had any notion of his future career. He har-

* Dissenters who had come into sharp conflict with the Orthodox Church and its authorities.

boured no idea of going to St. Petersburg, or even into European Russia, from which Siberians feel themselves cut off. Probably the idle and wandering life of a pilgrim attracted him for its own sake; it seemed pleasanter than the uninterrupted labour of the peasants at his home. His fate was decided by a chance meeting with a young missionary-monk, a well-informed, deeply religious man, as pure and as naive as a child.

He believed in Rasputin's sincerity, and presented him to Bishop Theophan, who, in his turn, brought the impostor to St. Petersburg.

Any ordinary peasant would have become confused by life in the capital. He would have lost himself in the intricate web of Court, society and official relations.

No ordinary muzhik would have had the courage, particularly while everything was as yet strange to him, to show such ease and independence in such surroundings.

Incidentally, the easy manner and familiar tone which this former horse-stealer adopted even towards the most highly-placed personages, was a very considerable factor in his success. Rasputin went in and out of the Tsar's palace as calmly and unconstrainedly as if it had been his own cottage at Pokrovskoe. This made a deep impression. People were apt to think that nothing short of real saintliness could cause a simple Siberian peasant to show no sign whatever of servility before an earthly power. But this muzhik was not slow to observe, remember, and turn over in his mind everything that was of use to him in the noisy and crowded capital.

He almost flawlessly analysed certain characters, quickly perceiving the weak points of those whom he desired to influence, and adapting himself to them.

At Tsarskoe Selo he appeared in the guise of a righteous man who had consecrated himself to God; in society drawing-rooms, among his female admirers, he was much less circumspect; and finally, at home or in a private room at a restaurant, in the intimate company of his associates, he gave full vent to his drunkenness and wanton debauchery.

In certain — incidentally, very small — circles of the highest ranks of St. Petersburg society, occultism of every kind was cultivated. People sought after thrilling sensations at spiritual *séances,* and were drawn towards everything that was piquant and unusual in the realm of unwholesome mysticism. In this environment Rasputin was assured of marked success.

He tried to hide his connection with sectarianism, yet on coming into closer contact with him people instinctively felt that, still deeper than his occult powers, there lay within him some other disturbing force which attracted them.

This element was Khlystism, with its intoxicating, sensual mysticism.

Khlystism is essentially sexual in character; it is a blend of the coarsest animal passion with a belief in the highest spiritual revelation.

The 'prayer-meetings' of the Khlysts combine, in an intense degree, religious ecstasy and erotic abandon. The Khlysts believe that at the height of their hysterical excitement the Holy Spirit descends among them, and that the licentious union of the sexes which is the customary end of their ceremonies is nothing else than an act of 'God's blessing.'

Khlystism is without doubt a survival of pagan times. The ceremony begins with a slow rhythmic dance, which changes to a mad whirl. There is a blinding glitter of candles in the room during 'prayer,' and the inevitable climax is a wild, amorous debauch. It would seem that in the dark recesses of the national consciousness there may still linger some feeling or memory of bygone times which has taken the form of a sacrilegious distortion of the Christian faith.

It is characteristic that the Khlysts have never severed their official ties with the Orthodox Church. They attend the services, acknowledge the sacraments, and frequently partake of Holy Communion.

Rasputin justified all his monstrous debauchery with typical Khlyst reasonings; and sometimes instilled into women the belief that contact with him was far from being a sin.

He went from house to house, overwhelmed by invitations. Some desired to see him out of curiosity; others especially in the early days, were interested by stories of his saintliness; while others, again, with a morbid strain in them, were at once infatuated by him.

After he had acquired an influence in political circles he was; still more eagerly besieged. His good graces were sought, he was given presents and bribes, he. was 'wined and dined.'

His sojourn in St. Petersburg was one long holiday, one continuous debauch. Life had indeed changed for this one-time fugitive horse-stealer.

It was natural that in the end his head should be turned by the realisation of his power, by the servility of those who surrounded him, by the unusual amount of money at his disposal, by all this undreamed of luxury. His cynicism passed all bounds. How could it be otherwise? Could he stand on ceremony with those who had waited in his hall, and with women who were ready to kiss, with reverence, his dirty hands? The more he felt his strength the less he respected those who surrounded him.

But his popularity was very restricted. He moved only within the limited circle composed of his female admirers, and of those persons connected with the Government who needed his support. All the saner elements of St. Petersburg disapproved of him. Satiated with debauchery and drunk with power, he degenerated, and lost all perspicacity and prudence.

His end was a fitting condition to the whole of his life; his body, which to the last had resisted both poison and bullet, was thrown into the waters of the Neva. The Siberian wanderer, who had set out on too venturesome a path, would have met with a similar end in any case, yet had he met it in his native village, it is doubtful whether anyone would have troubled to search for his remains in the waters of the Tura.

· · · · · · ·

There would seem to be no inherent connection between Rasputinism and Bolshevism. Yet the link is there, and it is a very strong one.

Rasputin was the personification of that obscure power which rises from the lowest depths of life and is pregnant with the seeds of disintegration and disruption of all moral principles. He was the forerunner of coming infamies and terrors.

'A muzhik in his greasy boots,' he would say of himself, entered the palace, and traipsed about the Imperial parquets.

With those 'greasy boots' he trampled down the people's ancient faith in the purity and justice of the Tsar's calling. Throughout the whole of his career, there lurked in the person of Rasputin the seeds of approaching Bolshevism with its ignorance, greed, cynicism and depravity, with its dark passion for power, its denial of responsibility before God or man.

Rasputin became a weapon in the hands of Russia's enemies. But were the Germans her only enemy? Or did there stand behind Rasputin some other power? — a power which sought the political enfeeblement of Russia and her moral disintegration and destruction, in order to strengthen its own diabolical hold on her? Rasputin duped the Empress and the Emperor who trusted him. The Bolsheviks duped the whole of the Russian people, who blindly followed them in some sort of wild, intoxicated, Khlystic ecstasy of revolution.

Unknown to himself, Rasputin was, in a sense, the first 'Commissary' of Bolshevism. He had drawn near to the throne in order to trample on its might and extinguish its majesty.

Others followed him. . . .

Rasputinism paralysed the supreme power because it did not meet with a strong and organised opposition among influential people prompted solely by ideas of duty and by purely moral motives.

Bolshevism likewise met with no obstacle. Flabbiness, confusion, vanity, party blindness and self-seeking, the absence of a united national idea, the illusion of revolution — hung like a poisonous mist over those Russians who found themselves in power after the fall of the monarchy. Under cover of this mist the enemies of Russia stealthily crept up and dealt her the long premeditated blow.

Stunned and bewildered, the people readily fell into their hands.

Bolshevism dropped its anchor in a foul and muddy pool. It caught the refuse of every class of society. It brought with it a whole army of aliens for whom Russia could never be a home — for whom Russia was, and is, a stranger's house, given over to them to be plundered and defiled.

A great country became the home of the most appalling depravity and the most monstrous crimes.

Unheard-of outrages were inflicted on a defenceless people. Russia was transformed into a laboratory for the preparation of poisons destined for the destruction of all mankind.

In the whole world there was not — nor has there yet been found — a power ready to rise up unhesitatingly in defence, not of the Russian people only, but of all that is best in morals and in culture.

Civilised countries live in close contact with the leprosy of Bolshevism; they stretch out a hand to the servants of the devil and are not choked by the moral rot and stench which, like poison gas, are spread over the entire earth by that criminal organisation — the Third International.

Peoples and their governments do not seem to understand that Bolshevism is something more than a mere form of administration closely fitted into the framework of the Soviets; they do not realise that first and foremost it is a moral perversion — a terrible and complicated disease of mankind of to-day, a disease which stifles conscience, duty and honour.

Bolshevism paralyses and destroys the heritage of long centuries of spiritual culture; it gradually transforms man into a civilised brute, governed by his lowest instincts and devoid of all needs of a higher order.

Bolshevism is the most determined enemy of Christianity. It is as if the powers of darkness were endeavouring to storm the heavens. It was not without meaning that the communists staged a 'trial of God' and repudiated and condemned Him.

The Church, the mainstay and the crown of Russia, alone withstood the onslaught of the revolution.

She overcame, within herself, the virus of Rasputinism which had done its best to poison her; she has not yet yielded to force or threats, or to the disintegration and corruption of Bolshevism. She has saved, and is saving, the soul of the Russian people, with all its high moral qualities. She is destined to face the formidable task of Russia's moral cleansing.

Purification is essential; without it no new life can be built up, no new system of government can be established. Any form of government which is not founded on all that is best in the spiritual life of the people will prove frail and fleeting, and will end in a repetition of the terrible calamity of 1917, when a throne which had stood firm for centuries collapsed, having lost — thanks to Rasputin — its moral authority.

Documents exposing Bolshevism and the Soviet Government are published in all languages. A whole new literature has appeared — a literature which by no means exhausts the terrible truth.

The whole world reads books which are written in blood, and yet remains indifferent not only to the position of Russia, but to its own ultimate fate.

Humanity of to-day is blind to everything save the small concerns of the moment, petty personal interests and the thirst for immediate success. It closes its eyes to the spectacle of a great country, exhausted and bleeding, struggling alone against the powers of darkness.

Is not this also a form of Rasputinism, which has gained possession of our epoch, and of the whole of mankind to-day?

Paris, 1926.

RASPUTIN

THE END OF RASPUTIN

CHAPTER I

HOW I MADE RASPUTIN' ACQUAINTANCE

My first meeting with Rasputin was at the G.s' house in St. Petersburg in 1909.

I had known the G.'s for years, my particular friend being their daughter, M.

As everything connected with the name of Rasputin is apt to excite a feeling of disgust, I would like to add a few words concerning M. to distinguish her from the Rasputin clan.

She was exceptionally pure-minded, good-natured, and responsive, and unusually impressionable. But there was much nervous exaltation in her character; and thanks to this, her spiritual impulses always predominated over her reason. Religion played the chief part in her life, but her religious feelings were tinged with an unhealthy mysticism.

Trustful to excess, she was totally incapable of judging either people or facts. When anything surprised her, she blindly yielded to the impression which it made on her. She remained wholly under the influence of those in whom she had once believed, and she did not readily distinguish good from evil.

In these circumstances it was not a matter for surprise that Rasputin should be a frequent visitor at the G.'s.

When I returned from abroad, in 1909, I found that M. was one of his ardent admirers. She sincerely and firmly believed in his uprightness and spiritual purity; she regarded him as one of God's elect, as an almost supernatural being. Her infatuation for the *starets** did not surprise me in the least.

* See note on page 248

Rasputin, with his natural perspicacity, was not slow to see in her his future devotee. He divined her spiritual leanings, and gained her complete confidence. M.'s purity prevented her from seeing the grime and horror that hung about the man. She was too naive to form any true estimate of his actions. Her greatest joy lay in the full spiritual subjection of her personality.

She was happy to have found a 'Holy Guide.' Not only did she fail to analyse the qualities of this 'teacher,' but she timidly withdrew into herself whenever she felt anyone trying to expose him. The ideal, which she had formed in her imagination, of 'the divine *starets*' blotted out the true Rasputin from her sight.

At our first meeting after my return, she began to talk about him. She described him as a man of rare spiritual strength, filled with God's blessing, who had been sent into the world to cleanse and heal our hearts and to guide our wills, thoughts, and conduct.

I remember that I adopted a sceptical attitude, although at that time I had nothing particular against Rasputin — indeed I had heard very little about him. Knowing M., I decided that she was simply passing through one of the usual phases of enthusiasm typical of her highly-strung nature.

But something in her words seemed to arouse my curiosity. I asked her many questions. With great animation and enthusiasm M. proceeded to tell me more about 'the shining personality of the *starets*'

Her story was one long eulogy. Rasputin was a healer; he interceded for mankind; he was an altruist; a peacemaker, a comforter of the sorrow-stricken; he was a new apostle, God's chosen emissary; he stood on a different plane from the rest of mankind; he knew no human weaknesses nor vices, and his whole life was spent in asceticism and prayer.

M.'s fervour and conviction did not inspire me with any faith in the miraculous gifts of the *starets*, but they increased my curiosity and roused in me a desire to meet him. I told her that I should like to make the acquaintance of this remarkable man. She was quite delighted with my suggestion, and the meeting was not long delayed.

Some days later I drove up to the G.s' house on the Winter Canal, where this first meeting was to take place. When I entered the drawing-room, Rasputin had not yet arrived. M. was seated with her mother at the tea-table. Both were very nervous and excited;

especially the daughter, who seemed to be in a state of suppressed anxiety. I felt that she was nervous about the first impression that Rasputin would make on me, and that at the same time she desired that I, like herself, should be inspired with veneration for him. Both mother and daughter seemed to be in a state of devout tension, as if the arrival of a wonder-working ikon was awaited in the house.

This attitude still further excited my curiosity and desire to see this 'wonderful man.' We did not have to wait long. The door leading from the hall soon opened, and Rasputin walked in, with a mincing gait. He came straight towards me, and with the words, 'Good day, my dear,' made a movement as if to embrace me. I drew back. With a sly, sickly smile, he went forward to M. and her mother. He embraced them both without my ceremony, kissing them with an air of gracious condescension.

My first glance at him filled me with dislike of his appearance; there was something repugnant about him. He was of medium height, thick-set yet rather thin, with long arms, His big head was covered with an untidy tangle of hair. Above his forehead there was a bald patch which, as I subsequently learnt, came from a blow administered to him when he was beaten for horse-stealing. He seemed to be about forty years old. He was wearing a long coat, wide trousers and long boots. His face was of the post ordinary peasant type – a coarse oval, with large, ugly features overgrown with a slovenly beard, and with a long nose; his small grey eyes looked out from under bushy eyebrows with piercing yet shifty glances. His whole bearing attracted attention; he appeared unconstrained in his movements, and yet there seemed to be something dissembled about him – something suspicious, cowardly and searching. All these details did not, of course, strike me at our first meeting.

He greeted us, and sat down for a moment. Then he rose and for some time walked about the room with his quick, short steps, muttering incoherently to himself. His voice was thick, and his pronunciation indistinct.

We drank our tea and looked at him in silence – M. with enraptured attention, I with curiosity and distrust.

At last he came to the tea-table, settled down in an armchair by my side, and began to submit me to a searching scrutiny.

A conversation about nothing in particular was started, Rasputin, apparently wishing to maintain the tone of one inspired from above, held forth in a dictatorial manner. His speech was quick, voluble, yet often faltering. He quoted scripture texts which had no connection with each other, and his words gave the impression of something involved, if not chaotic.

As he talked I carefully watched his expression. There was certainly something unusual in this muzhik's features.

The longer I examined him, the more I was struck by his eyes; they were amazingly repulsive. Not only was there no trace of spiritual refinement in the face, but it called to mind that of a cunning and lascivious satyr. The peculiarity of his eyes was that they were small, almost colourless, and too closely set in large, exceptionally deep sockets; so that from a distance they were not visible — they seemed to get lost in the depths of their recesses. Hence it was often difficult to see whether they were open or not, and only the feeling that a needle was piercing through you told you that he was looking at you and examining you closely. His keen and penetrating gaze did, in fact, convey a feeling of some hidden, supernatural power.

His smile, too, was arresting; it was sickly yet cruel, cunning and sensual. Indeed, the whole of his being was redolent of something unspeakably revolting, hidden under the mask of hypocrisy and cant.

M. was full of excitement at the presence of Rasputin. Her eyes shone; her cheeks burned with a nervous flush. She and her mother did not take their eyes off him; with bated breath they caught at every word the *starets* uttered.

At last he rose, enveloped us all in a would-be loving and caressing glance, and turning to me, said, while he pointed to M., 'What a true friend you have in her. Listen to her, and she will be your spiritual wife. Yes . . . she has spoken well of you, told me many things; and now I see for myself that you are suited to each other. . . . My dear, — I do not know your Christian name — you will go a long way, a very long way.'

And with these words he left the room.

I also took my leave, absorbed in my impressions of this enigma.

A few days later, I heard from M. that Rasputin had taken a great liking to me, and that he wanted to meet me again.

* * *

CHAPTER II

ANXIETY AMONG LOYAL SUBJECTS OF THE THRONE

SOON after my first meeting with Rasputin I left for England, and went up to Oxford.

On one occasion, when I was visiting an English Princess closely related to the Empress Alexandra Feodorovna, our conversation turned on him.

The Princess listened to my stories about him with great interest. She fully realised the danger to Russia involved in his proximity to the Court; and after briefly sketching the mental characteristics of the Empress Alexandra Feodorovna, she expressed a fear that certain of those traits, especially her leaning towards morbid mysticism, might cause grave complications in the future if Rasputin were to remain near the Royal Family. At that time my parents lived in St. Petersburg and spent the summer at Tsarskoe Selo.

My mother was much liked by the Empress Alexandra Feodorovna and was often with her. Rasputin's proximity to the Emperor and Empress greatly perturbed her, and in her letters to me she often mentioned her anxiety. She also communicated her fears to the Grand Duchess Elizabeth Feodorovna, a friend of many years' standing.

The Grand Duchess, who resided in Moscow, shared all her apprehensions, and during her rare visits to St. Petersburg she exerted every effort to persuade the Emperor and Empress to dismiss the pernicious *starets*.

At that time the danger of Rasputin's presence at Tsarskoe Selo was not generally realised. His appearance at the Court was probably a mere chance; and only later, when the enemies of Russia and of the dynasty found a field of action ready prepared for them — realising how all powerful Rasputin had become, and to what an extent 'autocracy' was in his hands — were they able to make use of him for their own ends.

My mother was one of the first openly to oppose Rasputin. She had a long conversation with the Empress, and quite frankly told her all that she thought on this matter.

Her words made a great impression on the Empress, who

apparently understood my mother's sincerity, and felt the justice of her conclusions. In parting from her, the Empress, in most touching terms, expressed a wish to see her as often as possible.

But Rasputin's friends were not slumbering. They fully realised the danger of such an intimacy, and contrived to win back their control over the Empress's sick imagination, and gradually to alienate her from my mother.

Many members of the Imperial Family, with the Dowager Empress Marie Feodorovna at their head, also tried to influence the Emperor and Empress; but in vain.

And then began a struggle between those who were sincerely devoted to Russia and the Throne, and those who shamelessly used Rasputin's influence to gain access to the Emperor and Empress, and so further their own selfish ends and secret political schemes.

From childhood I had been accustomed to look upon the Imperial Family as people apart, different from ourselves. I held them in veneration, as beings of a higher order, girt with a sort of halo that set them beyond all criticism. Any aspersion cast upon them filled me with indignation, and I paid no attention to the storied I heard of Rasputin's relations with the Court.

In the autumn of 1912 I came down from Oxford and returned to my home in Russia.

I had many plans for the future; but they were still rather vague. My meeting with Princess Irina Alexandrovna* altered my fate. In a short time our engagement was announced.

At the outbreak of war I was in Germany with my wife and parents. By order of the Kaiser Wilhelm we were arrested in Berlin. We escaped by a miracle and reached Copenhagen, where we found the Dowager-Empress, who brought us safely to St. Petersburg.

The enthusiasm provoked by the declaration of war had already begun to subside, and many people were pessimistically inclined. Tsarskoe Selo was enveloped in gloom. The Emperor and Empress, cut off from the world, out of touch with their subjects, surrounded by the Rasputin clan, were deciding questions of world-wide importance.

Could this forebode anything but disaster?

* The daughter of the Grand Duke Alexander Mikhailovich and the Grand Duchess Xenia Alexandrovna.

CHAPTER III

RASPUTIN IS REVEALED TO ME

AND so there was no hope that the Emperor and Empress would ever understand the full truth about Rasputin, and dismiss him from the Court.

What other steps, therefore, could be taken to deliver the Emperor and Russia from this evil genius?

The thought arose; 'There is only one way; to put an end to the criminal *starets*.'

The idea first entered my head after a conversation with my wife and mother as far back as 1915, when we had been discussing the terrible effects of Rasputin's influence.

The subsequent march of political events made me turn to it again, and it took firm root in my mind.

The representations made by the members of the Imperial Family against Rasputin were followed by a number of open demonstrations of a public character, both by individuals and by various organisations. Reports were submitted, resolutions were drawn up, and collective appeals were made to the Supreme Power. But the Emperor and Empress remained deaf to all supplications, advice, warnings and threats. The more Rasputin was opposed, the more convincing the evidence against him, the less attention was paid to the matter at Tsarskoe Selo. He was indeed impregnable. He made such adroit use of his assumed mask of hypocrisy that no credence whatever was given there to reports of his profligacy. An eloquent illustration of this is afforded by the following incident.

General Dzhunkovski, Vice-Minister of the Interior, wishing to confront the Empress with clear proof that the stories of Rasputin's revolting behaviour were only too true, showed her some photographs taken during one of his lewd orgies in a St. Petersburg restaurant. On seeing this incontrovertible evidence the Empress was terribly indignant, and ordered immediate and searching inquiries to be made regarding the identity of the person who had dared to sully Rasputin's reputation by posing as the *starets*.

At a time when patriotic Russians were in despair at their failure to destroy the root of evil, the German party — having in the *starets* such a valuable assistant — naturally triumphed.

Already at the outbreak of the war Rasputin was almost at the summit of his influence and power. During the period that followed, honourable and devoted servants of the Crown were one by one dismissed, even those who were on terms of personal friendship with the Emperor himself; and their places were filled by Rasputin's nominees.

Meanwhile, innumerable lives were lost at the front. With magnificent, unheard-of heroism, the Russian troops went submissively to their death.

Spread over a vast front of some thousands of *versts*, they were fighting under conditions which no other soldiers in the world could have endured. Beset by terrible frosts, often deprived of all rations, they held the snow-filled trenches, never dreaming of retreat. Certain sections, owing to shortage of ammunition, fell under the enemy's fire without ever being able to reply. Whole regiments endeavoured to repulse attacks with their bare fists. Others went over the top armed only with sticks and stones.

The Russian army did not 'grouse;' it knew neither fatigue nor the fear of death, whether in defending its own territories or in sacrificing itself in support of its allies.

For instance, before the Battle of the Marne, the whole army of General Samsonov, with full knowledge that it was going to certain death, broke into Eastern Prussia, in order to draw part of the enemy forces from the French to the Russian front. The Germans, alarmed at this unexpected advance, reduced their forces on the Western front. The French gained a victory; but the Russian troops in Eastern Prussia were sacrificed in order to ensure it.

Russia felt these sacrifices. She felt how the life-blood flowed from her, the blood of her best and bravest, who were gladly dying for their country and for the common cause.

The people became doubly anxious. Was everything possible being done for the army? Were those at the base, to whom was entrusted the responsibility of supplying and arming the troops, conscientiously carrying out their duty ? There were rumours of peculation and even treachery.

As soon as the Emperor, thanks to Rasputin's intrigues, had transferred the Grand Duke Nicholas Nikolaevich to the Caucasian front, and had himself assumed the supreme command, the *starets* began to be an almost daily visitor at Tsarskoe Selo, where he gave his advice on affairs of State. His meetings with the Empress usually took place in Vyrubova's house.

Not a single important event at the front was decided without a preliminary conference with the *starets*. From Tsarskoe Selo instructions were given to General Headquarters on the direct telegraph line. The Empress insisted on being kept fully informed by the Emperor on the military and political situation. On receiving this information, sometimes secret and of the utmost importance, she would send for Rasputin, and confer with him. When it is remembered by whom Rasputin was surrounded, it ceases to be surprising that almost every one of our attacks was known to the Germans beforehand, and that they should have been aware of all plans and changes contemplated in military or political spheres.

Germany took the necessary measures to secure her victories and to prepare our destruction.

I decided to attach no particular importance to all the disturbing rumours which were rife, but first of all to obtain irrefutable evidence of Rasputin's treason.

My opportunities for this reconnaissance could not have been more favourable.

The G.'s were at that time living on the Moika, next to the Grand Duke Alexander Mikhailovich's palace, into which I had moved pending the completion of alterations in our own house.

As I have already said, M. and I were very old friends. She often invited me to visit her, but I seldom went, for I had no desire to enter the sphere of Rasputin's influence, still less to have my name connected with those of his friends who constantly gathered at her mother's house.

Now, however, since I was bent on completely unravelling the mystery of Rasputin's character and actions by means of a closer acquaintanceship with him, I decided to take advantage of M.'s invitations.

Incidentally, it was interesting to discuss in detail with M. herself the state of affairs in Russia. Knowing her blind adoration of Rasputin I could not, of course, attach any weight whatever to her views, but I knew that they were an exact reproduction of opinions held at Tsarskoe Selo.

I telephoned to her, to arrange a visit, and at the appointed hour I went to see her. M. told me that Rasputin was constantly asking about me.

'He is very anxious to see you,' she said. 'He is coming here one of these days; I will let you know which.'

My further conversation with her convinced me that Rasputin still enjoyed the unlimited confidence of the Emperor and Empress, and continued to play the part of their most trusted adviser on political and family matters.

M. again sang his praises. Full of emotion, she told me how the *starets* humbly endured 'slander' and 'persecution,' and that by these unmerited sufferings he redeemed our sins.

Her enthusiasm prompted me to touch upon Rasputin's adventures. 'How do you explain this good man's habit of defiling his saintliness with drunken revels ?'

M. was indignant. She blushed deeply and replied with some heat:

'You surely realise that all those tales are nothing but black and slanderous lies? He is surrounded by envy and malice. Evil-minded people invent charges and purposely distort facts, in order to blacken him, an innocent man, in the eyes of the Emperor and Empress. . . . It is all too terrible.

'But,' I answered, 'you must be aware that there are proofs in the shape of photographs and the tested evidence of witnesses, leaving no doubt whatever that he is by no means the holy man you make him out to be. . . . Why, for instance, should the gypsies be talking about his visits to them, his drinking and dancing with them? . . . Besides, many people have met him there. . . . And in the Villa Rodé restaurant, where he goes most of all, there is even a private room bearing his name. . . . How do you explain all that?'

'There you are ! You talk like everyone else, and you believe it !' exclaimed M. indignantly. 'Remember that even if he does all these things, it is with a special purpose; he wants to harden himself morally; and by resisting temptation, to stamp out all baser desires.'

'And the ministers he appoints and dismisses? Is that also to stamp out desires, and to perfect his morality?' I asked, with a smile.

M. became angry at this, and said that she would complain about me to Grigori Efimovich.*

It made my heart ache to see the unfortunate girl's fanatical belief in the purity and infallibility of this disreputable adventurer. She would not accept my proofs of his depravity. Every word of mine seemed as if shattered on the rock of her enslaved intelligence. I realised that she had lost the power of independent judgment, and that she dared not look upon her idol with a critical eye.

I then tried to make clear to her, from another point of view, the harm that his presence did to the Royal Family.

'Very well, then. We will assume, for the moment, that all this talk about his behaviour is pure invention. But you cannot ignore public opinion in Russia and throughout Europe. Both here and abroad Rasputin is regarded as a scoundrel and a spy. . . . His nearness to the Throne upsets the whole country and alarms our allies. . . . Is not that a sufficient reason for securing his removal from the presence of the Emperor and Empress?'

'Nobody has the right to criticise the actions of the Emperor and Empress. What they do concerns no one,' she replied hotly. 'They stand by themselves, above all public opinion.'

'And supposing,' I said, 'that Grigori Efimovich is an unconscious weapon in the hands of Russia's enemies, who carry out through him their criminal plans for the ruin of Russia — what then? Would you, even under those conditions, still consider his presence useful at Tsarskoe Selo?

'And besides, you yourself have told me that Grigori Efimovich not only prays and speaks of religion with the Emperor and Empress, but that he also discusses with them the most important affairs of State. You know very well that not a single decision is taken without his approval, not a minister is appointed without his knowledge. Remember that whatever his spiritual qualities may be, good or bad, he is first and foremost an unenlightened and uneducated muzhik. Why, he can scarcely write. What can he understand about complicated questions of war, politics and internal administration? What advice can he give on these matters? And if he does give such advice, then there are obviously people behind him who are secretly directing him. You do not know these people or their aims. What right, then, have you to affirm that all the actions

* Rasputin

of Grigori Efimovich are good and helpful?

'Again I tell you, the proximity to the Throne of a man with such a terrible reputation undermines the authority of the Tsar everywhere. Dissatisfaction grows, indignation is universal, and if those at the head of the State do not realise this, events may happen which will overthrow everything.'

M. looked at me with a pitying expression, as if I were an innocent child, and in answer to my impassioned speech, said:

'You talk like this simply because you do not know or understand Grigori Efimovich. Get to know him better, and if he takes a liking to you, then you yourself will become convinced of his exceptional and wonderful qualities. He cannot be mistaken in people. God Himself has given him such perspicacity that just by looking at a person he can immediately read his thoughts. That is why he is loved at Tsarskoe Selo; and of course they trust him in everything. He helps the Emperor and Empress to discern every person's character; he protects them from fraud, from every dangerous influence. . . . If it were not for Grigori Efimovich, everything would have been ruined long ago !' she concluded, in a tone of absolute conviction.

I put an end to this fruitless conversation. I said good-bye and went away.

On reaching home, I began to turn over in my mind my future course of action. This discussion only served to strengthen my conviction that it was impossible to fight against Rasputin's influence with mere words. Logic was of no avail. The dearest arguments would not convince those whose judgment was clouded.

I realised that no more time must be wasted in talk; it was necessary to take action, deliberately and with energy, while all was not yet lost.

* * *

CHAPTER IV

THE RESOLVE TO DO AWAY WITH THE *starets*

I DECIDED to consult certain influential people and to tell them all I knew of Rasputin's doings. The impressions that I carried away from these conversations were very discouraging.

In the past I had so often heard them denounce Rasputin in the most bitter terms, attributing to him all our evils and misfortunes, and maintaining that, if it were not for him, the position might still be saved. But when I suggested that it was time to pass from words to deeds, I was told that his importance at Tsarskoe Selo had been greatly exaggerated by empty rumours.

I do not know whether their evasive attitude was dictated by their fear of losing their posts, or whether they light-heartedly hoped that nothing terrible would happen, and that time would put everything right. But in either case I was astonished at the absence of any alarm for the country's fate. It was clear that their addiction to a quiet life, and an eager desire for their own welfare, impelled them to avoid any kind of decisive action which would necessitate departure from the beaten track. I think they were all convinced of one thing; that the old order of things would in any case remain unchanged. They relied on this order, as if it were as firm as a rock; and the rest — whether their country would emerge victorious from this terrible war, whether all the blood poured out by Russians would be spilt in vain, whether a disastrous defeat would be the tragic end of the nation's enthusiasm — did not worry them overmuch.

Least of all were they capable of realising that an appalling catastrophe was drawing nearer and nearer, and had already assumed definite shape.

True, I did meet certain people who shared my fears; but they were powerless to help me. One of them, an elderly man who held a responsible post at the time, said to me: 'My dear fellow, what can one do, when the entire Government, and those who are in close contact with the Emperor, are, without exception, Rasputin's nominees?

'The only way out is . . . to kill the blackguard. But unfortunately there isn't a man in Russia to do that. . . . If I were not so old I'd do it myself. . . .'

When I saw that there was no help forthcoming from any direction, I decided to act independently.

No matter what I was doing, no matter to whom I was talking, I was haunted by one persistent idea, the idea of delivering Russia from her most dangerous internal enemy.

I would often awake in the middle of the night, and pace up and down the room.

How can one kill a man, and deliberately plan his murder?

The thought oppressed and tormented me. . . . Until a voice within me said:

'Every murder is a crime and a sin, but in the name of your country you must take this sin on your conscience. You must take it without faltering. At the front, millions of innocent men have been killed. . . . While here there is only one man who must die, and of all the enemies of your country, he is the most pernicious, the most cynical, the most vile. By his abominable deceit he has made the Russian Throne his fortress, and no one has power to drive him forth. . . . Come what will, you must destroy him. . . .'

All my doubts and hesitations vanished. I felt a calm resolution, and gave myself over to the set purpose of destroying Rasputin. The idea took deep and firm root in my mind, and guided all my subsequent actions.

* * *

CHAPTER V

MY INQUIRIES

I MENTALLY ran through the list of those of my friends to whom I could entrust my secret, and chose two. They were the Grand Duke Dmitri Pavlovich and Captain Sukhotin.

The Grand Duke was at G.H.Q., but he was soon to arrive in St. Petersburg. Captain Sukhotin, who was undergoing treatment for wounds received in action, I saw almost daily. I decided not to delay any longer, but to confer with him at once. I outlined my plan in general terms, and asked him if he wished to take part in carrying it out. He consented without the slightest hesitation, telling me that he agreed with my views and shared my fears.

On the same day the Grand Duke Dmitri Pavlovich arrived from G.H.Q. As soon as I had returned home from my visit to Sukhotin, I telephoned to the Grand Duke, and arranged to call and see him at five o'clock that afternoon.

I was sure that he would support me, and be willing to take part in the fulfilment of my plan. I knew how he detested Rasputin, and how deeply he felt for the Emperor and Russia. For very many reasons I attributed great importance to his participation in the plot.

I realised the necessity of being prepared for the most distressing possibilities, the most fateful issues; but I was buoyed up by the hope that the destruction of Rasputin would save the Tsar's Family, and that the Emperor, roused from the spell which had been cast on him, would lead the country to a decisive victory, at the head of his united people.

The crucial moment of the war was drawing near. In the spring of 1917, the Allies proposed to launch a general attack on all fronts. Russia was energetically preparing her army for this move. But a purely technical preparation on the front and at the base was insufficient to inflict a decisive blow on the enemy. It was essential that there should be a strong feeling of unanimity between the Supreme Power and the people.

Yet the shadow of Rasputin continued to hang like a cloud over G.H.Q. and St. Petersburg.

Needless to say, Germany was not slumbering. While putting down barbed-wire entanglements in front of her lines, she was busy weaving her terrible nets within Russia herself.

Germany had made a close study of the internal situation in Russia for many years before the war. At the time when the Kaiser Wilhelm, foreseeing the inevitability of a general European war, was making every effort to bring about a Russo-German alliance, he warned the Emperor Nicholas against Rasputin and advised him to see no more of this dangerous and pernicious man. The German Emperor realised that Rasputin's proximity to the Throne compromised not only the Russian Tsar but monarchy as a whole. After the proposals for alliance had been rejected, however, and especially after war had been declared, the Kaiser made very adroit use of Rasputin's influence. The German General Staff, all unseen, held him in their hands, by means of money and the most subtle intrigues. Simultaneously the Germans exerted every effort to provoke a revolution in Russia; they sent their agents into our midst, and gave all kinds of support to revolutionary organisations abroad which were constantly preparing the ground and watching the moment for an attack.

In point of fact, the Germans had counted on a Russian revolution before August, 1914. There were persistent reports that just before war was declared, Count Pourtalés, the German Ambassador in St. Petersburg, had informed his Government, in a telegram which had been intercepted and deciphered, that the most favourable moment for hostilities had arrived, since Russia was on the brink of revolution. The contents of the telegram made it quite clear, moreover, that Germany had sent into Russia huge sums of money for propaganda.

In the earlier phases of the war, the great patriotic response of the Russian people upset these calculations. The Germans began to make suggestions for a separate peace; but they none the less continued their revolutionary propaganda.

I was looking forward with impatience to my meeting with the Grand Duke Dmitri Pavlovich; and at the appointed hour I went to the palace.

I found him alone in his study and at once proceeded to tell him what I had in mind.

I gave him my views in detail on the situation, told him of my intentions, and asked him whether he would be ready to co-operate with me.

As I had expected, he at once agreed, saying that in his opinion Rasputin's death was the only effective means that remained of saving Russia from imminent disaster. He told me that he had long been tormented by the necessity of settling accounts with the *starets*, but that he had not been able to conceive how this could be done.

In the course of our conversation I gave the Grand Duke an account of my talk with M. He was not in the least surprised, as he was well aware of the attitude which prevailed at Tsarskoe Selo.

He had to return to G.H.Q. in a few days' time.

He told me that his stay there would probably be a short one, as he was not liked there, and his influence was feared. He added that, Voeikov* made every effort to keep him away from the Emperor, who was completely in his hands.

He then gave me his views of what was going on at G.H.Q. He had noticed that there was something wrong with the Emperor; every day he became more indifferent to his surroundings, and to the course of events.

'In my opinion,' he concluded, 'that is all part of some evil plot. I am almost sure that he is being given drugs which obscure his intelligence and weaken his will-power. . . . All this is terrible . . . it's a nightmare.'

At this point our conversation was interrupted by the arrival of guests, and we had to postpone it.

But we had arranged that by the time he next returned from G.H.Q. – he expected it would be between the 10th and the 15th of December – I should work out a detailed plan for Rasputin's destruction, and prepare everything for its fulfilment.

On this we parted; everything, in principle, was settled.

I returned home, moved by strange feelings. The idea which had so disturbed and tormented me had now begun to pass from the realm of my own thoughts into reality. Not so very long ago it had overwhelmed me like some confused delirium. But now I was no longer alone; I had adherents, friends with me. Everything was now decided, everything clear. And I felt an immense spiritual relief.

In the evening Sukhotin came to see me.

I told him of my conversation with the Grand Duke Dmitri Pavlovich, and we settled down to discuss our plan of action.

It was decided that first of all I should get into close touch with

* General Voeikov, the Commandant of the Palace.

Rasputin, obtain his confidence, and try to learn from his own lips as many details as possible concerning his participation in political events.

Afterwards, we intended to try our utmost — not by extreme measures, but by peaceful persuasion or by the promise of large sums of money — to sever his connection with Tsarskoe Selo.

If these attempts should meet with complete failure, it only remained for us to destroy the criminal *starets*.

At this point the question arose, how and where should we carry out this sentence on him?

I suggested that the three of us should draw lots; and that whoever was chosen by destiny should contrive an entrance into Rasputin's flat, and shoot him there.

* * *

Palace Commandant Major-General Vladimir Nikolaevich Voeikov standing behind Tsarevich Alexis, with Alexis' tutors. Circa Summer 1916.

Back row Left to Right: Pierre Gilliard, (French); Vladimir Voeikov; Charles Sidney Gibbes (English); Professor Pyotr Petrov (Russian).

CHAPTER VI

RASPUTIN AMONG HIS FEMALE ADMIRERS

A FEW days later, M. said to me on the telephone:
'Grigori Efimovich is coming to see us tomorrow. He very much wants to meet you. We both insist on your coming too.

I shuddered on receiving this invitation. The means of pursuing my design was presenting itself of its own accord, but in adopting it I was forced to deceive one who was genuinely attached to me. M. could not suspect my reasons for keeping up an acquaintance with Rasputin; she should on no account suspect them.

But having arrived at a definite decision I could not and would not go back on it.

When I entered the G.s' drawing-room on the following day, I found M. and her mother there. They had long cherished the hope that Rasputin and I would become friends; and they were clearly agitated at the prospect of our second meeting.

He arrived very soon afterwards.

He had changed a great deal since we first met.

The environment in which this muzhik was living, cut off from the healthy physical labour which was natural to him, sunk in absolute sloth and spending his nights carousing, seemed to have laid its inevitable mark on him.

His face was puffy, his form seemed to have become lax and flabby. He was no longer clad in an ordinary peasant's coat, but in a blouse of pale blue silk, and wide velvet trousers. There was something extraordinarily repugnant about his whole appearance. Yet he seemed very much at ease.

As soon as he caught sight of me he screwed up his eyes and smiled sweetly, saying how glad he was to meet me. He hurried towards me and embraced me. His touch sickened me, but I controlled myself and made a show of being very pleased to see him.

I noticed that with M. and her mother his manner was even more familiar than before. He clapped them on the shoulder or on the back, and did not even deign to answer when they asked him to sit down and take tea.

He seemed preoccupied that day. He paced restlessly up and down the room, and several times asked M. whether there had been no telephone message for him.

He eventually sat down beside me and began to ask questions. What was I doing? Where was I serving? Should I soon be going to the front? His patronising tone exasperated me, but I had to appear amiable and humour him.

M. followed our conversation with the deepest attention.

When he had completely satisfied his curiosity about me, he reeled off a series of disjointed and meaningless phrases about God and love for one's neighbour. I tried to grasp his meaning, in the hope of discovering something original, or eccentric. But the more I listened the more convinced I became that he was using exactly the same expressions as at our first meeting, four years before.

As I listened to his senseless mumblings, I watched the reverent and attentive faces of his admirers, who seemed fearful of missing a single syllable of his disjointed 'sermon.' To them, of course, it seemed to hold a profound and hidden meaning.

Into what depth of mental and moral abjection, I thought, can people sink. Here is this impudent scoundrel shamelessly hoaxing them — and they don't want to be undeceived. That's just it; they don't want to be undeceived. They are pleasantly intoxicated with his narcotic suggestions. An ignorant muzhik sprawling in armchairs, spouting forth the first words that come into his head, is something new for them, something unexpected; it excites their nerves, fills up their time, and perhaps even induces in them a state of hysterical ecstasy. . . . And this muzhik is not only playing on feminine weakness; he is fooling the whole country; he is juggling with the fate of millions of people, and leading to disaster all Russia and her unfortunate Tsar.

I remembered my conversation with the Grand Duke Dmitri Pavlovich concerning the drugs with which the Emperor's faculties were being deliberately undermined. . . . Incidentally, he was not the only person who had told me about those stupefying Tibetan herbs.

Rasputin was on very friendly terms with a certain Badmaev who was living in St. Petersburg at that time. Badmaev, who hailed from Tibet, gave himself out to be a fully qualified doctor, but he had not fulfilled the requirements which Russian law imposes on medical practitioners. He treated patients in secret; and as he demanded large fees both for his advice and for his medicines — which by the way, he prepared himself —* he had succeeded in amassing a considerable fortune. On several occasions he had been charged with the criminal offence of quackery, but in spite of that he remained in St. Petersburg and continued his surreptitious treatment of those credulous people who consulted him.

Whether Badmaev was really one of the true Tibetan 'Lamas,' versed in all the secrets of Tibetan medical lore — which is based on centuries-old study of the properties of various herbs — or whether he was merely an astute charlatan with a superficial knowledge of medicine as practised in his country, it is difficult to say. His mode of life showed him to be a typical adventurer of the lowest grade, in search of money and prominence. He was on very good terms with the dregs of the political underworld in St. Petersburg, such as the notorious journalist and sharper, Manusevich Manuilov, and Prince M. M. Andronikov, whose shady intrigues and swindles were completely exposed after the revolution.

Badmaev strove by every means in his power to gain influence in political spheres, and as soon as Rasputin began to play a prominent *rôle* at Tsarskoe Selo, the Tibetan adventurer lost no time in making his acquaintance and forming the closest of friendships with him.

Rasputin's doctoring of the Emperor and Tsetsarevich with various herbs was, of course, performed with the aid of Badmaev, who was undoubtedly familiar with many remedies unknown to European science.

The sinister Tibetan and the still more sinister *starets* . . . it was indeed a formidable alliance.

These were my thoughts as I watched Rasputin's easy and confident postures; and I felt that nothing now could arrest my purpose.

In the meantime, his conversation — or, to be more exact, his monologue — continued.

His religious vapourings gave way to a theme more directly con-

* It is not the custom in Russia for medical practitioners to dispense for their patients.

cerned with himself. He began to enlarge on 'the unjust attitude of people who were ill-disposed towards him' — people who spent their whole time in slandering him, and in trying to blacken him in the eyes of the Emperor and Empress. He volunteered his conviction that he was a *porte-bonheur*, and that all who were on friendly terms with him were pleasing in the sight of God, whereas those who opposed him were always punished.

I had more than once heard him boast of possessing the gift of healing, and I had come to the conclusion that the easiest way of approaching him would be for me to ask him to treat me. I told him that for many years I had been in the hands of various doctors, but that none of them had given me permanent relief.

'I'll cure you,' said Rasputin, after he had listened with the greatest attention to the tale of my illnesses and the various cures that I had tried. 'I'll cure you . . . Doctors ? — They don't know anything. All they do is to stuff you with medicine — anything will do. . . . And you only get worse. But I know better than that, my dear. With me everybody gets well. I heal in God's way, and in God's name. There's no trash with me. You wait ! You'll see for yourself. . . . '

Just then the telephone-bell rang. Rasputin stopped talking. He was obviously excited.

'I expect that's for me,' he said — and then addressing M. as if she were his servant — 'Go and see,' he commanded.

M. got up and obeyed him. She did not seem to be in the least put out by his tone.

As a matter of fact, it really was a telephone message for Rasputin. It was only a short conversation, and he looked glum and ill at ease when he returned to us. . . . He took his leave in silence, and hurried away.

This second meeting with him left me in a rather doubtful frame of mind.

I decided that I would not seek an opportunity of meeting him again, for the time being; I would wait until he himself expressed a desire to see me.

On the evening of that same day I received a note from M., in which she begged me, on Rasputin's behalf, to forgive him for interrupting our conversation by his unexpected departure, and invited me to call on her on the following day at the same hour. She further asked me, at the request of the *starets*, to bring my guitar with me; he was very fond of gypsy songs, and having learnt that I sang, had expressed his desire to hear me.

I saw that I had interested him, and that he wanted to get into closer touch with me.

I no longer hesitated to go to the G.s', for I attached great importance to my next meeting with the *starets*.

I made my way there at the appointed hour, taking my guitar with me. As on the first occasion, I got there before Rasputin had arrived.

I took advantage of this to ask M. why he had left so suddenly the day before.

'He was told that an important matter had taken an undesirable turn,' she replied. 'But now, thank Heaven! everything is arranged. Grigori Efimovich got angry, and shouted at them; and they took fright and gave in to him.'

'Where did this happen?' I asked.

M. was silent. I saw she did not want to answer.

'At Tsarskoe,' she said at last, very reluctantly. 'I won't tell you anything more. You'll soon hear for yourself.'

Shortly afterwards I discovered that the matter which had so upset Rasputin was the appointment of Protopopov to be Minister of the Interior.

Rasputin's party wished at all costs to carry this appointment through; but the Emperor would not consent to it. Rasputin, however, had only to go to Tsarskoe, and — as M. had put it — 'to get angry and shout at them,' for everything to be done as he wished.

'Do you also take part in the appointment of Ministers?' I asked M.

She blushed, and said, with some embarrassment: 'We all help Grigori Efimovich as much as we can, whenever occasion arises. After all, it is difficult for him to manage alone; he has so much to do — he must have assistance.'

In the midst of these explanations Rasputin arrived. He was talkative and in excellent humour. 'Forgive me, my dear, for yesterday,' he said to me. 'These things can't be helped. . . . Bad people have to be punished, and so many of them have sprung up lately.' And turning to M. he continued: 'I've put everything straight. I had to go down there myself. The first person I ran into was Annushka.* All she could do was to whimper and whine. "It hasn't come off," says she. "You are the only hope, Grigori Efimovich. Thank God you've come!" '

'I went in. I saw that "she" ** was angry and sulky, while "he" *** was pacing the room. But after I'd shouted a bit they calmed down. As soon as I threatened to go straight off and have done with 'em, they gave in completely.

'Somebody had said to them, "This is all wrong, and that's all wrong." What do "they" understand about it all?'

'If they'd only pay more attention to me ! I know he's**** a good man and believes in God, and that's all that matters.'

Rasputin glanced at us all in his confident and self-satisfied way, and turned to M.

'Now let's have some tea! Why aren't you looking after us?'

We went into the dining-room. M. poured out tea for us, offering Rasputin every imaginable kind of sweetmeat and pastry.

'There's a dear, kind girl for you,' he said to me. 'She always thinks of me, and gets, what I like. . . . Have you brought your guitar?'

'Yes, I have it here.' 'Well, sing us something, and we'll sit and listen.'

It cost me a great effort to force myself to sing before him, but I took the guitar and sang a few gypsy songs.

'How well you sing!' he approved. 'You put your soul into it . . . lots of soul. Give us some more!'

So I sang a few more, some sad and some gay, and after each one Rasputin pressed me to go on.

At last I finished.

'Then you like my singing?' I said to him. 'But if you only knew how depressed I feel! I have plenty of energy. I long to work hard, yet I can't. I so soon get tired and ill.'

'I'll cure you in no time,' he answered. 'Just you come to the gypsies with me, and we'll soon have done with this illness of yours.'

'I've been,' I said, with a smile, 'but somehow it didn't seem to do any good.'

Rasputin laughed.

'Ah, but it's quite a different thing to go with me, my dear . . . it's

---

* *Madame Vyrubova* (on previous page)
** *The Empress*   *** *The Emperor*   **** M. Protopopov

much more amusing with me . . . everything's much better!' And he began to tell us, with full details, how he spent his time singing and dancing with the gypsies.

M. and her mother showed surprise and embarrassment at such candour from the 'holy' *starets*.

'Don't you believe him!' they said. 'He's just making fun of us; he's running himself down on purpose.'

This attempt to protect his reputation made him very angry. He banged on the table with his fist, and spoke to them so sharply that both mother and daughter at once became mute.

He turned to me again.

'Well, what about it? Coming with me? I'll cure you, I tell you ... you'll see for yourself. I'll cure you, and you'll feel grateful for it. ...' Yes, and we'll take her along with us too,' he said, pointing to the daughter.

M. blushed crimson. Her mother, in confusion, began to reproach him. 'Grigori Efimovich, what is the matter with you? Why do you slander yourself, and drag my daughter into it as well? What should she be doing there? She comes to you for prayer, and you want to take her to the gypsies! That's not the way to talk.'

'What!' said Rasputin, glaring angrily at her, 'you know quite well that anybody can go anywhere with me; there's no sin in that. What are you cackling about?'

'My dear,' he said, turning to me again, 'don't you listen to her. Do as I say, and everything will be all right.'

His proposal to visit the gypsies did not suit me at all; but I could not refuse outright, so I gave him an evasive answer, reminding him that I was in the *Corps des Pages*,* and could not, therefore, frequent such places.

But Rasputin insisted, assuring me that he could disguise me so that no one would recognise me, and that nobody would be any the wiser.

I still refused to pledge myself; but I promised to telephone to him later on in the evening.

There was no doubt that I had aroused his interest, for at our parting he patted me on the shoulder and said:

'I want to see more of you . . . much more of you. Come and have tea with me one day — only let me know beforehand. . . .'

*A military school in St. Petersburg.

CHAPTER VII

A VISIT TO THE STARETS

ON arriving home I found Captain Sukhotin eagerly awaiting my return from the G.s'.

My second meeting with Rasputin had encouraged me in the hope that my acquaintance with him would eventually become sufficiently close to enable us to carry out our design. But what it cost me to attain our object by such means!

My meetings with him left one with an overpowering feeling of contamination; all this worship of a coarse and insolent muzhik by his hysterical female admirers seemed so monstrous.

Incidentally, in my last conversation with him I had been unpleasantly surprised at Rasputin's suggestion to M. that she should join in his carousals. I could not shake off the depressing feeling that there might be no limit to the influence of this scoundrel, or to the subjection of those weak characters upon whom it was exercised: was he capable of sparing the purity and innocence of an unreasoning faith in him?

That evening I telephoned to the *starets* and him that I could not go with him to the gypsies, as on the following day I was down for an examination at the *Corps des Pages*.

Preparation for these examinations really did take up a great deal of my time, and I did not meet Rasputin again for a considerable period.

One day, as I was driving past the G s' house, I met M. She stopped me, and said:

'You ought to be ashamed of yourself. Grigori Efimovich has been waiting all this time for you to go and see him, and you have completely forgotten him! But if you look him up he will forgive you. I am going to visit him to-morrow. Shall we go together?'

I fell in with her suggestion.

On the following day, at the appointed hour, I drove over to call for M. I was still uneasy at the thought of her visiting the gypsies in company with Rasputin, and I wondered what she would answer if I asked her point-blank whether she would do so.

When we had settled ourselves in the car I said to her:

'What am I to understand by Grigori Efimovich's offer to take you with us to the gypsies at Novaya Derevnya?* What does he mean?'

M. became confused, and did not give me a direct answer. I felt that conversation on this subject was extremely unpleasant to her, and I refrained from pursuing it.

When we reached the Fontanka my companion asked me to stop the car, and to tell the chauffeur to wait for us round the corner. It was not possible, she explained, to visit Rasputin openly. He was guarded by the secret police, who kept a record of his visitors. M. knew how intensely my family disliked the *starets*, and spared no effort to keep my relations with him secret.

We arrived, on foot, at the front entrance to No. 64 Gorokhovaya Street, crossed the courtyard, and went up to Rasputin's flat by the back staircase.

On the way M. told me that the guard was stationed on the main staircase, and that it comprised men appointed by the Prime Minister himself, as well as by the Minister of the Interior and even by certain banks — she did not know exactly which.

She rang the bell.

Rasputin himself opened the door, which was carefully locked and chained.

We found ourselves in a small kitchen, crammed with baskets and boxes, and all sorts of stores and provisions.

A young girl was seated near the window. She was thin and pale, with a strange, wandering look in her big dark eyes.

Rasputin was dressed in a light-blue silk blouse embroidered with wild flowers, and in loose trousers tucked into his long boots. As soon as he caught sight of me he said:

'You've come at last! I was beginning to get angry with you. Here I've been waiting I don't know how many days, and never a sign of you.'

We left the kitchen and went into his bedroom. It was small and simply furnished. In one corner, along the wall, there was a narrow

* The Gypsies' settlement in St Petersburg.

bed; on it lay a cover of fox fur — a present from Vyrubova. Near by, there was a huge chest. In the opposite corner hung *ikons*, with lamps burning in front of them. Here and there on the walls were portraits of the Tsar and of the Tsaritsa, and gaudy coloured prints depicting scenes from the Holy Scriptures.

From the bedroom Rasputin took us into the dining-room, where tea was laid out.

The *samovar* was already boiling. On the table were glass dishes of jam and fruits, and quantities of plates filled with cakes, biscuits, sweets and nuts. In the middle stood a basket of flowers.

The furniture was of massive oak — high-backed chairs, and a cumbersome sideboard loaded with crockery. Paintings, badly executed in oils, adorned the walls; over the table hung a bronze chandelier with a large glass shade. There was a telephone near the door leading to the hall.

The whole contents of the flat, from the cumbersome sideboard to the crowded and abundantly stocked kitchen, bore the stamp of *bourgeois* wellbeing and prosperity. The lithographs and badly-painted pictures on the walls were fully in keeping with the owner's taste.

The dining-room obviously served as Rasputin's reception-room, in which he spent the greater part of his time when at home.

We sat down at the table, and Rasputin served us with tea.

Conversation hung fire at first. I felt that the *starets* was in a suspicious mood. Or perhaps he was put out by the continual ringing of the telephone bell, which constantly interrupted our conversation.

M. was very restless. She kept getting up from the table, moving away from it, and returning to her seat.

The telephone was not the only source of interruption. Rasputin was several times called away to an adjoining room serving as his study, where people awaited him with various requests. All these calls on his patience irritated him. He was nervous and ill-humoured.

During one of his temporary absences from the dining-room a huge basket of flowers, with a note pinned to it, was brought in.

'Are these really for Grigori Efimovich?' I asked M.

She nodded, by way of assent. At that moment Rasputin returned. He took no notice of the gift, but sat down next to me and poured out tea. 'Grigori Efimovich,' I said to him, 'people bring flowers to you just as if you were a *prima donna*!'

He laughed.

'Idiots. . . . They can't leave me alone. They bring fresh flowers every day; they know I love 'em'.

'Eh! you,' he said, turning to M., 'go into the other room; I'm going to have a chat with him.'

M. meekly got up and went out.

As soon as we were alone Rasputin moved closer to me and took my hand.

'Well, my dear,' he said, in a caressing tone, 'do you like my flat? Does it appeal to you? Well, mind you come more often. . . . You'll be all the better for it.'

He stroked my arm and steadily looked me in the eyes.

'Don't be afraid of me,' he said insinuatingly. 'When you know me better, you'll see what sort of a man I am. . . . I can do anything. . . . If the Tsar and Tsaritsa obey me, surely you can . . . I shall be seeing them soon, and I'll tell them that you've been to tea with me here. . . . It'll please 'em.'

This idea did not appeal to me in the least. I knew that the Empress would immediately tell Vyrubova — who would at once look upon my 'friendship' with the *starets* with extreme suspicion, for she had on several occasions heard me refer to him in the most candid and disapproving terms.

'No, Grigori Efimovich,' I said, 'don't say anything about me at Tsarskoe Selo. The less people know about my being here the better. Otherwise there will be gossip. It might get to the ears of my family, and I can't bear any sort of domestic scene or unpleasantness.'

Rasputin agreed, and promised to say nothing. Our conversation then turned on politics. He began to criticise the Duma.

'They're always speaking ill of me there, and the Emperor gets upset. . . . Well, anyway, their babblings won't last much longer. I'll dissolve the Duma soon, and send all the deputies to the front. . . . I'll show 'em! . . . Perhaps they'll remember me then.'

'Grigori Efimovich, can you really dissolve the Duma? How?'

'Oh! That's a simple matter, my dear. Just you get to know me better, and help me, and then you'll learn all about it. . . . But I'll tell you this here and now. The Empress is a very wise ruler. . . . With her I can do anything, I can get whatever I like. But as for him — well, he's a child of God. There's an Emperor for you! Why, he ought just to play with children and flowers, and get busy in a vegetable garden — not rule the country; that's a bit difficult for him, and so we help him, with God's blessing.'

It made me writhe to hear the supercilious disdain with which this conceited muzhik-horse-thief spoke of the Emperor of Russia. But I controlled myself, and very quietly suggested to Rasputin that perhaps he himself was sometimes deceived by those who surrounded him; he could not always, perhaps, be sure whether they were giving him good or bad advice in their attempts to attain their ends through his influence at Tsarskoe Selo.

'How can you know, Grigori Efimovich, what these various people are trying to get out of you, and what objects they have in view? They might be just using you as a pawn for their own foul purposes.'

Rasputin smiled indulgently. 'D'you want to teach God what to do? It wasn't for nothing that He sent me to help His anointed. . . . I tell you they'd be completely lost without me. I don't beat about the bush with them. If they don't do what I tell them I just bang the table with my fist and get up and go; and then they chase after me and start begging: "Don't go away, Grigori Efimovich; we'll obey you in everything if you will only stay with us. . . ." So there you are, my dear; you see how they love and respect me.

"The other day,' he continued, 'I told them that a certain man must be given a post, but they kept putting it off. So at last I threatened to leave 'em. "Very well," says I, "I'll go off to Siberia; and then you'll all rot away, and you'll be causing the death of your boy. If you turn your back on God you'll face the Devil." That's how it's done, my dear. Yet there are all sorts of puppets swarming around Tsarskoe Selo, whispering to them that Grigori Efimovich is a bad man who wishes them evil. . . . Why should I? They are good and God-fearing people.'

'But, Grigori Efimovich, it is not enough that the Emperor and Empress love you,' I said. 'You surely know what evil things people say of you? And their stories are believed not only in Russia, but abroad also. They write about you in the newspapers there. . . . And if you really do love the Emperor and Empress, then I think you ought to leave them and go back to your home in Siberia for good. .

. . Otherwise, you may some day meet with sudden violence; and what will happen then?'

'No, my dear, you know nothing about it, or you wouldn't be talking like that,' answered Rasputin. 'The Lord wouldn't allow that to happen. If it was His will to bring us together, it means that it was necessary. And as to what these puppets say, or what they write in foreign newspapers, I spit on 'em. Let 'em talk. They'll only ruin themselves.'

Rasputin got up and began to pace up and down the room with nervous steps.

I watched him closely. He was morose and preoccupied.

Suddenly he wheeled round and came up to me. He bent over me, and with his face close to mine, stared me fixedly in the eyes.

I was harrowed by his gaze. There seemed to be an immense power behind it.

Without taking his eyes off mine, he stroked my back, and with a crafty smile asked me, in a soft and insinuating voice, whether I would like some wine. I assented. He produced a bottle of madeira and, pouring out a glass for himself and one for me, drank my health.

'When will you come here again?' he asked.

But at that moment M. came in, and reminded him that it was time for him to go to Tsarskoe Selo, and that the car was waiting.

'Here I've been chatting away, forgetting that they were waiting for me. Well, never mind; it isn't the first time. Sometimes they telephone and telephone, and send for me; but I don't go straight away. . . . I just arrive unexpectedly, and you should see how glad they are. They appreciate me all the more.'

He turned to me and said: 'Well, good-bye, my dear.' Then glancing at M., he said, pointing to me, 'He's got brains. He'll go a long way, if his mind doesn't get warped. . . . If he'll only listen to me . . . all will be well. Isn't that the truth? . . . Well, you just explain things to him, so that he thoroughly understands. Goodbye, goodbye I Come again soon. . . .' And he embraced me.

After his departure, M. and I left by the same back way by which we had entered. Coming out on the Gorokhovaya, we proceeded towards the Fontanka, where the car was awaiting us.

On the way home, M. again confided to me her feelings for Rasputin. 'Isn't it nice at Grigori Efimovich's? Don't you find that in his presence you forget everything worldly?' she said. 'He seems to bring such wonderful calm to your soul.'

I was forced to agree with her; but I added:

'I think, you know, that Grigori Efimovich ought to leave St. Petersburg as soon as possible.'

'Why?' she asked.

'Because otherwise it will end by his being killed I am quite convinced of this, and I advise you to do everything in your power to influence him in that direction. It is essential that he should go away.'

'No! No!' she exclaimed, terror-stricken. 'That can never happen. . . . God will not take him from us! Don't you realise that he is our only consolation and support? If he were no longer with us, everything would be lost. The Empress believes that as long as Grigori Efimovich is there, no harm can come to the Tsetsarevich; but that as soon as he goes away, her son will inevitably fall ill. This has already happened, on more than one occasion; and Grigori Efimovich has had to come back. And the strange thing is, that as soon as he did come back, the boy began to get better.

'Grigori Efimovich himself says: "If I am killed, the Tsetsarevich will not live: he is sure to die."

'There have already been a number of attempts on Grigori Efimovich's life, you know, and God has preserved him,' she continued. 'And now he is so careful and is so well guarded that we need not feel anxious about him.'

At that moment we arrived at the G.s* house.

'When shall I see you again?' asked M.

I suggested that she should ring me up after her next meeting with Rasputin, for I was most anxious to hear what impression my last conversation had made on him.

I thought over all that I had just heard, both from Rasputin himself and from M., and considered it side by side with our intention of removing the *starets* from the Tsar's family by peaceful means.

It had now become clear to me that there was no possible way of persuading him to leave St. Petersburg, never to return. He was too firmly established; he valued his position too highly. The strong guard which followed him everywhere gave him unwavering confidence in his absolute security. Money, with which he might otherwise have been tempted, was hardly likely to induce him to forego all those unlimited privileges which he enjoyed.

'Rasputin,' I thought, 'has plenty of means of obtaining all the money he wants for his carousing and drinking. Besides, it is quite possible that he has means of getting more wealth than we could offer him. . . . If he really is a German agent, or something of that kind, Germany will not grudge him gold for her own advantages, for her own victory.'

I was forced to the conclusion that it would be necessary to resort to extreme measures in order to deliver Russia from this evil genius.

* * *

CHAPTER VIII

A HYPNOTIC SÉANCE

MY work at the *Corps des Pages* left me few leisure hours. I would return home very tired; but there was no time for rest — I had to confront the task which we had set ourselves, and to take all the steps necessary for carrying it out.

The thought of Rasputin preyed on me like a disease. I could not dismiss him from my mind. I was impelled to consider from every point of view the decision we had taken, and to try to fathom the personality of the *starets* and his mysterious and forbidding influence.

I seemed to see a monstrous plot against Russia, and in the midst of it stood Rasputin, who, by the will of inexorable fate, had become a dangerous weapon in the hands of our enemies.

'Does he fully realise the meaning of it all?' I asked myself.

'No, of course not. He is incapable of understanding how complicated is the web in which he is entangled. He cannot realise the subtle and diabolical ingenuity of those who are directing his actions.'

An ignorant muzhik, hardly able to read and write — there was much that he could not analyse or understand. His head had been turned by his unexpected success, and he had become more avaricious, more cynical, more unprincipled than ever.

His boundless influence in high places, the fawning adoration of hysterical women, his continual orgies, and a life of degenerate and unaccustomed ease, had extinguished in him the last sparks of conscience and deadened all fear of consequences. Cunning and extremely observant, he undoubtedly possessed great hypnotic power. On watching him closely, the least superstitious person would feel that there was something satanic in his powers.

More than once, when I have looked him in the eyes, I have felt that apart from all his vices he was possessed by some sort of demon, and that he often acted unconsciously, as if in a trance.

This frenzy invested certain of his words and actions with a peculiar authority; so that persons lacking in strength of mind and of will fell readily under his power. His position as the most trusted friend and counsellor of the Tsar's family increased his hypnotic influence, particularly over those who were inclined to be impressed by the halo of power which thus surrounded him.

But who were these unseen people who guided his actions, and who were able to exploit him so well for their own ends?

Their real aims and identity were probably all but unknown to him. He was generally very vague about people's identity, and he had the habit of giving everybody nicknames. Whenever he spoke of these mysterious persons he referred to them as 'zeleni'.* He had probably never even seen them, but communicated with them at third or even fourth hand.

He had once casually remarked to me: 'The "zeleni" live in Sweden; when you go there you shall meet them.'

'Are there any "zeleni" in Russia?' I had asked.

'No, only "zelenenkie" — their friends and ours — and all of 'em clever people,' he had replied.

Such were my reflections on this mystery — which was probably much more complicated than he himself realised — while I was awaiting the promised telephone call from M.

She rang me up at last, and told me that Rasputin wanted me to go with him to the gypsies.

I had succeeded in resisting his first invitation, and I hoped to be able to evade it again this time.

I proffered the same excuse — my examinations at the *Corps des Pages* - and added that if Grigori Efimovich wanted to see me I would go and take tea with him. We accordingly arranged that on the following day I should call for M. as before, and that we should go to Rasputin's flat together.

My second visit to the *starets* proved still more interesting than the first.

We were alone together almost the whole time.

He was particularly well-disposed towards me and I reminded

---

* 'Zeleni' is the Russian for 'green.' 'Zelenenki' is the diminutive form of the same word.

him of his promise to give me advice on the score of my health.

'I'll cure you in a few days. You just wait and see. Come into my study; nobody will interfere with us there. Let's have some tea first, and then with God's help we'll begin. I'll pray, and drive your illness out of you. You just listen to what I say, my dear, and all will be well.'

After tea he took me to his study. It was the first time I had seen it. It was a small room furnished with a couch and armchairs upholstered in leather, and an enormous writing-table littered with papers.

The *starets* told me to lie down on the couch. He stood in front of me, looked me intently in the eyes and began to stroke my chest, neck and head. He then suddenly knelt down and – so it seemed to me – began to pray, placing his hands on my forehead. He bent his head so low that I could no longer see his face.

He remained in this position for a considerable time. Then he suddenly jumped to his feet and began to make passes. He was evidently familiar with certain of the processes employed by hypnotists.

His hypnotic power was immense. I felt it subduing me and diffusing warmth throughout the whole of my being. I grew numb; my body seemed paralysed. I tried to speak, but my tongue would not obey me, and I seemed to be falling asleep, as if under the influence of a strong narcotic. Yet Rasputin's eyes shone before me with a kind of phosphorescent light. From them came two rays which flowed into each other and merged into one glowing circle. This circle now moved away from me, now came nearer and nearer. When it approached me it seemed as if I began to distinguish his eyes; but at that very moment they would again vanish into the circle, which then moved further and further away.

I was conscious that the *starets* was speaking but I could not make out his words; I could only hear a vague murmur.

Such was my condition as I lay motionless, unable to call out or stir. Yet my mind was still free, and I realised that I was gradually falling into the power of this mysterious and sinister man.

But soon I felt that my own inner force was awakening and was of its own accord resisting the hypnosis.

This force grew stronger within me, enveloping my whole being in an invisible armour. Into my consciousness floated a vague idea that an intense struggle was taking place between Rasputin and myself, and that my own personality in battling with his made it impossible for him to dominate me completely.

I tried to move my hand; and it obeyed me. But I did not alter my position; I waited until Rasputin himself should tell me to do so.

By now I could clearly distinguish his figure, face and eyes. That terrible circle had completely disappeared. . . .

'Well, my dear, that'll be enough for the first time,' he said.

He kept a close watch on me, but evidently he was able to note only one aspect of my sensations; my resistance to the hypnosis had escaped him.

There was a self-satisfied smile on his face, and he spoke to me in the assured tone of a person conscious of his entire mastery over another. He was obviously convinced that I had been completely subjugated by him, and that he could henceforth count me among his submissive followers.

With a brusque movement he pulled my arm. I sat up, feeling dizzy and weak. With an effort, I rose from the couch and took a few steps about the room; but my legs seemed half-paralysed, and would not fully obey me.

Rasputin continued to observe every movement I made. 'This is God's grace,' he said. 'Now you'll see how soon it will heal you, and drive all your illness away.'

We parted, and he made me promise to visit him again very soon. After this hypnotic *séance* I repeatedly went to him, sometimes with M., sometimes alone. The 'treatment' continued, and his confidence in me grew day by day.

Sometimes we had long conversations together. He looked upon me as his friend; he was firmly convinced of my belief in his divine mission, and counted on my unreserved co-operation and support. Hence he did not consider it necessary to weigh his words, and one by one he showed me all his cards. He had such faith in the strength of his influence that the idea did not even occur to him that I was not completely in his power.

'You're a clever chap,' he said to me once. 'It's easy to talk to you; you take everything in at once. Say the word, and I'll make you a minister.'

A suggestion of this kind from Rasputin greatly disconcerted me. I realised how easy it was for him to obtain anything, and I also knew what a scandal might ensue.

'I'll willingly help you; but don't make me a minister,' I answered with a smile.

'What are you laughing at?' he asked. 'D'you think I can't do it? — I can. I can do anything — anything I want, and everybody obeys me. Just you wait! You'll be a minister.'

His persistent and serious tone really perturbed me. I already saw the universal astonishment which would be caused by the announcement in the press.

'Grigori Efimovich, for Heaven's sake, don't!' I begged. 'Think! How could I possibly be a minister? And anyway, why should I want to be one? . . . It would be ever so much better if I could help without anyone knowing about it.'

'All right! Have it your own way,' he finally agreed. 'But it doesn't often happen that people talk like that. They're always at me. It's "Arrange this" and "Arrange that"; they all want something or other.'

'But how do you manage to satisfy them all?' I asked.

'I send 'em to one or other of the ministers, or else I give 'em a note to somebody who's in a position to fix things up. And sometimes I send 'em straight to Tsarskoe Selo. . . . That's how it's worked!'

'And do all the ministers do as you tell them?'

'Every one of 'em,' exclaimed Rasputin. 'Every one! . . . How shouldn't they, when they owe their appointments to me? They know perfectly well that if they cross my path it'll be all the worse for them. Why, the Prime Minister himself daren't stand in my way. It was only the other day that he offered me fifty thousand roubles through a friend of his, if I'd replace Protopopov. . . . He's afraid to come to me himself, bless him! So he sends his friends instead! . . . And what about Khvostov?* There's a scoundrel for you! Always running after me, he was; and as soon as I'd appointed him he got uppish and turned against me. I got him dismissed, of course, just as

---

* In 1914, thanks to Rasputin's intrigues, M. A. A. Khvostov, who was then Governor-General of Nizhni-Novgorod, was made Minister of the Interior. He subsequently became convinced of the evil influence exercised by the *starets*, and resolved to poison him. Kurlov, Chief of the Police, whom he regarded as his associate in this project, supplied him with a harmless drug, and afterwards denounced him. Khvostov was forced to resign his portfolio; and, but for his influential position, proceedings would have been taken against him.

he deserved. And now he realises his mistake, and he's sorry for it. . . . And so,' added Rasputin, after a short pause, 'you can judge for yourself. The Empress herself is a friend of mine. . . . How can they do anything else but obey me?

'They're all afraid of me, everyone of 'em. . . . I've only got to bang my fist down, and there's no more fuss.' And he glanced at his horny hand, not without some degree of pride.

'That's the only way to deal with your aristocrats' — he had a special way of pronouncing this word — 'They can't get over me stalking about the palace in my greasy boots. Their trouble is that they're so proud. And it's pride that's the beginning of all our sins. If you want to be pleasing in the sight of God, first of all kill your pride.

'Mark my words, my dear,' he continued with a queer smile, 'the women are worse than the men; you've got to begin with them. Yes. . . . I take them to the baths — it doesn't matter who they are — and when I've got 'em there: "Now take off your clothes," I say, "and wash the muzluk." And if they start putting on airs or making a fuss, I soon stop all that nonsense. . . .'

I listened to him with horror; but I kept silent, fearing that any questions or comments might interrupt his monstrous story — the rest of which is quite unprintable. He was obviously rather drunk, and was enjoying his disclosures.

He poured himself out another glass of madeira and added, with a cough:

'But what about you? Why are you drinking so little? Surely you're not afraid of wine? Why, it's the best medicine in the world. It cures every disease, and it isn't made up by the chemist either. It's God's own remedy — and it strengthens you, body and soul. God has given me such strength, that there's no limit to it. Do you know Badmaev? I'll introduce you to him. He's got every remedy you could wish for. He's a real doctor, he is. Botkin and Derevenkie* are no good at all. They just write down some rubbish or other on bits of paper, and they think the patient's getting well — while all the while he's getting worse and worse. Badmaev's medicines are nature's own. They come from the forests and mountains, and they're planted by God Himself — and God's blessing is in them.'

'Grigori Efimovich,' I interrupted: 'And the Emperor and Tsetsarevich, why aren't they treated with these medicines?'

* Physicians-in-ordinary to the Imperial Family.

'What do you mean, "not treated" with 'em? Of course they are. She* and Annushka** see to that. They're all afraid that Botkin will find out — but I tell them: "If one of your doctors finds out about my medicines, the patient won't get better, but very much worse. So they're on their guard; and they do everything on the sly.'

'What sort of medicines do you give the Emperor and Tsetsarevich?'

'Different kinds, different kinds. They give "him" tea to drink; and from this tea the blessing of God comes down on him and gives peace to his soul — and everything is well with him, and he's happy.

'And after all,' continued Rasputin, 'he's no Tsar-Emperor. He's just a child of God. You just wait and see; things'll be arranged quite differently.'

'What are you talking about, Grigori Efimovich? What will be different?'

'Oh, you're far too inquisitive. You want to know everything, don't you? You just wait. You'll learn everything in time.'

I had never known Rasputin so communicative. The wine had obviously loosened his tongue. I was loth to miss the opportunity of extracting from this criminal *starets* as many details as possible of his diabolical plan. I encouraged him to drink. For a long time we replenished our glasses in silence, Rasputin tossing off the contents of his at a gulp, while I just lifted mine to my lips and replaced it behind a dish of fruit which stood between us.

When one bottle of strong madeira had been emptied, he rose and stumbled across to the sideboard for another. Again I filled his glass, and pretended to fill my own.

Then I cautiously resumed our conversation at the point where it had broken off.

'Grigori Efimovich, do you remember telling me a little while ago that you wanted me to help you? I am ready to do so; but if I am to be of any use, you must explain what you have in mind.

Just now, for instance, you were saying that "everything will be different"; but I don't know why, or in what way.'

Rasputin looked at me intently, with his eyes half-closed, and thought for a moment.

'This is what will happen,' he said. 'There's been enough fighting,

* The Empress
** Madame Vyrubova.

enough bloodshed; it's time all this mess was cleared up. What! Aren't the Germans our brethren? Our Lord said: "Love thy enemy as thy brother." But what sort of love is this? He* won't budge an inch, and even she's** obstinate. Here again somebody's giving 'em bad advice, and they're listening to it. But what's the use of talking about that! Once I order them to do a thing, and show 'em that I mean it, they'll do it right enough. But we're not quite ready yet.

'When it's all settled, we'll hail Alexandra as Regent for her young son and we'll send "him" to Livadia for a rest. . . . There! Wont that be a treat for him? to be a market-gardener! He's worn out – he must have a rest. . . . Yes, and mark you, down there in Livadia, among the flowers, he'll be nearer to God; and he's got plenty to pray about – the war, for one thing, and all it has cost. A whole life of prayer won't be enough to wipe out that.

'If it wasn't for that confounded woman*** who stuck a knife into me, I should have been on the spot and would never have let it come to bloodshed. . . . But without me here your cursed Sazonovs and the rest of 'em succeeded in fixing up the whole business. And look at the harm they've done.

'Now the Empress herself – she's a wise ruler, a second Catherine. Why, she's been governing alone for some time past. You just watch; it'll be better later on.

'She has promised to get rid of all the chatterboxes first of all. To the devil with the lot of them! Think of it! They've dared to go against the Lord's Anointed. But we'll knock 'em on the head all right. It's

---

* The Emperor

** The Empress

*** A peasant girl named Guseva. Several unsuccessful attempts had been made on the life of Rasputin. In 1914 Guseva – who had lived with him for some years, but had finally forsaken him for his enemy, the monk Heliodor – stabbed him in the abdomen. The wound was so serious that he lay at the point of death for many weeks, and, but for his marvellous physique, he would probably not have recovered. When charged with the crime, Guseva declared that he was nothing more than a seducer of women. She was sent to a lunatic asylum. For these and other interesting details concerning the private life and baneful influence of the *starets*, the reader is referred to Dr. E. J. Dillon's book. *The Eclipse of Russia* (Messrs J. M. Dent & Sons, Ltd, 1918,) and to Sir Paul Vinogradov's admirable article on Rasputin in the Encyclopaedia Britannica, vol xxxii, p 249, 1922 Edition (Translator's note)

right. It's high time they were sent to the devil's mother. . . . Every single one of 'em who shouts out against me will only be the worse off for it in the end.'

Rasputin grew more and more heated. Excited by wine and by his plans, it did not seem to occur to him to hide anything from me. 'I'm just like a baited animal; everybody wants to get his teeth into me. I stick in the throat of all your aristocrats. With the people it's different. They respect me, because I'm a peasant — in a peasant's coat and boots — and I've raised myself to be the adviser of the Tsar himself, and of the Tsaritsa too. It's the will of God. The Lord gave me power to read the innermost thoughts of men.

'Only a short time ago General Russki sent some people to see me. I didn't beat about the bush with 'em. "What have you come for?" I said. . . . Well, well — I promised to arrange it. He's a good man.

'They're all at me to liberate the Jews. And why, thinks I, shouldn't I? They're no different from us. . . . We're all God's creatures.

'So, you see,' he continued, 'how much work there is. And there's nobody to help me. I've got to do everything myself . . . and you can't be everywhere at once. You've got brains, and you'll help me. I'll introduce you to the right people, and you'll be able to make quite a little pile. . . . But I don't suppose you need money. I expect you're richer than the Emperor himself. All the same, you can give it to the poor — everybody's glad to get an odd penny. . . .'

Rasputin's discourse was interrupted by a sudden ring of the bell. He began to fidget. He was evidently expecting some visitor or other, but he had been carried away by our conversation and had forgotten the appointment. He had remembered it now, and he seemed very nervous and anxious that the newcomers should not find me with him.

He jumped up from the table and led me to his study, and hurriedly left the room. I heard his quick, uncertain steps as he passed through the hall. He bumped into something and knocked it over, with a loud curse. He could hardly keep on his legs, but his head was still clear. I marvelled at the strength of the man.

The voices of the newcomers reached me from the hall. There seemed to be several of them. They went into the dining-room. I went to the study doors, which opened into the hall, and listened;

but the conversation was carried on in low tones and was very difficult to follow. I cautiously pushed the two halves of the door apart, and in the chink thereby formed I could see right across the hall into the dining-room, of which the doors had been left open. Rasputin was sitting at the table, just where he had been while talking to me.

There were five men sitting quite close to him, while two others were standing behind his chair. Some of them were writing rapidly in their notebooks.

I carefully examined these mysterious visitors. They were all unpleasant to look upon. Four of them were typically and unmistakably Jewish in appearance. The remaining three were singularly alike; they were fair-haired, with red faces and small eyes. One of them I seemed to have seen somewhere or other, but I could not remember where. Some of them were sitting in their overcoats.

In their presence Rasputin had completely changed. Sitting in a careless, sprawling attitude, he was holding forth to them, with an air of importance.

The whole group looked like some meeting of conspirators. They wrote, conferred in whispers, and read out from various papers.

The thought flashed through me: 'Can these be the "zelenenkie" of whom Rasputin had spoken?'

Remembering all that I had heard from him I had no doubt that before me was an assembly of spies. In this very ordinary room, with the *ikon* of the Saviour in the corner, and the Imperial portraits on the wall, the fate of millions of Russians was apparently being decided.

I felt a desire to leave this sinister flat as quickly as possible, but Rasputin's study had only the one exit, and to go out of the room unnoticed was impossible. After what seemed to be an eternity Rasputin at last returned to me with a pleased, self-satisfied look on his face. I hurriedly took my leave of him, and departed.

CHAPTER IX

HOW WE DECIDED TO ACT

MY meetings with Rasputin, and all that I had seen and heard, had firmly convinced me that he was at the root of all the evil, and the primary cause of all the misfortunes which had befallen Russia.

Rasputin's death would put an end to that diabolical power which held the Emperor and Empress in its toils.

It seemed as if fate had led me to this man, that I might see with my own eyes the part he played, and the goal towards which his unbounded influence was urging us all.

What, then, was the use of waiting?

Was it possible to spare Rasputin, who was driving Russia and the dynasty to their doom, and by his treachery was swelling the list of casualties in the war?

Was there even one honest man who did not sincerely wish for his death?

There was no shadow of doubt; everyone desired the death of the criminal *starets*, and the sooner the better.

And so the question was no longer: 'Should Rasputin be killed?' but: 'Could *I* undertake this responsibility?'

It was necessary to take decisive measures. This abominable play of 'friendship' could not be kept up any longer.

Our original plan of shooting him in his own flat now seemed impracticable, in view of the extreme tension throughout the country. The war was at its height, the army was preparing an offensive, and the open assassination of Rasputin might be interpreted as a demonstration against the Tsar and his family.

It was not a propitious moment for open measures. It seemed to me necessary that Rasputin should vanish in such a way that no one should know how or whither he had gone;, and it was most important that those responsible for his disappearance should remain unknown.

I felt that Purishkevich and Maklakov, who fully realised the evil influence of Rasputin, would be able to give me good advice. Their public denunciations of him in the Duma were still fresh in my memory.

Men who had exposed Rasputin with such vehemence could not fail to share my views and to approve my intentions. I believed that they would help me.

I approached Maklakov first. I made an appointment with him, and went to his flat. Our conversation was very brief. I explained my plan to him in very few words, and asked him his opinion.

Maklakov avoided giving me a clear answer. His hesitation and mistrust could be felt in the question which he put to me:

'And why have you come to me, in particular?'

'I heard your speech in the Duma,' I replied. It was clear that he inwardly approved of my plan; and I was at a loss to understand the reason for his evasive attitude. Was it due to lack of confidence in me as a man whom he knew only by name, or was it simply his fear of being involved in a dangerous enterprise? Whatever might be the explanation, a short talk with him sufficed to convince me that his assistance was not worth counting on. I realised that he was too cautious to venture on decisive action. However bitterly he might feel against Rasputin, his apprehensiveness would always gain the upper hand.

On my return home I telephoned to Purishkevich, and arranged to go and see him on the following morning.

My interview with Purishkevich was of a very different kind. I had hardly begun to speak of Rasputin and of my intention to do away with him, when he exclaimed, with characteristic vivacity and fervour:

'Why, that has long been a dream of my own, I am ready with all my heart to help you if you want me; but it isn't as easy as you think. You can't get at Rasputin without slipping through a whole crowd of officials and spies who surround him.'

'All that has already been arranged,' I answered. I explained to him how I had got into touch with the *starets*, and told him of our conversations.

Purishkevich listened with great interest. I mentioned the Grand Duke Dmitri Pavlovich and Captain Sukhotin, and told him of my conversation with Maldakov.

Purishkevich fully shared my opinion that Rasputin must be put away secretly.

While fully realising the difficulties of carrying out our plan, he did not for a moment doubt its necessity or its immense political significance. He was firmly convinced that the root of the evil lay in Rasputin, and that only by his removal could the country be saved from inevitable collapse.

Purishkevich was not in the least surprised at Maklakov's excessive caution. He said he would take an early opportunity of talking things over with him, and that he would try to win him to our side.

Having assured myself of Purishkevich's co-operation, I took my leave. We arranged that on the following evening he should visit me at the Moika, to work out a general plan of action.

By 5 p.m. next day the Grand Duke Dmitri Pavlovich, Purishkevich and Captain Sukhotin had duly assembled at my house.

After lengthy discussion we came to the following conclusion:

Rasputin must be done away with by means of poison, this being the method which would leave fewest traces of his assassination.

My friends fully agreed that his destruction should bear the character of a sudden disappearance, and that it should be kept a close secret.

Our house on the Moika was chosen as the place where our project was to be carried out. A suite of rooms there was being adapted for my own use, and would serve our purpose better than anything else. My associations with Rasputin would afford me an opportunity of persuading him to come and visit me.

This decision caused me much heart-searching. The prospect of inviting a man to my house with the intention of killing him horrified me.

Whoever the man might be — even Rasputin, the incarnation of crime and vice - I could not contemplate without a shudder the part which I should be called upon to play — that of a host encompassing the death of his guest.

My friends fully understood my feelings. After much discussion, however, we arrived at the conclusion that where the destiny of all Russia was concerned, all considerations or feelings of a personal nature should be set aside.

Our decisions were final; but one or two complications arose. The house alterations to which I have referred could not be completed before the middle of December. Both the Grand Duke Dmitri Pavlovich and Purishkevich were due to leave for the front before then, although they would be returning to St. Petersburg by the time the rooms were ready. In this respect everything fitted in quite well, but for over two months I had to face the repugnant task of keeping up my relations with Rasputin.

It had been difficult enough hitherto to associate with a man whose destruction I considered essential, but the prospect of continuing to associate with him now that we had passed definite sentence upon him was still more painful.

Purishkevich proposed a fifth accomplice – a Dr. Lazovert, who served in his detachment. We agreed.

Our second meeting took place in the Red Cross train commanded by Purishkevich. Here we discussed and arranged all the details of our joint action, and definitely adopted the following plan:

I was to continue to visit Rasputin, losing no opportunity of strengthening his confidence in me; and some day I was to invite him to my house, in such conditions that his visit could be kept an absolute secret.

On the day that Rasputin should choose to come to me, I was to call for him towards midnight, and drive him to the Moika in an open car, with Dr. Lazovert as chauffeur.

While Rasputin was drinking tea, I was to administer a solution of cyanide of potassium, which would cause his immediate death. His body was to be put into a sack, driven out of town and thrown into the water. A closed car would be required for this purpose, and the Grand Duke Dmitri Pavlovich suggested that we should make use of his. This was particularly expedient, for the Grand Duke's flag, attached to the bonnet of the car, would safeguard us from every suspicion and delay.

While Rasputin was in my house I was to be alone with him. The others should be waiting in an adjoining room, so that they could come to my help in case of necessity.

Whatever might be the outcome of our project, we agreed to deny, at all costs, our complicity in the murder of Rasputin or in an attempt on his life.

The place where Rasputin's body was finally to be disposed of was to be selected after the return of the Grand Duke Dmitri Pavlovich and Purishkevich to St. Petersburg.

They both left for the front a few days afterwards. Captain Sukhotin and I met almost daily after their departure. Before he left St. Petersburg, Purishkevich had asked me to do my utmost to obtain Maklakov's close co-operation in our plans; and I accordingly went to see him again.

I was agreeably surprised at finding a change in his attitude. Instead of giving me evasive answers, he expressed his full approval of everything we had planned. But when I suggested that he should join us, he replied that towards the middle of December he would probably have to go to Moscow for a few days on very urgent business. I interpreted this to mean that while expressing his full sympathy with us in words, he wished to avoid all action which might implicate him in our plot. All the same, I gave him a detailed description of our plans. He listened with the greatest attention, agreeing with all our arguments, and concurring in our proposed line of action . . . but he showed no desire to render any active assistance.

He said good-bye to me with great kindness, and wished us complete success. Incidentally he made me a present of a loaded stick.

'Take this,' he said, with a smile, 'in case you might ever want it.'

* * *

DMITRI PAVLOVICH - VLADIMIR PURISHKEVICH - SERGEI SUKHOTIN

FELIX YUSSOUPOFF

CHAPTER X

RASPUTIN ACCEPTS MY INVITATION

IN the meantime I was completing my course at the *Corps des Pages*, and Colonel Fogel continued to coach me.

I went to see Rasputin now and then, in order to keep up relations with him. The repulsion with which he inspired me increased with the necessity of visiting him and talking to him.

One of these visits took place a few days before the return of the Grand Duke Dmitri Pavlovich and Purishkevich to St. Petersburg.

Rasputin was in very good humour.

'Why are you in such good spirits?' I asked him.

'Well, I've brought off a very nice little deal. We shan't have to wait long now. Our turn's coming.'

'What's it all about?' I asked.

'What's it all about? What's it all about?' he repeated, trying to mimic me. 'You're afraid of me, and you've stopped coming to see me. I've got lots of interesting things to tell you. . . . But I won't, just because you're afraid of me. You're afraid of everything. If you weren't, I'd tell you.'

I explained to him that I had been preparing for my examinations at the *Corps des Pages*, and that the sole reason why I had not been to see him was that I had not had a moment to spare.

He merely repeated: 'I know, I know. You're afraid of me. Your parents won't let you come. Your mother's hand-in-glove with "Lizbeth"* They both of 'em think of nothing else but how to get me away. But they won't manage that. No attention'll be paid to 'em. They like me at Tsarskoe. And the more I'm spoken against, the more they love me; so that's that!'

'But, Grigori Efimovich,' I said, 'you behave quite differently at Tsarskoe Selo. While you're there you only talk about God; and that's why they have faith in you.'

* The Grand Duchess Elizabeth Feodorovna.

'And why shouldn't I speak to them of God, my dear? They're God-fearing people, and they like such, talk. They understand and forgive everything, and they appreciate me. . . . And as to people saying bad things about me — it's all waste of breath; they won't be believed. I've often said to 'em, "People will revile me, but remember how Christ was persecuted. He also suffered for truth's sake." And so they hear what everybody's got to say; but they act for themselves, as their conscience bids them.

With him*, though, it's sometimes difficult. As soon as he gets any distance away from home he begins to listen to evil-minded people. I've had a worrying time with him just lately.

' "We've had enough bloodshed," I tell him. "Russians, Germans, Frenchmen — we're all brethren. And this war is God's punishment for our sins." But that's as far as we get. He's obstinate. All he does is to repeat his "It would be shameful to sign peace!"

'And where's the shame, if you're saving your brethren? Millions of people will be killed, I tell you. . . .

'Now "she" is a good and wise ruler. . . . As for "him" — what does he understand? It's not his line. He's a child of God: that's what he is.

'The one thing I'm afraid of,' continued Rasputin, 'is that Nikolai Nikolaivich may stop it all if he finds out! All he wants is to go on fighting, sending people to their death, to no purpose. But he's a long way off now, and his arms are short — he can't reach us. That's why he was sent all that way — so that he shouldn't meddle and get into difficulties.'

'But I think it was a great mistake,' I said, 'to remove the Grand Duke Nikolai Nikolaivich. All Russia worshipped him.'

'That's just why he was sent off. He got too uppish and aimed too high! The Empress at once realised which way the wind was blowing.'

'That's not true, Grigori Efimovich; the Grand Duke Nikolai Nikolaivich is not at all that kind of man. He had no ulterior motives; he was just doing his duty towards Russia and the Tsar. Since he went away everything has gone from bad to worse. It was a mistake to deprive the army of their beloved leader at such a critical time.'

'Now, don't you be too clever. If it was done, it means it had to be done, and that it was the right thing to do.'

* The emperor

Rasputin rose to his feet and began to pace thoughtfully up and down the room, muttering to himself. Suddenly he stood still. He came quickly towards me and brusquely seized me by the arm. There was a strange light in his eyes.

'Come to the gypsies with me,' he said. 'If you come — I'll tell you everything, down to the last detail.'

I agreed, but at that moment the telephone-bell rang. Rasputin was then and there summoned to Tsarskoe Selo. I took advantage of this interruption to suggest that he should come and spend the evening at my home in a few days' time.

He had long shown a desire to make the acquaintance of my wife, and thinking that she was in St. Petersburg, and that my parents were still in the Crimea, he said he would come with pleasure.

As a matter of fact, my wife had not yet arrived in St. Petersburg; she was still in the Crimea with my parents. But I thought that Rasputin would more readily accept my invitation if he were unaware of this.

I then took my leave of him.

The Grand Duke Dmitri Pavlovich and Purishkevich returned from the front a few days afterwards.

We had several discussions, at one of which it was decided that Rasputin should be invited to our house on the Moika on December 16th.*

I telephoned to him and asked if he would come on the evening of that day. He agreed, on condition that I should go and fetch him myself, and that I should drive him back. Further, he asked me to approach his flat by the back staircase, promising that he would warn the dvornik** that a friend would be calling for him at twelve o'clock that night. He took these precautions with the object of leaving the house unnoticed.

It surprised and appalled me to think how readily he agreed to everything; it seemed as if he himself were helping us in our difficult task.

The appointed day drew near. I asked the Grand Duke Dmitri Pavlovich to select a place on the Neva where it would be possible to dispose of Rasputin's body.

---

* The date on which my wife would have returned from the Crimea, if illness had not prevented her from doing so.

** The house-watchman.

He came back to me that evening, having spent several hours in the search. We sat and talked for a long time. He spoke to me of his recent visit to G. H.Q. He was very depressed at finding the Emperor so thin and aged, so apathetic and indifferent to all that was happening.

His words brought back to my mind all that I had heard from Rasputin. It seemed as if Russia were about to be engulfed in an abyss. We felt convinced of the justice of our decision to destroy the man who had so multiplied all the sufferings of our unhappy country.

Grand Duke Nikolai Nikolaivich of Russia

CHAPTER XI

THE CELLARS AT NO. 94 MOIKA

IN the morning of the 16th. (New Style-29th) of December, during an interval in my work, I drove to our house on the Moika, in order to give final instructions.

The room in which Rasputin was to be received that evening was situated in the basement of the house, and had just been redecorated. It had to be arranged in such a way as to give the impression of being habitually used; otherwise Rasputin's suspicions might be aroused, for it would seem strange to him to be conducted into a cheerless and uncomfortable vault.

On my arrival I found the upholsterers there, laying carpets and putting up curtains.

There were no signs of furniture as yet, and I went up to the store-room to select what was suitable.

The newly-decorated room had originally formed part of the wine-cellar. In the daytime it was a rather dark and gloomy chamber, with a granite floor, walls faced with grey stone, and a low vaulted ceiling. Two small narrow windows, level with the ground, looked on to the Moika. A low arch divided the room into two parts, one of which was rather narrow, while the other was wide and spacious, and was intended for use as a dining-room. From the narrower part, the entrance door opened towards a spiral staircase. On the first landing of this staircase there was a door opening into the courtyard, while a little higher up was my study.

Anyone entering these rooms, therefore, would first come into the narrower portion. Here, in shallow recesses, were two big Chinese vases of red porcelain, which stood out in striking relief against the sombre grey walls.

I ordered some antique furniture to be brought down from the store-room, and we began to arrange the dining-room. I can still picture the whole scene, down to the smallest detail.

There were carved chairs upholstered in mellowed leather, small ebony cupboards full of secret recesses and drawers, massive oak chairs with high backs, and here and there little tables levered with coloured fabrics, bearing ivory goblets and Italian *objets d'art*.

I have a particularly vivid recollection of an inlaid cupboard, the interior of which was a labyrinth of mirrors and little bronze columns. On this cupboard stood a XVIIth crucifix of rock-crystal and silver, of Italian workmanship.

In the dining-room there was a large open fireplace of red granite; over it were a number of gilt cups and old Majolica plates and a group carved in ebony. The floor was spread with a large Persian carpet; and in front of the labyrinth cupboard and crucifix was a huge white bearskin.

In the middle of the room we placed the table at which Grigori Rasputin was to drink his last.

In arranging the room I was assisted by our house-steward, and by my servant. I ordered them to prepare, by eleven o'clock that evening, a meal for six persons. They were to get a good supply of biscuits and cakes, and wine from the cellar. I explained to them that I was expecting visitors, and that as soon as they had prepared tea they were to withdraw to the service-room until I should send for them.

When all these arrangements had been completed I went up to my study, where Colonel Fogel was already awaiting me.

I worked with him until about six o'clock, and then went to my temporary quarters at the Grand Duke Alexander Mikhailovich's Palace. After a hurried meal there I returned to my home at Moika No. 94.

* * *

CHAPTER XII

THE LAST VISIT TO GOROKHOVAYA STREET

BY eleven o'clock everything was ready.

The *samovar* stood on the table, with various cakes and sweetmeats for which Rasputin had a great liking. On one of the sideboards was a tray with wines and glasses.

I was still alone in the house as I cast an eye over the room and its arrangements.

Antique lanterns, with panes of varied colours, lit the room from above; the heavy dark-red curtains were drawn. In the open fireplace a huge fire was burning; the logs crackled and threw out sparks on the stone hearth.

The room was almost underground, and was ordinarily of a rather gloomy aspect; but now, thanks to the lighting and furnishings, it was astonishingly cosy. Moreover, the stillness which reigned lent an air of mystery, a sort of detachment from the world. It seemed that whatever might happen here would be hidden from mortal eyes and buried for ever in the silence of these stone walls.

A bell rang. It told me of the arrival of the Grand Duke Dmitri Pavlovich and the rest of my associates. I went to meet them. They looked confident and in good spirits, but they all talked rather loudly and seemed unnaturally gay, as if their nerves were on edge.

We passed into the dining-room. The arrangement of it greatly impressed my friends, particularly the Grand Duke Dmitri Pavlovich, who had seen it the day before, when nothing was as yet ready.

They all stood in silence for a while, as they examined the scene of the approaching event.

I drew from the labyrinth cupboard a box containing poison, and took from the table a plate of cakes; there were six — three with chocolate, and three with almond icing.

Dr. Lazovert put on rubber gloves and took out the crystals of cyanide of potassium. He crushed them, and having removed the upper layers from the chocolate cakes, sprinkled each of them with a strong dose of poison, afterwards replacing the tops.

We followed his movements with strained attention. A tense silence reigned in the room.

All that now remained to be done was to shake some powdered crystals into the wine-glasses. We decided to do this at the last possible moment, so that the poison might not lose strength by evaporation. The total amount of poison applied was enormous: the doctor assured us that the dose was many times stronger than would be required to cause death.

To make everything appear natural it was necessary that there should be a number of used cups on the table, as though people had just taken tea. I had explained to Rasputin that when we had visitors tea was served in the lower dining-room, and that after the others had gone upstairs I sometimes remained below, reading.

We slightly disarranged the table and the room, drawing back the chairs, and pouring a little tea into the cups. I further arranged with the Grand Duke Dmitri Pavlovich, Sukhotin, and Purishkevich, that within ten minutes of my departure they should go upstairs to my study and turn on the gramophone, selecting the most cheerful records they could find. My object was to keep Rasputin in good humour, and to clear his mind of all suspicion. For I could not entirely rid myself of the fear that the underground situation of the rooms might put him on his guard.

When all these preparations had been completed, Dr. Lazovert and I left the room. He changed into chauffeur's clothes and went to start the car, which was standing at the side entrance in the courtyard, while I put on a voluminous fur cloak and a fur cap with ear-pieces, which served to conceal my face.

We got into the car and drove off.

My head was a whirl of thoughts. I was sustained by my hopes for the future. During those few short minutes of my last drive to Rasputin's I lived through a whole life of emotions.

The car stopped outside No. 64 Gorokhovaya Street.

On entering the courtyard I was at once challenged by the *dvornik*.

'Whom do you want?'

On learning that I wanted to see Grigori Efimovich he was unwilling to let me pass, and insisted that I should give my name and explain why I was calling at so late an hour.

I replied that Grigori Efimovich himself had asked me to come at this particular hour and to go up to him by the back staircase. The *dvornik* looked me over with distrust, but nevertheless allowed me to pass.

The staircase was in darkness, and I had to feel my way. I had not even any matches with me. With great difficulty I at last succeeded in finding the entrance to Rasputin's flat.

I rang, and in reply heard his voice from behind the closed door: 'Who's there?'

I shuddered. 'Grigori Efimovich, it is I. I've come to fetch you,' I answered.

I heard him moving and bustling about. The door was chained and bolted, and I felt uneasy as the chain clanged and the heavy bolt grated at his touch.

He led the way and I went into the kitchen. It was in darkness, and I felt that someone was watching me from the adjoining room. Instinctively I turned up my collar and pulled down my cap.

'What are you muffling yourself up like that for?' asked Rasputin.

'Why, didn't we decide that no one should know about to-night?' I replied.

'True, true. I haven't told anybody here, and I've sent off all the *tainiki*.* Come on; I'll get ready.'

We went into his bedroom, which was partially lit by a lamp in the corner, in front of the *ikons*. Rasputin applied a match to a candle. I noticed that the bed was disarranged — he had evidently just been resting. His fur coat and beaver hat were in readiness. On the floor was a pair of snow boots.

He was dressed in a white silk blouse embroidered with cornflowers and girded with a thick raspberry-coloured cord with large tassels, wide trousers of black velvet, and long boots, brand new. Even his hair and beard were carefully combed and smoothed. As he drew nearer to me I felt a strong smell of cheap soap. He had obviously paid special attention to his toilet that day, certainly I had never before seen him so clean and tidy.

* Agents of the secret police.

'Well, Grigori Efimovich, isn't it time we were off? It's already nearly one o'clock.'

'Shall we go on to the gypsies? What d'you say?' he asked.

'I don't know — perhaps,' I answered.

'But there won't be anybody special at your place to-night?' he said, with a note of uneasiness in his voice.

I calmed him by telling him that he would meet no one whom he disliked, and that my mother was still in the Crimea.

'I don't like her, your mother. And she can't stand me, I know ... she's a friend of Lizbeth.* They're both digging pits for me, and slandering me. ... The Empress herself has told me time and again that they're my worst enemies. ...'

'And what d'you think?' he added unexpectedly. 'Protopopov drove round here this evening, and made me promise that I'd stay at home during these next few days. "They want to kill you," he said. "Evil-minded people are plotting against you." Ah, well! Let 'em plot. They won't succeed — they haven't got a long enough reach.

'But what's the use of talking about it! Let's go!'

I picked up his coat from a chest and helped him into it.

'Money — I've forgotten my money,' he said, in a fluster. He went to the chest and opened it. I moved nearer and, looking into it, I saw a number of parcels wrapped in newspaper.

'Surely that isn't all money?' I asked.

'Of course it is — nothing but bank-notes; I got 'em to-day,' he answered without hesitation.

'Who gave them to you?'

'Various kind people. I just fixed up a little affair, and out of gratitude they made a donation to the Church.'

'I suppose there's a good deal of money there?'

'Why should I bother to count it? I haven't time. I'm not a banker! That's a job for Mitka Rubinstein;** he's got pots of money. Besides, to tell you the truth, I can't count it. I just said to 'em, "Bring fifty thousand, otherwise I shan't worry over you." Well, and they sent it. Perhaps they've given more! How should I know?

'It'll make a nice little wedding present for my daughter,' he continued. 'She's going to be married soon, to an officer with four

---

* The Grand Duchess Elizabeth Feodorovna.
** A notorious St. Petersburg financier.

St. George's Crosses* He earned 'em, too. And there's a fat little job waiting for him. "She"** has promised to give her blessing.'

'But, Grigori Efimovich, didn't you say that this money was a donation to the Church?'

'Well, what about that? There's nothing to be surprised at! Marriage is of God, isn't it? The Lord Himself gave His blessing at Cana, in Galilee. And as to the particular use to which this money is put, isn't it all the same to Him — to God?' replied Rasputin, with a cunning leer.

I could not help being amused at the naive insolence with which Rasputin played with the words, of the Holy Scriptures.

He took some money from the chest, which he then carefully locked. He blew out the candle, and the room was again in semi-darkness — illuminated only by the lamp which burned fitfully before the *ikon* in the corner.

I was suddenly overwhelmed by a feeling of infinite pity for this man.

I felt disgusted and ashamed at the thought of the vile means and appalling deception with which I was luring him to my home. Here was my victim — standing before me, suspecting nothing, trusting me.

At that moment I was filled with the deepest contempt for myself; I asked myself how I could have decided to commit such a hideous crime; and I could not understand how it had happened.

He trusted me. . . . But what had become of his insight? What had happened to his instinct? It seemed as if fate had somehow clouded his reason, and blinded him to our intentions.

But then I saw, with amazing clearness, one scene after another from the life of Rasputin. All my qualms of conscience, all my remorse vanished, and gave place to a steadfast determination to complete the task which we had undertaken.

I hesitated no longer.

We walked towards the dark landing, and Rasputin closed the door behind him.

The lock grated noisily, and a harsh, ominous echo rang down the deserted staircase. We were in total darkness.

I felt a vice-like grip on my arm.

---

* A high military decoration awarded for gallantry in the field.
** The Empress Alexandra Feodorovna.

'I'll show you the way,' said Rasputin as he led me down. His grasp hurt me. I wanted to protest and shake it off; but I felt numb. . . . I do not remember anything that he said to me, or whether I replied. At that moment there was only one thing I desired: to get into the open air as soon as possible, to see as much light as possible, and not to feel the touch of that terrible hand.

As soon as we got downstairs my horror left me, and I again became cool and collected.

We got into the car and drove off.

I looked through the rear window to find out whether we were followed. Not a soul was to be seen in the darkness.

We proceeded by a circuitous route, and on reaching the Moika, we turned into the courtyard, and drew up at the side entrance.

RASPUTIN

CHAPTER XIII

THE NIGHT OF THE 16TH DECEMBER

ON entering the house I heard my friends' voices, and the sounds of a popular American song on the gramophone. Rasputin stopped to listen.

'What's this going on? A party?'

'No; my wife has friends with her. They will go away soon, so for the time being let's go down to the dining-room and have some tea.'

We went downstairs. Rasputin removed his fur coat and proceeded to scrutinise the room and furniture.

He was particularly interested in the labyrinth cupboard. He showed quite a childish delight in it, and returned to it again and again, opening and shutting the small doors and examining the interior. He refused at first to take either tea or wine.

'Does he suspect anything?' I wondered; but I there and then decided that in any case he should not leave the house alive.

We sat down at the table and talked. We discussed mutual friends, the G.'s and Vyrubova, and we touched upon Tsarskoe Selo.

'Grigori Efimovich, why did Protopopov come to you? Is he in constant fear of a plot against you?' I asked.

'Yes, I'm a stumbling-block to a good many people, because I'm always telling the truth. . . . Your aristocrats don't like the idea of a common muzhik wandering about the Palaces. It's all sheer envy and malice. But why should I be afraid of them? . . . they can't do any harm to me: I'm proof against evil designs. They've had more than one try, but the Lord laid their plans bare. Take Khvostov. He tried it on, but he was punished and dismissed. They daren't even touch me. They'd only get into trouble.'

His words sounded ominous.

But nothing could now dismay me. During the whole of that conversation I had only one idea in my head: to make him drink wine out of those poisoned glasses, and to eat the poisoned cakes.

He exhausted his ordinary topics after a time, and asked for some tea.

I poured him out a cup, and pushed a plate of biscuits towards him. Why I offered him the biscuits, which were not poisoned, I cannot explain.

It was only some time afterwards that I took the plate of poisoned cakes and passed them to him.

He declined them at first.

'Don't want 'em; they're too sweet,' he said.

However, he soon took one, then a second.... Without moving a muscle I watched him take them and eat them, one after another.

The cyanide should have taken immediate effect; but to my utter amazement he continued to converse with me as if he were none the worse for them.

I then suggested that he should sample our Crimean wines.

Again he refused.

Time passed. I began to get impatient. I poured out two glasses, one for him, the other for myself. I placed his glass in front of him and began to drink out of my own, thinking that he would follow my example.

'Well, let me try it,' said Rasputin, stretching out his hand for the wine. It was not poisoned. Why I first gave him the wine in an unpoisoned glass I am also at a loss to explain.

He drank it with obvious pleasure, praised it, and asked if we had much of it. On hearing that we had a whole cellar full, he showed great astonishment.

He became animated. 'Now give me some madeira,' he said.

I got up to take another glass, but he protested: 'Pour it into this one.'

'But that's impossible, Grigori Efimovich. You can't mix red wine with madeira.'

'Never mind; pour it out into this, I tell you.'

I had to give way.

By an apparent accident, however, I soon managed to knock his glass to the floor, where it smashed.

I took advantage of this to pour wine into one of the glasses containing cyanide of potassium. Having once begun to drink he made no further protest.

I stood in front of him and followed each movement he made, expecting every moment to be his last.

But he drank slowly, taking small sips at a time, just as if he had been connoisseur.

His face did not change; but from time to time he put his hand to his throat as if he found slight difficulty in swallowing. He got up and moved about the room and when I asked him whether anything was the matter, 'Oh, nothing much,' he said, 'just an irritation in the throat.

There was a nerve-racking pause.

'That's very good madeira. Give me some more,' said Rasputin, holding out his glass.

The poison still had no effect. The *starets* continued to walk about the room.

I took no notice of the glass which he held out to me, but seized another poisoned one from the tray. I poured wine into it, and passed it to him.

He drained it: and still the poison had no effect.

There remained the third and last glass.

In despair, I began to drink myself, hoping to induce him to drink more and more. We sat opposite each other in silence.

He looked at me with a cunning smile. I seemed to hear him say:

'You see! It doesn't matter how you try; you can't do me any harm.'

But all of a sudden his expression changed into one of fiendish hatred. Never before had he inspired me with such horror.

I felt an indescribable loathing for him and was ready to throw myself upon him and throttle him. I felt that he knew why I had brought him there, and what I intended to do to him. A mute and deadly conflict seemed to be taking place between us. I was aghast. Another moment and I should have gone under. I felt that confronted by those satanic eyes, I was beginning to lose my self-control. A strange feeling of numbness took possession of me. My head reeled. . . . I saw nothing. . . . I do not know how long this lasted. . . .

Rasputin was still sitting in the same position. His head was bent, and he was supporting it with his hands. I could not see his eyes.

I regained my presence of mind and offered him some tea.

'Yes, give me a cup; I'm terribly thirsty,' he said in a weak voice.

He raised his head. His eyes were dim, and he seemed to be avoiding my glance.

While I was pouring out tea, he got up and paced the room. His eyes fell upon the guitar, which happened to have been left in the room.

'Play something,' he begged. 'Play something cheerful. I love the way you sing.'

It was difficult to comply at such a moment . . . and he was asking me to sing 'something cheerful.'

'I'm not in the mood,' I said, as I took the guitar.

He sat and listened attentively at first; but as I continued, his head drooped towards the table. The moment I stopped he opened his eyes and looked at me with a calm and sad expression in them.

'Sing another,' he said.

I sang again.

My voice sounded strange in my ears. Time passed. . . . The hands of the clock pointed to half-past two. This nightmare had lasted over two hours.

'What will happen if my nerves don't hold out?' I wondered.

Upstairs, too, patience had evidently become exhausted.

The sounds from that quarter became more pronounced, and I was afraid that my friends would come down.

'What's all that noise?' asked Rasputin, lifting his head.

'Probably it's the guests going away,' I replied; 'I'll go up and see.'

As I entered the study, the Grand Duke Dmitri Pavlovich, Purishkevich, and Sukhotin rushed towards me with revolvers in their hands.

Questions showered on me.

'Well! It is done? It is all over?'

'The poison has had no effect,' I said.

They gazed at me in mute astonishment.

'Impossible,' exclaimed the Grand Duke. 'The dose was amply sufficient.'

'Did he take it all?' asked the others.

'Every bit of it,' I answered.

We began to discuss what to do next, and decided that we would go downstairs together, throw ourselves on Rasputin, and strangle him. We were carefully making our way down the staircase, when I suddenly realised that by doing this we should ruin everything. The unexpected appearance of strangers would at once warn Rasputin of our intentions, and there was no telling how matters would end. It had to be remembered that we were not dealing with an ordinary type of man.

I called my friends back into the study and told them of my apprehensions. With great difficulty I persuaded them to leave me to finish with Rasputin alone. For a long time they would not agree; they had qualms on my behalf.

But finally I took the Grand Duke's revolver and went down to the dining-room.

Rasputin was sitting at the table, just as I had left him. His head was sunken and he was breathing heavily.

I went quietly up to him and sat beside him. He took no notice of my approach.

A few minutes passed in silence, and then he slowly raised his head and looked at me. His eyes were dim; with a dull, lifeless expression in them.

'Are you feeling unwell?' I asked.

'Yes, my head is heavy, and my stomach is burning. Give me another glass — that will ease me.'

I poured him out some madeira; he drank it at a gulp, and at once revived and regained his good spirits.

I exchanged a few sentences with him and saw that he was perfectly conscious, and that his mind was working normally. All of a sudden he suggested that we should go to the gypsies. I refused, on the ground that it was too late.

'What does that matter! They're used to it! They sometimes wait up for me all night. I'm sometimes kept at Tsarskoe Selo on important business, or just talking about God . . . but afterwards I drive over to them in the car. The body also has to have a rest sometimes . . . isn't that true? With God in thought, but with mankind in the flesh. That's the idea,' said Rasputin, with a significant wink.

A conversation of this kind was the very last thing which I could have expected from him at that moment.

Here I had been sitting all that time with a man who had swallowed an enormous dose of the most deadly poison; I had been watching every one of his movements in the expectation of a fatal issue; and now he was suggesting that we should go to the gypsies!

But what amazed me most was that in spite of his instinctive knowledge and insight, he should now be so utterly unconscious of his approaching end.

How could his sharp eyes fail to observe that, clenched in my hand behind my back, was a revolver which in an instant would be aimed at him?

As this thought flashed through my mind, I looked round for some reason or other, and my glance fell on the crystal crucifix. I rose and went up to it.

'What are you doing over there so long?' asked Rasputin.

'I love this cross; it's a very beautiful thing,' I answered.

'Yes, it's a nice thing. Cost a lot of money, I'm sure.... How much did you pay for it?'

He came towards me and, without waiting for an answer, he continued:

'But this is what takes my fancy most.' And again he opened the labyrinth cupboard and began to examine it.

'Grigori Efimovich, you had better look at the crucifix, and say a prayer before it.'

Rasputin looked at me in amazement, and with a trace of fear.

I saw a new and unfamiliar expression in his eyes, a touch of gentleness and submission. He came right up to me, looking me full in the face, and he seemed to read in my glance something which he was not expecting. I realised that the supreme moment was at hand.

'God give me strength to end it all,' I thought, and I Slowly brought the revolver from behind my back. Rasputin was still standing motionless before me, his head turned to the right, and his eyes on the crucifix.

'Where shall I shoot?' I thought. 'Through the temple or through the heart?'

A streak of lightning seemed to run through my body. I fired.

There was a roar as from a wild beast, and Rasputin fell heavily backwards on the bear-skin rug.

I heard a noise on the staircase: my friends were hurrying to my aid. In their haste they caught against the main switch just outside the room, and I suddenly found myself in darkness.

Someone stumbled against me and called out in fright.

I did not move; I was afraid of stepping on to the body in the dark.

The light was switched on at last.

They all rushed towards Rasputin. . . .

He was lying on his back. His face twitched now and then; his hands were convulsively clenched; his eyes were closed.

There was a small red spot on his silk blouse.

We bent over him and looked at him closely.

Some of those present wanted to fire at him again, but were restrained by the fear of leaving unnecessary traces of blood.

In a few minutes Rasputin became quite still.

We examined the wound. The bullet had passed through the region of the heart. There could be no doubt about it; he was dead.

The Grand Duke Dmitri Pavlovich removed the body from the bear-skin to the stone floor. We switched off the electric light, closed and locked the dining-room door, and went upstairs to my study.

We all felt elated, so convinced were we that the events of that night would deliver Russia from ruin and dishonour.

Drawing from a Russian newspaper reporting the death of Rasputin.

FELIX YUSSOUPOFF

CHAPTER XIV

DEATH WHICH WAS NO DEATH

IN conformity with our plan, the Grand Duke Dmitri Pavlovich, Captain Sukhotin and Dr. Lazovert had now to stage a fictitious return of Rasputin to his own flat — in case the secret police had followed him on our drive to my house. Sukhotin had to disguise himself in Rasputin's fur coat and cap, and drive off in Purishkevich's car with the Grand Duke and the doctor in the direction of the Gorokhovaya.

Rasputin's clothing had to be conveyed to the Warsaw station, where it was to be burnt in Purishkevich's Red Cross train — the car being left there. From the station they were to take a cab and drive to the Grand Duke's palace; there they were to pick up his closed car, in which they were to return to the Moika.

Rasputin's body was then to be conveyed in that car from my home to the Petrovski Island. We requested the doctor, who acted as chauffeur, to drive as fast as possible, and to try and cover his tracks.

Purishkevich and I remained behind. While awaiting the return of our companions we talked and dreamed of the future of our country, now for ever delivered from her evil genius.

We believed that Russia was saved, and that with Rasputin's disappearance a new era had dawned. We believed that we should everywhere find support; and that all those who were near the seat of power, delivered from the intrigues of this upstart, would henceforward work in friendly unison. We could not then foresee that those whose hands had been thus freed would assume such a criminally frivolous attitude both towards his death and towards the duties which confronted them.

We did not for a moment realise that personal interests, base truckling, and the thirst for power and reputation would so effectively stifle all feelings of duty and patriotism.

The death of Rasputin opened out limitless possibilities before those who were in positions of influence and power. But not one of them desired or was able to take advantage of the favourable moment.

I refrain from naming those people; some day their attitude towards Russia will be set down at its real value.

But that night we were in an excited frame of mind. We had passed through nerve-racking experiences. We had fulfilled an onerous duty towards our Emperor and our country. Gloomy forebodings were far removed from us.

In the midst of our conversation I was suddenly seized by a vague feeling of alarm; I was overwhelmed by the desire to go down to the dining-room. I went downstairs and unlocked the door.

Rasputin lay motionless, but on touching him I discovered that he was still warm.

I felt his pulse. There was no beat.

From his wound drops of blood trickled, and fell on the granite floor.

It was an awe-inspiring and revolting sight.

I cannot explain why, but I suddenly seized him by both arms and violently shook him. The body rose, leant sideways, and fell back into its former position, the head hanging lifelessly to one side.

I stood over him for a little time longer, and was on the point of going away when my attention was arrested by a slight trembling of his left eyelid. . . . I bent down over him, and attentively examined his face. . . . It began to twitch convulsively. The movements became more and more pronounced. Suddenly the left eye half-opened. . . . An instant later the right lid trembled and lifted. . . . And both eyes . . . eyes of Rasputin — fixed themselves upon me with an expression of devilish hatred.

My blood froze in speechless horror. I was petrified . . . I wanted to run, to call for help; but my feet would not move, and no sound came from me.

I stood riveted to the floor as if in a nightmare.

Then the incredible happened. . . . With a violent movement Rasputin jumped to his feet. I was horror-stricken. The room resounded with a wild roar. His fingers, convulsively knotted, flashed through the air. . . . Like red-hot iron they grasped my shoulder and tried to grip me by the throat. His eyes were crossed, and obtruded terribly; he was foaming at the mouth.

And in a hoarse whisper he constantly repeated my name.

I cannot convey in words the fear which possessed me.

I tried to tear myself away, but his iron clutch held me with incredible strength. A terrible struggle ensued.

This dying, poisoned, and shot-ridden creature, raised by the powers of darkness to avenge his destruction, inspired me with a feeling so terrifying, so ghastly, that the memory of it haunts me to this day.

At that moment I understood and felt in the fullest degree the real power of Rasputin. It seemed that the devil himself, incarnate in this muzhik, was holding me in vice-like fingers, never to let me go.

But with a supreme effort I tore myself free.

Rasputin groaned, and fell backwards, still gripping my epaulet, which he had torn off in the struggle. I looked at him; he lay all huddled up, motionless.

But again he stirred.

I rushed upstairs, calling on Purishkevich, who was in my study, to come to my aid.

'Quick! quick! the revolver! He is alive!' I shouted.

I myself was unarmed. I had given my revolver to the Grand Duke Dmitri Pavlovich. At the door of my study I met Purishkevich, who had heard my desperate call for assistance. He was amazed to learn that Rasputin was still alive, and hurriedly took out his revolver from its holster. At that moment I heard sounds behind me. I realised that it was Rasputin, and in an instant I found myself in my study. Here on the writing table, I had left the loaded stick, which Maklakov had given me 'in case I might ever want it.' I seized it and rushed out.

Rasputin, on all-fours, was rapidly making his way up the staircase, bellowing and snorting like a wounded animal.

Suddenly he gathered himself up and made a final leap towards the wicket door leading to the courtyard.

In the full certainty that the door was locked, and that the key was in the possession of those who had left us, I stood on the staircase landing, firmly grasping the loaded stick.

But to my horror and surprise, the wicket-door opened, and Rasputin vanished through it into the darkness.

Purishkevich immediately rushed after him. Two shots rang out, resounding all over the yard.

I was beside myself with the idea that he might escape us. I rushed to the main entrance and ran along the Moika quayside, towards the courtyard, hoping, in case Purishkevich had missed him, to stop Rasputin at the gates.

There were three entrances to the courtyard, and only the centre gates were unlocked. Through the railing I saw that it was just to those gates that Rasputin, led by instinct, was heading.

A third shot rang out, and a fourth. . . .

Rasputin stumbled and fell near a snow-heap. Purishkevich ran up to him, stood still for a few seconds, and evidently having decided that everything was now over, and that Rasputin was killed, with rapid steps turned back to the house. I called out to him, but he did not hear me.

After looking round and finding that the streets were empty, and that the shots had not attracted attention, I entered the courtyard and went up to the snow-mound where Rasputin was lying.

He showed no signs of life. On his left temple gaped a large wound, which, as I afterwards learned, was caused by Purishkevich's heel.

But in the meantime people were approaching me from two sides. A policeman came through the gates straight to the spot where Rasputin was lying, and my two servants ran towards me from the house. All three had been alarmed by the shots.

I stopped the policeman on the way. While speaking to him I was careful to keep my face turned towards the snow-mound, so that he should be forced to turn his back on the spot where Rasputin was lying.

'Your Highness,' he said, recognising me, 'I heard shots. Has anything happened?'

'No, nothing serious. A stupid business. I had some friends with me to-night, and one of them drank rather too much, and began shooting and making all this disturbance. If anybody asks you what's been going on, just say that everything is all right.'

As I talked to him I led him towards the gates. I then returned to the spot where Rasputin was lying. My servants stood there. Purishkevich had told them to carry the body into the house. I went closer to the mound. Rasputin lay in a different position.

'My God, he is still alive,' I thought.

Terror seized me at the mere idea that he would again jump and seize me by the throat, and I hurried into the house.

I went to my study and called Purishkevich, but he was not there. That bloodcurdling whisper of my name rang in my ears all the time. I staggered to my dressing-room to get a drink of water. Purishkevich ran in.

'Here you are! I've been looking for you everywhere!' he exclaimed.

Everything swam before my eyes, and I thought I was about to fall. Purishkevich seized me by the arm and led me to the study.

We had hardly entered when my servant hurried in and announced that the policeman with whom I had spoken wanted to see me again, and that this time he had come through the main entrance, avoiding the courtyard.

It appeared that the shots had been heard at the district police-station, and that the policeman had been instructed to give an explanation by telephone. His first version had failed to satisfy the local authorities, and they insisted on being given all the details.

As soon as he caught sight of the policeman, Purishkevich quickly went up to him and, raising his voice, said: 'You have heard of Rasputin? — the man who has been betraying our country, our Emperor, and our soldiers at the front? He's been selling us to the Germans . . . do you hear?'

The policeman was struck dumb with surprise. He did not in the least understand what was wanted of him, and he remained silent.

'Do you know who I am?' Purishkevich went on, excitedly. 'I am Vladimir Mitrofanovich Purishkevich — Member of the Imperial Duma.

'Those shots which you heard killed Rasputin, and if you love your country and your Tsar — you must not breathe a word about it.'

I was horror-stricken at this conversation, but it was quite impossible to intervene and put an end to it. Everything had happened too quickly, and too unexpectedly. Purishkevich seemed to be seized by a kind of nervous exaltation. Obviously, he himself did not realise what he was saying.

'You have done a good deed. I will say nothing. But if they make me give evidence on oath, I shall say all that I know — there'll be no help for it. It's a sin to swear falsely,' the policeman answered at last.

With these words he left us. From his demeanour it was clear that what he had just learned had deeply affected him.

Purishkevich ran after him. When they had gone my servant told me that Rasputin's body had been carried from the courtyard to the bottom of the spiral staircase. I was feeling ill. My head was still reeling, and I could scarcely move. But I pulled myself together, and mechanically taking up the loaded stick from the table, made my way out of the study.

On going downstairs, I saw Rasputin lying on the lower landing.

Blood was flowing freely from his many wounds. The chandelier at the top of the staircase lit up his head, and threw into full relief his mutilated and blood-spattered face.

I wanted to close my eyes. I wanted to get away as far as possible from this revolting scene. And yet I felt irresistibly drawn towards it. The impulse was so strong that I could not struggle against it.

My head was bursting asunder. My thoughts were confused. I was beside myself with rage and spite.

Some sort of paroxysm seized me.

I rushed at the body and began battering it with the loaded stick. . . . In my frenzy I hit anywhere.

At that moment all laws of God and man were set at naught.

Purishkevich subsequently told me that it was such a harrowing sight that he would never be able to forget it.

I lost consciousness.

In the meantime the Grand Duke Dmitri Pavlovich, Captain Sukhotin and Dr. Lazovert returned in the closed car.

On hearing from Purishkevich all that had happened, they decided not to disturb me.

They wrapped the body in a cloth, placed it in the car, and drove off to Petrovski Island.

From a bridge there, the remains of Rasputin were thrown into the water.

* * *

On 19 October 1918 an American newspaper reported that Lazovert had claimed he was part of the assassination group that killed Rasputin and had arrived in America '. . . *to report to President Wilson on present conditions in Russia . . .*' and that, '*the monk was killed because he was considered to be employed by German money to influence the czarina in bringing about peace between Russia and Germany, and it was from patriotic motives that he was removed.*', which Lazovert denied in a letter to the Editor.

HELPED KILL RASPUTIN

COLONEL / DOCTOR
STANISLAUS de LAZOVERT

Chief surgeon heading the Red Cross Sanitary Corp organised in the Russian Army by Vladimir Purishkevich, of the State Duma.

He was responsible for the provision of potassium cyanide that was meant for Rasputin. After the assassination, he left Russia immediately to join the White Army in Odessa.

Eventually Lazovert moved to Paris. He accomplishing various medical missions and his wife worked as a nurse. They finally moved permanently to America.

Lazovert became involved in the oil industry pertaining to Romanian and Egyptian concerns, from which his ownership of oil wells and his contacts placed him in good stead to assist British Intelligence during World War II. His involvement would have had a tremendous impact on severing the major source of oil for the German war effort from Romanian oil fields. He died in 1976.

His memoirs, written shortly after he arrived in Paris, are fairly straightforward and in line with Felix Youssoupoff's account; hence they do not involve British Intelligence or implicate Oswald Rayner in the murder of Rasputin.

Letter to the Editor of The New York Times:

"The American press prints and reprints my statements with regard to the assassination of Rasputin and other events in Russia. I will appreciate your courtesy in permitting me to say, through your esteemed publication, that I never issued these statements, and did not give out any interview with regard to the present conditions in Russia." - DR STANISLAUS DE LAZOVERT

From Source Records of the Great War Volume V published by National Alumni 1923. A comprehensive source emphasising the more important events, recorded as narratives from the subjects themselves. Here translated from the Polish and transposed as accurately as possible.

By Dr Stanislaus De Lazovert:

The shot that ended the career of the blackest devil in Russian history was fired by my close and beloved friend, Vladimir Purishkevitch, Reactionary Deputy of the Duma. Five of us had been arranging for this for months. On the night of the killing, after all had been arranged, I drove to the Imperial Palace on an automobile and persuaded this black devil to the home of Prince Yusupoff, in Petrograd. That night Purishkevitch followed him into the gardens joining Yusupoff's house and shot him to death with an automatic revolver. We then carried his riddled body in a sheet to the River Neva, broke the ice and cast him in.

The story of Rasputin and his clique is well known. They sent the army to the trenches without food or arms, they left them there to be slaughtered, they betrayed Rumania and deceived the Allies, they almost succeeded in delivering Russia bodily to the Germans. Rasputin, as a secret member of the Austrian Green Hand, had absolute power in Court. The Csar was a nonentity, a kind of Hamlet, his only desire being to abdicate and escape the whole vile business. Rasputin continued his life of vice, carousing and passion. The Grand Duchess [ELIZABETH FEODOROVNA] reported these things to the Czarina and was banished from Court for her pains.

This was the condition of affairs when we decided to kill this monster. Only five men participated In It. They were the Grand Duke Dmitri Pavlovich, Prince Yusupoff, Vladimir Purishkevitch, Captain Sukhotin and myself.

Prince Yusupoff's palace is a magnificent place on the Nevska. The great hall has six equal sides and in each hall is a heavy oaken door. One leads out into the gardens, the one opposite leads down a broad flight of marble stairs to the huge dining room, one to the library, etc. At midnight the associates of the Prince concealed themselves while I entered the car and drove to the home of the monk. He admitted me in person.

Rasputin was in a gay mood. We drove rapidly to the home of the Prince and descended to the library, lighted only by a blazing log in the huge chimney-place. A small table was spread with cakes and rare wines — three kinds of the wine were poisoned and so were the cakes. The monk threw himself into a chair, his humor expanding with the warmth of the room. He told of his successes, his plots, of the imminent success of the German arms and that the Kaiser would soon be seen in Petrograd.

At a proper moment he was offered the wine and the *starets* devoured the cakes. Hours passed. The monk was even merrier than before. We were seized with an insane dread that this man was inviolable, that he was superhuman, that he couldn't be killed. It was a frightful sensation. He glared at us with his black, black eyes as though he read our minds and would fool us.

And then after a time he rose and walked to the door. We were afraid that our work had been in vain. Suddenly, as he turned at the door, some one shot at him quickly. With a frightful scream Rasputin whirled and fell, face down, on the floor. The others came bounding over to him and stood over his prostrate, writhing body. It was suggested that two more shots be fired to make certain of his death, but one of those present said, "*No, no; it is his last agony now.*" We left the room to let him die alone, and to plan for his removal and obliteration.

Suddenly we heard a strange and unearthly sound behind the huge door that led into the library. The door was slowly pushed open, and there was Rasputin on his hands and knees, the bloody froth gushing from his mouth, his terrible eyes bulging from their sockets. With an amazing strength he sprang toward the door that led into the gardens, wrenched it open and passed out.

As he seemed to be disappearing in the darkness, Purishkevitch, who had been standing by, reached over and picked up an American-made automatic revolver and fired two shots swiftly into his retreating figure. We heard him fall with a groan, and later when we approached the body he was very still and cold and — dead.

We bundled him up in a sheet and carried him to the river's edge. Ice had formed, but we broke it and threw him in. The next day a search was made for Rasputin, but no trace was found.

* * *

CHAPTER XV

WHY A DOG WAS KILLED

WHEN I finally regained consciousness I felt as if I had just emerged from a serious illness — as if, after a violent storm, I were drinking deep breaths of pure, fresh air.

My servant and I proceeded to obliterate all traces of blood which might betray us.

When everything incriminating had been cleaned and put in order, I went out into the courtyard to take further precautions.

Some sort of explanation for the shots had to be provided. My plan was a simple one; I would announce that one of my visitors, on leaving the house, had noticed a dog in the courtyard, and that being rather the worse for liquor, he had fired at it.

Accordingly, my servant took one of the dogs into an outbuilding in the inner courtyard and shot it. He then dragged its body over Rasputin's trail, so as to frustrate any subsequent blood-analysis, and threw it on the snow-mound where not so long before the dead *starets* had lain.

In case police dogs might be used, we poured camphor on the bloodstains which were visible in the snow.

I then assembled all those of my household who had been chance witnesses of what had happened, and explained to them its significance.

They listened in silence, and from their expressions it was clear that they were all determined to say nothing whatever about it.

It was already nearly 5 a.m. when I left the house for the Grand Duke Alexander Mikhailovich's palace.

The feeling that the first step towards Russia's salvation had been taken filled me with energy and inspired me with an unclouded belief in the future.

On entering my room at the palace, I found my brother-in-law, Prince Theodore Alexandrovich, there. He had been sitting up all night expecting my return.

'Thank God you've come at last I . . . Well, what has happened?'
'Rasputin is killed, but I can't say anything more just now. I'm too tired.'

Foreseeing that on the following morning I should be interrogated, and that measures would perhaps be taken against me, I felt that I should have need of all my strength. I went to bed and fell into a deep sleep.

ALEXANDER MIKHAILOVICH

Married in 1894 to the Tsar's sister Xenia Alexandrovna, she was also his first cousin's daughter His family knew him as Sandro.

He was a naval officer of some Distinction, with a love for the Arts. After he escaped Russia he became an archaeologist.

THEODORE ALEXANDROVICH

Third child and second son of Alexander Mikhailovich and therefore a nephew of the Tsar. He escaped Russia in 1919 with his father on the British rescue ship HMS Marlborough. In exile he married Irina Pavey, the daughter of Paul Alexandrovich of Russia (a son of Alexander II).

CHAPTER XVI

ENTHUSIASM AT ST. PETERSBURG

I SLEPT soundly until ten o'clock.
I had hardly opened my eyes when I was told that the Chief of the Police of the Kazan district, General Grigoriev, wanted to see me on very urgent business.

I hurriedly rose, dressed, and went into the study, where General Grigoriev was awaiting me.

'Your visit,' I said, 'is probably connected with shots which were heard in the courtyard of our house?'

'Yes, I have come to learn from you at firsthand full details of what occurred. Was not Rasputin a guest here yesterday evening?'

'Rasputin? He never visits me,' I replied.

'The shots heard from your courtyard are nevertheless associated with his disappearance, and the Prefect of Police has ordered me to make immediate inquiry into what happened at your house last night.'

This association of the shots on the Moika with the disappearance of Rasputin foreshadowed grave complications.

I had carefully to weigh and estimate the effect of every word I used before I could give any answer to the question which was put to me.

'But what is the source of your information that Rasputin has disappeared?' I asked.

General Grigoriev told me that early in the morning an inspector, accompanied by the policeman on duty in the neighbourhood of my house, had come to him and reported that at 3 a.m. a number of shots had been fired. The policeman had inspected his beat, but had found everything quiet, the streets empty, and the *dvorniki* asleep at the gates. Suddenly someone had hailed him with the words, 'Come quickly; the Prince wants you.' The policeman had complied, and had been conducted to my study. There he had seen me, with another person. The latter had come towards him and asked:

'Do you know me?'

'No, sir, I do not,' the policeman had replied.

'Have you ever heard of Purishkevich?'

'Yes, sir.'

'I am Purishkevich. Do you love the Tsar and your Fatherland?'

'Yes, sir.'

'If you love them, swear that you will tell no one; Rasputin is dead!'

After this conversation the policeman had been conducted out of the house. He had at first returned to his post, but later, out of fear, he had decided to report the incident to his superiors.

I listened attentively, and tried to preserve an expression of utter surprise. All those in the plot had solemnly sworn not to divulge our secret, and I was bound by this promise. We had then hoped to conceal all evidence of the assassination; the political situation demanded that Rasputin's disappearance should remain a mystery.

'What an incredible story!' I exclaimed, when General Grigoriev had finished. 'How tiresome that just because this policeman did not understand what was said to him, so much unpleasantness may arise. . . . I will tell you at once, in detail, what really happened.

'Last night a number of friends and acquaintances came to supper with me. Among them were the Grand Duke Dmitri Pavlovich, M. Purishkevich, and a number of officers. A good deal of wine was consumed, and everyone was in excellent humour.

"When my guests began to leave, I suddenly heard two shots from the direction of the courtyard. I went out and saw one of our yard dogs lying dead on the snow. One of my friends, excited by wine, had fired his revolver as he left the house and had accidentally killed the animal.

'Fearing that the shots might have attracted the attention of the police, I sent for the policeman on duty, in order to explain them to him. By this time all the guests had departed with the exception of Purishkevich. When the policeman entered, Purishkevich hurried towards him and began speaking with him in an undertone. I noticed that the policeman became confused. I do not know what was actually said, but from your words it is now clear to me that Purishkevich, who was also rather excited, spoke of the dog that had been killed, and, comparing it with Rasputin, regretted that it had not been the *starets* instead. The policeman obviously did not grasp his meaning. . . . That's the only explanation I can suggest for this misunderstanding. I sincerely hope that everything will soon be cleared up satisfactorily; and if it is true that Rasputin has vanished, I trust that his disappearance will not be associated with the shots at our house.'

'Yes, it's all clear to me now. But tell me, Prince, who were your guests other than the Grand Duke Dmitri Pavlovich and M. Purishkevich?'

'I must decline to answer that question. The whole of this affair, trivial as it is, may take a serious turn. They are my friends. . . . There are their families to think of; their official positions might be prejudiced in spite of their innocence.'

'I am very grateful, Prince, for your information,' said the General. 'I shall drive straight to the Prefect and report to him all you have told me. Your explanation clears up the incident, and completely guarantees you from unpleasant consequences of any kind.'

I requested General Grigoriev to tell the Prefect that I would like to see him, and asked him to let me know at what time I could be received.

As soon as he had gone, I was called to the telephone. It was M. 'What have you done with Grigori Efimovich?' she asked.

'With Grigori Efimovich? What a strange question?'

'What! Wasn't he with you yesterday?' she exclaimed, in alarm. 'Then where is he? Come and see me quickly, for God's sake! I am in a terrible state of mind.'

The prospect of that conversation with M. oppressed me beyond words. What could I say to one who was so genuinely attached to me, who had such confidence in me, never doubting a single word that I uttered?

How should I look her in the eyes when she asked: 'What have you done with Grigori Efimovich?'

But I had to go, and within half-an-hour I arrived in the G.s' drawing-room.

An atmosphere of distress pervaded the house. On all sides there were anxious and tear-stained faces. M. was hardly recognisable. She ran towards me and, in a voice trembling with emotion, said:

'Tell me, for God's sake, where is Grigori Efimovich? What have you done with him? They say that he was killed in your house, and that you are his murderer.'

I tried to calm her, and told her in detail the story that I had prepared.

'Oh, how terrible it all is! Both the Empress and Anya* are sure that he was killed during the night, and that it was done in your house, and by you.'

'Ring up Tsarskoe at once. If the Empress will receive me, I will explain everything to her. Ring up as quickly as possible,' I insisted.

M. did as I asked. She was informed that the Empress would see me.

Just as I was leaving in order to proceed straight to the Empress, M. called me back. Apart from her alarm at the disappearance of Rasputin, her face now showed traces of a new anxiety.

'Don't go to Tsarskoe, don't go!' she implored. 'Something dreadful will happen to you. They will never believe that you had nothing to do with it. They are all in a terrible state of mind. They say that I've betrayed them. Oh! why did I listen to you? I oughtn't to have telephoned. It was a great mistake. Oh, what have I done?'

Her anxiety on my behalf and her whole attitude towards me showed such affectionate devotion that it cost me a supreme effort to restrain myself from confessing everything to her. It was torture to me to have to deceive her; she was so kind, and she trusted me so implicitly.

She came close up to me, and timidly looking at me with her kind, innocent eyes, made the sign of the Cross over me.

'God preserve you! I will pray for you,' she said in a low voice.

Suddenly a bell rang. It was a telephone call from Tsarskoe; Vyrubova was speaking.

The Empress was not feeling well, and could not receive me. I was to send her a written report of all I knew concerning the disappearance of Rasputin.

'Thank God! I'm so relieved that you are not going there,' said M.

I bade her good-bye and went out into the street. I had only taken a few steps when I met one of my friends of the *Corps des Pages*. He ran up to me in great excitement.

'Felix!' he exclaimed. 'Have you heard the news. Rasputin is killed!'

'Impossible! Who killed him?'

* Vyrubova.

Anna Vyrubova, Lady in waiting, c1905

'They say it happened at the gypsies, but nobody yet knows who did it.'

'I hope to God it's true,' I said.

He went on his way, very pleased with himself at having been the first to give me such a sensational piece of news, and I went back to the palace, expecting to find a reply from the Prefect of Police.

The reply was awaiting me. General Balk would see me immediately.

When I arrived at his office I found the place in a great turmoil. The General was in his room, sitting at a writing-table. He looked very worried.

I told him that I had come in order to clear up the misunderstanding that had arisen over Purishkevich's words. I added that I was anxious to lose no time in doing so, since I was proceeding on leave that evening for the Crimea, where my family were awaiting me; I did not wish to be detained in St. Petersburg by interrogations and various other formalities.

The Prefect replied that the explanations which I had given to General Grigoriev were entirely satisfactory, and that he did not foresee any difficulties over my departure, but he had to inform me that he had received orders from the Empress Alexandra Feodorovna to search our house on the Moika, in view of the suspicious shots in the night and of rumours of my association with the disappearance of Rasputin.

'My wife is a niece of the Emperor,' I said. 'Members of the Imperial Family, and their residences, are inviolable; and measures against them cannot be taken except by order of His Majesty the Emperor himself.'

The Prefect was obliged to agree with me on this point, and in my presence he at once gave instructions, by telephone, countermanding the search.

This greatly relieved me. I had been obsessed by the feeling that in getting the rooms in order overnight a good deal had escaped us, and that it was therefore necessary at all costs to postpone any such search until after we had carried out a thorough inspection and had removed every trace of what had really occurred.

I took my leave of General Balk and returned to the Moika, breathing more freely now that this difficulty had been overcome.

My fears turned out to be well-founded. On examining the dining-room and stairs by daylight I noticed brown stains on the floor and carpets. My servants and I removed every trace that was to be found. We worked with a will, and soon completed our task.

But we were unable to remove stains which were visible near the entrance to the courtyard, where the blood had soaked into the stone flags. Our only resource would be to explain that they had been caused by the dead dog.

But suppose they should make a search after all, and should make a chemical analysis of these stains? Matters might then take a very serious turn. It was essential therefore that we should find some means of concealing these traces.

We accordingly decided to paint them over with oil-colour of the same tint as the stones, and to cover the whole with a thick layer of snow. It seemed that we had now done everything possible to throw off the examining authorities on a false scent.

It was already two o'clock in the afternoon, and I went to lunch with the Grand Duke Dmitri Pavlovich. He told me in general terms how they had disposed of Rasputin's body.

On returning to the Moika in the closed car, the Grand Duke had found me unconscious. His first impulse was to remain with me until I recovered. But there was no time to spare, for dawn was approaching.

Rasputin's body, closely wrapped in a cloth and tightly bound with cord, was placed in the car. The Grand Duke acted as chauffeur. Sukhotin sat beside him, and Purishkevich, with Dr. Lazovert and my servant, sat behind. They stopped as soon as they reached the Petrovski bridge. The sentry's box stood out in the distance. Fearing that the noise of the motor and the powerful rays of the lamps might attract attention, the Grand Duke stopped the engine and extinguished the lights.

Complete confusion reigned. They were on edge with excitement. In their nervous haste they omitted to attach weights to the body before throwing it into a large fissure in the ice, and they even failed to remove the outer garments.*

To crown these misfortunes, the car at first refused to start. But after a brief delay the Grand Duke managed to set it in motion. In turning, he drove quite near to the sentry-box. Its occupant was fast asleep. The party drove back without further incident.

In conclusion, the Grand Duke expressed the opinion that in all likelihood the body had already been carried down to the sea by the river current.

I then gave him an account of my adventures and conversations during that morning.

Captain Sukhotin came in after lunch. We asked him to go and find Purishkevich, and to bring him to us at the Palace. That evening Purishkevich was leaving for the front** with his hospital train, and I was leaving for the Crimea; while on the following day the Grand Duke was to proceed to G.H.Q.

It was essential, therefore, that we should all meet, and agree upon a common line of action in the event of the detention, arrest, or cross-examination of any one of us.

---

* They had not had time to remove all the clothing and burn it, as had been originally decided.

** Purishkevich, protected by his popularity in the army and by his title of member of the Duma, returned to the front that evening.

After discussion we agreed to uphold the explanations which I had already given to Grigoriev, to M. and to the Prefect of Police. Whatever happened, whatever new proofs might be found against us, we were to maintain this attitude.

We had taken the first step. The way was now open for those who realised all that had been happening and were in a position to continue that struggle against Rasputinism which we had begun. For the time being we ought to stand aside.

And on this decision we parted.

* * *

CHAPTER XVII

INTERROGATORIES AND DEPOSITIONS

ON leaving the Grand Duke Dmitri Pavlovich's palace, I returned home to Moika 94 to discover whether anything fresh had arisen. When I arrived there I was told that in the course of the day all my servants had been cross-examined. I did not know the result of these inquiries, but the accounts which my servants gave of them tended to reassure me.

Nevertheless, I did not like the look of things. I was afraid that I might be delayed by various formalities and so prevented from being with my family at Christmas-time. I resolved, therefore, to call on the Minister of Justice, M. Makarov, to ascertain how matters stood.

The Ministry of Justice, like the Prefecture of Police, was in a state of great excitement. The Minister was in conference with the Public Prosecutor, whom I met coming out of the door of M. Makarov's room as I went in. He regarded me with unconcealed curiosity as we passed.

I had not met M. Makarov before, and I liked him at first sight. He was a thin, elderly man with grey hair and beard, a kindly appearance, and a soft voice.

I explained the object of my visit, and at his request repeated, from the very beginning, with full details, the story which by now I had learned by heart.

When I reached that part of it which bore reference to Purishkevich's conversation with the policeman, M. Makarov interrupted me with the words:

'I know Vladimir Mitrofanovich very well. He never drinks. If I am not mistaken, he is even a member of the Temperance League.'

'I can assure you,' I answered, 'that on this occasion Vladimir Mitrofanovich betrayed both himself and the League of which you state he is a member. He found it difficult to refuse wine; I was giving a house-warming and we all pressed him to drink with us. As he was unaccustomed to it, a very few glasses sufficed to affect him.'

When I had finished my explanation, I asked M. Makarov whether my servants were immune from further cross-examination and unpleasantness, as they all felt rather anxious, in view of my departure that evening for the Crimea.

The Minister reassured me on this point. He said that in all likelihood the police authorities would make no further inquiries, and that for his part he would neither sanction a search of the house, nor attach any importance to rumours or gossip in the town.

Just as I was departing, I asked the Minister whether I might leave St. Petersburg. He replied in the affirmative, and once again expressed his regret that I should have been subjected to so much trouble and unpleasantness through such a misunderstanding.

From the Ministry of Justice I went to my uncle, M. Rodzianko, the President of the Imperial Duma. He and his wife had known beforehand of our resolve to put an end to Rasputin, and they were impatiently awaiting a full account of what had happened. On entering their drawing-room I noticed that they were both agitated and were discussing something or other with raised voices. My aunt came up to me with tears in her eyes; she embraced me and made the sign of the Cross over me. My uncle also welcomed me in his voice of thunder, and embraced me.

I particularly appreciated such warmth of affection. Far away from my own people, completely alone, I was passing through a very difficult period. This fatherly attitude cheered and calmed me.

But I could not stay long with them, as my train was leaving at nine o'clock that evening, and I had not yet packed. I gave them a brief account of the assassination and then took my leave.

'We shall now stand aside and leave further action to others,' I said, as we parted. 'Please God that by common endeavour the Emperor may be given an opportunity of realising the truth before it is too late. It would be difficult to imagine a more favourable moment.'

'I am convinced that the assassination of Rasputin will be regarded as a patriotic deed,' replied Rodzianko, 'and that everyone will unite to save Russia from ruin.'

From the Rodziankos' I went to the palace of the Grand Duke Alexander Mikhailovich.

As I entered the hall the door-keeper informed me that a lady to whom I had given an appointment for seven o'clock was already awaiting me in the study.

I had not given any such appointment. This unlooked-for visit greatly surprised me, and I asked for a description of the lady's appearance. I learnt that she was dressed in black; and that her face could hardly be seen, as she was wearing a very thick veil.

My misgivings prompted me to pass into my bedroom, to examine my mysterious visitor.

What was my astonishment, on looking through the chink in the folding doors, to recognise one of the most fervent admirers of Rasputin!

I called the door-keeper and instructed him to tell my uninvited guest that I was out and should be returning very late that evening. I quickly packed and then went up to dinner.

On the stairs I met my friend Oswald Rayner, an English officer whom I had known since our Oxford days. He realised the truth of all that had happened and was very anxious on my behalf. I assured him that up to the present everything was well.

At dinner there were the three elder brothers of my wife, who were to accompany me to the Crimea, their tutor — Mr. Stuart, Mlle. Evreinova—one—of the Ladies-in-waiting to the Grand Duchess Xenia Alexandrovna, Rayner, and a number of others.

They were all excited by the news of the mysterious disappearance of Rasputin, and the most unlikely rumours were discussed. Some of those present did not believe in the death of the *starets*; they maintained that he was alive and that everything said to the contrary was sheer invention. Others quoted 'reliable sources,' even 'eyewitnesses,' in support of their assertion that he had been killed during a debauch at the gypsies. Others, again, confidently announced that he had been killed in my house on the Moika, and that I had participated in his murder. The less credulous among them thought it hardly probable that I had taken an active part in the assassination itself, but held that in any case I was aware of all the details; and they plied me with questions. Searching glances were directed at me from all sides, in the hope of reading the truth in my face. But I kept calm, and joined in the general rejoicing, and thanks to my demeanour these suspicions were gradually allayed.

In the meantime the telephone-bell rang incessantly. Throughout the whole of St. Petersburg my name was associated with the disappearance of Rasputin. I was rung up by relations, by friends, by members of the Duma, and by representatives and directors of various industries and factories, who announced that their employees intended to form a guard for me in case of need.

To one and all I replied that the rumours of my participation in the murder of Rasputin were false, and that I knew nothing about it.

My train was due to start in half-an-hour. After saying good-bye to the rest of the company I entered the car with my brothers-in-law — Prince Andrew, Prince Theodore, and Prince Nikita, their tutor, and Rayner.

On arrival at the station I noticed a large force of the Palace Police collected on the steps of the main entrance. This astonished me. 'Had an order been issued for my arrest?' I wondered. We left the car and went up the steps. When I was level with the colonel of the gendarmes he came up to me, and in an excited voice said something quite unintelligible.

'Could you speak a little louder, Colonel?' I said. 'I can't hear what you say.'

He pulled himself together and, raising his voice, said:

'By Her Majesty's orders, you are forbidden to leave St. Petersburg. You must return to the Palace and remain there until further instructions.'

'I'm sorry to hear that,' I replied; and turning to my companions, I repeated to them the Imperial command.

My arrest came as a complete surprise to them. Prince Andrew and Prince Theodore decided that they would not go to the Crimea, but would remain with me; Prince Nikita alone should leave, accompanied by his tutor.

We went to see them off. The police followed us. They seemed afraid that I might board the train and get away.

We presented an unusual spectacle as we proceeded along the platform. The public stood still, their eyes turned upon us with curiosity.

When I entered the carriage to say a few words to Prince Nikita, the police again showed uneasiness. I calmed their fears by telling them that I had no intention of evading them, but simply wanted to say good-bye to those who were leaving us.

The train started, and we went back to the car.

'It is strange to feel oneself arrested!' I thought, 'I wonder what is in store for me?'

Everyone at home was astonished at our return and could not understand what it meant.

I was tired out by the events of the day, and as soon as I reached my room I lay, down. I asked Prince Theodore and Rayner to stay with me for a while.

While we were talking Prince Andrew ran into the room and announced the arrival of the Grand Duke Nicholas Mikhailovich.

This late visit forboded ill for me. He had apparently come to find out from me full details of all that had happened, and he had arrived just at a moment when I felt tired, wanted to sleep, and was not in the mood for such conversations.

There were strange contradictions in the character of the Grand Duke Nicholas Mikhailovich. A learned historian, a man of great intellect and independence of mind, in his dealings with people he at times adopted a tone of excessive banter. He was inclined to be garrulous, and to speak of matters on which he should have preserved silence.

He detested Rasputin, and fully realised how harmful he was to Russia. In his political outlook he was an extreme Liberal. He sharply criticised current events; he had even suffered for such free expression of his thoughts, and had previously been dismissed from St. Petersburg to Grushevka, his estate in the Province of Kherson.

Prince Theodore and Rayner had hardly closed the door behind them when the Grand Duke entered from the opposite side of the room. He turned to me with the words:

'Well, now, tell me; what have you been up to?'

I feigned astonishment and said:

'Surely you don't believe these rumours about me? Why it's all a crass misunderstanding. I've really nothing whatever to do with it.'

'Tell that to others, not to me! I know everything, every detail — even the names of the women who were at the party!'

His last words showed me that he knew absolutely nothing, and that he was merely pretending to be well-informed in order that he might trip me up. I told him exactly the same story of my house-warming party, and the shooting of the dog.

Apparently he believed my tale, but to preserve himself against error, he smiled knowingly at me as he left. It was clear that he not only knew nothing, but that he was intensely annoyed at having failed to get any information out of me.

After he had gone Prince Andrew, Prince Theodore and Rayner rejoined me. I told them that in the morning I should move to the Grand Duke Dmitri Pavlovich's palace in order to be with him until our fate was decided. I fully explained to them what answers they were to give if they should be cross-questioned. They promised to follow my instructions to the letter, and then bade me good-night and left.

The events of the previous night passed before my eyes, one thought succeeding another, until at last my head grew heavy with fatigue, and I fell asleep.

* * *

Grand Duke Dmitri Pavlovich

Grand Duchess Alexandra Georgievna of Russia died in 1891 less than a week after giving birth to Dmitri Pavlovich. In 1902 his father Paul of Russia (a son of Alexander II,) was banished from Russia. This meant he and his sister Maria became very close and remained in Russia under the protection of their paternal uncle Sergei Alexandrovich and his wife Elizabeth Feodorovna.

Youssoupoff connects Pavlovich as an integral cog in the plot to kill Rasputin. Pavlovich was in his prime at 25 years old and if the others may have been a bit older, they could certainly count on the energy of Pavlovich to see the task to its end at all costs. He had grown up around Alexander Palace and was arguably the only person of similar age to the princesses that they saw regularly, during their relative seclusion.

He was regarded as a son by the Imperial couple and would have seen first hand the effect that Rasputin was having on the Imperial Family, and been *au fait* with the goings on at the palace during the war years when the Tsar moved to the front leaving the Tsarina at the mercy of the seemingly malevolent Rasputin.

* * *

Oswald Rayner

British Intelligence learned that Protopopov, Stürmer and Rasputin were the leading Germanophiles. The assassination of two prominent politicians would not have been a consideration but the elimination of Rasputin, that was entirely different. Soon after this discovery, British Intelligence officers Captain Stephen Alley, Captain John Scale and Lieutenant Oswald Rayner began meeting with Prince Youssoupoff at the Moika Palace.

* * *

CHAPTER XVIII

AT THE PALACE OF THE GRAND DUKE DMITRI PAVLOVICH

EARLY the following morning I moved to the palace of the Grand Duke Dmitri Pavlovich. He was very surprised to see me; he had felt certain that I had left for the Crimea on the previous evening.

I told him of my arrest and of my decision to come and stay with him in view of the complications that had arisen, and of the possibility of measures being taken against us both. I also recounted to him my conversations with the various people whom I had met. In his turn he told me all that he had done during the previous day. In the evening he had gone to the Mikhailovski Theatre, but he had been obliged to leave, as he was warned that the audience was about to give him an ovation. On returning home from the theatre he had learned that at Tsarskoe Selo he was credited with having taken a leading part in the assassination. He had then telephoned to the Empress Alexandra Feodorovna, and requested her to receive him; but she had categorically refused.

After chatting a little longer with him I went to the room which had been allotted to me. I sent for the newspapers and went through them, looking for references to what had occurred. There was nothing beyond the bald statement that 'on the night of the 16th - 17th of December the *starets*, Grigori Rasputin,' had been killed.

The morning passed quietly, but at about one o'clock, just as we were having lunch, General Maximovich, A.D.C. to the Emperor, telephoned to the Grand Duke to inform him that he was under arrest by order of the Empress, and was requested not to leave his palace. He added that he would shortly arrive in person, and communicate further details.

The Grand Duke returned to the dining-room very much perturbed by this conversation.

'Felix,' he said, 'I am arrested by the orders of the Empress Alexandra Feodorovna. . . . She has no right to take this step; the Emperor alone can issue such an order.'

General Maximovich arrived in the midst of our discussion. He was shown into the study. When the Grand Duke entered the room the General met him with the words:

'Her Majesty requests Your Imperial Highness not to leave your palace. . . .'

'What does this mean? — Arrest?'

'No, it is not arrest, but Her Majesty nevertheless insists that you should not leave your palace.'

The Grand Duke replied, with deliberation:

'I maintain that this is arrest! Inform Her Majesty that I submit to her command.'

With these words he left the study.

In the course of the day the Grand Duke Dmitri Pavlovich was visited in turn by nearly all the members of the Imperial House who were in St. Petersburg at that time. They were deeply concerned over his arrest and over the fact that the Empress Alexandra Feodorovna had so far exceeded her powers as to give orders that a member of the Imperial Family should be deprived of his liberty on the mere supposition that he was a party to the murder of Rasputin.

On the same day the Grand Duke received a telegram from the Grand Duchess Elizabeth Feodorovna at Moscow, again associating my name with the disappearance of Rasputin. Aware of the ties of friendship between us, and not suspecting that he himself had taken an active part in the destruction of the *starets*, the Grand Duchess requested him to tell me that she was praying for me and blessed my patriotic action.

This telegram seriously compromised us. Protopopov intercepted it, and sent a copy of it to Tsarskoe Selo to the Empress, who immediately concluded that the Grand Duchess Elizabeth Feodorovna also was in the plot.

The telephone-bell rang incessantly, and the person who rang up most frequently was the Grand Duke Nicholas Mikhailovich; he gave us the most incredible news. He came to see us several times a day. He affected to know everything, and tried to trip us up at every turn. Seeking by every possible means to discover the whole truth, he pretended to be our ally, in the hope that we should heedlessly commit ourselves.

He was not satisfied with conversations on the telephone and his constant visits to us. He took a most active part in the search for Rasputin's body.

During one of his visits he incidentally informed us that the Empress Alexandra Feodorovna was fully persuaded of our complicity in the death of Rasputin and was demanding that we should be shot out of hand, but that everyone was restraining her. Even Protopopov had advised her to await the Emperor's arrival from General Headquarters. A telegram had been despatched to the Emperor, and he was expected at any moment.

On the same day that we heard this news from the Grand Duke Nicholas Mikhailovich. M. communicated to me the no less unpleasant information that attempts were afoot against our lives, and advised us to take all possible precautions. It appeared that on the previous evening she had been an involuntary witness of how, in Rasputin's flat, twenty of his most ardent followers had sworn to avenge him.

It was a particularly exhausting day for both the Grand Duke Dmitri Pavlovich and myself, and we felt relieved when all our visitors had left. It had been difficult to keep a constant guard on ourselves in the presence of others, to preserve our serenity and to endeavour, by our own calm attitude towards events and rumours, to dispel all suspicion of our participation in the murder.

Now that we were alone we talked for a long time, exchanging our impressions of all that we had heard.

I had never before known the Grand Duke so simple and so sincere. The horror through which we had lived had left a deep mark on his sensitive nature, and I felt happy to be at his side, sharing his enforced solitude during this period beset with anxiety.

* * *

CHAPTER XIX

THE BODY RECOVERED

ON the morning of the following day, December 19th, the Emperor arrived from G.H.Q.

Those in attendance upon him said that on receiving the news of Rasputin's death his mood was more cheerful than since the outbreak of war.

He himself evidently felt and believed that the disappearance of the *starets* had freed him from those heavy fetters which he had lacked the strength to cast off. But with his return to Tsarskoe Selo his mood abruptly changed, and once again he fell under the influence of those who surrounded him.

All sorts of rumours continued to circulate in the town. All classes of society lived on them, believed in them, and were deeply affected by them.

News of our impending execution reached the workmen of large factories, and caused great fermentation among them. They held meetings at which they passed resolutions to the effect that they would save us, and would organise a secret guard to protect us.

Although we were on the footing of persons under arrest, and except for members of the Imperial Family no one was supposed to be admitted into the Sergei Palace, our friends and acquaintances nevertheless managed to visit us. Officers of various regiments came, with the assurance that their commands to a man were ready to defend us. They had been deeply affected by the event, and submitted to the Grand Duke various plans based on decisive action, to which he could not, of course, agree.

On this day we were visited by an unusual number of people. Members of the Imperial House had been arriving at the palace since the early morning. On going into the study we found them assembled there, and they inundated us with questions. On the previous day their attention had been so entirely preoccupied by the arrest of the Grand Duke that they did not discuss anything else. Now, however, they wanted to know full details of Rasputin's mysterious disappearance — but they only heard from us the same story.

The Grand Duke Nicholas Mikhailovich arrived just before dinner and told us that Rasputin's body had been found in an ice-hole below the Petrovski Bridge.

In the evening General Maximovich returned, to inform the Grand Duke Dmitri Pavlovich, in the name of the Emperor this time, that he was under arrest.

We passed an uneasy night. At about 3 a.m. we were awakened with a warning that suspicious persons were in the palace, having gained access by the back entrance. They had explained to the servants that they had been sent to guard the premises, but as they had no written authority they were expelled, and palace servants were posted at all the entrances.

On December 20th almost the whole of the Imperial Family assembled again for tea. They reopened their discussion of the Grand Duke Dmitri Pavlovich's arrest, now officially confirmed by the Emperor. Not one of them was reconciled to such treatment of a member of the Imperial Family. They regarded it as an affair of State, and as an event of the gravest significance.

It did not occur to anyone that there were more serious questions at issue — that on the Emperor's actions during the next few days hung the destiny of the country, the fate of the Throne and dynasty, and the outcome of the war, which could not end in victory without complete harmony between the Supreme Power and the people.

The end of Rasputin had brought into the foreground the question of the end of Rasputinism, the necessity of a new trend in politics which were now or never to be disentangled from criminal intrigues.

After the members of the Imperial House had left, General Laiming, the Grand Duke Dmitri Pavlovich's former tutor, came in. He lived in the palace, and often visited us. He gave us full details of the recovery of Rasputin's body from the river.

The official inquiry into the disappearance of Rasputin had been entrusted to Colonel Globachev, Chief of the Secret Police. He informed the Public Prosecutor at the St. Petersburg Courts of

Justice that after a thorough search, 'a black snow-boot, size number eleven, covered with recent blood-stains,' had been found on the Petrovski Bridge. This snow-boot was taken to Rasputin's flat, where it was recognised as the property of the murdered man. Further, the snow on the bridge bore numerous footmarks and traces of motor tyres right up to the parapet itself.

Thus, according to Colonel Globachev, the clues to the discovery of the murderers should be sought not at Moika No. 94, but at the opposite end of the town — on the Petrovski Bridge.

Following on this report, further searches were made, and the Petrovski Bridge was re-examined. All the higher officials of the administrative and of the judicial world repaired there. The bare enumeration of the posts which they occupied is in itself proof of the importance in which Rasputin was held, and shows what a 'national disaster' his death seemed in the eyes of the Government and of the Supreme Power.

At the inspection of the bridge — according to the official report on the murder of Rasputin — there were present; 'The senior officials of the Ministry of Justice, with the Minister at their head; the Public Prosecutor of the St. Petersburg Courts of Justice; the Deputy Public Prosecutor; the Examining Magistrate for cases of special gravity; and a representative of the Ministry of the Interior.'

All these important State officials concentrated their attention and zeal on solving the problem which mystified them.

They interrogated the policeman on duty, the watchman at an ale-house near by, the watchman from the Home for Aged Artists of the Imperial Theatres . . . but all to no purpose.

There followed a further and most minute search. On this occasion a fresh clue was found — a piece of matting bearing traces of blood. Further, attention was drawn to the fact that at one point on the bridge-railing the snow had been displaced in such a way as to justify the assumption that some object had lain there. This circumstance tended to confirm the opinion that the murder of Rasputin must have taken place here, on the Petrovski Bridge, a deserted spot on the very outskirts of the town — and nowhere else; certainly not on the Moika, which was at the opposite end of St. Petersburg.

There were two main reasons which impelled the examining authorities to favour this theory. In the first place, they maintained that if the body had been conveyed through the streets, traces of blood would have been discovered somewhere along the route taken. Yet the whole town had been searched and no bloodstains had been found.

Secondly, there was the discovery of the victim's snow-boot. It could hardly be supposed that before the body was conveyed from the actual scene of the crime it was clothed so completely that even the snow-boots were not forgotten.

The examining authorities accordingly reconstructed the crime on the following lines: Rasputin was killed on the bridge itself. His body lay over the balustrade for a time, and was then thrown down into the ice-hole, just opposite the spot where the bloodstained piece of matting had been found, and where the snow had been brushed away from the railing.

Divers were immediately summoned. The bottom of the river was searched for two-and-a-half hours, but the body was not discovered.

The divers maintained that the current of the Neva, exceptionally strong at this point, might have carried it under the ice far beyond the Petrovski Bridge. Their work was interrupted for a time by the heavy frosts. The bridge was roped off, and a guard was placed at its approaches.

But in the meantime, one of the river police, while making a hole in the ice, chanced to notice the sleeve of a beaver fur coat frozen to the under surface.

He promptly reported this to his superior officer. Orders were given to cut through the ice, and a quarter of an hour afterwards the body of Rasputin was taken from the water, having been found at a point about thirty *sazhens** distant from the Petrovski Bridge.

The body was covered with such a thick layer of ice that it was difficult to recognise the features.

When this coating of ice had been carefully removed, the examining authorities saw the mutilated remains of Rasputin. The head of the dead man was found to be broken in a number of places, and tufts of hair had been torn out here and there. In its fall from the bridge the body had probably struck head-foremost against the edge of the ice-hole. The beard had frozen to the clothing; on the face and chest there were clots of congealed blood; one eye was blackened.

* A *sazhen* is equivalent to 7 feet.

The arms and legs were tightly bound round with rope, and the left fist was tightly clenched. The body was wrapped in a beaver coat thrown over the shoulders. The loose sleeves, floating up. and freezing to the ice, had revealed the presence of the corpse.

As soon as an official report of this discovery had been drawn up, the body was covered with sacking and removed to a wooden shed on the river-bank.

In the meantime, there arrived at the Petrovski Bridge the Minister of the Interior, M. Protopopov; the Officer in Command of the St. Petersburg Military District; the Officer in Command of the Secret Police, and various administrative officials. The Public Prosecutor's Office was instructed to draw up a full report on the external appearance of the body and on the circumstances attending its discovery.

The Deputy Public Prosecutor, M. Galkin, who was entrusted with this task, temporarily transferred his office to a private house in the neighbourhood of the Petrovski Bridge.

At 11 am. the examining authorities, accompanied by a number of high officials, proceeded to the shed and began a minute inspection of the body.

After the clothes had been removed, two wounds caused by firearms were observed; one in the region of the breast, near the heart, the other in the neck. The doctors stated that each of them would undoubtedly have been fatal.

A domestic servant was summoned to identify the body, and recognised it as being that of Grigori Rasputin of No. 64 Gorokhovaya Street, who had disappeared, leaving no trace, on the night of December 16th.

At midday Rasputin's two daughters and the fiancé of one of them, Lieutenant Papkhadze, were admitted. The daughters applied for permission to have the body removed to their home, but the authorities refused.

The news that Rasputin's remains had been found spread through the town like wildfire. A file of carriages and cars streamed to the Petrovski Bridge, but the authorities gave strict instructions that no one should be admitted into the shed where the body was lying.

Soon afterwards a wooden coffin was brought in, and the body was placed in it. Before this was done, however, it was twice photographed; first with its clothing, and then without. The ropes with which the legs and arms had been bound, the beaver coat, and certain other articles were sealed up and filed as material evidence.

The body, in its coffin, was then taken to the Chesma Asylum for further examination.

Long before the arrival of the persons who had been appointed to conduct the autopsy, the whole of the district in which the Asylum is situated was surrounded by a strong force of police, mounted and on foot.

The post-mortem continued until nearly 1 a.m. and was conducted in the presence of rows of prominent officials, including a representative of the Ministry of the Interior. The operation was performed by one of the professors of the Judicial Department of the Military Medical Academy, assisted by a number of police doctors.

For two hours the body was submitted to a most minute examination. Apart from the two wounds caused by the shots, a number of livid bruises were discovered.

In the stomach was found a ductile mass, dark-brown in colour ... but its analysis was never made, for the Empress Alexandra Feodorovna commanded that the examination should cease.

It is not known what other orders were given, but at about 2 a.m. General Grigoriev, who had been present at the autopsy, directed that a car should be sent to the Asylum. In the meantime, a richly-decorated oak coffin had been brought to the mortuary. The remains were placed in it, and conveyed in the car to a destination unknown. The route was divulged to no one; Rasputin's body was removed by agents of the Secret Police.

* * *

CHAPTER XX

DISAPPOINTMENT

ON the evening of December 21st, we were astonished by the sudden appearance of soldiers at the Sergei Palace. We learned that they were a guard sent by the military authorities by order of the President of the Council of Ministers, who had been informed that Rasputin's adherents were preparing an attempt on our lives.

At almost the same moment, another 'guard,' of a totally different kind, sought admission. An agent of the secret police presented himself to General Laiming, alleging that he had been sent by M. Protopopov, Minister of the Interior. He declared that M. Protopopov had received information that the life of the Grand Duke Dmitri Pavlovich was threatened, and had instructed him, with the men under his command, to guard the palace.

The Grand Duke, on hearing of this, said that he had no need of any Protopopov guards, and asked General Laiming to insist on their producing papers in proof of their assertion. They had no documents of any kind, and were immediately turned away from the palace. This, however, did not prevent them from keeping a watch on us from without, and from noting everyone who entered and left the building.

Not content with their observations from outside, Rasputin's adherents made fresh attempts to gain access to us. On the second floor of the palace, which communicated with the lower floor* by a circular staircase, the Anglo-Russian Hospital was housed. Most suspicious individuals began to appear there, under pretext of visiting the wounded. Lady Sybil Grey, who was in charge of the hospital, advised us to close the staircase entrance, and to place a sentry at that point. We acted on her suggestion.

* The Grand Duke Dmitri Pavlovich at this time occupied the lower floor.

We seemed to be living in a beleaguered fortress; we could only follow events from a distance.

We read the papers, and listened to the accounts and conversations of our visitors.

Each proffered his own opinion of what was happening. We encountered almost invariably a fear of any bold initiative, a passive awaiting of what the morrow would bring.

Those who were in a position to act were too timorous to come out into the open. They seemed to be counting on some chance intervention which should decide the destiny of Russia.

Even those who served their country and Emperor in the name of duty, envisaged that duty only in the narrow frame of the routine of a ministry or government department. In spite of their assiduity in the performance of their official tasks, they lacked the breadth of view which would have enabled them to realise the supreme importance of the moment; they did not venture to overstep the recognised limits of their authority. Devotion to the Emperor, as felt by the most sincere among them, meant little more than a desire to please him, a blind obedience tempered with the fear of compromising themselves by association with anything that savoured of opposition.

It is a characteristic fact that the handful of men who were in positions of influence in the Government independently of Rasputin's aid, and had nothing whatever in common with him, were afraid to visit us at the Sergei Palace.

Yet it was only by the combined action of all who by their parentage or position could influence the Emperor, that successful results could be attained.

If the Emperor, on learning of the death of the *starets*, travelled from G.H.Q. in a cheerful frame of mind, it necessarily follows that he realised Rasputin's harmful influence in Russia.

But he was unable to maintain this attitude after he had regained the atmosphere of Tsarskoe Selo, where feelings ran so high against us that we were threatened with the severest form of punishment, as was reported to us by so many of our friends.

In such circumstances what could be effected by people who singly expressed their opinions to the Emperor and were then content to stand aside, conscious of having done their duty?

Firmly convinced of the futility of struggling against fate, the

Emperor Nicholas II at the end of his reign was weighed down not only by disturbances and failures of a political nature, but by all those morbid influences which surrounded him and stifled in him every possibility of active resistance.

To awaken his own initiative and encourage his independence the influence of his immediate surroundings would have had to be directly opposed by some very powerful and solidly organised force.

If he had seen that the majority of the Imperial Family and all honest men holding high office in the State were harmoniously united in striving to save the Throne and Russia, it may well be that he would not only have responded to their exhortations, but would have been grateful to them for their moral support, and for having freed him from the chains which had bound him.

But from what elements could this solidly organised force be drawn?

Where could people be found who were ready to sacrifice their own interests?

Long years of Rasputin's influence, with its surreptitious intrigues, had contaminated those who stood high in the government service, had fostered a widespread distrust, and had tainted even the best and most honourable with scepticism and suspicion.

Some recoiled before serious decisions; others no longer believed in anything; while others, again, simply did not bother their heads. . . .

After bidding our visitors farewell, the Grand Duke Dmitri Pavlovich and I would remain alone, reviewing all that we had heard during the day — conversations, rumours and facts; and we would exchange our impressions.

Our deductions were far from encouraging.

One by one our bright hopes were extinguished — those hopes which had been our inspiration in putting an end to Rasputin and had supported us through the nightmare of that unforgettable night of December 16th.

As if I were reading a book, I turned over page after page of all that had passed; my acquaintance with Rasputin, the gradual growth of my resolve to destroy him, the appalling deception to which I had been obliged to resort, and the immense efforts it had cost me to preserve the role which I had assumed.

With what youthful fervour we had believed that with one blow we could triumph over evil!

To us it had seemed that Rasputin was merely a cancerous growth, and that with its removal the Russian Monarchy would be restored to health. We would not admit that this cancer had become so deeply rooted that its work of destruction would baffle even the most radical measures.

It would have been still more depressing to realise then that Rasputin's appearance on the scene was not merely an unfortunate chance, but that it was inexplicably connected with some hidden process of disintegration which had already affected part of the Russian State organism. . . .

Those days of arrest in the Sergei Palace taught us how difficult it was to change the course of history even when inspired by the most sincere intentions, when ready for any sacrifice.

But we still hoped for better things, right up to the very last.

And the whole country hoped for, and believed in, this improvement. A huge wave of patriotism had swept over Russia. Enthusiasm was especially marked in both the capitals.

Every newspaper was full of eulogistic articles.

The recent event was interpreted as heralding the extinction of an evil power which had brought Russia to the verge of ruin. Expression was given to the most sanguine hopes for the future, and on this occasion the voice of the press seemed to be a genuine reflection of the thoughts and feelings of the whole country. But this freedom of speech was short-lived. On the third day special orders were issued to the whole of the press, forbidding all mention of Rasputin. Public opinion, however, found expression by other means. The streets of St. Petersburg wore a holiday air; men stopped each other, and, whether acquainted or not congratulated each other on what had happened. It was no uncommon sight to see people going down on their knees and crossing themselves as they passed the palace of the Grand Duke Dmitri Pavlovich or our house on the Moika.

Thanksgiving services were held in churches throughout the town. In all the theatres the public demanded the National Anthem, and encored it with enthusiasm. Our health was drunk in private houses, at officers' messes, and in the restaurants. Workmen gave three cheers for us at the factories.

We received numerous letters of congratulation, couched in the most touching terms. People wrote to us from every quarter; from the front, from various towns and villages, from factories, and from public institutions. Partisans of Rasputin also wrote to us, swearing to avenge the death of the *starets* and to kill us.

The Grand Duchess Marie Pavlovna, sister of the Grand Duke Dmitri, in giving us her impressions of Pskov — which was the headquarters of the Northern Front — told us that the death of Rasputin had raised the morale of the army, and had inspired the belief that the Emperor would now dismiss the Rasputin coterie surrounding him, and gather round him honest and faithful people in their stead.

One word from the Emperor, his summons to a new life — even if it entailed fresh sacrifices for the sake of the country — and everything would have been forgotten, and forgiven....

One day, M. Trepov, President of the Council of Ministers, sent for me.

I had great hopes of this meeting, but I was to be disillusioned.

I was driven, under escort, to the Ministry of the Interior.

M. Trepov had sent for me by order of the Emperor, who desired at all cost to discover who had killed Rasputin.

He greeted me very kindly, reminded me of his intimacy with my parents, and asked me to look upon him, not as an official, but as an old friend of my family.

'You have probably sent for me by order of the Emperor?' I asked.

He nodded in assent.

'And it follows that anything I may tell you will be repeated to 'him?'

'Why, certainly. I cannot lie to my sovereign.'

'Then you surely do not imagine, after what you have told me, that I would confess to the murder of Rasputin, supposing that I had killed him? Or that I would give away those who were guilty of it, if I knew them?

'Tell His Majesty that those who destroyed Rasputin did so with the sole purpose of saving the Tsar and their country from inevitable ruin.'

'But,' I continued, 'is valuable time to be lost in tracking down Rasputin's murderer?

'Consider for a moment the significance which all Russia attaches to the destruction of this criminal, the enthusiasm which has everywhere been evoked. The Rasputin government clique has been thrown into complete confusion. And the Emperor? I am convinced that in his inmost soul he also rejoices over what has happened, and is waiting for help from you all. Get together and act, while there is yet time! Surely some of you realise that we are on the brink of a terrible catastrophe, and that if the Emperor is not forcibly extricated from this magic circle in which he is confined, then he himself, all the Imperial Family, and all the rest of us will be swept away by the wave of revolution.

'Disaster is inevitable, unless it be averted by a sweeping change of policy from above.'

The Minister listened to me with astonishment and attention. He was evidently unaccustomed to such plain speaking.

'Tell me, Prince,' he said suddenly. 'How did you acquire such self-control and presence of mind?'

I made no reply; and he said nothing more.

My conversation with the President of the Council of Ministers was the last appeal which we made to high government officials.

* * *

CHAPTER XXI

BANISHMENT

OUR fate was as yet undecided.

At Tsarskoe Selo there were endless conferences to determine what treatment should be meted out to us.

On December 21st. my father-in-law, the Grand Duke Alexander Mikhailovich, arrived in St. Petersburg. On learning of the danger which threatened us he had travelled from Kiev, his headquarters as Commander-in-Chief of the Russian Air Service. He came straight to the Grand Duke Dmitri's palace, and then went on to Tsarskoe Selo.

The result of his interview with the Emperor was that later in the day General Maximovich arrived at the Sergei Palace, with the Emperor's orders that the Grand Duke Dmitri Pavlovich should immediately leave St. Petersburg for Persia, where he was to report to General Baratov, Commander-in-Chief of the Persian Division. His late tutor, General Laiming, and Count Kutaisov, A.D.C. to the Emperor, were to accompany him.

At 11 p.m. the Prefect of Police came to announce that the Grand Duke Dmitri's train would leave at two o'clock in the morning.

I also was ordered to leave St. Petersburg. My place of confinement was to be our estate Rakitnoe in the Province of Kursk.

My train was to leave at midnight.

I was placed under the surveillance of Captain Zenchikov, an officer-instructor of His Majesty's *Corps des Pages*, and we were to be accompanied to Rakitnoe by Ignatiev, the Assistant-Director of the Secret Police.

Both Captain Zenchikov and Ignatiev had received strict instructions from Protopopov himself to keep me in complete isolation.

The Grand Duke Dmitri Pavlovich and I were very loath to part.

Those few days which we had passed together under arrest in his palace had seemed like so many years. We had lived through and thought over so much. We had begun by entertaining so many hopes for changes which would benefit Russia, and we had ended by burying so many of them.

And now fate was forcing us apart; and we did not know when we would meet again, or in what circumstances. The outlook was gloomy. We were oppressed with evil forebodings.

At 11.30 p.m. the Grand Duke Alexander Mikhailovich came for me and drove me to the station.

The public was not admitted to the platform. The station was guarded by a strong force of police.

As he took leave of me, the Grand Duke said that he himself was leaving St. Petersburg in the morning, and that his train would overtake me. . . .

With a heavy heart I entered the carriage. . . .

The third bell rang, the engine whistled shrilly, the platform drifted by and then disappeared. And soon afterwards St. Petersburg vanished into that winter night. The train hurried on its lonely way through the snow-covered fields sleeping in the darkness.

And I too was alone save for the thoughts which crowded my brain, and the monotonous sound of the wheels as they carried me on.

* * *

CONCLUSION

AND then began the break-up of Russia.
First the Emperor's abdication.

Then the agony of the Provisional Government, doomed from the day of its birth.

Finally, with the roar of guns and the rattle of rifles bombarding both capitals, came the Bolsheviks — and the terrible, bloodthirsty power of the Third International threatening the peace of the whole world.

Through how many horrors our country has lived; how many millions of lives have been lost; how many memorials of our culture have been destroyed.

An emigration unexampled in history followed. Masses of people, equivalent to the population of a whole State, left their country and are scattered in exile all over the world.

This wandering of homeless Russians has continued for years, and no one of us knows when the hour of return will come. Shall we live to see it, or will it be only for our children that the glorious morn of Russia's delivery will dawn?

Exiles always live on hopes of the future and on memories of the past — more perhaps on the past, for the future no one can foresee.

Each of us cherishes visions of the past; memories of dear ones long since dead; memories of a mode of life that is over; visions of our country, so beautiful, so mighty, and so vast, from its icebound northern shores to the radiant south.

Memory unfolds to us scene after scene, and fills us with yearning for all it depicts — Russia's vast plains, her towns and cities crowned by the church domes shining with gold, the Eastern contours of ancient chapels and battlements, the peace and spaciousness of life in the past.

Mighty Russia has sunk into an abyss. She was mighty not only by virtue of her territories and her military resources, but in the part which she played in politics and history and in the advancement of civilisation.

Foreigners, for the most part, did not know her. The familiar stories of a 'barbarous country' ruled by despotic tsars with the aid of knout and whip are nothing more than crude inventions, often fabricated by those political exiles mostly of alien origin, from whose midst came Trotski, Lenin and Zinoviev.

The western world, unhappily, gave credence to these stories and did not see the real Russia or know her history. It had forgotten that for centuries Russia had been Europe's bulwark against the Mongolian hordes, that she had borne the whole weight of the Tartar yoke, that she had finally cast it from her and under the leadership of the great Muscovite Tsars had been formed into a united and powerful State. The western world had forgotten Peter the Great and Catherine and their successors, whose chief aim was the enlightenment and cultural development of the country. Under the patronage of the Tsars, universities and high schools were founded, science flourished, and art, literature and music attained a level which even now is the admiration of the old world and the new.

There are probably few foreigners to-day who are aware that the daughter of Peter the Great — the Empress Elizabeth, founder of Russia's first university — abolished the death penalty, and that since her time it was never inflicted except by military courts, on political criminals who threatened the safety of the realm.

It pleased fate that after three hundred years of great creative work, a tragic end should overtake that Russian dynasty which the poet Pushkin, in his drama *Boris Godunov*, describes as 'The Romanovs; the hope of our native land.'

Rasputinism, like some leprous disease, held the last reign in its clutches. It struck down Imperial Russia, together with her last Tsar, whose memory is cherished to-day by everyone of us, with the deepest pain and sorrow.

If 'victors are not judged,' no mercy, in the majority of cases, is shown to the vanquished.

And the Tsar, who witnessed the downfall of Russia, and who, with all his family, met with such a terrible end — is not he one of the vanquished, in the eyes of the world?

He wielded a power which was greater than himself, and he was crushed beneath it when it collapsed on its century-old foundations.

The Emperor's reign might have been one of the most glorious in our history if Russia had not been struck down by revolution almost on the eve of victory, in a war which had entailed countless sacrifices and had demanded the most heroic exertions.

If Russia had conducted the war to a successful end, she might have become the most powerful State in the world; her Emperor might have become the Supreme Arbiter of Europe, like his predecessor Alexander I after his triumphal entry into Paris in 1815.

But the Russian Empire collapsed when almost on the threshold of victory, and the Russian Emperor perished at the hands of base criminals.

In the minds of most people, the terrible end of his reign has overshadowed all that he achieved and all that he had set out to accomplish — not for Russia alone.

The noble aim of universal peace belongs to the Russian Tsar. The son of an Emperor Peacemaker, he cherished the same ideal; he endeavoured to serve humanity by calling the Hague Conference to realise his dream.

It was not through any fault of his that civilisation was not henceforth delivered from the horrors of war. To-day, the League of Nations, seconded by the efforts of particular statesmen, spare no pains in averting war. But few people now remember that the first person who conceived this idea on broad, universal lines, devoid of any self-seeking, was the crowned head of the greatest Empire in the world.

The reign of Nicholas II saw the completion of the great reforms inaugurated by his grandfather, the Tsar-Liberator Alexander II.

Representative institutions were formed. Religious freedom was granted. The peasants were given full ownership of their land and were freed from that last survival of serfdom, corporal punishment.

The prohibition of the sale of spirituous liquors in Russia was the direct result of the Emperor's own initiative. Apart from its beneficial effect on their physique and morals, this measure soon opened out new vistas of prosperity for the Russian peasants. The People's Savings Bank overflowed with deposits. Indeed, the peasants grew so rich and needed money so little, that during the war they were unwilling to market their surplus produce; and in consequence of this, there was a shortage in certain food commodities just before the Revolution.

During the reign of Nicholas II a project of universal education and a bill for the establishment of district councils were submitted to the legislative chambers.

Yet everything failed, and perished.

Fate was against the Emperor. In the midst of his dreams of universal peace he was drawn into the Japanese war, and later into that terrible world-war which, by its death-roll, has dwarfed all previous struggles.

Victory held out to him the promise of a further expansion of the Empire. Constantinople was to come under his sway, and all the Slav races were to be united in an alliance under the powerful protection of Russia. . . . But instead of this, whole provinces were torn away from her. . . .

The long-cherished dream of the Russian people, that Eastern Christianity should be reinstated in its foremost sanctuary – the Cathedral of St. Sophia in Constantinople – might have been realised in the reign of the Emperor Nicholas II. He awaited with impatience the triumphant moment when the Cross should be raised above that dome which for centuries had supported a Crescent implanted there by force. . . .

But the catastrophe of the Revolution resulted in the defilement of the majority of Russia's ancient churches, by the diabolical power of the Soviets. The cathedral of 'The Holy Virgin of Kostroma, known as Feodorovskaya,' at Tsarskoe Selo, which had been built under the directions of the Emperor himself, and was held by him in special veneration, was turned into a place of amusement for Communists.

One of the most devout of Russian Tsars, the Emperor had set his heart on the restoration of the Patriarchate in Russia. And yet it was in his reign that the Metropolitan Pitirim, thanks to Rasputin's criminal intrigues, was appointed to the Holy Synod – an office of which he was thoroughly unworthy. The Church's best representatives were passed over, while those who were tainted received advancement.

The Emperor loved his people, and was cut off from them. He was drawn to the pure, unsophisticated soul of the simple Russian peasant. And fate forced upon him, in the guise of a peasant, one who was not only a criminal, a wastrel, and a horse-thief, but an utter traitor – one who brought the Emperor and all Russia to their ruin.

The Emperor longed for a son and heir whom he might train to succeed him, and to whom he could leave a throne that had been well secured.

After long years of waiting a son was born, an intelligent, capable boy; but from the day of his birth he was afflicted with an incurable illness which at any moment might cause his death.

The father did not pass on his crown, he abdicated for himself and his son.

He abdicated on behalf of his son because he would not be parted from him, because he did not wish to see a sick child on a throne already shaken by rebellion.

Few monarchs have bestowed such love and care upon their families. The Emperor Nicholas II was attached to his wife and children with all his heart and soul. Yet it was the Empress, who was devoted to her husband, and was ready to sacrifice everything for his well-being, who was the cause of his failures and fatal mistakes.

She blindly believed in Rasputin, and was completely dominated by his influence. She had implicit faith in the healing powers of those drugs of Badmaev which, in reality, were administered to the Emperor and Tsetsarevich for purposes quite different from those she supposed.

During the whole of his life, the Emperor Nicholas II was dogged by a merciless fate. With his gentle submission to his destiny, could he develop a resolute will which would know neither hesitation nor retreat?

It may be that doubt first arose in his mind during the festivities which accompanied his coronation, when the triumphal path of the young Emperor, who had repaired to the ancient capital to receive the blessing of the Church on his reign, was strewn with the mutilated bodies of the victims of the terrible catastrophe on the Khodynka.* (see the next page for this footnote)

The simple-minded Russian people looked upon this catastrophe as an omen of evil to come. And the evil came. . . .

All the horrors of his imprisonment, all the insulting behaviour of the revolutionary authorities, the Emperor bore with unaffected gentleness, with true humility, with the high-mindedness of one who was every inch a Tsar.

And with unaffected gentleness, with majesty, he died. In honour of conquering kings, memorials are raised, imposing statues are erected, to foster the respect and admiration of their subjects.

But in memory of the Emperor Nicholas II and of his tragic end the Russian people, if the hour of their deliverance sees their moral regeneration, will build a cathedral where they will pray for the soul of the martyred Tsar and seek forgiveness for the grievous sins and monstrous crimes committed in the name of revolution.

* In his book *Russia* (2nd impression, Cassel & Co, 1905, vol II, p 40), Sir Donald Mackenzie Wallace thus describes this appalling catastrophe — 'A day or two after the Coronation I saw Khodinskoe Pole (Khodynka) a great plain in the outskirts of Moscow, strewn with hundreds of corpses. During the previous night enormous crowds from the city and surrounding districts had collected here in order to receive at sunrise, by the Tsar's command, a little memento of the coronation ceremony, in the form of a packet containing a metal cup and a few eatables, and as day dawned, in their anxiety to get near the row of booths from which the distribution was to be made, about two thousand had been crushed to death. It was a sight more horrible than a battlefield, because among the dead were a large proportion of women and children, terribly mutilated in the struggle.'
— (Translator's note)

* * *

APPENDIX

The Emperor's natural kindness, his greatness of soul, his profound and unselfish love for Russia, were manifested not only in the hour of his martyrdom, but in the manner and motives of his abdication. His last manifesto, together with his farewell order to the Army, are documents of human interest apart from their historical significance.

Whatever mistakes the Emperor may have committed while under the influence of his fateful delusions, the welfare of his country was his constant and unchanging care.

It must in justice be acknowledged that most of the Russian Tsars who were described in Europe as 'eastern despots' were inspired with a high sense of duty towards their subjects.

An interesting comparison may be drawn between the maxims of two monarchs each of whom history has styled 'Great.'

'L'Etat, c'est Moi,' said Louis XIV of France.

Peter I of Russia addressed his subjects thus: 'Ye are to know, then, that Peter setteth no value on his own life — if Russia should yet live.'

The Emperor Nicholas II was ever faithful to the precept of his great ancestor. In his abdication, as in his subsequent refusal to save his own life, Russia was his only thought. I append the Emperor's manifesto and his farewell order to the Army, in order to recall their contents to remembrance.

MANIFESTO ANNOUNCING THE ABDICATION OF THE EMPEROR NICHOLAS II.

At this time of intense struggle against an external enemy who for nearly three years has been striving to enslave our country, it has pleased the Lord God to send down on Russia a fresh and grievous trial.

The disturbances which have begun in our midst threaten to have a disastrous effect on the further progress of this stubbornly fought war.

The destiny of Russia, the honour of Our heroic army, the welfare of the people, and the whole future of Our beloved fatherland demand that the war shall be conducted at all costs to a victorious end.

A cruel foe is exerting his last strength, and the hour is at hand when Our valiant army, with the help of Our glorious Allies, will finally overthrow him.

In these decisive days in the life of Russia, We have deemed it Our duty to facilitate the close union of Our people and the rallying of all their forces for the swift attainment of victory; and in agreement with the Imperial Duma, We have decided to renounce the Throne of Russia, and to divest Ourselves of the Supreme Power. Not wishing to part from Our beloved Son, We bequeath the heritage to Our Brother, the Grand Duke Michael Alexandrovich. Blessing him on his accession to the Throne of the Russian Empire, We adjure Our Brother to rule in full and unbroken harmony with the people's representatives in the legislative assemblies, on principles which they shall determine, and to take an inviolable oath that he will do so.

In the name of Our dearly-beloved country We call upon all faithful sons of the Fatherland to fulfil their sacred duty to it by obeying the Tsar in this time of grave national crisis and to help Him, together with the representatives of the people, to lead Russia into the path of victory, prosperity and glory.

May the Lord God help Russia. Nicholas

* * *

THE LAST MESSAGE OF THE EMPEROR NICHOLAS II TO THE TROOPS.

Issued by the Chief of Staff of the Commander-in-Chief.
8th March, 1917, Order No. 371*

After his abdication and before his departure from the zone of the army in the field, the Emperor Nicholas II bade farewell to the troops in the following words:

'I address you for the last time, my well-beloved troops. Now that I have renounced the Throne of Russia on my own behalf and that of my son, the supreme power has passed to the Provisional Government established on the initiative of the Imperial Duma.

'May God aid it to lead Russia along the path of glory and prosperity! And may God aid you, valiant troops, to defend our country against the evil enemy.

'For two and a half years you have hourly endured the hardships of military service; much blood has been shed, great efforts have been made; and the day is already at hand when Russia, united with her brave allies by the desire for victory, will break down the enemy's last resistance. This unprecedented war must be fought out to a completely victorious finish.

'Whoever thinks of peace at this moment, whoever desires peace, is a traitor to his country. I know that this is the feeling of every honest soldier.

'Do your duty. Defend our great country valorously. Comply with the orders of the Provisional Government. Obey your officers, and remember that any slackening of discipline is merely a service rendered to the enemy. I firmly believe that unbounded love for our great country abides in your hearts. May the Lord God bless you, and may St. George the Great Martyr lead you to victory.

NICHOLAS.

G.H.Q.   8th March, 1917.
   Signed :
    General Alexeiev,
      Chief of Staff.

* The Provisional Government refrained from publishing this Order of the Emperor. It remained unknown to the army and to the nation.

FELIX YUSSOUPOFF

THE YOUSSOUPOFFS FELIX AND IRINA LEAVING RUSSIA
FOR EVER - ONOARD H.M.S. MARLBOROUGH, 1919

END OF BOOK TWO

BOOK THREE

After the Bolshevik Revolution Bykov left the army and moved to Leningrad in 1918. During the 1920s he would write several historic works on Ekaterinburg, where for a time he had been in charge of the ex-royal family during their imprisonment, acting as the Chairman of the Ekaterinburg Soviet. During World War II he was living in Leningrad and survived the blockade of the city during World War II. He died in 1953.

Bykov's first-hand account, begins at the February revolution until the capture of Ekaterinburg by the Czech troops of the White Army. It was first published in Russian in 1926 with the title *The Last Days of Czardom* and later in 1934 the English title appeared as *The Last Days of Tsar Nicholas*.

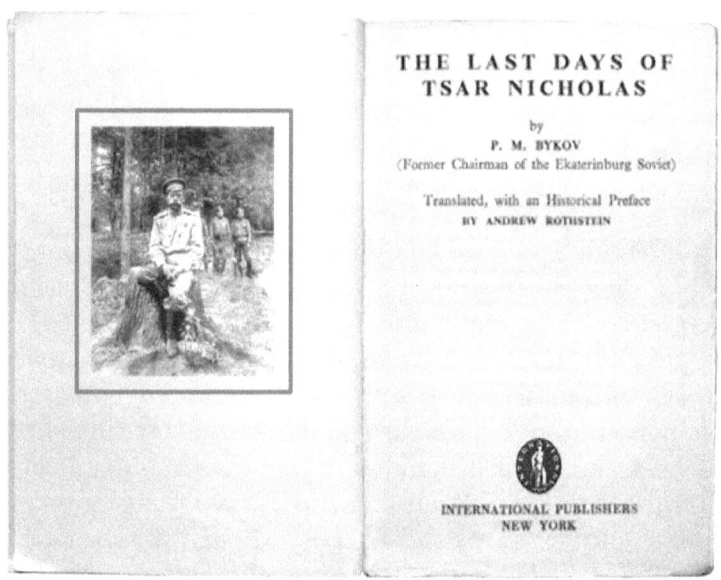

English Edition published 1934

Original book published in Russia and edited and prefaced by A. Tanyaev, in Sverdlovsk. Published by International Publishers in New York. First published in 1934 in the UK, by Martin Lawrence Ltd., London and also by Western Printing Services Ltd., Bristol. Pages: 90

PAVEL MIKHAILOVICH BYKOV

Bykov's book describes how the prisoners at Ekaterinburg were communicating with the monarchists, namely through the conduit of Dr Derevenko who was allowed to attend to Alexis at Ipatiev House unhindered. He gives several examples of plots that were foiled by the Bolshevik guards which only General Dieterichs has partly corroborated with rescue letters to and from the Tsar that do exist. Bykov gives valuable insight in to the circumstances that led to the decision to execute them all and this book was removed from circulation in Russia so that it could not be bought, or obtained from a library. It was the first report from a significant Bolshevik that put on paper the admission of what had happened to the ex-royal family as well as their aides in Ekaterinburg and at Perm.

END OF BOOK ONE

THE LAST DAYS OF TSAR NICHOLAS

by

P. M. BYKOV

(Former Chairman of the Ekaterinburg Soviet)

Translated, with an Historical Preface

BY ANDREW ROTHSTEIN

INTERNATIONAL PUBLISHERS
NEW YORK

Printed in Great Britain by
Western Printing Services Ltd., Bristol.

CONTENTS

CHAPTER		PAGE
	PREFACE	391
I.	ON THE EVE OF REVOLUTION	410
II.	THE OVERTHROW OF THE AUTOCRACY	416
III.	THE ARREST OF THE ROMANOVS	426
IV.	IN THE OLD NEST	433
V.	AT TOLBOLSK	440
VI.	THE HERMOGENES AFFAIR	447
VII.	TOBOLSK AFTER THE NOVEMBER REVOLUTION	453
VIII.	HOPES OF LIBERATION	459
IX.	THE SOVIET URALS	465
X.	NO ROAD PAST THE URALS	470
XI.	AT THE CAPITAL OF THE URALS	478
XII.	THE LAST DAYS OF THE ROMANOVS	482
XIII.	THE EXECUTION OF THE ROMANOV FAMILY	488
XIV.	THE EXECUTION OF THE FORMER GRAND DUKES	492
XV.	SEARCHING FOR THE ROMANOVS	497

PREFACE

THE TRUTH ABOUT NICHOLAS ROMANOV

I. *The Legend*

DURING the Yussupov libel action, which drew such a striking picture of manners and morals at the Court of Nicholas II, the last Russian Tsar, Sir William Jowitt, K.C., let fall a remark deserving of wider fame. He asked the injured lady: "It is about time somebody tried to show a true picture of that devoted couple who, according to the best of their beliefs, were doing their best for Russia?" And Princess Yusupova (*née* Romanova), naturally answered: "Yes."

Just as naturally the *Morning Post*, summing up the case after the verdict, did its best to restore the reputation of "the illustrious dead." Simple, credulous and bigoted—obstinate, credulous, simple—more sinned against than sinning—such are the harshest judgments which the Diehards' paper ventures to pass upon "that tragic pair." Nor is this the first occasion for such attempts to whitewash Nicholas Romanov and his wife.

The publication in 1929 of the letters exchanged by Nicholas and his wife, Alexandra, afforded an unexpected opportunity of which the defenders of the Romanovs fully availed themselves. No effort was spared in the attempt to draw the picture of two simple, kindly, charming souls, whose love for each other soared far above earthly affairs of State, and whose very ignorance and innocence left them helpless in the grip of a system stronger than themselves.

Dr. Hagberg Wright wrote: "The character of the Tsar emerges morally enhanced from the severe ordeal of having his private life laid bare to the world. No impartial historian will in the future pay any attention to the accusations of duplicity and cunning which flooded the press after the Revolution. . . . It is quite impossible to avoid a feeling of sympathy with a man overburdened from the outset with the weight of care thrust upon him." (Introduction to *Letters of the Tsar to the Tsaritsa*.)

Mr. J. C. Squire followed in the same strain: "He had a strong sense of duty, a generous nature, a great capacity for affection, a desire to serve his people, no malice, no liking for cruelty and slaughter: adversity sweetened his character, and at the worst moments he never complained. But he was not intelligent, he was not educated, he did not know what was going on in Russia, and he was a poor judge of men. . . . There is no sign at all in these letters that the Tsar ever came near realising the efficiency that is called for in modern civic, military and industrial organisation. If things were going badly anywhere, his only idea of a remedy was a stroke of the pen and the appointment of somebody who was bien-pensant, and whom his wife did not dislike." (*Observer*, February, 1929.)

A reviewer in the *Daily Telegraph* (March 1, 1929) took up the burden: "Nicholas II is revealed as a kind-hearted, affectionate creature; weighed down by a sense of responsibility to which he was utterly unable to rise; dependent for his inspiration upon an irresponsible wife, who was in her turn the victim of an unscrupulous adventurer. . . . Devotion to his home, and trust in a deep, superstitious religion—these were the prevailing consolations of a weak and wavering intellect." A writer in the *Evening Standard* thought that the "Letters" show "how inherently good and yet how utterly futile was this tragic figure." And so on.

After these moving sentences, the apologists need only say a few words about the execution of the Romanovs at Ekaterinburg, in June 1918. "A horrible deed . . . which humanity will always condemn" (Hagberg Wright); "They were too simple to understand, and too honourable to fly, and their death was the death of the Babes in the Wood" (J. C. Squire); "The last, terrible tragedy of Ekaterinburg" (the *Daily Telegraph* reviewer).

So, little by little, by means of suppressing truth and suggesting falsehood, has been built up a complete legend of Nicholas II. And this legend has not any abstract or academic purpose. Its object is intensely political—to serve the ends of the White counter-revolutionaries and their foreign supporters in fighting the Soviet Union. The legend of the kindly Charles I, ungratefully executed by his rebellious subjects, played a similar counter-revolutionary part against the English Republic of the seventeenth century. The story of Louis XVI and Marie Antoinette helped many a noble adventurer in the Courts of Europe in the eighteenth century.

2. *A Kind-hearted, Affectionate Creature*

Unfortunately for the apologists, other documents from the pen of Nicholas Romanov have been made available by the November Revolution. The Tsar's letters to his mother, to Stolypin, to other officials: his marginal autograph comments on State papers laid before him by his ministers and diplomats: the diaries and memoirs of high court officials, have all become the property of the historian within a few years of Nicholas' death. It took a couple of centuries to destroy the Charles Stuart legend, and a century to destroy the legend of the simple, honest, liberal Louis XVI. The documents already published by the Soviet Government are sufficient to ensure that the Nicholas Romanov legend will die more easily, once they become known.

In April 1895 a meeting of textile workers on strike at Yaroslavl was attacked by soldiers, and thirteen strikers were shot. "I am very satisfied with the behaviour of the troops at Yaroslavl during the factory disturbances," wrote the kindly Nicholas (within twelve months of his accession) on the margin of the official report. In the spring of 1903, there were terrible massacres of Jews at Kishinev and elsewhere. General Kuropatkin, Minister for War at the time, has the following entry in his diary for April 14, 1903 (just afterwards): "Before leaving (the Palace), Plehve sat with me for an hour. We talked about the disorders at Kishinev and Kronstadt. *Just as his Majesty had done*, Plehve said that the Jews ought to be taught a lesson, that they have got above themselves and are taking the lead of the revolutionary movement" (*Krasny Arkhiv*, 1922, Vol. II, p. 43).* On another occasion General Dratchevsky reported in person on the pogrom at Rostov. "How many were killed ?" asked the Tsar. "Forty." "So few? I thought there were more," said Nicholas regretfully.

---

* *Krasny Arkhiv* (*The Red Archives*) is the official publication of the Central Archives Department of the R.S.F.S.R.

The first Revolution of 1905 left an imperishable trace of the Tsar's kindly and affectionate character—on the margins of his State papers. On August 6, 1905, General Trepoff reported to him that the Cossacks had "unfortunately" beaten with their nagaikas a group of doctors, who were under arrest on the charge of assisting the peasants of Saratov in the recent disorders. Nicholas underlined the word "unfortunately" in thick blue pencil, put a question mark at the side, and underneath wrote : "Very well done !" (*Krasny Arkhiv*, 1925, Vols. XI-XII, p. 435.) On November 5 he was informed that 162 "anarchists" were stirring up strikes in Vladivostok. "They should all be hanged," wrote this simple but kindly monarch. (Ibid., p. 436.)

The suppression of the peasant revolts against the feudal Junker barons of the Baltic Provinces was particularly ferocious, and the punitive expeditions sent out by the Imperial Government earned an unenviable reputation for themselves throughout the world. On December 14, one of the generals engaged in this work reported that he had spared the town of Tukkum, as the rebel authorities there had surrendered their arms, the Socialists had fled, and he himself was short of ammunition. "That is no reason. He should have destroyed the town," we find on the margin, in the handwriting of Nicholas II. {Ibid., p. 439.) But a fortnight later he was consoled. On reading a report (December 30, 1905) that Riga had been captured with the slaughter of many thousands of workers, and that "Captain Richter not only shot, but also hanged the chief agitators," Nicholas did not attempt to conceal his admiration. " Fine fellow!" he wrote, opposite this part of the report. {Ibid., p. 437.)

The suppression of the Revolution was followed by a new wave of Jewish pogroms. On February 16, 1906, the Cabinet asked Nicholas for permission to investigate the reports that a recent butchery of Jews at Gomel was facilitated by the commander of the local garrison, who had supplied the local "Black Hundred" with arms. "How does this concern me?" wrote the lovable autocrat, his character sweetened by adversity. There was indeed good reason for his remark, since he had publicly enrolled himself a member of the Black Hundred (the "Union of Russian Folk") and wore their badge at State functions, received their President, Dr. Dubrovin, as a friend, subscribed to their funds, and so on. Later, it is hardly necessary to add, he exercised his Imperial clemency and, out of the "generous nature" extolled by Sir John Squire, pardoned most of the chief ring-leaders of the pogroms.

3. "*A Strong Sense of Duty.*"

It might be urged that these remarks and actions were not the result of firm and consistent policy, but merely the first, ill-considered and impetuous reactions of a combatant in the endless struggle to maintain the Tsardom. The fact that the Tsardom could not be maintained except by such methods, and in the spirit breathed by the marginal notes of Nicholas Romanov, is undeniable. But apologists go a little too far when they say that the Tsar did not understand "the efficiency that is called for in modern civic, military and industrial organisation," and thought that "a stroke of the pen" was all that was necessary to get out of a difficult position. Nicholas shows, in his marginal writings and otherwise, that for him violence and frightfulness were not incidents of passion, but the instruments of cold policy.

In May 1905 the Moscow City Council summoned a national conference of Mayors to discuss the growing menace of revolution. Such an assembly would stand politically for the right of the bulk of the British Conservative Party. Nicholas wrote on the margin of the report: "I hope this conference will not be allowed. They have been chattering enough already." (*Krasny Arkhiv*, 1925, Vols. XI-XII, p. 434.) Later in the year, when he heard that the Sebastopol Town Council had been parleying with the local revolutionaries, he wrote in his simple way: "I am amazed at the Sebastopol Town Council interfering in other people's business. Reducing rebels to obedience is the task of the military authorities. . . . They will be treated as traitors and perjurers. N." (Ibid., pp. 434-5.) When the general commanding a punitive force in the Caucasus reported, a little later, that he had suppressed the revolt without bloodshed, the Tsar said "That is no good! In such cases one must always shoot. . . . *One must always shoot, General!* " Is this the philosophy of a kindly innocent sitting on the throne?

In 1905 Nicholas put his principles into practice. The following ingenuous explanation of the pogroms organised in over 100 towns by the Black Hundreds, as the first blow of the counter-revolution, is contained in a letter to his mother, the Dowager Empress Marie

Feodorovna, dated October 27, 1905. The fact that the Black Hundreds are not mentioned in the letter, despite the Tsar's intimate personal connection with them, is characteristic—as indeed is the whole letter: "During the first days after the manifesto, the bad elements strongly raised their heads; but then began a powerful reaction, and the whole mass of loyal people took heart, the result was comprehensible, and as is customary with us: the people revolted against the impudence and insolence of the revolutionaries and Socialists " (this within a month of the all-Russian General Strike!)" and as nine-tenths of them are Jews, all the hatred fell upon them—hence the Jewish pogroms. It is amazing with what *unanimity and suddenness* this happened in all the towns of Russia and Siberia. In England, of course, they say that these disorders were organised by the police, as usual—the old, well-known story. But it was not only the Jews who caught it, the Russian agitators, engineers, lawyers and all other rotten elements came in for it too. The incidents at Tomsk, Simferopol, Tver and Odessa showed clearly what an infuriated crowd can do, when it surrounded houses in which revolutionaries had shut themselves up, and set fire to them, killing everyone who came out." (*Krasny Arkhiv*, 1927, Vol. XXII, p. 169.)

Is this political lunatic, smacking his lips over the pogroms of Jews, engineers, lawyers "and all other rotten elements," a Babe in the Wood?

As the counter-revolution developed, the philosophy of "one must always shoot" gained the ascendancy more and more. On December 1, 1905, Nicholas writes to his mother: "From all sides voices begin to call louder and louder that it is time for the Government to begin acting energetically. This is a very great success! Witte was only waiting for this, and now he will begin to crush the revolution decisively—at all events, so he told me. . . . He is ready to order the arrest of the chief leaders of the rebellion. *I told him long ago about this*, but he constantly hoped to do without drastic measures." (Ibid., p. 178.)

A year later, Nicholas' own ministers were desperately trying to persuade the man that there had been enough shooting. But his strong sense of duty made this difficult. On February 6, 1907, we read in the memoirs of General A. A. Polivanov (at that time Assistant War Minister) that the Cabinet discussed the continuing executions by decision of field courts-martial, and the likelihood of the forthcoming session of the Duma opening with a general attack on the Government because of these atrocities. It was agreed that a circular ought to be issued stopping the practice, followed up by a public Ukaz, or decree, on the eve of the session. But the Cabinet reckoned without the Tsar.

On February 13, Polivanov entered in his diary: "His Majesty has not agreed to the publication of an Ukaz on February 19, abolishing the field courts-martial, but has been pleased to order a circular limiting their scope." Two days later, when the War Minister was with the Tsar, the latter told him that the slightest attack on the Army in the Duma "must meet with a categorical (terrible) rebuff, and it can always be pointed out that the Army does not engage in politics, but fulfils a painful duty."*

In this piece of advice Nicholas showed indeed his " strong sense of duty." That sense inspired him all through his life with the high watchword of: " One must always shoot, General." It was so right up to the very eve of the abdication forced from him in March 1917, when he despatched General Ivanov, one of the most notorious martinets in the Army, with a picked punitive force to subdue the " Socialists " in revolt at Petrograd. Ivanov's expedition only came to nought because the rifles began to go off in the wrong direction.

4. "*A Desire to Serve His People*"

We have seen that Nicholas delighted in the slaughter of his political opponents (this term covering the category of workmen on strike), and that this delight sprang from his adherence to the fine old Romanov tradition that the autocracy must meet its difficulties with bullet, bayonet and knout—not at all by "a stroke of the pen," as naive British essayists like to think. Did he remain true to the other Romanov tradition—the maintenance of absolutism, single and unimpaired? In 1865 his grandfather, Alexander II, wrote (in a personal letter to his son): "Constitutional forms, after the manner of the West, would be the greatest possible disaster for us, and would have as their first result, not the unity of the State, but the dispersion of our Empire into fragments."

* A. A. Polivanov, Memoirs, vol. i, pp. 18-20 (Military Publishing Board, Moscow, 1924).

In 1883 Nicholas' father, Alexander III, wrote to his chief adviser Pobedonostsev: "I am too deeply convinced of the scandalous nature of the representative elective principle ever to permit its introduction into Russia, in the form in which it exists throughout Europe." What were the political opinions of Nicholas II ?

Almost on the morrow of his accession, Nicholas gave the answer. One of the innumerable addresses of loyal congratulation on his marriage came from the Tver Provincial Zemstvo, a body created by Alexander II to create the impression that representative government was beginning. In reality, the Zemstvo was a mere occasional meeting of the nobility and gentry, with a few selected peasants. The address expressed the hope that such bodies "will be allowed to voice their opinions in matters in which they are concerned"—not a very revolutionary demand. On January 30, 1895, in the Winter Palace, Nicholas gave his reply to the assembled deputations from the provinces: "It has come to my knowledge that during recent months there have been heard in some meetings of the zemstvos the voices of those who have indulged in *the senseless dreams that the zemstvos could be called to participate in the government of the country*. I want everyone to know that I will devote all my strength to upholding, for the good of the nation, the principle of absolute autocracy, as firmly and strongly as did my lamented father." The phrase about "senseless dreams" ran like an electric shock throughout the entire country, and was never forgotten.

But perhaps it was merely an awkward turn of phrase, some youthful gaucherie—or, more natural still, a sentiment placed in the mouth of the robot Tsar by some evil adviser? Nicholas II gives the reply to this also, through his own intimate documents, in which no minister assisted.

On December 24, 1898, he wrote the following on the Foreign Minister's report concerning the situation in Crete: "It is very important at the earliest possible time to *limit*, as far as possible, *the application of the representative principle in Crete*, which the Crown Prince George asked particularly of me while I was still in Denmark. With this I am fully agreed." (*Krasny Arkhiv*, 1926, Vol. XXII, p. 250.) The italics are in the original.

From the beginning of his reign, Nicholas began an attack on the democratic and autonomous constitution of Finland, which had been secured by that country as the price of its union with Russia in 1809. In 1899 Nicholas and the Governor-General of Finland, Bobrikov, were making active preparations for the abolition of the separate Finnish battalions and the introduction of the Russian military regulations. On March 7, 1899, Nicholas wrote in a private letter to Bobrikov: "We have inherited a monstrous crookedly-built house, and the painful task has fallen upon us of rebuilding it (or its wing)." But mass demonstrations, monster petitions, and other signs of popular discontent soon warned the autocrat that he must hasten slowly, and in a further letter of March 19, 1899, the man whom Dr. Wright absolves from "the accusations of duplicity and cunning" wrote: "It seems better to me, until we have got them finally in hand, to let them amuse themselves with trifles, like little children. In time, of course, we shall not let all their tricks pass so unpunished." (*Krasny Arkhiv*, 1928, Vol. XXVII, pp. 229- 230.)

On December 6, 1901, Nicholas assembled at one of his palaces the superior officers of the Corps of Gendarmerie. "I am very glad to see you, gentlemen," said this servant of his people. " I hope the alliance established to-day between myself and the Corps of Gendarmes will grow stronger year by year." It did indeed, such being the logical corollary of the policy of absolute autocracy in a country of rapidly-increasing class antagonism at home and Imperialist aggression abroad.

Despite the attempts of his apologists to represent Nicholas as ignorant of "what was going on in Russia," he was well aware of the essential principles on which the Tsardom rested, and in particular of the importance of the economic enslavement of the peasantry as the foundation-stone for the maintenance of autocracy. In a letter to his mother, on November 11, 1905, Nicholas wrote: "As you of course know, agrarian disorders have begun in Russia. This is the most dangerous phenomenon of all, on account of the ease with which the peasants can be incited to take the land from the landowners, and also because everywhere there are insufficient troops. The Army is returning from Manchuria slowly, on account of the stoppage on the Siberian Railway." (*Krasny Arkhiv*, 1927, Vol. XXII, p. 173.) On January 11, 1906, Count Witte, his Prime Minister, reported on the desirability of alienating compulsorily a certain proportion of the State, Imperial and private lands, lest worse befall: "I do not approve," wrote Nicholas at this stage.

Witte's report pointed out that it was a choice between giving up part of the land in order to retain undisturbed possession of the remainder, as in 1861, or else run the risk of losing all. "*Private property must remain untouched*," was the Tsar's comment.

Forced to grant a moderately liberal constitution, the Tsar literally felt himself a captive. When he heard that a deputation of British M.P.'s was on its way to Russia, to congratulate Muromtsev, the President of the new Duma, Nicholas relieved his feelings in a letter to his mother (September 27, 1906): "Some comic deputation is on its way from England with greetings to Muromtsev and the rest of them. Uncle Bertie" (Edward VII) "and the British Government have let us know that, to their great regret, they can do nothing to prevent them coming. Wonderful liberty! How angry they would be if a deputation came from us to the Irish, and wished them success in their struggle against the Government!" (*Krasny Arkhiv*, 1927, Vol. XXII, p. 202.)

One of the most illuminating documents—in the Emperor's own hand—is his reply, on December 10, 1906, to a memorandum from "Hangman" Stolypin, submitting proposals for abolishing the more glaring disabilities of the Jews, and pointing out that Nicholas had as good as promised this in his Manifesto of October 17, 1905.

Nicholas wrote: "Peter Arkadievich! I return you the memorandum on the Jewish question unconfirmed.

"Long before it was submitted to me, I may say that I thought and meditated on this question day and night. In spite of the most convincing arguments in favour of a decision in the affirmative, an inner voice ever more insistently repeats to me that I should not take this decision upon myself. So far my conscience has never deceived me. Therefore, in this case also, I intend to follow its dictates.

"I know you, too, believe that 'the Emperor's heart is in God's hand.'

"So be it. I bear a terrible responsibility before God for all authorities set up by me, and at any time I am ready to answer for them to him." (*Krasny Arkhiv*, 1924, Vol. V, p. 105.)

An interesting reflection of Nicholas' mood during the period of counter-revolution was his note (December 8, 1907) on report of the Russian Minister at Teheran, describing the growing revolutionary movement in Persia after the establishment of a Medjliss (Parliament):

"The Shah can save Persia only by immediately scattering the Medjliss and other revolutionary gatherings. This is the only reply." (*Krasny Arkhiv*, 1927, Vol. XXII, p. 251.)

It will be noticed that this remark not only breathes the spirit of his instructions regarding Crete, nine years before, but also follows directly from his declaration about "senseless dreams," at the very beginning of his reign. Nine years later, on the eve of the Revolution, we find his letters to his wife Alexandra imbued with exactly the same "ideals." On December 13, 1916, he describes his conversation with Trepov: "He set forth his plan concerning the Duma—to dismiss it on December 17 and convoke it again on January 19, in order to show them and the whole country that, in spite of all they have said, the Government wants to work with them. If in January they begin to cause confusion and trouble, he proposes to pour thunders on their heads (he briefly summarised his speech) and finally to close the Duma. . . . I did not deny the logical character of his plan, and also one advantage struck me, namely, that, if everything happens as he thinks, we should get rid of the Duma two or three weeks sooner than I thought, the middle of January instead of the beginning of February. So I approved this plan, but exacted a solemn promise from him to keep to it and to hold out." (*Krasny Arkhiv*, 1923, Vol. IV, p. 185.)

Even two or three weeks' more freedom from the hated Duma, which was a living reminder of his winged words 20 years before, was worth the price of finally alienating a huge volume of public opinion in the midst of a great war. Whatever Nicholas II may have been deficient in (Count Witte said that he had "the average education of a Colonel of the Guards," and even Sir John Squire finds that "he was not intelligent, he was not educated"), he cannot be accused of lacking definite and clear political views. Autocracy must be maintained: representative institutions are an affliction sent by the devil—or by "engineers, lawyers, and other rotten elements": the peasants must stay as they are, and the principle of private property rest inviolate; the Jews must not only be kept in their place, but from time to time "taught a lesson": the other nationalities subject to the Romanov Empire must be "taken in hand." From this political creed naturally sprang the practice which we have already seen at work: "One must always shoot," and in the application of that practice Nicholas II developed very early the taste for blood, examples of which have also been quoted.

None of these characteristics were very original—they were all to be found, on a grander scale, a hundred years before, in the mad Paul and his sons, Alexander I and Nicholas I—but at all events they were well-defined. There is no excuse for the sentimental slobber of the apologists.

5. *"Too Simple and Too Honourable"*

There remain one or two other facts about Nicholas to be established. We have already seen how little the anxiety to absolve him from " accusations of duplicity and cunning " squares with the Tsar's cynical letter to the Governor-General of Finland. That was at the beginning of his reign: no less illuminating, towards its end, is the following letter to his wife, dated December 14, 1916, and dealing with the same joint preparations with Trepov for dissolving the Duma mentioned a little earlier. "It is disgusting to have to deal with a man whom you do not like and distrust, like Trepov. But first of all we must find a successor for him, and then push him out after he has done the dirty work. I mean to dismiss him when he has closed the Duma. Let all the responsibility and all the burdens fall on his shoulders, not on the shoulders of the man who takes his place." (*Krasny Arkhiv*, loc . cit., p. 189.)

This sage remark, well worthy of Machiavelli's "Prince," gives ample food for reflection to the propagandists for whom Nicholas Romanov is an "inherently good" and tragic figure. It is also a text for the lickspittles of monarchy everywhere.

It was not only in home affairs that there was displayed this double-facedness, of which Homiakov, the reactionary President of the Third Duma, said: "He doesn't lie, but he doesn't tell the truth either." In relation to the Tsar's "gallant Allies," the same features show themselves. As early as 1903, Kuropatkin's diary (February 3) shows that the war against Germany-Austria was in contemplation: "To-day I received a rescript of great importance from the sovereign, in which he informs me that, in the event of a conflict between Russia and the European Powers, he will assume the supreme command of all the armies himself, and proposes to appoint me Commander-in-Chief of the armies of the South-western front, ranged against Austria-Hungary." (*Krasny Arkhiv*,

1922, Vol. II, pp. 29-30.) It was shortly after this period, as is well known, that began the movement for a rapprochement with Great Britain and France.

However, this did not prevent the following entry being made in the diary of General Kuropatkin, under the date January 3, 1904: "I reported on the despatch of a Kalmuk, 2nd Lieutenant Ulanov, to Tibet, to find out what is happening there, and in particular what the English are doing. The sovereign was pleased to direct that this should be a private venture, at his own risk. He ordered me to advise Ulanov to 'inflame the Tibetans against the English.' His Majesty said that I should not tell Lamsdorff of these instructions." (*Krasny Arkhiv*, 1923, Vol. II, p. 101.) Lamsdorff was Foreign Minister, and in that capacity working for a closer understanding with Great Britain. No doubt Nicholas decided not to "disturb" him by revealing his friendly advice to Lieutenant Ulanov.

The correspondence between the Tsar and the Tsaritsa during the war throws further light on that "devoted couple." True, the letters quoted below come from the pen of Alexandra: but in each case the context shows that there could have been no difference between Nicholas and his wife on this point; in the first, because Alexandra treats as a matter of course an event already known to both : in the second, because the opinions voiced are those of Rasputin, than whom there was no higher authority on earth for Nicholas.

The first letter, dated January 5, 1916, runs : "Mita Benk said at Paul's that Masha had brought a letter from Erny. A said that she knows nothing, but Paul declared it was true. Who could have told him ? . . . It is unpleasant that again my name and the name of Erny are mentioned." (*Correspondence of Nicholas and Alexandra Romanov*, Vol. IV, pp. 19-20, Moscow, 1926.)

"Mita Benk" was Dmitri Benckendorff, a member of the Board of the Russian Bank for Foreign Trade. "Paul" was the Grand Duke of that name, " Masha" was Marie Vassilchikova, a lady-in- waiting. And "Erny" was Ernst Ludwig, Grand Duke of Hesse—Alexandra's brother, with whom she was in constant communication throughout the war, and with whom Vassilchikova had recently established contact through Sweden, bringing Alexandra letters from him and from other German princes.

But the great Ally of the British Empire went further than mere "correspondence with the enemy." In the Tsaritsa's letter of June 5, 1916, we find : "In the opinion of our Friend, it is a good thing for us that Kitchener has perished, as later on he might have caused harm to Russia, and it is no loss that his papers perished with him. You see he is always frightened of England, what she will be like at the end of the war, when peace negotiations begin." (*Ibid.*, p. 289.) The Tsaritsa makes no comment on this interesting opinion, further than to mention that her friend Anna Vyrubova had been commissioned to tell it to the Tsar during a recent visit, but had forgotten to do so. After the Yussupov case, it is hardly necessary to add that the "Friend" spoken of so reverently is none other than the monk Rasputin.

Previously the Imperial consorts had only exchanged the most banal of reflections on the disaster to the *Hampshire*—"How terrible, and what a loss for the English," and "The loss of Lord Kitchener must really be very painful for Georgy " (May 25); "But such is life, particularly in wartime" (May 26). It was left for Rasputin to express, and Alexandra to convey, the real feelings of the Romanov Court: nor is there any trace of protest or dissent on the part of Nicholas.

In passing, it should be mentioned that the extraordinary callousness of Alexandra's letter had its precedents—in the famous remark of Nicholas after the Hodynka catastrophe (June 1896), in which nearly 2,000 people who had assembled to celebrate the coronation, were crushed to death, that he did not see why the feast and the ball at the French Embassy, fixed for that day, should be countermanded : and in Nicholas' tranquil continuation of his pleasure trip after Stolypin, his Prime Minister, had been killed at the theatre in his presence (1911).

One cannot pass over in silence Sir John Squire's last desperate effort to save the reputation of his clients by the sublimely ridiculous remark that "they were too simple to understand and too honourable to fly; and their death was the death of the Babes in the Wood." Nicholas' diary shows that very soon after the Revolution he was contemplating flight : "March 23, 1917. Cleared up my books and things, and began to set aside everything I want to take with me, if I have to go to England." The narratives of the Whites themselves—E. Semchevskaya, the wife of a General Staff Officer ("Dvuglavy Orel," Berlin, 1921, Vol. XV), Kerensky (*From Afar*,

Paris, 1922), Gilliard, tutor to the Tsarevich (in his diary published at Reval in 1921), Sokolov, who conducted the official White investigation into the circumstances of Nicholas* execution (Berlin, 1925), General M. K. Dieterichs, formerly of the Imperial suite—all show that at that time the Provisional Government, by agreement with the British Ambassador, made a determined attempt to smuggle the Romanov family away to England. The attempt was frustrated only by the vigilance of the Petrograd Soviet. Bykov, in the pages which follow, tells the story of this period briefly but convincingly.

Throughout his captivity, and particularly after the establishment of the Soviet Government in November 1917, Nicholas was in close touch with numerous monarchist organisations, composed chiefly of ex-officers and wealthy merchants, who were plotting to get the Romanov family away (Tobolsk, Tiumen, Ekaterinburg). At Ekaterinburg itself, Nicholas and Alexandra kept up a constant correspondence with an "underground" group of thirty-seven ex-officers, headed by three or four Grand Dukes, sending their notes in loaves of bread, on the wrappers of parcels, and even in a cork. General Dieterichs publishes the text of a letter from Nicholas, containing an exact description of the house in which they were confined, the strength of the armed guard, posts of the sentries, and so forth. The authorities intercepted an exact plan of the house, with notes in Nicholas' handwriting, between the inner and outer linings of an ordinary envelope. And Nicholas' own diary for 1918 (*Krasny Arkhiv*, 1928, Vol. XXVII, p. 136.) contains the following entry: " June 14, Thursday. . . . We spent a disturbed night, and sat up in our clothes. All this took place because recently we received two letters informing us that we must be ready to be rescued by some devoted persons ! But days passed, and nothing happened, while the delay and uncertainty have been very worrying."

If the Romanovs did not escape, it was not because they were as innocent as the Babes in the Wood, but because the workers of Siberia and the Urals in 1918 were as watchful as the people of Paris in 1792.

6. *Some Conclusions*

It is, perhaps, unnecessary to revert to the opinions quoted earlier, and to show how little the portrait of Nicholas II, drawn by himself and his most intimate associates, corresponds with the rosy picture delineated by his apologists. Only brazen impudence or inexcusable ignorance can explain the legend of the "Illustrious" Nicholas II.

F. A. Golovin, the moderate Liberal who was elected President of the Second Duma, wrote the following character sketch in 1912, after years of personal contact with the Tsar and observation of his actions:

"I positively affirm that the generally accepted view of Nicholas II as a foolish, weak-willed, insignificant creature who understands nothing of what goes on around him, a tool in the hands of the Court clique by which he is surrounded, is quite baseless.

"True, he does not shine by his intelligence, nor does he possess a strong will; he is little prepared, apparently, for the difficult task which has fallen to his lot; but still it would be wrong to treat him as a nonentity acting not by his own will or understanding. Nicholas II is a poor copy of the bad qualities of Alexander I. The latter was for long considered a weak-willed man subjected to outside influence, first of Speransky, then of Arakcheyev; but later historical researches have shown that this view was a mistake. His natural cunning, duplicity and cowardice prompted him to act by stealth, hiding behind someone else's back, pretending that this person was using the Emperor's name without the Emperor's knowledge or consent.

"Nicholas II acts in exactly the same way. Also by nature cunning, doublefaced and cowardly, he readily consents to let another s head bear the brunt of the popular hatred aroused by his own internal policy.... He always acts deliberately, crookedly, often malignantly sneers at society, yet at the same time maintains a cowardly screen of dissembled simplicity. To maintain the greatest possible power in his own hands, he sticks at nothing. The interests of the dynasty and of petty personal pride are for him above the interests of the State." (*Krasny Arkhiv*, 1926, Vol. XIX, pp. 125-126.)

To this severe description, every word of which is borne out by the evidence previously quoted, must be added the qualities which Golovin, himself a supporter of capitalism, of the church and of monarchy, did not think it necessary to condemn—absolute devotion to the principle of autocracy, an inveterate fear and hatred of the oppressed peasants, workmen and subject nationalities, a callous belief in the efficacy of mass bloodshed which bordered on criminal lunacy, and the grossest superstition—which, beginning with an unshakeable confidence in his divine right and inspiration, degenerated in the days of Iliodor and Rasputin into miracle-working and amulet-worshipping. A cold-blooded scoundrel, the most degenerate representative of a decaying dynasty and a corrupt society—no milder language can give a just appraisal of the character of Nicholas II.

He was not executed because of his character, however, nor even directly because of his past crimes. The execution was first and foremost an act of social defence, at a critical moment in the history of the Revolution, when open rebellion fomented from without and armed intervention by hostile Powers were threatening a restoration and counter-revolution, as unmistakeably as did the Austrian–Prussian–British attack on revolted France in 1792. Nicholas Romanov and his family were shot (and countless hundreds of thousands were done to death during his reign without world-wide protests or armed intervention) in order to crush the symbol of the old order and to warn off would-be aspirants to the throne. If the highest interests of the British Empire justified Amritsar, the Black-and-Tans, the bombing of villages in Iraq and Waziristan, the drowning of women in Gambia (not to speak of intervention in Russia and in China)—and this is the claim of all "constitutional" British parties—a hundred times more did the interests of the workers' and peasants' Revolution of November 1917 justify the execution of the Romanovs. And when the apologists of Nicholas II, avoiding both an examination of his political record and an authentic study of his character, attempt to condemn his execution, and create hostility to the Soviets—by referring to the undoubted fact that he loved his wife and children, and was loved by them in return, that he sometimes conferred favours on those who sought them, and frequently expressed human emotions—then it is timely to remind them of the biting reply given by Macaulay to an earlier generation of apologists for reaction and counter-revolution.

"The advocates of Charles, like the advocates of other malefactors against whom overwhelming evidence is produced, generally decline all controversy about the facts, and content themselves with calling testimony to character. He had so many private virtues! And had James the Second no private virtues? Was Oliver Cromwell, his bitterest enemies themselves being judges, destitute of private virtues? And what, after all, are the virtues ascribed to Charles ? A religious zeal, not more sincere than that of his son, and fully as weak and narrow-minded, and a few of the ordinary household decencies which half the tombstones in England claim for those who lie beneath them. A good father! A good husband! Ample apologies indeed for fifteen years of persecution, tyranny and falsehood !

"We charge him with having broken his coronation oath; and we are told that he kept his marriage vow! We accuse him of having given up his people to the merciless inflictions of the most hot-headed and hard-hearted of prelates; and the defence is, that he took his little son on his knee and kissed him! We censure him for having violated the articles of the Petition of Right, after having, for good and valuable consideration, promised to observe them; and we are informed that he was accustomed to hear prayers at six o'clock in the morning! It is to such considerations as these, together with his Vandyke dress, his handsome face, and his peaked beard, that he owes, we verily believe, most of his popularity with the present generation.

"For ourselves, we own that we do not understand the common phrase, a good man, but a bad king. We can as easily conceive a good man but an unnatural father, or a good man and a treacherous friend. We cannot, in estimating the character of an individual, leave out of our consideration his conduct in the most important of all human relations; and if in that relation we find him to have been selfish, cruel and deceitful, we shall take the liberty to call him a bad man, in spite of all his temperance at the table, and all his regularity at chapel." (*Essays*, 1860 edition, London, Vol I, pp. 36-37.)

The requisite changes made, there is little that need be added in reply to the advocates of Nicholas Romano.

It remains only to commend to the earnest attention of the reader the little book by P. M. Bykov, Chairman of the Ekaterinburg (now Sverdlovsk) Soviet in 1918, in which the last days of the Romanovs are described by an eye-witness and a participant in the great Russian Revolution.

ANDREW ROTHSTEIN.

March, 1934.
*Seventeenth anniversary of the
overthrow of the Romanov tyranny.*

ANDREW ROTHSTEIN, COMMUNIST LEADER (1898-1994)

He was a Londoner, born to Jewish parents, and studied at the esteemed Balliol College in Oxford; that being the very same also attended by Yussupoff and Oswald Rayner. In 1917 he served in the army and was part of the detachment that was kept at Archangel after the war ended.

The purpose of his regiment not being demobbed, was so that they could resume hostilities against the newly formed Soviet republic in the Churchill backed enterprise to assist the White movement to remove the Bolsheviks from power.

Instead of willingly accepting the task, Corporal Rothstein led a refusal to conform with soldiers' strikes as their representative.

In 1920 he became a founding member of the Communist Party of Great Britain and the London correspondent for the Soviet news agency TASS.

In his magazine The Call, (May 9, 1918,) he described the wasted opportunities for bringing about peace in Europe to end the tremendous suffering of world war, labelling the allied leaders the 'Enemies of Humanity' and asked *"Do the workers now see how they are deceived?"* In simpler terms, he saw everything as a socialist war against the 'bourgeoisie' and in due course came to be regarded as one of the foremost world experts in Marxism.

* * *

PAVEL BYKOV

THE LAST DAYS OF TSARDOM

CHAPTER I

ON THE EVE OF REVOLUTION

THE Romanov dynasty for the first time came face to face with the danger of losing its throne in 1905. The Imperial Government, with the active help of French finance, succeeded in crushing the revolution and saving the dynasty. All power remained as before in the hands of Tsarism. But the situation thereafter changed considerably.

The Russian bourgeoisie had long wielded economic power. After 1905 it began to acquire more and more influence in the political sphere also. In this it was assisted by the "Constitution of the Third of June" (1907), which opened the gates of political activity wide before the bourgeoisie. All the bourgeois parties Cadets, Octobrists, etc.—were in effect legalised, and their press enjoyed great freedom. They rapidly gained the upper hand in municipal authorities, congresses of various kinds, the Duma and other public bodies, making them the base of their ever-growing political influence.

Side by side with this the bourgeoisie drew closer to the Tsardom, which was adapting itself more and more to the service of the capitalist development of the country. To a certain degree, one might say, the Tsardom was becoming bourgeois. By 1914 the Russian bourgeoisie beyond all doubt partially exercised political power, and its attitude frequently determined the policy of the Imperial Government.

The war at first welded the Russian bourgeoisie even more closely to Tsardom, and established full harmony and agreement between them. But within three or four months this unity was shaken. The autocracy proved bankrupt in face of the vast problems created by the war. The Russian troops suffered one defeat after another, thanks to the absence of a sufficient quantity of rifles, cartridges and shells. The position in the rear was little better. Here was beginning to make itself felt one of the most serious consequences of the war—economic collapse, produced to a large extent by the incapacity of the Government to grapple with wartime difficulties. All this made a Russian victory in the war most uncertain, and drove the Russian bourgeoisie along the path of opposition to the Tsarist Government.

The bourgeoisie was interested in a successful outcome of the war. From the very outset it had transformed the public bodies under its control (the All-Russian Union of Zemstvos, the All-Russian Union of Towns, etc.) into auxiliaries of the State military and civil machine. They were more mobile than the State bodies, and soon became of great importance in the prosecution of the war. The Government was obliged to give recognition to their work and to grant them fairly extensive powers. But the bourgeoisie considered that this was insufficient, and insistently demanded an even larger share in the leadership and organisation of the war.

The retreat from Galicia of the Russian troops in April 1915, forced the Government to make concessions. In the summer a Special Conference for Public Defence was set up at Petrograd, representatives of manufacturers, of the Duma, etc., participating. From that time onward war economy was in effect under the control of the bourgeoisie. But this was not enough. The bourgeois representatives in the Duma, in the name of the so-called "Progressive Bloc" which commanded a majority, put forward the demand for a "responsible ministry."

Thus the bourgeoisie desired not merely to control war economy through the Special Conference, but to establish its political control over the country. The latter became all the more urgently necessary, in its eyes, because in Court circles the pro-German tendency, striving for an understanding with Germany and a separate peace, began to grow in strength.

Rumours of negotiations behind the scenes disturbed the patriotically-inclined bourgeoisie no less than defeats at the front or chaos and collapse in the rear. Nevertheless, the Duma could not make up its mind to enter on an active struggle with the Tsar's Government, fearing thereby to excite a mass movement which seemed even more dangerous than the maintenance of the autocracy. The Duma's opposition was therefore extremely moderate, and in the main of a verbal character.

The bourgeoisie, therefore, failed to achieve its object of a responsible ministry by peaceful methods. The Court camarilla, headed by Rasputin, held power firmly in its own hands and would not tolerate any further concessions. Nicholas II, weak-willed and intellectually limited, was entirely under its influence and a mere pawn in the hands of his wife, who in her turn, as is well known, was exceptionally dominated by Rasputin.

In fact, the autocracy of Rasputin was established. His omnipotence may be judged from the fact that, during the last two or three years before the overthrow of the autocracy there was scarcely a single change in the Cabinet made without his knowledge and consent. This seizure of power by Rasputin was accompanied by an unheard-of corruption of the Tsarist machine, which became the field of operations for all kinds of adventurers and blackmailers. Even such a double-dyed monarchist as Purishkevitch was forced to admit that "our Government is nothing but a kaleidoscope of mediocrity, egotism, careerism of individuals who live only for to-day and are mindful only of their own interests."*

In circumstances of extending economic collapse and of unending reverses and defeats of the Russian Army, the administration of the Rasputin clique increased the dissatisfaction of all sections of the people with the Government. The bourgeoisie took advantage of this, and of its position in the Duma, to concentrate the attention of the masses on its exposure of the activities of the so-called "dark forces."

The autumn of 1916 saw discontent rising to serious dimensions. Even amongst the loyal nobility the policy of the Imperial Government no longer met with the old unquestioning support. The Conference of the Nobility on November 28 declared its support of the moderate demands of the Progressive Bloc.

After the nobility came the turn of the Tsar's relatives—the Grand Dukes, who implored the Tsar to take steps to save the dynasty from destruction otherwise inevitable. The Grand Duke Alexander Michaelovitch anxiously wrote to Nicholas II : "We are passing through the most perilous moment in Russian history.... There are some forces inside Russia which are leading you, and consequently

* *The Murder of Rasputin* (from the Diary of V. Purishkevich), p. 5.

Russia, to inevitable destruction."* There followed a letter of warning from another relative, the Grand Duke Nicholas Michaelovitch, who told the Tsar that he was "on the eve of a new era of disorder." He assured Nicholas that, "if it were only possible to eliminate the constant interference of dark forces in every sphere, the regeneration of Russia would begin at once, and the lost confidence of the vast majority of your subjects would return."† The Grand Duke George Michaelovitch went even further, hinting at the necessity, in the interests of the Dynasty, of forming—true, in a very remarkable fashion—a "responsible ministry."

However, Nicholas was deaf to all these entreaties and counsels. He would not agree to any diminution of his autocratic power, while his wife simply refused to hear any talk of it. "Whoever wants a responsible ministry is a fool," she wrote to Nicholas, referring to the letter from the Grand Duke George.‡ As for the letter from the Grand Duke Nicholas Michaelovitch, who had plucked up courage to mention the danger of the influence of "dark forces," and in particular of herself, Alexandra Feodorovna wrote to her husband: "Please order Nicholas Michaelovitch to leave: he is a dangerous element here in town." And the Grand Duke was in consequence banished from Petrograd to his estates.

Invariably meeting with this resistance from Nicholas, this section of the ruling class began to seek other ways of saving themselves and the dynasty. In their eyes, the chief culprit for the increasing national collapse, and for the influence of "dark forces" over the Tsar was Rasputin. Only his elimination could save the dynasty. Therefore in their midst arose the idea of murdering Rasputin. The Grand Duke Dimitri Pavlovitch, together with Prince Yussupov and the noted monarchist Purishkevitch, made up their minds to take this "heroic" step.

They intended to draw into their plot V. Maklakov, one of the prominent Cadet leaders, and thereby to impart to their enterprise the character of a broad public undertaking. But Maklakov, while not objecting in principle to their "worthy object, took fright and refused to participate, on the plea of an urgent call out of Moscow. According to Purishkevitch, Maklakov said that "he could hardly be of much practical use in the liquidation of Rasputin. But thereafter,

* *Nicholas II and the Grand Dukes* (Correspondence between the last Tsar and his relatives). State Publishing Agency, 1925, pp. 117-118.
† Ibid, pp. 146-7.   ‡ Ibid, P. 20.

of much practical use in the liquidation of Rasputin. But thereafter, if matters did not go smoothly, and we were caught, he was not only ready to help us with legal advice, but would willingly come forward as our counsel, should matters come to a trial. 'But this is what I earnestly ask you,' added Maklakov warmly. 'If you succeed, be kind enough to send me an urgent telegram, saying for example : " When do you arrive ? " I will understand that Rasputin no longer exists, and that Russia can breathe freely.' "*

Thus the hope of saving the autocracy by killing Rasputin was shared by the leadership of the chief bourgeois Opposition party, which was unofficially cognizant of this terrorist undertaking.

On December 17, 1916, Rasputin was killed in the house of Prince Yussupov, where he had been invited to a specially organised dinner-party. But the salvation of the Tsardom did not, of course, follow. The changes in the Cabinet which took place subsequently displayed the firm determination of the Tsarist Government to carry on its previous policy, reckoning neither with the bourgeois opposition, in the shape of the Progressive Bloc, nor with opposition tendencies in its own midst.

Influenced by this, some representatives of the bourgeoisie, and also some military circles, began to discuss—at first secretly, later more and more openly—the idea of coming to a settlement by means of a palace revolution. "This idea," says Kurlov, "found support even amongst certain members of the Imperial House."†

However terrified the bourgeoisie at the possibility of a mass movement in consequence of such a revolution, it was still driven to this decision as the sole possible guarantee of victory in the war. P. Miliukov, in his History of the Second Russian Revolution, states that there existed two groups which were discussing the details of the forthcoming revolt. One, consisting apparently of military men, was headed by General Krymov. The other was composed of "some members of the Executive of the Progressive Bloc, together with some provincial and municipal public men." This group, according to Miliukov, "discussed the question of the part to be played by the Duma after the revolution. After discussing various possibilities, this group also decided on the regency of the Grand Duke Michael Alex-

* *The Murder of Rasputin*, p. 26.
† *The End of Russian Tsarism* (Memoirs of General P. G. Kurlov), State Publishing Agency, 1924, p. 280.

androvitch, as the best means of establishing in Russia a constitutional monarchy. A considerable number of members of the first Provisional Government took part in the discussions of this group."*

This, in general terms, was the political programme of the conspirators. What measures they were prepared to take to achieve their object is recounted by General Denikin in his memoirs. It was proposed that, during one of Nicholas' visits to General Headquarters, General Krymov with a special detachment should attack the Imperial train and request the Tsar to abdicate. In the event of Nicholas proving obstinate, he was to be "physically eliminated." The plan was to be carried out in February 1917.

While preparations for this palace revolution were being pushed ahead, and were becoming known fairly widely, the Imperial Government, without knowing in detail the plans of its opponents, was preparing its counterblow. The details are described by General Kurlov, according to whom the counterblow resolved itself into the dissolution of the Duma, while the masses were to be kept in check by publishing "a law granting land to the peasants . . . establishing the equality of the whole people in civil rights . . . and declaring the equal rights of all nationalities."†

That such a plan really existed can partially be seen from the evidence of Protopopov, Minister for the Interior, before the Extraordinary Commission of Inquiry, set up by the Provisional Government after the February Revolution in order to investigate the illegal activities of politicians of the old regime. Apparently the Imperial Government linked the plans indicated with the idea of a separate peace with Germany, which of course was not mentioned by Kurlov and Protopopov for obvious reasons.

But neither the palace revolution nor the counterblow materialised, owing to the fact that in February 1917 a third power, the working class, intervened in the struggle for power, and prevented the fulfilment of either plan. Thereafter events turned out quite differently from the wishes of the bourgeoisie or the hopes of the Tsarist Government.

* P. N. Miliukov: *History of Second Russian Revolution*, Vol. i, Part I, Sofia, 1922, p. 36.

† *Op. cit.*, pp. 284-5.

CHAPTER II

THE OVERTHROW OF THE AUTOCRACY

WHILE the bourgeoisie was organising a palace revolution in order to continue the war "to a complete victory," the masses of workers and soldiers who bore the full burden of the consequences of the war were also moving into struggle against the autocracy. But their demands went much further than the moderate "reforms" which constituted the programme of the Progressive Bloc. The bourgeoisie saw in this—not without foundation—a sign of the approach of revolution, with which it associated the ideas of defeat in the war and its own and the dynasty's destruction. Therefore it was no less alarmed than the Tsardom at the daily growth of revolutionary ferment amongst the workers and in the army. V. Shulgin, the prominent monarchist, quotes the following interesting conversation with the Cadet Shingarev:

"The situation is growing worse every day," said Shingarev anxiously to him at the beginning of January 1917. "We are moving towards the abyss. Revolution means destruction, and it is towards revolution that we are going. The railways are in a disastrous condition again, and there are serious complications at Petrograd in regard to the food supply. We must hold out to the spring : but I am afraid we shall not hold out."

"We must hold out," Shulgin replied. "But how ? Even if our insane Government makes concessions, even if it forms a responsible Ministry, this will not be satisfactory. Popular feeling has already passed over our heads, it is already well to the left of the Progressive Bloc. The country gives heed to those who are most to the left, not to us. . . . It is too late."*

Seeing the rise of revolution, the bourgeoisie took every possible step to avert it. While appealing to the workers to keep calm, it implored the Government to make concessions to the demands of the Progressive Bloc, which alone, in its opinion, could save the situation. And even when the left wing of the bourgeois Opposition—the pro-war Social-Democrats—proposed a workers' demonstration in support of the Duma on February 27, i.e., in support of the Progressive Bloc itself, the bourgeoisie were so terr-

---

* V. Shulgin : *Days*, p. 86 ; *Priboi*, Leningrad, 1925.

ified that their leader Miliukov hastily published an Open Letter to the workers of Petrograd, pleading with them to abandon the demonstration, which, in his words, was nothing but a "perfidious device" of the enemy.

On the very same day as Miliukov's appeal (February 10), Rodzianko, the President of the Duma, was doing his best to persuade the Tsar of the peril with which approaching events were pregnant, and of the necessity of making concessions.

"Save yourself, your Majesty," said Rodzianko. "We are on the eve of tremendous events, whose outcome cannot be foreseen. What your Government and you yourself are doing is irritating the people to such an extent that anything is possible."

But, confident of himself and of the time-honoured methods of crushing revolution, the "Lord's Anointed" put off the annoying Rodzianko with his usual phrase: "The Lord will provide—everything will be all right." "The Lord will provide nothing," retorted the pious Rodzianko. "You and your Government have spoiled everything. A revolution is inevitable."

The demonstration appointed for February 27, which so frightened the bourgeoisie, did not take place. This was not because the workers listened to the appeals of Miliukov, but because the proposal of the jingoes was sharply rebuffed by the internationalist organisations, who regarded the demonstration as support of the Duma's demand for a "responsible ministry " and a "fight to a finish." Such demands no longer satisfied the workers, and they refused to follow the jingoes. The revolutionary ferment, however, began thereafter to extend day by day with overwhelming force. By the beginning of March it had seized, upon literally all the workers of Petrograd, and began to break out spontaneously in strikes. On March 8 tens of thousands of workers struck. On March 10 their numbers already ran into hundreds of thousands. From the very first, the movement was of a clearly expressed political character.

As soon as it became clear that the movement was assuming such wide proportions, the bourgeoisie, in the person of the Duma, and individual politicians of the old regime began straining every nerve to save the situation.

Rodzianko, the Grand Duke Michael Alexandrovitch, the Prime Minister Galitzin, and others sent Nicholas one telegram after another on the seriousness of the situation and the necessity of forming a "responsible Ministry," as a concession to save the Tsardom and put an end to the movement. These telegrams made no impression on the Tsar: he put off his unwelcome advisers with quiet obstinacy. He replied to his brother Michael thanking him for his advice, but adding, with great self-assurance, that he knew himself how to act. In a telegram to Prince Galitzin, written out in his own hand, Nicholas stated that at present he saw no possibility of making any changes in the Cabinet, and demanded the suppression of the. revolutionary movement and of the mutinies among the troops.

"During these days," writes N. Sokolov, "Nicholas was tranquil, and in no way showed the shadow of any anxiety."*

On March 11 and 12 all the workers of Petrograd were already in the streets and the Army joined the movement. By the evening of March 12 the entire capital was in the hands of the insurgents, with the exception of the Governor's building, the Admiralty, the Winter Palace and the fortress of Peter and Paul. On the same day the Petrograd Council of Workers' Deputies (the Soviet) was organised, and simultaneously was formed the Provisional Committee of the Duma. But the Tsar as before could not comprehend the events which were developing, and did not realise that his own head was at stake. In response to the insistent demands of General Habalov, commander of the forces of the Petrograd Military District, for the despatch of reinforcements, Nicholas issued on March 11 a decree for the suppression of the insurrection, as though it were a question of some strike or other.

"I order that this very day the disorders in the capital, intolerable at this most difficult time of war with Germany and Austria, be brought to an end. Nicholas."†

But Nicholas' decree was too late. The capital was already in the hands of the revolting workers and soldiers.

Faced with the fact of the overthrow of Tsarism, the bourgeoisie hastened to take the leadership of the revolution into its own hands. The most important question was how to delay the progress of the revolution, how to save the Tsardom by sacrificing Nicholas.

On March 14 a secret consultation of the members of the newly-

* N. Sokolov: *The Murder of the Imperial Family*, p. 6 (*Slovo*, Berlin, 1925).
† *The Fall of the Tsarist Regime*, Vol. 1, p. 190.

formed Provisional Committee of the Duma took place. They all agreed in declaring that the monarchy must be maintained, and that Nicholas alone must be sacrificed in order to save Russia. A. Guchkov, the Octobrist leader, enlarged on this theme as follows: "It is extremely important that Nicholas II should not be overthrown by violence. Only his voluntary abdication in favour of his son or brother can ensure the firm consolidation of the new order without great convulsions. The voluntary abdication of Nicholas II is the only means of saving the Imperial regime and the Romanov dynasty."*

The representatives of the bourgeoisie overwhelmed the Tsar with telegrams begging him to "renounce" the throne in favour of his son Alexei, with Michael Alexandrovitch (his brother) as Regent. Nicholas now no longer displayed his former obstinacy, as even he at last had realised that power was no longer in his hands. On March 13 he had already decided to leave General Headquarters in order to join his family at Tsarskoye Selo, but his train was stopped by orders from Petrograd, and he had no alternative but to go to Pskov, the road to which was open. In this way the last of the Romanovs came to be personally convinced, even before his abdication, that he had lost his power.

On March 14 Nicholas arrived at Pskov, and on the same day signed an act of abdication, in favour of his son. Later on, as we shall see, he thought better of this decision.

Meanwhile, at Petrograd, the interests of the Duma and the Soviet had come into conflict. The Provisional Committee had decided to send Rodzianko and Shidlovsky on its behalf to the Tsar at G.H.Q., with instructions to procure from Nicholas an act of abdication in favour of his son, and appointing the Grand Duke Michael Alexandrovitch as Regent. News of this decision came to the Petrograd Soviet, which during these days was in permanent session at the Taurida Palace. On behalf of the Soviet, Chkheidze demanded that the Provisional Committee should give an explanation and the text of the act of abdication which it had adopted. When it had made itself acquainted with this text, the Petrograd Soviet rejected the formula transferring power to a new autocrat, and demanded the proclamation of a Republic.

* J M. Paleologue: *Imperial Russia on the Eve of the Revolution*, p. 355 (Moscow 1923).

While these negotiations were continuing, two of the Duma leaders, A. I. Guchkov, and V. V. Shulgin, obtained on March 15 a special train at the Warsaw station and left for G.H.Q. in order to "persuade" Romanov to "renounce" his authority.

Shulgin describes the comedy of Nicholas' abdication thus:

"We arrived at nine in the evening. A few lines away stood a brightly lit-up train. We understood that this was the Imperial train.

"Someone came up at once. 'His Majesty is expecting you.'

"He led us across the rails. We entered: it was a large drawing-room car, green silk on the walls, a few tables here and there. A tall, lean old yellow-grey general with shoulder-knots came forward. It was Baron Frederiks.

"His Majesty appeared in the doorway. He was wearing a grey Caucasian tunic. He seemed calm.

"We bowed. His Majesty greeted us and shook hands. If anything, his movement was friendly. With a gesture, he invited us to be seated. He sat down on one side of a small square table, which was pushed up against the green silk wall. Guchkov sat on the other side. I took my place by Guchkov, diagonally from the Tsar. Opposite the Tsar sat Baron Frederiks.

"Guchkov was the spokesman. His speech had seemingly been well thought out, but he mastered his agitation with difficulty. He spoke jerkily and low.

"The Tsar sat leaning slightly on the silken tapestry and looked straight in front of him. His expression was quite calm and impenetrable. The only thought that might be guessed from his face was, 'This long speech is unnecessary.'

"During this period General Russky entered. He bowed to the Tsar and, without interrupting Guchkov, took his place between Baron Frederiks and myself. At that moment, I think, I noticed that in a corner sat another general, with dark hair and white epaulettes. This was General Danilov.

"Guchkov again grew agitated. He had reached the point that possibly the only way out was to abdicate the throne.

"Guchkov ended. The Tsar replied. After the anxious tones of Guchkov, his voice sounded calm, simple and precise. Only his guardsman's accent was a little foreign.

"'I have decided to renounce the throne. Up to three o'clock to-day I thought I could abdicate in favour of my son Alexei. But now I have changed my decision in favour of my brother Michael. I trust you will understand the feelings of a father.'

"The last phrase was uttered in lower tones.

"The Tsar rose, followed by all. Guchkov handed him the draft. Nicholas took it and went out. After a little time he returned, and, handing Guchkov a document, said : 'Here is the text.'

"It was in two or three copies on quarter-sheets of note-paper, such as were used at G.H.Q. for telegrams. The text was typewritten."*

Guchkov, in the words of A. Blok, was amazed that the abdication was made so easily. The scene produced a painful impression on him by its drabness, and it came into his head that he was dealing with an abnormal individual, with a lowered sensitiveness and intelligence. The Tsar, according to Guchkov's impression, was completely unconscious of the tragic significance of events. The most iron self-control might have broken down, but his voice appeared to tremble only when he spoke of separation from his son.†

The abdication of Nicholas, like his renunciation of his original decision to abdicate in favour of his son, was undoubtedly dictated by considerations of personal safety. This can be seen, incidentally, from the letter of Alexandra Feodorovna (the Empress) to Nicholas on March 17, in the postscript of which she wrote : "Only this morning we heard that everything had been handed over to Misha, and Baby is now safe—what a relief !"‡

Even before Nicholas' abdication in favour of his brother became known, P. Miliukov, in the name of the Provisional Government which had just been formed, announced at a meeting in the Taurida Palace that power would be vested in a Regent, the Grand Duke Michael, while Alexei would be the Heir-Apparent.

This information caused great discontent and indignation among the workers and soldiers of Petrograd. The feeling was so strong that it already threatened to find expression in a movement against the bourgeoisie itself. Miliukov gives one of these facts. "By the end of the day (March 15)," he writes, "the excitement caused by my ann-

---

* Shulgin, op. cit., pp. 175-180.
† A. Blok : *The Last Days of Imperial Power*, p. 107, Petrograd, 1921.
‡ *Family Correspondence of the Romanovs* (*Red Archives*, Vol. iv, p. 221).

ouncement of the Regency of the Grand Duke Michael had greatly increased.... Late at night a large body of extremely agitated officers entered the Taurida Palace, and declared that they could not return to their units unless P. N. Miliukov withdrew his statement."*

Terrified by the rising wave of this movement, the bourgeoisie hastened to yield its positions.

The day after the abdication—March 16—as soon as Guchkov and Shulgin arrived in Petrograd, and while they were still at the station, they were called up on the telephone by Miliukov, who requested them, in the name of the Provisional Government, not to make known the act of abdication.

Shulgin gives this conversation as follows:

"Yes, it is I, Miliukov. Don't make known the manifesto. Serious changes have been made."

"But how?... I have already announced it."

"To whom?"

"Why, to all here. Some regiment or other, the people.... I have proclaimed Michael Emperor."

"You should not have done that. Feelings have become much worse since you left. We have received the text: it is quite unsatisfactory. Don't take any further steps. There may be great misfortunes."†

While this conversation was going on, Guchkov had left to announce the "glad news" at a meeting in the railway workshops, at which there were 2,000 workers present. Shulgin decided to go and warn Guchkov, but, fearing that the act of abdication might be taken away from him and destroyed, he handed it over beforehand to a messenger specially despatched by Bublikov, a member of the Duma. While Shulgin was looking for him, Guchkov was arrested by the railway shopmen, who demanded that he should destroy the act of abdication. They did not find the document in his possession. He was then despatched, under a guard of armed workers, to the carriage of the commissary for the North-Western Railway. After 'politely detaining' Guchkov for twenty minutes, the commissary let him go directly the workers had calmed down.

This incident is also described in his memoirs by G. Lomonosov,

---

* P. Miliukov, *op. cit.*, Vol. I, Part I, p. 52.
† Shulgin, *op. cit.*, p. 189.

who met Lebedev, the man entrusted with the act of abdication. The following conversation took place between them:

" 'Where is the act?'

" 'Here it is,' whispered Lebedev hoarsely, pushing a document into my hand. ' Guchkov has been arrested by the workmen.'

" 'What?' I asked confusedly, sticking the act of abdication into a breast pocket.

" 'I will tell you in the Ministry.'

"We enter Bublikov's room in silence.

" 'Well, how goes it?' asked Bublikov.

" 'Guchkov is arrested. . . . Here's the act of abdication.'

"However sensational the news of Guchkov's arrest might be, the eyes of everyone, forgetful of his fate, were fixed on the scrap of paper I placed on the table.

" 'Yes, and what has happened to Guchkov?' asked Bublikov after a moment's silence.

" 'When his train arrived at Petrograd, he was met here by a fair crowd, and he made two speeches while still in the station. Then he went to a meeting in the workshops. When I arrived, he was already there, while Shulgin and the management were sitting in the station-master's office. There was word that feelings were running high in the workshops. We were very anxious. Then they informed us from the shops that Guchkov had been arrested, that they hadn't found the document on him, and that they are going to search the other deputies, in order to destroy the act.'

" 'Why?'

" 'The comrades want to overthrow the Tsar and everything else, apparently. The abdication isn't enough for them.'

" 'Well, and then?'

" 'Then I was given the document, and taken away quietly through alleys and byways to the other side, and got away. . . . They are looking for the document all over the city. They may come here too. It must be hidden.'

" 'Put it in the safe, and put a guard over it.'

" 'No, put it somewhere inconspicuous, and not in this room.'

"The document was concealed among the dusty old piles of official journals on a what-not in the secretarial room."*

* Professor G. V. Lomonosov, *Recollections of the Revolution of March, 1917*, pp. 28-29, Stockholm-Berlin, 1921.

In this way, having no opportunity of saving the monarchy, the bourgeoisie put its trust in an unknown future, and tried at least to save the act of abdication, which has ever since remained a lost document.* On the same day, March 16, a second comedy, of the abdication of Michael, was arranged. There were present, in addition to the Grand Duke Michael Alexandrovitch, the following members of the Provisional Government : Prince Lvov, P. Miliukov, A. Kerensky, N. Nekrasov, I. Tereschenko, I. Godnev, V. Lvov, A. Guchkov, and in addition the following members of the Provisional Committee of the Duma : M. Rodzianko, V. Shulgin, N. Efremov, M. Karaulov, and others. The meeting took place under very conspirative conditions, as, knowing the discontent prevalent among the masses of workers and soldiers, those present were more than concerned for their lives and for the life of the new "anointed."

There were two points of view expressed, for and against the renunciation of the succession by Michael. The first was put forward by Rodzianko and Kerensky. Both declared that the proclamation of the new Tsar would call forth even greater anger and discontent among the masses, and would inevitably lead to civil war. Furthermore, they pointed out, to accept the throne under such conditions would endanger the life of the Grand Duke himself.

"I have no right to conceal here," said Kerensky at the close of his speech, addressing Michael, "what perils you personally incur in the event of your deciding to accept the throne. . . . In any case I cannot answer for the life of your Highness."† This argument seemed most convincing to Michael, and, as we shall see, decided the question of the throne.

Miliukov represented the second point of view, and earnestly opposed the abdication. In his speech he declared that, "although those are right who say that the acceptance of power involved risk to the personal safety of the Grand Duke and the ministers themselves, but this risk must be run in the interests of our country," as, in his opinion, "the Provisional Government alone, without a monarch, is a frail bark, which may sink in the ocean of national disorder : and the country will then be in danger of complete anarchy."‡

* Translator's Note—It was discovered in 1929 in the archives of the Academy of Sciences at Leningrad.
† Shulgin, *op. cit.*, p. 197.
‡ Miliukov, *op. cit.*, Vol. i, Part I.

Only Guchkov supported Miliukov. The majority supported the necessity of Michael renouncing the throne and leaving the question of the monarchy open until the Constituent Assembly, which must, in their opinion, independently settle it. Then Guchkov, says Paleologue, made his supreme effort, addressing himself personally to the Grand Duke and appealing to his patriotism and courage. He urged on him the necessity of immediately producing to the Russian people the living image of a national leader. "If you fear to assume immediately the burden of the Imperial crown, your Highness, take at any rate the supreme power in the capacity of 'Regent of the Empire' for the time that the throne is vacant—or, what would be an even finer title, in the capacity of 'Protector of the People' as Cromwell was called. At the same time you could give the people a solemn undertaking to hand over authority to the Constituent Assembly as soon as the war is over."*

Michael turned out to be more sensible than was expected of him, and decided not to assume the crown out of consideration for his head. He signed an act of renunciation in the sense desired by the majority at the meeting. In drawing it up, their chief concern was to leave the way to the throne open, if possible, for members of the Romanov dynasty. But legal niceties did not help them. The Romanovs never succeeded in regaining the throne they had lost.

To-day, rewriting in exile the history of bygone days, the representatives of the bourgeoisie doubt whether they correctly solved this important problem of the end of the Romanov dynasty. At all events, they did everything possible to sustain the falling monarchy : and, if they were not successful, this of course was not their fault. Even Nicholas, in his farewell manifesto to the army, dated March 21, could express nothing but his gratitude to the bourgeoisie for its efforts. Declaring that he had renounced all power, he wrote : "Submit to the Provisional Government, obey your officers, and may God assist the Provisional Government to lead Russia along the path of glory and well-being."†

---

* Paleologue, *op. cit.*, pp. 363-364.
† Sokolov, op. cit., p. 7.

*   *   *

CHAPTER III

THE ARREST OF THE ROMANOVS

WHILE Guchkov and Miliukov were begging Michael on their knees to assume supreme power, the Executive Committee of the Petrograd Soviet, at its session of March 16, resolved to request the Provisional Government, together with the Council of Workers' Deputies, to arrest the Romanovs.

The question of how to effect the arrests was entrusted to the Military Commission of the Soviet to work out. The Executive Committee appointed its chairman, Chkheidze, and Skobelev to negotiate with the Provisional Government. For four days the Provisional Government was silent, hesitating to give a final reply to the Soviet. During this time the workers and soldiers, impatient of delay, grew more and more insistent on the arrests being carried out. On March 19 the Executive Committee was forced again to discuss the question, and, in order to bring pressure on the Provisional Government, took the decision "immediately to instruct the Military Commission to take steps for the arrest of Nicholas Romanov."

This had its effect on the Provisional Government. Fearing independent action by the Soviet, it decided on the very next day to "deprive Nicholas and his wife of their liberty."

Such a step on the part of the Provisional Government was still provoked not so much by the pressure of the Soviet as by the desire to preserve the life of the crowned degenerate. The best witness of this is Kerensky, who says : "The attitude of the soldiers and workmen of the Moscow and Petrograd districts was extremely hostile to Nicholas. Demands for his execution were addressed directly to me. Protesting in the name of the Government against such demands, I said privately to myself that I would never play the part of a Marat. . . . The workers' feeding of hatred was very deep-seated." This was the reason which prompted the Provisional Government to arrest the Tsar and Alexandra Feodorovna. By depriving them of their liberty, the Government was thereby placing a guard over their lives.

Prince Lvov, who was at that time Prime Minister, says the same : "It was necessary to defend the former bearer of supreme authority from the possible excesses of the first torrent of revolution."*

On March 21, representatives of the Provisional Government—Bublikov, Vershinin, Gribunin and Kalinin, members of the Duma—arrived at Mogilev, where the former Tsar was living. They announced to Nicholas, through General Alexeiev, that he was arrested and must leave for Tsarskoye Selo, where the former Tsaritsa was living with her family. During the revolutionary days the children of the Romanovs were suffering from measles, and this prevented Alexandra Feodorovna from being with Nicholas at the moment critical for the dynasty. Exercising a considerable influence over him in all affairs of State, she would hardly have allowed him to part company with the crown so easily. Like Nicholas, she continued to misunderstand events to the very end. She invariably rejected as nonsensical rumours, unworthy of attention, the warnings of her intimates that the movement which had begun threatened the very existence of the autocracy. Even when faced with facts, she stubbornly refused to believe in the possibility of a revolution. "When the valet Volkov," writes Sokolov, "pointed out that even the Cossacks in Petrograd were unreliable, she calmly replied: 'No, it is not so. There can be no revolution in Russia. The Cossacks will not turn traitor.' "†

Similarly she would not believe the announcement that Nicholas had abdicated. The Grand Duke Paul Alexandrovitch states that even on March 16 she knew nothing of this fact, and that when he read her the manifesto of abdication, Alexandra Feodorovna exclaimed: "I don't believe it. It is all lies, newspaper inventions, I believe in God and the army. They have not abandoned us yet.' ‡

A few days earlier, relying on the same God and army, she had tried to visit her husband at G.H.Q. But the stations were in the hands of the insurgent soldiers of that very army on which she pinned her hopes, and she did not succeed in meeting Nicholas for the purpose of influencing him. Then she sent him telegram after telegram, but these were returned to her with the inscription in blue pencil: "Whereabouts of addressee unknown."

At length on March 22 the addressee himself was brought to Tsarskoye Selo.

* Sokolov, *op. cit.*, pp. 11-12.
† Ibid, p. 9.
‡ *Nicholas II and the Grand Dukes*, p. 145.

The detention of the Romanovs under arrest at Tsarskoye Selo did not by any means, of course, eliminate the danger to the life of the "anointed" and his family. This was well understood by the Provincial Government itself. The decision, to arrest the Romanovs was involved in their minds with a more far-reaching plan. Even before the decision had been made, Miliukov, on the instructions of the Provisional Government, was negotiating with the British Ambassador Buchanan on the possibility of transferring the former Tsar to England. Buchanan, after making the necessary enquiries of London, reported that his Government was ready to receive the former Imperial family in Great Britain, and that a British cruiser would be sent to transport them. In a special note sent to the Minister for Foreign Affairs, Buchanan stated that "the King and his Majesty's Government will be happy to offer the Emperor of Russia a refuge in Great Britain."*

Kerensky was entrusted with the task of transporting the Romanov family across the frontier, and he readily agreed to assume the role of saviour of the last Tsar. All these preparations for the escape of the Romanovs abroad were made in the strictest secrecy, only a few knowing of their existence. By effecting the arrest, the Provisional Government desired to lull the vigilance of the masses, in order to present them with a *fait accompli*. On the very day when the decision was taken to deprive the former Tsar and his wife of their liberty, Prince Lvov, the head of the Government, sent the following telegram to General Alexeiev at G.H.Q.: "The Provisional Government has decided.to grant to the former Emperor permission to leave Tsarskoye Selo without let or hindrance in order to travel to Murmansk."†

We do not know whether the promised cruiser was awaiting the Imperial refugees in the port of Murmansk, but they did not succeed in taking advantage of the offer of the British gentlemen.

On the evening of March 22, the Executive Committee of the Petrograd Soviet was informed that the Government intended secretly to "evacuate" Nicholas and his family to England. It resolved at all costs to arrest them, even though this might involve a rupture with the Provisional Government. Immediately wireless messages were sent to all towns, ordering the detention of Nicholas

---

* A. Kerensky, *From Afar*, p. 191 (Paris, 1922).
† *Russian Chronicles*, Book V.

Romanov. Instructions were given for troops loyal to the Soviet to occupy all railway stations, while commissaries with extraordinary powers were despatched to the stations of Tsarskoye Selo, Tosno and Zvanka. In order to protect the country for the future against similar attempts to smuggle the Romanovs abroad, the Soviet decided on the Trubetskoy bastion of the fortress of Peter and Paul as their place of detention.

One of the Socialist-Revolutionaries active in the March Revolution, S. Mstislavsky, describes this page of the Russian Revolution as follows:

"At the session of the Soviet (March 22) the chairman, Chkheidze, put the following question to the vote:

" 'Shall we permit the departure of the Imperial family? Who is against?'

"All hands went up as one, in a nervous sweep.

" 'If so, we must take steps to see that such attempts are made impossible once for all. The Provisional Government may try again at the first convenient moment. The Republic must be safeguarded against the Romanovs returning to the historical arena. That means that the dangerous persons must be directly in the hands of the Petrograd Soviet?' Again unanimously adopted."*

Finally it was decided to send to Tsarskoye Selo a detachment of the Semenovsky Regiment and of the machine-gunners, under Mstislavsky.

The Petrograd Soviet had accurately summed up the situation so far as the watch over the Romanovs was concerned: it was in unreliable hands. The Provisional Government had committed it to the notorious General Kornilov, who was at that time commander of the forces of the Petrograd District.

On their arrival at Tsarskoye Selo, the Soviet's plenipotentiaries met with a decisive rebuff at the hands of the local authorities.

The latter refused to hand over Nicholas, considering it their duty to carry out the instructions of General Kornilov, who had given orders that Nicholas must not be yielded up. But Mstislavsky himself was already far from this in his thoughts. The militant mood in which he had left the Soviet had evaporated, and the plenipotentiary "emissary" confined himself to an "agreement" with the guard—to check the sentries and disconnect the telephone and

* S. Mstislavsky: *Five Days*, p. 45 (Moscow, 1922).

telegraph. However, it would have been awkward to leave Tsarskoye without seeing Romanov, and Mstislavsky demanded that the "prisoner" be shown to him. It was not easy to penetrate into the Alexandrovsky Palace to visit the "imprisoned" Romanovs. Admission was only by permits with the name of the bearer, signed by the same Kornilov. After long negotiations with the officers of the Guard, who attempted to dissuade him from such an "extraordinary measure," they finally summoned the chief Master of Ceremonies, Count Benckendorff. The old man proved still more obstinate than the officers, and flatly declared that he would not show the Emperor to mutineers. The insistence of Mstislavsky, however, and the real strength of the detachment which had come from Petrograd, finally forced the loyal subjects to make a concession and agree to an "inspection."

" I was accompanied on the 'inspection,' " writes Mstislavsky, "by the commander of the inner guard, the battalion commander, the guard officer on duty, and the orderly officer. . . . When at last the door opened with a reluctant grunt, and we entered the vestibule, we were surrounded—respectfully but inquisitively—with a crowed of courtier flunkeys, who seemed fantastic on the background of the 'simple' events of those revolutionary days. A vast officer-in-waiting, as heavy as Trubetskoy's Alexander on the square, in a bearskin hat like a tub; pages; court negroes, in crimson velvet coats embroidered in gold, with turbans and sharp-pointed curved shoes ; equerries in cocked hats and red capes, bordered with stamped Imperial eagles, stepping noiselessly with the soft soles of their patent-leather shoes; resplendent in snow-white gaiters, the footmen ran before us up the carpeted staircase. . . .

"Everything as it used to be, just as if in this far-off vast palace there had not sounded even a distant echo of the revolutionary storm which had swept over the country from end to end. And when, having ascended the staircase, we passed on through drawing-rooms, ante-rooms, banqueting rooms, passing from carpets to glittering parquet, and then back again to carpets which dulled the insolent ring of my spurs—at every door we found lackeys, petrified in pairs, in the most varied costumes according to the room to which they were attached : now the traditional black frock-coats, now Polish surcoats, black, white, red shoes, stockings and gaiters. And at one of the doors we found two handsome lackeys with ridiculous crimson scarves on their heads, caught up with tinsel clasps, and frock coats with white shoes and stockings.

"In the upper corridor (under the glass roof), which had been transformed into a picture gallery, we found a small crowd of courtiers awaiting us, Benckendorff at their head. The courtiers were in black coats buttoned up to the chin. Six or eight paces from the place we met the retinue, another corridor crossed ours at right angles: it was along this that the former Emperor was to come out to me.

"I took my stand in the middle of the corridor, Benckendorff to my right, Dolgorukov on my left, with another whom I did not know by sight. A little way behind me stood the officers who had come with me.

"Somewhere to the side a lock clicked. Benckendorff grew silent and with trembling hands smoothed his grey whiskers. The officers sprang to attention, hastily buttoning up their gloves. Rapid steps with the faint ring of spurs were heard.

"He (Romanov) was in a khaki summer tunic of the Life Hussars, without a cap. Twitching his shoulder as always and rubbing his hands as though washing them, he stopped at the point where the corridors met and turned his face towards us—bloated and red, with swollen, inflamed eyelids, surrounding in a heavy frame the dull, leaden, bloodshot eyes. After standing awhile as though in indecision, he rubbed his hands again and moved towards us. It seemed as though he was going to speak. We looked one another straight in the eyes, coming nearer at his every step. There was dead silence. The fixed yellow features of the Emperor, which resembled those of a tired, harassed wolf, suddenly lit up: in the depths of his pupils there blazed up a vivid, deadly hatred, which as it were melted their leaden indifference for an instant. . . .

"Nicholas stopped, stood first on one foot then on another, and, turning round sharply, went back, twitching his shoulder and limping.

"I freed my right hand, which had been tucked into my belt, raised it to my fur cap in parting from the courtiers, and, speeded by the hissing and foaming of Benckendorff, retraced my steps. My companions maintained a crushed silence. And only in the vestibule one of them, reproachfully shaking his head, said: 'It was wrong of you not to take off your cap. His Majesty looked as though he

wanted to speak to you, but when he saw how you were standing...'
And another added: 'Well, now look out. If ever the Romanovs come to the throne again, you will remember that minute: they will find you even at the bottom of the sea.' "*

The Mensheviks and Socialist-Revolutionaries, who at that time dominated the Petrograd Soviet, proved true to themselves as always : loud words about committing Nicholas to the Trubetskoy bastion of the fortress of Peter and Paul, a bold plan for a descent on Tsarskoye Selo, and . . . an inspection of the arrested Tsar in his own palace.

Still, the detention of the Romanovs under arrest was from that time onwards under the control, to a certain extent, of the Petrograd Soviet.

The Government was forced to reckon with the actions of the Soviet, and temporarily to give up the fulfilment of its intentions of smuggling the Romanovs away to England.

* S. Mstislavsky, *op. cit.*, pp. 57-60.

* * *

CHAPTER IV

IN THE OLD NEST

FROM March 22 the whole family was under arrest in the Alexandrovsky Palace at Tsarskoye Selo, formerly the permanent residence of the Imperial family in pre-revolutionary years.

Tsarskoye Selo (now Detskoye Selo—the "children's village") is a small town about thirteen miles south of Petrograd. The Alexandrovsky Palace, situated in a park, is near the Great Palace, in which Catherine II lived. The Imperial family occupied one of the wings, while the main palace, in which were situated the reception rooms, was unoccupied. Their suite took up their residence in another wing. Count and Countess Benckendorff, the Lady-in-Waiting, Baroness Buxhoeveden, Countess Hendrikova, the lady reader Schneider, Count Frederiks, Prince Dolgorukov (Chief Marshal of the Court), the tutors Gilliard and Gibbs, Doctor Botkin and a few others shared the confinement of the former Imperial family.

The detention of the Romanovs at Tsarskoye Selo did little to assure the masses. They continued to insist on more severe treatment for the former Imperial family, as the best safeguard for the revolution against possible attempts at a Monarchist restoration. "The execution of Nicholas II and the transference of his family from the Alexandrovsky Palace to the fortress of Peter and Paul or to Kronstadt," writes Kerensky in his memoirs, "these were the furious, sometimes frenzied, demands of hundreds of delegations, deputations, and resolutions which poured in upon the Provisional Government, and in particularly upon myself as the Minister responsible for the safekeeping of the Imperial family."* Naturally, the Provisional Government and the Kerensky himself were deaf to such demands of the masses, and furthermore the Provisional Government, even after its formal abandonment of the plan to send the Romanovs abroad, continued its secret negotiations, through Miliukov, with the British Government on this question. When Miliukov resigned in April, Kerensky states that negotiations for removing to England the inhabitants of the Alexandrovsky Palace "were continued with even greater determination by his successor,

* A. Kerensky: *From Afar*, p. 187.

M. I. Tereschenko."* However, in June the Provisional Government met with an unexpected disappointment: the British Government officially informed it that, pending the termination of the war, it was impossible to receive the ex-Tsar and his family within the confines of the British Empire.

Apparently the Romanovs were acquainted with all these negotiations behind the scenes, but the longer that negotiations continued the less hopes they maintained of seeing the promised shores of Great Britain. Gilliard writes in his reminiscences: "We thought that our imprisonment at Tsarskoye Selo would be of short duration, and awaited our embarkation for England. But the days passed, and our departure was constantly postponed.... We were only a few hours' journey from the Finnish frontier, and Petrograd was the only serious obstacle. It seemed to us, therefore, that by energetic and secret action we could without great difficulty reach one of the Finnish ports, and thereafter escort the Imperial family abroad. But none would take the responsibility, and everyone feared to compromise himself."†

In anticipation of assistance from their "loyal and devoted subjects," the Romanovs continued an uneventful existence. Twice a day—from 11 to 12 in the morning, from 2.30 to five in the afternoon, the family went out for exercise under the escort of soldiers of the Palace guard, drawn from reserve units of the First, Second and Fourth Guards Regiments. For recreation they chopped wood, broke up ice, swept the snow, and in the summer worked in the garden. There were no particular restrictions in their home life. The restrictions only applied out of doors and in the park, where the prisoners were not allowed to stir a step beyond the area fixed for their recreation.

The new surroundings made little impression upon Nicholas. Just as at the moment of abdication, he resembled a man with an obviously lowered sensitiveness and intelligence. Paleologue, relying on the reports of extremely well-informed persons, wrote in his diary on April 11: "The Emperor is still unusually indifferent and calm. He spends the day carelessly and peacefully in reading the papers, smoking cigarettes, playing patience or with the children. He

* Ibid, p. 192.
† P. Gilliard 2: *The Tragic Fate of the Russian Imperial Family*, p. 45 (Reval, 1921).

seems almost to experience a certain satisfaction from being relieved at last of the burden of power."*

The life of the Palace was varied from time to time by the visits of Kerensky, who came to check the guard and converse with the Tsar and his family. The surviving associates of the Romanov family bear witness to his great concern for the welfare of the prisoners, his frequent enquiries after their health, whether they suffered from any restrictions or insults at the hands of the soldiers, etc. His visits, of which there were eight or ten, always made the best possible impression upon the whole Imperial family and its attendants. Even Alexandra Feodorovna, who behaved with great arrogance and contempt to all surrounding her, said on one occasion to Volkov, the Court Chamberlain, "He is not a bad sort. He is a good fellow. One can talk to him."† But soon this friendly idyll which had sprung up between the "Imperial captives" and the first "Socialist Minister" came to an end.

The July events came. They had no immediate effect on the life of the Palace. It continued, quiet and peaceful, as before. But, in spite of the suppression of the July Demonstration, the general political situation in the country became more and more threatening for the Provisional Government, and therefore for the lives of the Romanovs.

"In the summer, in the first half of July," writes Lvov, "the Government arrived at the conviction that the presence of the Imperial family near Petrograd had become impossible : the country was obviously on the decline." Concerned for the preservation of the Imperial family, the Provisional Government decided to remove it from Tsarskoye to a more secluded spot, further from Bolshevik Petrograd and Kronstadt.

The necessity for such measures grew all the more obvious, in the eyes of the Provisional Government, because the "demoralisation" which had begun in the army also affected the garrison of Tsarskoye Selo. "Tsarskoye was the most sensitive spot of all for us of the Provisional Government," writes Kerensky. "The Bolsheviks carried on the most sedulous propaganda amongst the soldiers on guard there and demoralised them. The attitude of the soldiers was one of strained distrust. Merely because the officer of the guard, in accord-

---

* M. Paleologue, *op. cit.*, pp. 432-33.
† N. Sokolov, *op. cit.*, p. 23.

ance with an old Palace custom, received a half-bottle of wine from the Imperial cellars, and this came to the ears of the soldiers, there was a great scandal. The careless driving of some chauffeur who damaged the park railings with his car produced suspicion and rumours among the soldiers that there was a plot to carry off the Tsar. All this created a bad atmosphere . . . and deprived us of our real force, the Tsarskoye Selo garrison, which we had looked upon as a bulwark against the demoralised soldiery of Petrograd."

But the chief motive for transferring the Romanov family from Tsarskoye was nevertheless not these apprehensions. This, by the way, is pointed out by Gilliard in his reminiscences. He writes that, when Kerensky informed Nicholas of the Provisional Government's decision, he explained at the same time that it was necessary because the Government had decided on the most energetic measures against the Bolsheviks. As a result, he said, there were bound to be armed conflicts, in which the Imperial family might fall the first victims, and therefore he, Kerensky, felt it his duty to protect them against any such possibility.* Subsequent events in Petrograd partially confirmed this statement.

The Provisional Government selected Tobolsk as the place to which Nicholas should be transferred. Its remoteness from the principal centres of political struggle made it a most convenient spot, in which the Romanovs could live in peace and the hope of better times. True, the Romanovs themselves preferred the south, to cold and distant Siberia, and during one of Kerensky's visits they raised with him the question of their transfer to Livadia (the Imperial villa), in the Crimea. Kerensky replied that at present it was quite impossible. It will be understood that he refused this request of the Romanovs, not because he personally was unwilling, but because the workers and soldiers would not have allowed it. By fixing on Tobolsk, where for many years the Romanovs themselves had exiled revolutionaries to certain death, the Provisional Government might still hope that the masses would not interfere with its plan. It would seem that this motive played no minor part in the decision to remove the Imperial family to Tobolsk.

In the early part of August, Kerensky came to Tsarskoye and held a conference with the officers of the guard on the subject of the journey. The conference was held in secret, and only a very limited

* P. Gilliard, op. cit., p. 52.

circle knew of its decisions. Three companies of six officers and 330 other ranks, nearly all non-commissioned officers who had been at the front, and Chevaliers of St. George, were fixed upon. They were served out with new uniforms and new rifles, and personally inspected by Kerensky, who promised that all members of the detachment would receive special service pay during the whole period of their engagement—the purpose of which, however, was not revealed. Colonel Kobylinsky, the commander of the guard, was appointed to take charge of the detachment. This figure once again emphasizes how little concerned was the Provisional Government for the detention in custody of the Romanov family, and how in reality it was enabling them to escape from Tobolsk.

Gilliard, who knew Kobylinsky well, and knew well also the circumstances in which he had to work, writes in his reminiscences: "No one thought that, in spite of the revolution and of his service, as it were, in the enemy's camp, he continued truly and faithfully to serve his Majesty the Emperor, suffering the rudeness and the insolence of the guard. Kobylinsky did everything he could for the Imperial family, and it is not his fault if the short-sighted monarchist organisers did not appeal to him—the only man who had ample opportunity to organise the liberation of the Imperial family, and was only awaiting that help from outside which he himself could not summon, subjected as he was to the constant vigilance of his hostile soldiers.

By his "true and faithful service," Kolinsky soon won the good graces of the Imperial family, who saw in him one of themselves rather than a commander of the guard. Before departure, Nicholas gratefully wrote in his diary: "Kobylinsky is my best friend."

On August 12 the Imperial family were informed of their forthcoming departure. In the evening Kerensky and Michael Alexandrovitch came to say good-bye. Kerensky delivered a parting speech, suitable to the occasion, to the soldiers of the escort: "Remember," he said, "we do not hit a man when he is down. Behave politely, not as ruffians. Don't forget he was formerly the Emperor. Neither he nor his family must suffer the want of anything."*

On the morning of August 14 the Imperial family were tranported in motor-cars, under the escort of dragoons of the Third Baltic

---

* Wilton: *The Last Days of the Romanovs* (Berlin), p. 56.

Regiment, to the Alexandrovsky Station. On the same day, two trains under the Japanese flag bore the Tsar and his guards away to Siberia. "The Japanese Red Cross Mission" was the legend on the magnificent international sleeping-cars of the trains which tore headlong on the road to the Urals.

There travelled with the Imperial family Prince Dolgorukov, Tatischev, Doctor Botkin, the tutor Gilliard, and Countess Hendrikova. In addition, the Romanovs were accompanied by a numerous staff of servants, beginning with Nicholas' valet and ending with the kitchen-boy—thirty-five in all. Their distribution according to rank and profession was as follows : three valets, eight footmen, three cooks, one kitchen-boy, one butler, three kitchen-maids, one steward, three maids, two chambermaids, two nurses, two waiters, one writer, one hairdresser, one wardrobe-keeper, one lady reader, one governess. History probably can record no criminal furnished by his jailers with such a vast staff of servants as Nicholas enjoyed with the personal consent of Kerensky. This petty-bourgeois revolutionary cherished a truly lackey-like respect for the worst enemy of the people.

On the journey the Imperial family were accompanied by two representatives of the Provisional Government—Makarov and Vershinin. Every precaution was taken to prevent any incident on the way. The stations at which the trains halted were surrounded with a wide circle of troops from the local garrisons, and the general public and unnecessary railway employees temporarily excluded. No one was allowed out of the carriages at these halts.

In spite of all the precautions, the trains were stopped at two stations in order that their destination could be ascertained. At Zvanka the local railwaymen demanded an explanation, but quietly let the trains pass when they heard who was in them. At Peron a representative of the local authorities demanded that the commissaries of the Provisional Government should show their mandates and explain the purpose of the special trains. Here, too, Kerensky's signature had the effect of allaying suspicion, and the trains were allowed to continue their journey.

On the evening of August 17 they arrived at Tiumen, and the Romanovs were immediately transferred to the quayside by the river Tobol, where three steam-boats were in waiting: two large boats—the *Rus* and *Kormiletz*—and one steam-tug. The officers of the local garrison, headed by the commandant, were on parade at the entry to the quay, and saluted the ex-Tsar and his family when the latter were leaving their carriages.

The Imperial family and part of the guard were placed on the *Rus*, the remainder of the guard on the *Kormiletz*, while the tug served to maintain communications. By the morning all the luggage had been shipped, and at 5 a.m. on the 18th the steamers began their journey down the Tobol, towards Tobolsk. On the way they passed the village of Pokrovskoye, the birth-place of the Imperial family's "Friend"—Gregory Rasputin. The venerable man's house stood out from amongst the ordinary peasant's huts by reason of its size and its town style of architecture, and could be easily descried from the river. The Imperial family gathered on the deck while passing this spot and exchanged animated reminiscences of their departed "Friend."

They arrived at Tobolsk on the evening of the 19th. The house set aside for the ex-Tsar and his guard was being redecorated, and some days, therefore, had to be spent on board. During this enforced delay, the polite commissaries of the Provisional Government arranged an excursion up the river to the Aballaksky Monastery. Here a special service was organised for the Imperial family, in which they took part, surrounded by a sighing and weeping congregation.

Only on August 26 was the debarkation begun.

* * *

CHAPTER V

AT TOBOLSK

TOBOLSK, one of the oldest towns of Western Siberia, served for years as one of the "remote provinces" to which the Russian Tsars used to exile courtiers involved in palace intrigues and revolutions, and, later on, the best leaders of the working class.

The town stands at the confluence of the Tobol and the Irtysh, from which point there is a direct waterway to Obdorsk and the Arctic. Overland communications in the summer are bad, passing through tundra and swamps, but the winter road, with the help of reindeer, makes possible extensive connections with the Siberian towns. Tobolsk is linked to Tiumen, the nearest railway station, by fairly good waterways in summer, but separated by hundreds of miles of sledge path in the winter.

While fairly active as a commercial centre and halfway-house between European factory industry and the furs and fish of the far north, Tobolsk politically was always backward and reactionary.

After the March Revolution, a Soviet was set up here as everywhere else in Russia. Its majority was composed of Socialist-Revolutionaries and Mensheviks, for the most part exiles who for one reason or another had remained in Tobolsk. The Soviet had little influence, and power *de facto* was entirely in the hands of the provincial commissary of the Provisional Government and of the Town Council.

In the summer of 1917, before the Romanovs arrived, there existed in the town a united Social-Democratic organisation* which carried on a certain amount of propaganda amongst the semi-proletarian craftsmen. There were, in fact, very few Bolsheviks at Tobolsk, and only by August did they succeed in establishing a small group.

With the arrival of the Romanovs and their guards the Soviet and the local authorities faded into the background : those entrusted with the care of the former Tsar became all-powerful.

The Romanovs took up their quarters in a large and roomy house, formerly the Governor's, on Liberty Street, so renamed after

---

* I.e.—One of which both Bolsheviks and Mensheviks were members. (Translator).

the Revolution. Their retinue were allotted a dwelling opposite, in what was formerly the house of a merchant, Kornilov.

On the very first day after their arrival at Tobolsk there took place an incident which immediately produced strained relations between the guard and the prisoners. During the day the whole family, with their suite and accompanied by the representatives of the Provisional Government, went over to the Kornilov house unattended by any guard, and remained there for a long time inspecting the accommodation. A special meeting of the detachment was immediately held, at which Vershinin and Makarov were requested to explain why they had allowed this freedom to the former Imperial family. The alarmed representatives of the Provisional Government justified their action by referring to their instructions. From their explanations, it would seem that the instructions were to guard the Romanovs exclusively for their personal safety, and not as prisoners. This caused serious discontent among the soldiers. A resolution was passed not to take any notice of the Government's instructions. Vershinin and Makarov were requested to confine Nicholas Romanov under close guard, for which purpose sentries should be posted around and inside the house, additional posts established at night, and pickets in three shifts to patrol the adjoining streets. It was further decided immediately to begin the erection of a high fence, to enclose the house and the grounds, in which Nicholas and his family could walk twice daily—from ten to twelve and from two to four. It was further resolved to permit the Romanovs once a week, under armed guard, to visit the Church of Intercession of the Virgin close by.

The demands of the general meeting were accepted by the Government representatives, and that very day the fence was begun and the sentries were posted.

After two or three days, Vershinin and Makarov left for Petrograd. Shortly after their departure, Pankratov, a Socialist-Revolutionary, who had just been appointed commissary of the Provisional Government, arrived in their place. As from September 1 the whole detachment came under his command, including Colonel Kobylinsky. Pankratov held a fairly peculiar view of his position as commissary. In this respect his first meeting with the Imperial family, described by himself is very characteristic.

"On September 2," he relates, "I visited the Governor's house.

Not wishing to infringe the rules of politeness, I requested the valet of the former Tsar to report my arrival and to state that I wished to see his master. . . .

"Good morning," said Nicholas Alexandrovitch, stretching out his hand. 'Did you have a good journey ? '

" 'Thank you, yes,' I replied, grasping his hand.

" 'How is Alexander Feodorovitch Kerensky ? ' asked the former Tsar.

"There was a note of genuine sincerity, combined with sympathy and even gratitude" (as well there might be) "in this question. I replied briefly, and asked after the health of the former Tsar and all his family.

" 'Not bad, thank God,' he replied.

"After this exchange of mutual courtesies and enquiries after one another's health, the conversation turned to 'business.'

" 'Could you not allow me to saw wood ? ' he asked suddenly. 'I like that kind of work.'

" 'Perhaps you would like to have a carpenter's shop ? It is more interesting work,' I suggested.

" 'No, just see that they bring some logs into the yard and give me a saw," replied Nicholas Alexandrovitch.

" ' To-morrow it shall be done.'

" 'May I correspond with my relatives ? '

" 'Certainly. Have you enough books ? '

" 'Plenty, but why do we not receive our foreign journals; is this forbidden ? '

" 'Probably it is the fault of the post. I shall make enquiries. In any case your papers and journals shall not be held up."

" 'Will it not be cold here in the winter ? It is a big room," said the former Tsar.

" 'We must try and prevent that. I shall have all the stores examined and put right. 1 here is sufficient fuel, I said.

" 'If you have any requests, please inform me,' I said, taking my leave."*

The care and forethought displayed by the new commissary at their first meeting were not accidental. They were fully in keeping with the instructions of the Provisional Government, and with the

---

* V. Pankratov : *With the Tsar at Tobolsk* (*Byloe*, No. 25, 1924, pp. 199-200).

farewell speech of Kerensky himself before the detachment left for Tobolsk. During his tenure of office, Pankratov conscientiously observed the orders of his party colleague. True, in his zeal, he far outstripped the latter in servility, so that occasionally it was difficult to distinguish the commissary of the Provisional Government from a chief steward or other familiar of the Romanov family.

A Mme. Ersberg, who was with them at Tobolsk, writes about him in the following strain: "He was a kind and sincere man. He was well-disposed towards them and obviously pitied them. He liked the Grand Duchess Maria Nikolaevna particularly. Once she fell and hurt her eye.... When he heard of it, he came up immediately and was visibly disturbed. His attitude towards the ill-health of Alexei Nikolaevitch was similar. He was also most attentive to the Tsar. Sometimes he called on us and would tell the Grand Duchesses and Alexei Nikolaevitch about his exile in Siberia. They loved to listen to him."*

Under the watchful eye of this "kind and sincere commissary, the life of the Imperial family, surrounded with the cares of their numerous suite and the commissary himself, proceeded in calm and orderly fashion according to the regulations. The family had no lack of funds, as the Romanovs could at that period dispose freely of their vast resources. At the most modest estimate, the sums to their credit amounted to over 14 million roubles. This rendered possible pleasant conditions not only for the family, but for all their numerous servants.

One of the soldiers, P.M. Matveyev, writes of this blissful state as follows: "All the Romanovs' requirements in foodstuffs were bought in the market. If anything could not be procured there—sugar, for example—the offerings of the nuns from surrounding convents more than covered the deficiency. For the honour of drinking coffee in the former Tsar's kitchen these 'blacktails' came from nunneries far and wide with innumerable presents in the form of sugar, butter, cream, eggs and other delicacies. There could be no talk of payment, of course."†

Maintaining close contact with all their friends, the Romanovs in their turn saw to their welfare. In the correspondence between Alex-

---

* N. Sokolov, *op. cit.*, p. 32.
† From the unpublished manuscript of P. M. Matveyev: Tsarskoye Selo-Tobolsk-Ekaterinburg.

andra and Vyrubova we find, almost in every letter : "I am sending macaroni, sausages and coffee, though it is Lent" : "I am sending you some more flour; I hope the provisions I sent you through the Loshkarevs and Krarup," etc.* This shows that the connections between the family and the capital, whither special "volunteer courtiers," carrying mail and parcels, constantly travelled, were extremely well organised. This can incidentally be judged from the following incident. On one occasion a cargo of several chests, addressed to the Romanovs, arrived at Tobolsk. Colonel Kobylinsky requested the soldiers, for special pay, to unload the chests. Some of the heavy boxes were labelled : "Crockery," "Warm clothes," "Fruit," etc. In unloading, one of the boxes was broken, and was found to contain twenty quarters of spirits. The soldiers then decided to open the other chests. One of them was found to contain spirits, the remainder wines. This caused considerable feeling among the soldiers and the local inhabitants. All the wine and spirits were immediately poured into the Irtysh.

The Romanovs were very displeased with this, although, according to the guards, they had no lack of spirituous liquors; wine was always served at dinner, and a decanter of vodka for Nicholas.

Their friends also concerned themselves with the "spiritual food" of the prisoners, sending them books, journals and newspapers. "In addition to the Russian newspapers, Nicholas received English and French newspapers and magazines. Someone, who evidently knew the tastes of the former Tsar, used to send him very frivolous little journals."† The family passed the day in the garden, playing "gorodki," or sawing timber, for which purpose saws and hatchets were bought and logs brought in.

"In the evening," writes Gilliard, "all their friends gathered in the circle of the Imperial family. . . . Games were organised and every way attempted of dissipating the painful monotony of their life in captivity. The Emperor often read aloud, while the Grand Duchesses were engaged in some handiwork or playing with us. The Empress usually played one or two games of bezique with General Tatischev and then took up some work in her turn, or else stretched herself out in an arm-chair. And in this peaceful, purely family atmosphere we passed the long winter evenings."‡

* Vyrubova : *Memoirs*, p. 162.
† Pankratov, *op. cit.*, p. 209.   ‡ Gilliard, *op. cit.*, pp. 54-55.

As we see, life in exile at Tobolsk was not so bad. All the surviving intimates of the Romanovs who were there remark that the first six weeks or two months at Tobolsk were the best passed by the Imperial family during their whole imprisonment. According to their own words, the conditions were sufficiently close to those prevailing at Tsarskoye Selo, and the prisoners received all that was necessary.

If the soldiers of the guard on the very first day had not limited the territory of the former Imperial "Court" to the courtyard of the house, the Romanovs' stay at Tobolsk would have borne little resemblance to imprisonment. They might have passed their days, anticipating an early deliverance, far better than at Tsarskoye Selo.

Nicholas and his family, both personally and through their retinue, showed great persistence in asking for permission, not only to attend church, but to visit the town and the neighbouring country. They made such requests of Pankratov more than once. Personally he himself had nothing against such excursions, but he had to reckon with the hostility of the guard and the local population to any relaxation of the prison regime. This was the chief reason which led the "kind and sincere" commissary on every occasion to refuse the Romanovs' request. Had the attitude of the soldiers and the people been any different, he would certainly have granted it.

In his reminiscences, Pankratov records the following interesting conversation with Nicholas on this subject:

" 'I want to ask you to allow me to see the town with my family.'

" 'I should do so most willingly, had I the permission of the Provisional Government. Besides, there are other reasons.'

" 'You are afraid I will escape ? ' Nicholas Alexandrovitch interrupts me.

" 'Least of all that,' I reply. 'I am certain you would not even attempt such a thing.'*

One has to be a very simple person like Pankratov to express such certainty that even an attempt to escape on the part of the Romanovs is impossible. It was just at this moment that a number of monarchist organisations and groups were beginning to lay plans to carry off the Imperial family. The commissary of the Provisional Government was so ridiculous in his naivete that even the Imperial family were laughing up their sleeves at him. Even such a limited

* Pankratov, *op. cit.*

and dull intelligence as Nicholas, in spite of all his "sympathy and even gratitude" to Pankratov, treated him ironically, calling him "the little fellow" (Pankratov was not very tall).

And, if the Romanovs did not manage to escape after all, we shall see later that this could least of all be laid at Pankratov's door. On the contrary, by his behaviour he did all he could to procure the success of the flight.

* * *

CHAPTER VI

THE HERMOGENES AFFAIR

CLOSELY linked with the stay of the Imperial family at Tobolsk is the activity of one of the most prominent Russian monarchist ecclesiastics—Bishop Hermogenes.

Hermogenes was the closest confidant and lieutenant of Rasputin, and was widely known throughout Russia as a friend of the Imperial family. After the revolution he was left at liberty. As is well known, the Provisional Government was extremely tolerant and even sympathetic towards this species of open monarchist, sometimes even appointing them to new responsible posts.

Hermogenes was also not forgotten. The new "revolutionary" High Procurator of the Holy Synod, V. N. Lvov, appointed him Bishop of Tobolsk. This appointment took place before the transfer of the Romanovs, but, as has since transpired, had a definite object. On his arrival at Tobolsk, Hermogenes began prolonged negotiations with Petrograd for the transfer thither of the Romanovs, negotiations which actually ended successfully.

The few individual revolutionaries organised in the Tobolsk Soviet realised what part this monk might play in organising plots to set free the Romanovs. They drew the attention of the Government to this on more than one occasion. But all such attempts failed. The Provisional Government thought fit to maintain a discreet silence.

Very soon after the arrival of the Romanovs, former officers under assumed names began to assemble—for "rest" or "recreation," as they replied to the enquiries of the local authorities, who attempted to ascertain the reasons for these suspicious "guests" coming into the Tobolsk backwoods.

Most of them apparently arrived with false documents. Two officers, for example, who had arrived for two weeks' leave from the front, were called "Kyrillov" and "Mefodiev."* Another two officers arrested were, according to their documents, the brothers Raeovsky. One of them arrived in Tobolsk first, and was under observation. The second "brother," immediately on arrival, without visiting his

---

* Kyril and Mefodi (Cyril and Methodius) were the two missionaries to the Slavs to whom tradition ascribes the introduction of the Slavonic alphabet. (Translator.)

brother, called on Hermogenes. He was arrested on leaving the latter's house. A certificate was found on him issued by the "All-Russian Brotherhood of Orthodox Congregations." Under cross-examination he stated that he had brought Hermogenes a letter from Nestor, Bishop of Kamchatka. Later, when a search was made at Hermogenes' house, it was discovered that the letter brought by Raeovsky was from the former Dowager-Empress, Maria Feodorovna,[*] pressing Hermogenes to take charge of the plans to set free the Imperial family, as a preliminary to the restoration of the monarchy: "My Lord," she wrote, "you bear the name of St. Hermogenes, who fought for Russia : it is an omen. . . . The hour has come for you to save the Motherland, all Russia knows you: appeal, expose, condemn. May your name be glorified in the salvation of long-suffering Russia."

And Hermogenes began to glorify.

The Romanov family went to church in the mornings, when the streets were more empty. A special service was arranged for them. On November 3, the day of the old Imperial holiday—the succession of Nicholas Romanov to the throne—at the moment the family was leaving the church after the usual service, all the bells of the churches began to peal as though on a church holiday, and so continued until the family had entered their house. This was by order of the priest Alexei Vasiliev, who thus repeated the traditional ceremony attending the "outgoing of their Majesties." The incident caused some talk among the soldiers, but matters did not go any further.

In November an unknown monk was already distributing leaflets in the Cathedral, the barracks and the streets, calling on the people to help "our father, the Tsar," and "to make a stand for the Russian Orthodox faith." Simultaneously there suddenly appeared in the church attended by the Romanovs the "wonderworking ikon" of the Aballaksky Monastery. This ikon was usually transported to Tobolsk in summer-time, with special pomp and ceremony. Its "appearance" at Tobolsk at an unusual time was intended, apparently, to serve as a sort of "miracle." The Soviet had to interfere most emphatically before the ikon would "go" back to the monastery.

Finally, on December 6 (old style), at the same church, during the

[*] Died at Copenhagen, 1929. (Translator.)

presence of the Imperial family, the deacon made the old invocation of "long years of life to the reigning House," naming the Tsar, his wife, the Heir-Apparent and their daughters by their former titles in full. This attempt of the monarchists to assume the offensive quite openly caused great dissatisfaction and indignation among the soldiers and the more revolutionary circles of Tobolsk. The Romanovs were deprived of the right to attend church, and were requested to pray in future at home. The deacon Yevdokimov and the priest Vassiliev were arrested and brought to the Soviet.

Under examination they told a confused story, each throwing the blame on the other, but the directing hand of Hermogenes could be felt behind them. The Soviet did not show the necessary firmness in this matter, leaving both priest and deacon at their homes under "domestic arrest." Without the sanction of the Soviet, Hermogenes liberated them and sent them to "do penance" in a monastery. I here began a long correspondence with Hermogenes, who evaded a request to give evidence in person. In his letter to the Soviet, Hermogenes went into philosophical disquisitions and quotations from the Fathers to show that "from the Holy Writ, public law, the Church Canons and canon law, and likewise from the evidence of history, former kings, tsars and emperors deprived of the governance of their country do not lose their dignity, as such, and therefore the appropriate titles"; hence he did not and does not consider the conduct of the priest Vassiliev to be "criminal."

All the activity of Hermogenes amounted, in the main, to this mobilisation of feeling amongst the religiously-inclined section of the Tobolsk population, i.e., chiefly the merchants, tradesmen, well-to-do peasants and similar reactionary and "Black Hundred" elements. Any direct attempt to liberate the Romanovs proved, apparently, beyond his powers.

At one time, it is true, he attempted to make use of the "War Veterans League" which was formed at Tobolsk. At the head of this League, which was under the patronage of the merchant element, stood a certain Lepilin. He gave himself out to be a political exile, but it soon transpired that he was a habitual thief, blackmailer and provocateur, in whom even the Secret Police had lost all faith. Hermogenes made the League a grant of several thousand roubles, and thereby won great popularity in the organisation which was always ready to follow whoever gave most. But this was the sum-total of his relations with the League, as might have been expected. Hermogenes was too prominent a figure in Tobolsk to be able to take a more active part in such a risky undertaking.

But Hermogenes was not alone in his attempts to assist the Imperial family. Various monarchist organisations, groups and circles in the capital got to work directly the Romanovs arrived at Tobolsk. While they were detained at Tsarskoye Selo, close to revolutionary Petrograd and Kronstadt, there could be no thought of any attempt—the case was too hopeless. The monarchists themselves very soon recognised this. The leader of the Russian monarchists, the well-known Markov II, relates : "During their imprisonment at Tsarskoye Selo, I tried to get into touch with his Majesty the Emperor. In a note I sent through Julia Alexandrovna Den, the wife of a naval Officer, very devoted to the Empress and one of the Court ladies, I informed his Majesty of my desire to serve the Imperial family and to do everything possible to mitigate its sufferings. I asked the Emperor to let me know through Den whether he approved of my intentions, by sending me an ikon. The Tsar approved of my wishes : he sent me through Den the image of St. Nicholas."*

From further accounts it is clear that this first attempt to establish contact between the monarchists and the Romanovs did not go further than "St. Nicholas," as, in the words of another prominent monarchist, N. Sokolov, they "could undertake nothing during the first months after the Tsar's abdication owing to the general situation : the Right monarchists were subjected to persecutions more than any others."

This explanation of the monarchists' passivity is pure nonsense. It was not that they were subjected as alleged to some kind of persecution (the Provisional Government was least of all inclined to persecute them), but that the Romanovs were under the watchful eye of the soldiers and workers of Petrograd.

With the transfer to Tobolsk, the situation was completely changed. Instead of Petrograd and Kronstadt with their workers and soldiers, there was a nest of Siberian well-to-do peasantry, a spot far away from the revolutionary proletarian centres, a direct road to England. All this could not but revive among the monarchists attractive prospects of liberating their adored monarch.

* N. Sokolov, *op. cit.*, p. 95.

It was no accident that precisely in the autumn began active operations on the part of the monarchists with a view to setting free the Romanovs. Markov II states: "After long but enforced inactivity, we decided in September to send our representative to Tobolsk to establish contact with the Imperial family and, should circumstances require it, to carry them off. Our choice fell on N, an officer of the Crimean Regiment, whose Colonel-in-Chief was the Empress. He was a man sincerely and profoundly devoted to their Majesties. He was personally well known to her Majesty the Empress. The Tsar also knew him. . . .

"He left, I think, in September 1917, and informed us of his arrival at Tiumen. . . . We began to think of other officers to send to Tobolsk. Markov was despatched."*

Even before the monarchist organisation led by Markov II, preparatory steps with the same end in view were made by Mme. Vyrubova's "Rasputin Circle." A certain Boris Soloviev, son of the Treasurer of the Holy Synod and an old friend of Rasputin's, was put in charge. Soloviev had been a member of the Rasputin Circle since 1915. During the Revolution he turned up in the Duma building with the 2nd Machine-gun Regiment, and was appointed adjutant to Polovtzev, the chairman of the Military Commission of the Duma Committee. However, he did not break off connections with the Rasputin Circle, but on the contrary continued to be an active member.

In August 1917, when the Imperial family was already at Tobolsk, Soloviev went there on the instructions of the Circle. Here he tried to establish relations with Bishop Hermogenes, who had already "made contact" with the Romanovs. Shortly afterwards he married Matriona Rasputin, daughter of the monk, and, after a brief absence, returned to Tobolsk. The extracts from the diaries of both husband and wife which have been published by Sokolov show that their marriage took place only for considerations of a "business character." For Soloviev it meant that he returned to Tobolsk as a relative of the Rasputin family, and therefore would be less likely to attract the suspicions of the local authorities, notwithstanding that he was a former officer. He could settle down quietly near the place where the former Imperial family were confined, and make his preparations undisturbed. The young couple stayed at first with

* N. Sokolov, *op. cit.*, pp. 95-97.

Rasputin's widow at Pokrovsk. Soon, however, Soloviev selected Tiumen as his main residence, as a town conveniently situated for the surveillance of all coming to and from Tobolsk. He lived here under the name of Stanislas Korjenevsky.

Once settled at Tiumen, Soloviev established communications with the former Empress, and soon became an intermediary between her and the Rasputin Circle, transmitting letters, money and parcels to and from Tobolsk and Leningrad. At Tobolsk there lived two maids of the Empress Alexandra Feodorovna's, Utkina and Romanova, who had not been included in the list of servants and had arrived at Tobolsk after the Imperial family. They lived by themselves in private apartments. They were both devotees of Rasputin's, and through them Soloviev was able to establish contact with the former Tsaritsa. The latter trusted him both as Rasputin's son-in-law and as the emissary of Vyrubova's "Rasputin Circle."

Thus by the beginning of October the monarchist groups and circles had succeeded in establishing bases of operations for setting the Romanovs free.

If the escape of the Romanovs did not materialise, this is to be explained, as we shall see below, by the fact that its immediate organisers could not arrive at a satisfactory division among themselves of the vast sums which poured in for the purpose from Moscow, and came to mutual abuse and fisticuffs, losing completely out of sight the "adored person" of the monarch. No small part was played also by the circumstance that, after the November Revolution, control over the guard of the former Tsar passed from Kobylinsky and Pankratov to the Soldiers Committee. Had it not been for this, the Romanovs would probably have succeeded in escaping execution.

* * *

CHAPTER VII

TOBOLSK AFTER THE NOVEMBER REVOLUTION

TOBOLSK learned of the November Revolution a full fortnight after it had taken place, while the real meaning of the event was realised much later. The explanation is the general political situation at the time. For a long time the whole machinery of communications—the telegraphs and the railways—was under the control of organisations hostile to the Bolsheviks. The "Vikjel" (the All-Russian Executive Committee of Railwaymen), the "Peasant League" and other organisations supporting the Provisional Government, caused confusion in many distant parts of the country by their lying telegrams about the struggle in Petrograd. Tobolsk was among these districts, and for a long time knew nothing of the true state of affairs. This was helped on, of course, by the work of the Mensheviks and Socialist-Revolutionarie (sic) who at that time controlled the Tobolsk Soviet.

When the situation had been cleared up, contact with the capital restored, and the first decrees and regulations began to arrive, the Soviet again made an attempt to set up a Coalition Committee of the Town Council and Soviet : but nothing came of it. Until the first workers' detachments from Omsk and Ekaterinburg came to Tobolsk, at the beginning of 1918, the old authorities—the provincial commissary and the Town Council—still held sway, and even elections to the District Council were held.

This political situation at Tobolsk aroused comprehensible suspicions among the workers of the Urals and Siberia, and produced apprehensions as to the reliability of the guard, particularly of its commissary. "I began," writes Pankratov, "to receive anonymous threatening letters from the front, from Omsk, Krasnoyarsk, Ekaterinburg, and even from Tobolsk itself. They even threatened to send a whole division because I had let the Imperial family *get out of hand.' "* The Omsk Soviet on two occasions emphatically gave instructions through its military commissary that the former Tsar and his family were to be transferred to the convict prison, and that the provincial commissary was to be arrested : but in vain. Tobolsk and its commissary did not

---

* V. Pankratov : *With the Tsar at Tobolsk* (*Byloe*, No. 26, 1924), p. 213.

take any notice of instructions from Omsk, in spite of the fact that they were subordinate to Omsk in administration. But these attempts to resist the extending Soviet power were of a passive character, as power in Tobolsk began to pass more and more out of the hands of the agents of the Provisional Government in the measure that the masses realised the meaning of the events at Petrograd.

Commissary Pankratov for a long time endeavoured to keep the detachment in ignorance of events in the capital. But little by little echoes of the November Revolution began to penetrate into the mass of the soldiers.

The most "unsatisfactory" was the company of the 2nd Guards, where, under the leadership of 2nd Lieutenant A. Matveyev, a small but reliable group of revolutionary militants was set up, who had pledged themselves at one of their meetings to keep watch over the Romanov family, and, in the event of attempts to escape, not to allow either the former Tsar or his family to get away alive.

The influence of this group gradually spread to all the Guardsmen of the detachment. Even previously they had not paid a great deal of attention to Pankratov and his assistant Nikolsky : now they began to ignore them and even to display hostility towards them.

At the end of November a Soldiers' Committee was set up. With its organisation, effective control over the Romanovs passed into the hands of the soldiers. From this moment a drastic change began in the life of the prisoners. The life of the "Court," which up to that time had passed in an orderly and well-regulated fashion which no one infringed, began to undergo many changes and limitations. The Soldiers' Committee endeavoured to establish a more severe regime for the prisoners, doing away with the modifications and relaxations permitted by Pankratov and Kobylinsky. The Committee began with the friends and servants. The latter enjoyed considerable freedom in comparison with the Romanov family : they could go, not only into the town, but also into the surrounding districts. This had long aroused the dissatisfaction of the soldiers, and they had more than once warned Pankratov that, if Dolgorukov and the others did not stop "wandering round the town, they would get a hiding."* The Soldiers' Committee decided to establish the same conditions for them as for the Imperial family. The suite and servants, who had been living in a separate house opposite the former Governor's

* Pankratov, *op. cit.*, p. 217.

house, were transferred to the latter (i.e., the house in which the Imperial family lived). This measure was exceptionally timely, in connection with the attempts of the monarchists to organise the liberation of the Romanovs. Their communications with the Imperial family were now rendered much more difficult.

It was at this time also that there took place the incident of the wine poured into the Irtysh by the soldiers. Then, as a result of the priest Vassiliev's invocation of "long years for the reigning House" at the service of December 19, the Soldiers' Committee decided to forbid the family attending church, and to permit services to be performed at home instead, in the presence and under the observation of a sentry. With difficulty Kobylinsky succeeded in extorting permission from the Committee for the family to attend church on the twelve principal saints' days. This interference by the soldiers in the regime established for the Imperial family was well reflected in the diary of Countess Hendrikova. She writes: " January 27. We did not go to church. The soldiers decided to let us go to church only on the twelve holidays" : "February 15. The Soldiers' Committee did not allow them to go to church to-day either." "February 17. Yesterday and to-day, service at home."

In spite of the more severe conditions, the Romanovs and their suite continued to live fairly cheerfully. Matveyev, chairman of the Soldiers' Committee at the time, recalls the following scene : "Being orderly officer for the day, at about 11 p.m., I went out of the orderly officer's room, which was situated on the ground floor of the Governor's house, into the corridor. This corridor is crossed at right angles by another, leading to the staircase. I heard an extraordinary noise upstairs, where the Romanovs lived. It was some family holiday with them, and dinner had lasted until far into the evening. Finally the noise grew louder, and soon a cheerful company, consisting of the Romanov family and their suite in evening dress, came down the staircase. Nicholas headed the procession, in Cossack uniform with a colonel's epaulettes and a Circassian dagger at his belt. The whole company went into the room of Gibbs, the tutor, where they made merry until 2 a.m."

Hearing of this, the soldiers decided to make a search for arms in the Romanov's quarters. As a result, a Caucasian dagger was taken from Nicholas and sabres from Gilliard and Dolgorukov. Soon afterwards took place the affair of the epaulettes, which particularly excited the prisoners. On January 16 a joint meeting of the local garrison and the detachment passed a resolution forbidding officers and soldiers to wear epaulettes. The Soldiers' Committee decided that the former Tsar should also cease to wear epaulettes.

"Knowing how insulting this demand would be for him," writes Sokolol, "Kobylinsky stubbornly opposed the soldiers' wishes, threatening them with both the King of England and the German Emperor." But apparently the soldiers were not frightened by this, and continued to insist on their demands being carried out, threatening to use violence in the contrary event. Nicholas had to share the lot of all the officers of the guard, and take off his epaulettes without waiting for the help of the English King. In spite of the promise given to the representative of the Soldiers' Committee, Nicholas continued to wear epaulettes in his rooms, and, when the family set out for church the day after the epaulettes affair, Nicholas wore his under a felt cloak, and Alexei his under a Caucasian greatcoat.

"All these affairs were painful to me," writes Kobylinsky. "It was not life, but very hell. My nerves were strained to the extreme. . . . And when the soldiers passed a resolution that we officers must take off our epaulettes, I could stand it no longer. I realised that I had no more authority, and felt all my impotence. I went to the house and asked Tegleo to inform the Tsar that I must see him. The Tsar received me in his room. I said: 'Your Majesty, authority is slipping out of my hands. They have taken away our epaulettes, I can no longer be any use to you. If you will allow me, I will leave. My nerves have all gone to pieces. I can stand it no longer.' The Tsar passed his arm around my shoulders, and tears stood in his eyes. He said: "Eugene Stepanovich,* on behalf of myself, my wife and my children I ask you to stay. You see that we bear everything. You must bear it too.' Then he embraced me, and we kissed. I remained, and decided to bear it all."

Pankratov went through no less pain and suffering through these affairs. Like Kobylinsky, he understood that only nominal power was left to him, and that the soldiers were deciding everything. He

---

* *Translator's Note* Every Russian has three names—his first or "Christian" name, the name of his father with "vich" added (meaning "son of") and his surname. It is usual for acquaintances to address one another by the first two. Hence "Eugene Stepanovich" (Kobylinsky).

also began to think of resigning.

"My position," he writes, "was becoming extremely complicated and difficult, and the only hope which still lived within me was in the Constituent Assembly; but I doubted even if that were not too late. Still, I awaited the summoning of the Constituent Assembly, and had even prepared my petition asking to be relieved of my charge.

"The Constituent Assembly was my only hope. With what impatience I awaited its convocation!

"Even Nicholas II asked more than once: 'How soon will the Constituent Assembly meet?'"

" 'I think not later than the beginning of January, at all events," I replied."*

It was a deeply symbolical and historic picture: the Socialist-Revolutionary and the head of the monarchists, each praying on their knees for the Constituent Assembly to come and realise their hopes of a better future.

Doubt as to the exact status of the guard and lack of contact with the capital prompted the soldiers at one of their general meetings to resolve that delegates be sent to Petrograd to report to the central Soviet Government on the conditions under which the Romanov family were detained, and to ask for instructions. Delegates were elected, one from each company.

Their arrival at Tsarskoye Selo, before the committees of the three regiments from which they came, created a great impression. Thanks to the stories in the bourgeois Press about the conditions in which the Imperial family were living, the demoralisation of the detachment and the numerous attempts of the monarchists to set free the former Tsar, the broad masses of soldiers and workers in Petrograd were convinced that the Romanovs were no longer at Tobolsk.

After appearing before the Central Executive Committee of Soviets and the Council of People's Commissaries, and receiving the necessary instructions, the delegates returned to Tobolsk. At the first general meeting after their arrival they proposed that Pankratov and his assistant should be expelled from the detachment. But there were still many soldiers who objected, on the ground that Pankratov had not actively opposed the Committee. This aroused great feeling at the meeting, which dragged on very late and finally broke up without coming to a definite decision.

* V. Pankratov, *op. cit.*, pp. 217-18.

Anticipating events, however, Pankratov hastened to hand in his resignation to the Committee. "In view of the fact," he wrote, "that of recent date there has arisen friction between the companies of the Special Detachment, arising out of my presence as commissary appointed by the Provisional Government in August 1917 : and not wishing to aggravate this friction on a matter of public importance : I resign the charge committed to me, and request that written confirmation of the correctness of my motives be given me.—V. Pankratov. Tobolsk, January 24, 1918."

In reply to this letter, the Committee accepted the resignation, and issued a certificate to Pankratov in the following terms : "This is issued by the Soldiers' Committee of the Special Detachment to Vassili Semionovitch Pankratov, commissary for the guard of the former Tsar and his family, to certify that he resigned his post in view of the friction caused among the soldiers by his presence : and that the Committee recognises his motives as justifiable. Kireyev, *Chairman* ; Bobkov, *Secretary*. Tobolsk, January 26, 1918. Seal of the Soldiers' Committee."

With Pankratov there also resigned his assistant, Mikolsky. Control officially passed into the hands of the detachment.

"Everything depends on the soldiers," wrote Alexandra anxiously to her friend Vyrubova. "Thank God, they have left us our commandant."*

This was their only consolation. The retention of Kobylinsky left the only man who sympathised with the Imperial family, as, following the resignation of Pankratov and Nikolsky, a number of soldiers who had shown themselves insufficiently reliable were dismissed. Their place was filled by new soldiers from Petrograd.

---

* Vyrubova, *op. cit.*, p. 162.

*   *   *

CHAPTER VIII

HOPES OF LIBERATION

SOON after the delegates returned to Tobolsk, instructions for regulating the conditions and guard arrangements of the former Tsar began to arrive from the capital. The first important step taken by the centre was to transfer Nicholas and his family to soldiers' rations. This instruction came from the People's Commissariat of State Property, and was received in Tobolsk on February 23. The same telegram established restrictions on the amounts which the Romanovs might draw from their accounts in the various banks. Every member of the family might spend not more than 600 roubles a month, or 4,200 roubles for the whole family. Within the limits of this sum they were enabled to improve their diet, maintain servants, etc.

On receipt of these instructions, the Soldiers' Committee requested the Romanovs to adjust their expenses in strict accord with the sums indicated. As a consequence, the Romanovs had to dismiss ten servants and considerably reduce their expenditure on provisions.

The new regime came into force on March 1. On this day Gilliard entered in his diary: "The new regime has begun. As from to-day butter and coffee are excluded from our table, as articles of luxury." Two days later he wrote anxiously: "Now every day brings new restrictions on those surrounding the Tsar, as well as on the Imperial family. For a long time we have been unable to leave the house unless accompanied by soldiers: probably they will soon deprive us of this last shadow of liberty."*

The severities increasing day by day caused the Romanovs and their suite to await the assistance of the monarchists, of whose preparations they had been made aware, with feverish impatience. The Romanovs implored them to hurry, pointing out that every day made escape more difficult, and that the most favourable moment might be lost. In reply they received reassuring messages that within a few days their loyal followers would do their duty, and that they possessed sufficient forces for this purpose.

The former Empress gave particular credence to these messages,

* P. Gilliard, *op. cit.*, pp. 60-61.

and it was through her that all communications went on with the conspirators. According to the latter, she assured her family that a band of three hundred officers had already been formed at Tiumen, and was ready at any moment to go to their aid. Her faith infected all the members of the family and suite. On March 17 Gilliard entered in his diary that all the prisoners were insisting on Nicholas "remaining on the qui vive, in view of anticipated possibilities."[*]

The belief of the Romanovs in their early liberation was so great that when, a week later, a detachment of one hundred Red Guards arrived from Omsk, they were all convinced that amongst the soldiers were a number of loyal officers in disguise. "The empress pointed from the window to these Red Guards," Sokolov writes on the evidence of eye-witnesses, "and cried out: ' Good Russian men ! ' "[†]

Receiving information of forthcoming attempts to set them free from various monarchist organisations and groups, Alexandra had every reason to believe in early deliverance. Apart from individual monarchists who offered their services on their own initiative, they were in contact, as pointed out above, with Hermogenes, with the Rasputin Circle of Vyrubova, and with the Petrograd organisation controlled by Markov II. In January 1918 these were reinforced by the "Moscow Group of Russian Monarchists," who also sent their representative, a certain Krivoshein, to Tobolsk.

As we see, there were more than sufficient organisations concerned with the liberation of the Romanovs. But none of them was connected one with the other, and all acted independently, seeing first of all competitors in one another's persons. Not only did they pay very little heed to the combining of their activities, but on the contrary strove in some way or other to eliminate their rivals from such a high and honourable enterprise as the rescue of the Imperial family.

The Rasputin Circle had most funds of all the monarchist organisations, receiving money from all kinds of sources. From one banker and sugar-manufacturer alone, K. I. Yaroshinsky, the Circle received 175,000 roubles for this purpose. This, together with the intimate connexion of the Circle with the ex-Tsaritsa, immediately placed it at the centre of all activities.

The Petrograd organisation, on the contrary, was in the position

[*] *Ibid*, p. 61.
[†] N. Sokolov, *op. cit.*

of a "poor relation," as the November Revolution had deprived it of the resources which had previously flowed in generous volume from the public chest. Its leader, Markov II, attempted to come to an agreement with Vyrubova "for the common cause," but without success. Vyrubova politely declined the proffered services, giving Markov to understand, according to his account, that she wished to act independently.

When the Petrograd monarchists sent their people to Tobolsk despite this, Markov states that they were informed by the Rasputin Circle that "it was quite useless for them to try and establish contact with the Imperial family, that Vyrubova's people were already working there, and that we were quite unnecessarily interfering and by our misplaced zeal compromising the chances of a great undertaking. In order to impress their "poor relation" the more, reference was made to the opinion of her Majesty that their work was endangering the cause.

Similar relations sprang up between Soloviev, the representative of the Rasputin Circle, and Hermogenes. The latter was the favourite of Marie Feodorovna, the mother of the ex-Tsar, who was hostile to Alexandra Feodorovna, as is well-known. When Soloviev arrived at Tobolsk for the first time in August, and tried to make contact with Hermogenes, the latter refused to receive him, apparently also seeing in him a rival.

Particularly lamentable was the position of the "plenipotentiaries" of the various organisations.

First place in respect of contact with and assistance to the Imperial family was occupied, as might have been expected, by Soloviev. But the latter sought to draw advantages from his position as plenipotentiary first of all for himself, and only in the second place for the "adored" monarch. The evidence of a number of persons shows that, out of the large sums which he received, only a small amount was delivered to its destination : the greater part was appropriated by Soloviev. His right-hand man at Tobolsk was the priest already known to the reader—Alexei Vassiliev. This priest was distinguished by no less love of coin than his chief, and also pocketed a considerable portion of the money passing through his hands.

According to Dieterichs, Soloviev and Vassiliev reported to their centre that they had succeeded in constituting a strong band of three hundred men, and that consequently it was not necessary to send them any more officers, as the further expansion of the organisation was dangerous. They asked only for money, both for the Imperial family and for themselves. But, in spite of their warnings, new people continued to arrive from Petrograd, sent independently of Vyrubova's organisation.

Fearing that new hands might win away their profitable business, Soloviev and Vassiliev took steps to prevent them entering Tobolsk. They showed great determination and courage in defending their interests. At Tiumen they established a kind of toll-gate for all persons trying to visit Tobolsk with the object of seeing the Romanovs.

According to the evidence of the intimate associates of the Imperial family, who lived with the latter at Tobolsk, Soloviev forced all newcomers to work under his direction, achieving this either by tales of the strength of his organisation or by threats, if they disobeyed, to hand them over to the local authorities.

In this direction he was very successful. "The Petrograd and Moscow organisations," says Botkina-Melnik, "sent many of their members to Tobolsk and Tiumen. Many of them even lived there for months at a time under false names. But all of them fell into the hands of the organisation of Father Alexei and its chief leader, Lieutenant Soloviev, who had wormed his way into the confidence of the shortsighted monarchists.

The same fate befell Markov and N, the representative of the Petrograd officers' organisation. Both found in Soloviev and Vassiliev leaders worthy of themselves, no less ambitious than they in money matters and no more concerned for the fate of their beloved monarch. When, in the spring of 1918, the officer N returned to Petrograd, it could be seen from his report, in the words of Markov II, that "he had done absolutely nothing to establish contact with the Imperial family, and had not visited Tobolsk once while his Majesty the Emperor was there." Regarding the other officer, his namesake, Markov says that "he created the impression of a young man of unnecessary rashness, and extremely persistent and pretentious in money matters."*

These were the "good Russian men on whom the Romanovs pinned all their hopes of escape.

* Sokolov, *op. cit.*, p. 96.

It is difficult to say how much truth there was in the statement that the monarchists had three hundred men at their disposal at Tobolsk and Tiumen. At all events, if this figure refers to a strictly conspiratorial organisation, it is obviously exaggerated. One thing is certain, that they had men, and if nevertheless not even an attempt was made to rescue the Romanovs, this was only because the leaders were up to the ears in quite other matters.

Just at the time that the Romanovs were awaiting help with impatience, a dispute arose over the funds. Father Vassiliev renowned for his intimacy with the family, whom he confessed, and later for his "long years of life" prayer, soon became for the monarchists a central figure, side by side with Soloviev, and friends began sending parcels and money addressed to him at Tobolsk. The priest began to claim pride of place, and a correspondingly increased share of the sums sent for the "organisation." He met with a rebuff at the hands of Soloviev. As a result, they quarrelled and fought. Dieterichs writes of this: "While money came through Soloviev, Vassiliev behaved correctly. But later, apparently, he wanted to play the part of leader, and began to empty buckets of abuse on Soloviev, who replied in kind."*

This was the reason why they were unable to make timely use of favourable opportunities for rescuing the Romanovs. In the opinion of Botkina, one of these opportunities was in February, 1918, when the frame of mind of the guards was most favourable, she says. The detachment consisted in the main, it will be remembered, of old Guards N.C.O.'s and Chevaliers of St. George, "nearly all of whom were amicably inclined towards their Majesties. A whole platoon of riflemen, headed by Lieutenant Malyshev, declared that during their turn of duty they would allow the captives to escape in safety."†

Dieterichs thinks that the most suitable time for escape was from August to December, 1917. "But at this moment," the general complains, "the monarchist centre scarcely showed any sign of life. This period was the most favourable from the viewpoint of the attitude of the guard itself, particularly among the soldiers of the former 4th Imperial Rifles, the majority of whom themselves suggested that his Majesty should take advantage of their days on

---

* General M. K. Dieterichs : *The Murder of the Impend Family*, p. 73.
† T. Melnnik-Botkina : *Reminiscences* (Harbin, 1920).

duty to make his escape."*

It is difficult to say definitely which of these moments was the most suitable. But it is unquestionable that in either case a rescue could have been organised.

After letting slip two such convenient opportunities, the monarchists were deprived of a third chance, as we shall see—even in less favourable conditions. Just at that time the Party and Soviet authorities in the Urals and at Omsk decided to put an end to the unstable position at Tobolsk. In February a special commissary, V. A. Dutzman, was sent from Omsk to Tobolsk, with instructions to reinforce the watch over the prisoners. He was followed from Omsk by a detachment of one hundred Red Guards, under Demianov. On this day Gilliard entered in his diary : "These are the first Bolshevik soldiers in the Tobolsk garrison. Our last hope of escape is gone." †

Almost at the same time as Omsk, the Red Urals also stretched out their hands to the "captives of Tobolsk." This finally eliminated any danger of the escape of the Romanovs.

* Dieterichs, *op. cit.*, p. 72.
† P. Gilliard, *op. cit.*, p. 62.

* * *

CHAPTER IX

THE SOVIET URALS

FOR hundreds of years bent under scourge and rod, at the mercy of the Imperial favourites who governed the region, the Ural workers toiled at the plough and the blast-furnace, passing from the meadow to the primitive damp mine. It is not wonderful that the people of the mining Urals have for long years had a deep-rooted feeling of revolt against their factory servitude and the autocracy which maintained it. Numerous factory insurrections, repressed with merciless severity, brought out of the masses of Ural workers a number of champions who, by the time of the 1905 Revolution, had come together in groups of the Social-Democratic Party. For many years the Urals were the borderland in which the Bolsheviks felt the ground firmer under their feet than under that of any other revolutionary organisation. After the March Revolution of 1917, the Party came out of its underground existence with a reliable corps of leaders, permanently connected with the very rank and file of the working class. This, by the way, explains the comparative ease with which the November Revolution was carried out in the Urals.

Power passed into the hands of the Soviets actually some months before the insurrection in Petrograd. As early as August 1917, by resolution of the Regional Soviet, such large enterprises as the Viriakov Weaving Factory and the Kriaze-Petrovsky Works (Kyshtim district) were nationalised.

After the November Revolution Soviet reconstruction proceeded at an increased rate. The third Regional Congress of Soviets at Ekaterinburg, in February 1918, united all the Soviets of the Urals. At this Congress almost exclusively Bolsheviks, representing the Ural factories, were elected to the Executive Committee. The Presidium it elected was composed of the following : A. G. Beloborodov (chairman), G. N. Safarov, V. B. Didkovsky, I. Goloschekin ("Philip") and N. G. Tolmachev.

The question of the Romanovs at Tobolsk, and of the possibility of their escape, began to be discussed at private meetings of Party Committees and the Regional Soviet in February 1918. Reports from comrades of the influx of officers into Tiumen and Tobolsk, and of the existence there of organisations aiming at the liberation of the Romanovs, forced an even more attentive consideration of the question.

At the beginning of March the Presidium of the Regional Soviet decided to request the All-Russian Central Executive Committee to transfer the Romanovs to Ekaterinburg. Without awaiting a reply from the capital, it decided to send an expedition to Tobolsk to ascertain the local situation and make the necessary preparations for removing the Imperial family. A preliminary plan was drawn up for the purpose, according to which several groups of reliable Bolshevik workers were to go to Tobolsk and the surrounding country. It was anticipated that, in the event of their escape, the Romanovs would be taken either towards Obdorsk, where they could board a British ship, or by road through Ishim to the Far East. Two militant groups of Nadezhdinsk workers were accordingly sent in these directions, and travelled from their works through Nikito-Ivdel and Ukladovy Yurti to Berezov. Each group was instructed to watch all travellers from Tobolsk along the routes mentioned, and, in the event of the Romanovs escaping, to arrest them, come what may.

The arrival of Nadezhdinsk workers at Berezov naturally aroused the suspicion of the local authorities. The agents of the Provisional Government were still in control there, and the expedition was before long arrested.

Simultaneously a detachment of Ekaterinburg workers was sent to bar the road from Tobolsk to Tiumen. They stopped at the village of Goloputovskoe, where they gave themselves out to be merchants. Several officers who were connected with the organisations preparing the rescue of the Romanovs also lived here. Owing to some mistakes on the part of the group (abundance of new "Imperial" banknotes, badly-concealed weapons, treachery of a landlady), all its members were arrested and brought to a village meeting, where they were searched and documents were discovered which revealed their real business at Goloputovskoe. At the instigation of the officers and the wealthy peasants, all the members of the group were immediately killed. Later a punitive expedition was sent to Goloputovskoe, which inflicted a well-merited punishment on the Tsar's defenders.

The most successful was the expedition to Tobolsk itself, which was more secretly organised. One of the Ekaterinburg Party workers, Naumova, was sent first. Her mother lived in the Yalutorovsky district, and therefore her arrival did not arouse suspicions. She was soon followed by N. Hochriakov, a sailor, who came under the guise of her fiance. Later came Zaslavsky and A. T. Avdeyev, travelling separately with false commercial passports. This group was given extraordinary powers by the Regional Soviet, with a view to their taking all steps necessary to prevent the liberation of the Romanovs. At the beginning of April a small detachment of trustworthy Red Guards was sent to their aid, who came to Tobolsk travelling singly and in small groups. Part of them were Letts.

Rumours of the arrival of this group caused great disquiet at Tobolsk. The monarchists felt that this secret organisation represented a direct threat to themselves. The guard over the Romanovs was also disturbed. Dutzman and Demianov, who represented Omsk, and did not know what were the exact plans of the emissaries from the Urals, were anxious. Matters even went so far that Hochriakov was arrested. Only negotiations with Omsk and Ekaterinburg cleared up mutual distrust.

In these conditions it was no use speaking of transferring the Romanovs to the Urals, as both the guard and the Omsk representatives insisted on permission from Moscow. Taking account of the hesitancy of their Omsk comrades, however, the Urals representatives did all possible to win the confidence of all detachments, in which they partially succeeded.

At the same time, jointly with the other Communists in Tobolsk, they began a campaign for new elections to the Soviet. As a result of this campaign, the Mensheviks, Socialist-Revolutionaries and Cadets lost their seats in the Soviet, and Hochriakov, mentioned above, was elected chairman of the new Soviet. Henceforward that body began to play an active part in the watch over the Romanovs. At one of its first meetings the Soviet decided to transfer the Romanovs and their attendants up the "mountain," to the prison, where repairs were begun with this in view. Later on the necessity for this step disappeared as the All Russian Central Executive Committee decided to transfer the Romanovs from Tobolsk to Ekaterinburg.

At the same time as it sent its expedition to Tobolsk, the Ural Regional Executive began negotiations with the centre about transferring the Romanovs to the Urals. The Regional Military Commissary, Goloschekin, was sent to Moscow, whither the central Soviet Government had moved. At a session of the A.R.C.E C. he reported on the state of affairs at Tobolsk and the necessity of taking urgent steps with regard to the Imperial family. The Presidium of the A.R.C.E.C. decided to transfer Nicholas Romanov to Ekaterinburg, on condition that Goloschekin, an old Party worker well known to the Central Committee of the Party, took full personal responsibility. In order to organise the shifting of the ex-Tsar, the A.R.C.E.C. decided to send a special commissary, of which decision the Ural Soviet was informed through Goloschekin.

Gloomy reports were received at Ekaterinburg at this time from Hochriakov and Zaslavsky, to the effect that distrust towards them was growing amidst the guard and the Omsk representatives, and that the monarchists, now at Tobolsk in large numbers, were growing increasingly active.

In April, Goloschekin was sent on Party and Soviet business to Ufa. Here he met Yakovlev, the special plenipotentiary of the A.R.C.E.C., who was furnished with a mandate to transport Nicholas Romanov from Tobolsk to Ekaterinburg and deliver him to the Ural Regional Soviet on Goloschekin's personal responsibility.

At Ufa there was placed at Yakovlev's disposal, to guard the Romanovs en route, a cavalry detachment of workers of the Miniarsk factory, led by Zentsov. This had previously been called a detachment for the protection of public property. To this group were added sixty Ufa militants with a few machine-guns. In addition, Goloschekin, on his part, gave orders that Hochriakov, Zaslavsky, Avdeyev and all the detachment from the Urals at Tobolsk were to come under the orders of Yakovlev.

Some days later, Yakovlev with his detachment set out for Ekaterinburg via Cheliabinsk. Only on the road were the leaders and a few Party workers of the detachment told of the object of the expedition.*

Learning at Ekaterinburg how matters stood, Yakovlev left for Tiumen. Here he was met by Avdeyev, despatched from Tobolsk to seek reinforcements and additional powers, as the situation at Tobolsk grew worse daily. Avdeyev received from Yakovlev Goloschekin's instruction to join the new expedition, and returned to Tobolsk with Yakovlev, Zentsov and their force.

A little earlier, the Ural Regional Executive had received disquieting news from Tobolsk. Not having definite instructions

* Zentsov : *Reminiscences* (Ufa).

yet from Moscow, it decided to send a further reinforcement to Tobolsk, in shape of a company of Red Guards led by Brusiatsky. The new detachment was instructed to bring Nicholas Romanov to Ekaterinburg "alive or dead," for which purpose Brusiatsky was to work out a plan of action with Hochriakov and others at Tobolsk, combining all the forces supporting the emissaries from the Urals, and, if necessary, to open hostilities against the defenders of the Romanovs.

Brusiatsky's detachment passed through Tiumen a day or two before Yakovlev. Preliminary study of the mood of the neighbouring villages had shown that the well-to-do peasantry of these villages was quite prepared for the rescue of the Romanovs, and was ready to grant them and their supporters every assistance.

There was nothing surprising in this. In Tobolsk, thanks to the energy of the delegates from the Urals, it had been possible to create and maintain a firm Soviet authority. In the country, and even at Tiumen itself, this was not the case. Suffice it to say that at this time in Tiumen, in one and the same street, there were two staffs and two notices. One announced the recruitment of volunteers for the Red Army, the other flaunted the legend: "Volunteers enrolled for the People's Army." In the staff of the "People's Army" you could always meet officers, local and new arrivals. It was already a stable organisation, ready to attack the Soviet power in order to liberate the Romanovs.

Brusiatsky's detachment was moving forward fairly deliberately, and Yakovlev's cavalry soon caught it up. Both detachments, under Yakovlev's single command, went forward, and arrived at Tobolsk on April 22.

* * *

CHAPTER X

NO ROAD PAST THE URALS

THE arrival of the commissary from Moscow greatly agitated the family in the Governor's house. The "big mandate" of Yakovlev, stating that the whole guard over the Romanovs was subordinated to him, and that failure to carry out his orders would entail penalties up to and including death, caused a profound disquiet among the prisoners. On April 22 Gilliard wrote in his diary: "To-day arrived a Moscow commissary with a small body of troops: his name is Yakovlev. All are worried and depressed. A threat can be felt in the commissary's arrival, real even if as yet indefinite."*

The day after his arrival, Yakovlev visited their house and asked every prisoner if he had any complaints to make. No statement was made by the Romanovs. Yakovlev, however, ascertained that the transfer of the Imperial family was complicated by the sickness of Alexei, who was confined to his bed in consequence of an attack of hemophilia. In spite of this unexpected difficulty, Yakovlev decided to take Nicholas from Tobolsk, even if he went alone.

On April 25 Yakovlev informed Romanov that he had instructions to remove him from Tobolsk.

Nicholas replied sharply, without a moment's hesitation: "I shall go nowhere," turned on his heel and went to his room, where Alexandra and his closest friends (including Colonel Kobylinsky) were waiting. During the discussion which ensued, Kobylinsky expressed the belief that the ex-Tsar was probably being taken to Moscow, pointing out the calculations of time which Yakovlev had been making the day before, in connection with the necessity for returning to Tobolsk for the sick Alexei. This supposition seemed very probable to the participants of the family council, and it was decided that Nicholas must submit. Alexandra thereupon declared that she would travel with Nicholas, as she could not contemplate letting him travel alone: he might do "something foolish," she feared. "At this point," says Kobylinsky, "she said something about Rodzianko. Undoubtedly the empress was referring to his Majesty's act of abdication."†

* Gilliard, *op. cit.*, p. 63.
† N. Sokolov, *op. cit.*, p. 45.

Later on the same day, Yakovlev returned to the Governor's house and summoned Romanov. Nicholas came out accompanied by his wife. In reply to Yakovlev's enquiry whether Nicholas would submit to the Soviet Government's order to leave Tobolsk, Alexandra replied: "Yes, he will go, only I shall not let him travel alone, I will go too." Nicholas only asked when they must leave. It was decided to leave the same night.

As the river was still frozen over, the journey to Tiumen—260 versts—had to be covered by carriage. Yakovlev suggested to the Romanovs that they should take some persons with them, pointing out the desirability of as few as possible: the river Tobol would soon be opened up, and then it would be easy to transport the others, with the baggage, by steamer.

In his discussions with the Romanovs, Yakovlev, as Matveyev and Gilliard both affirm, stated definitely that they were going to Moscow. Alexandra Feodorovna expressed her doubt of this, as rumours of the transfer of the Romanovs to the Urals had been current at Tobolsk since the first emissaries from Ekaterinburg arrived. She asked Yakovlev whether this question had been definitely settled. Yakovlev replied in the affirmative. What his object was in saying this, when he had instructions to transport the family to the Urals, it is difficult to say.

On the eve of their departure rumours spread through the town that Yakovlev intended, notwithstanding his instructions from the Government, to transport the Romanovs not to the Urals but to Moscow. Yakovlev's conduct had already caused not a little suspicion, and forced the Urals delegates to pay some attention to these rumours. On their initiative, a special private meeting was summoned under the auspices of the Soviet Executive Committee. All present expressed their definite distrust of Yakovlev, and it was decided, if necessary, to attack his detachment on the road and carry off the Romanovs.

For his part, Yakovlev summoned a general meeting of the soldiers of the Tobolsk guard, in order if possible to win their confidence and support. It should be said that the soldiers were a little suspicious of Yakovlev, and demanded at the meeting that they should also accompany the Romanovs. Yakovlev firmly resisted this request, pointing out the reliability of his detachment. The soldiers insisted. Finally he agreed to take with him eight members of the guard, whom he personally selected then and there. By this means Yakovlev succeeded in making sure of the guard, thereby consolidating his position at Tobolsk.

At the family council of the Romanovs it was decided that Nicholas should be accompanied, in addition to Alexandra, by his daughter Marie, Doctor Botkin, Dolgorukov, Chemadurov (Nicholas' valet), Demidova (Alexandra's maid) and Sednev (the Grand Duchess' servant).

Although Moscow was, in the eyes of the Romanovs, preferable to the Urals, they nevertheless understood that in either case their hopes of escape were finally collapsing. Two days before their departure they sent to the Moscow monarchist organisation a cypher telegram, anxiously asking for advice and help. It said: "The doctors have demanded an immediate departure for the south, to a health resort. This demand greatly disturbs us. We think the journey is undesirable. Please give us your advice. The position is most difficult.'

Krivoshein, the monarchist already mentioned, says that the reply was approximately as follows: "Unfortunately we have no information throwing any light on the reasons for this demand. Not knowing the position of the patient and all the circumstances, it is extremely difficult to give definite advice, but we suggest that the departure be postponed as long as possible, and that you give way only in the last resort to a categorical demand from the doctors." Shortly afterwards a second telegram was received by the same means from Tobolsk: " We must submit to the doctors."*

In spite of their submitting to the "doctors' " orders, the Romanovs passionately hoped that the moment of departure would be postponed. Their last hope was that the flooding of the river Tobol, which was expected any day, would begin.

"I known, (sic) I am convinced," said Alexandra the evening before, that the river will overflow to-night, and then our departure must willy-nilly be postponed. This will give us time to get out of this terrible position. If a miracle is necessary, I am sure a miracle will take place."†

But there was no miracle.

At 4 a.m. on April 26 the carriages were in the courtyard of the Governor's house. The whole distance to Tiumen had to be covered

* N. Sokolov, *op. cit.*, p. 105. † *Ibid*, p. 46.

covered in open box-carriages (tarantass). Only one covered tarantass, resembling a coach, could be found.

At 6 a.m. the passengers took their seats. Yakovlev himself took his seat by Nicholas Romanov, Alexandra and Marie entered the covered carriage, the remainder took their places in the other box-carriages, and the expedition set out, surrounded by Yakovlev's cavalry and eight soldiers of the Tobolsk guard with two machine-guns.

At the outset they had to cross the river Irtysh. The ice was already weak, and the crossing involved a certain risk : the wheels were up to the axle in water. However, slowly but surely the whole train got across.

The halts had been determined beforehand, and the necessary vehicles collected from the surrounding country. Delay was only caused by the covered carriage, for which relays of horses had to be found. At the stopping-places Yakovlev was very attentive to the Romanovs, and spent the greater part of his time by Alexandra and Marie, distracting them by conversation.

They were to stay the night in the village of Bochalino, on the banks of the Tobol, at the point where the Tavda flows into it below the village of Iovlev. They arrived fairly late. A two-storied house had been prepared. Yakovlev's detachment was given charge of the outer guard, while the eight soldiers from Tobolsk were put on the inner guard. The Romanovs had camp-beds with them, thanks to which they were able to rest in the room allotted to them with a certain amount of comfort.

Zaslavsky had arrived at Iovlev a little earlier, with a small detachment and machine-guns. Yakovlev's group was followed by the Urals detachment, under the command of Brusiatsky: these also halted at Bochalino. They had finally come to the conclusion that Yakovlev was unreliable. At first the thought of taking away the Imperial family from him by force crossed their minds. Yakovlev, suspecting this did not wait to be attacked, but summoned Brusiatsky's second-in-command to himself and arrested him. No conflict took place as Yakovlev later set him at liberty, while Zaslavsky gave up the idea of an attack, thinking it more prudent to insist on the Romanovs being delivered at Ekaterinburg.

At 8 a.m. the expedition set out again. The ice on the river Tobol over which they now had to cross, had already begun to break up, and for safety's sake it was decided to cross on foot, part of the way over the ice, and in places, where there was open water, over hastily constructed bridges.

In the evening they arrived at Pokrovskoye. The relay of horses was drawn up just opposite the house of Rasputin. All the windows of the house were filled with people waving white handkerchiefs. Alexandra replied to these greetings from her tarantass.

At the last halt before Tiumen the travellers were met by Nemtzev, chairman of the Tiumen Soviet. After a talk with Yakovlev he returned to Tiumen, and shortly after him the detachment set out again. Some versts from the town they were met by a squadron of cavalry, sent out as an escort.

Late at night on April 27 they arrived at Tiumen, where a train was in readiness on the Ekaterinburg line. The Romanovs were placed in the middle coupes of a first-class car, while Yakovlev and a section of the guard took the end coupes. The loading of the baggage was completed by 1 a.m. Nemtzev arrived at the station about this time, and Yakovlev went with him to the telegraph office, to get on to the direct Moscow line. Returning, Yakovlev informed his colleagues and Avdeyev (whom he did not allow to leave the carriage) that, by order of the capital, he was to take the Romanovs not to Ekaterinburg but to Moscow, via Omsk-Cheliabinsk-Samara. Avdeyev succeeded in notifying his colleagues from the Urals of the change of route, and asked them to inform Ekaterinburg.

About 5 a.m. on April 28 the train carrying the Romanovs left for Omsk. Later on it was established that Yakovlev, knowing that execution awaited the Romanovs, decided to save them, and to alight with them on the way to Samara and to hide them for a time in the hills of the Sima district.

Even before Yakovlev left Tobolsk, the Presidium of the Ural Regional Council had despatched a special representative to Tiumen, with instructions to send regular information about the movements of the Romanovs, and to report at once when their train left for Ekaterinburg. According to their calculations, the train was to leave Tiumen in the early morning of April 28. Suddenly telegrams ceased to arrive from Tiumen, and the message expected at 6 a.m.— that the train had left—never came. The Presidium got no reply to its repeated enquiries until 10 a.m., when it was informed that the train had left Tiumen early in the morning with all lights extinguished in the direction of Omsk. This telegram was sent by Brusiatsky, who arrived at Tiumen with his detachment after Yakovlev had left.

A special meeting of the Presidium was immediately summoned, to which representatives of the regional committees of the Communist and left Socialist-Revolutionary Parties were invited. The meeting decided to declare Yakovlev a traitor to the revolution and to send out a telegram "to all, to all, to all."

This telegram, which was sent immediately, stated that the A.R.C.E.C. had instructed Yakovlev to organise and carry out the transfer of the Romanovs from Tobolsk to Ekaterinburg. In spite of this, and without the knowledge of the Ural Soviet, he had diverted the train to Omsk. The message ended by proclaiming Yakovlev a traitor and an outlaw.

At the same time the Regional Soviet entered into direct communication with Omsk, where an old Communist, Kosarev, was at that time chairman of the West Siberian Soviet. He was asked to take immediate and decisive steps to prevent the train proceeding to Siberia or to Cheliabinsk (through Kulomzino). The Omsk Soviet immediately sent a considerable force to Kulomzino, with instructions to stop Yakovlev's train and turn it back to Tiumen.

At this time the 4th Ural Regional Conference of the Russian Communist Party was taking place at Ekaterinburg. There were present 102 delegates from 57 Party organisations of the Urals, representing 30,278 Party members.

The Conference approved the action of the Party committee and the Regional Soviet, and in an unofficial meeting the majority of the local delegates declared in favour of the earliest possible execution of the Romanovs, in order for the future to forestall all attempts to set free the ex-Tsar and restore the Russian monarchy.

After directing the train towards Omsk, in spite of the instructions of Moscow and the Regional Soviet, Yakovlev endeavoured to convince Avdeyev, who was travelling in the same coupe, of the desirability of taking the Romanovs to Moscow. He argued that, when he was given this responsible task, he was personally instructed that it was necessary to protect the Romanovs against any hostile attempts, while he feared that Zaslavsky was determined to take their lives.

Avdeyev protested against Yakovlev's action, but was obliged to continue as his fellow-traveller to Omsk, being alone in the carriage and in effect a hostage from the Urals, not the plenipotentiary representative of the Ural Soviet.

When he came near to Omsk, Yakovlev learned from the railway staff of the telegram from the Regional Soviet. From them, too, he learned that Omsk was preparing to stop the train, and had sent armed forces for this purpose to Kulomzino, the junction for Cheliabinsk. Yakovlev held a conference with his assistants, and decided to halt the train at Liublinskaya, whence he, with a locomotive and one carriage, accompanied by a few of his comrades, left on the evening of April 28 for Omsk.

There the chairman of the West Siberia Soviet, in accordance with his conversation with Ekaterinburg, ordered him to carry the Romanovs to the latter town. Yakovlev insisted on a preliminary conversation by direct wire with Moscow. Together with the chairman, he called J. M. Sverdlov (chairman of the All-Russian Central Executive Committee) to the telegraph and explained the circumstances which had prompted him to change the route. An instruction was at once given by Moscow that he must take the Romanovs to Ekaterinburg, and hand them over there to the Ural Regional Soviet.

Seeing that he could not break through Kulomzino by force Yakovlev decided this time to submit. The train turned back from Liublinskaya and proceeded to Tiumen. Although the real reason for the change of direction was concealed from the Romanovs, and, and damage to the line given as the explanation, fragmentary conversations, together with what was not said, were sufficient to give them to understand that they were no longer bound for Moscow.

They passed through Tiumen at night. Brusiatsky with his whole detachment were waiting here. As soon as it became known that the tram had passed through without stopping, Brusiatsky had a special train assembled and set off in Yakovlev's wake.

At Kamyshlov, in the morning, Brusiatsky met Brainitsky, the commander of his regiment, who had been sent forward with a battalion to meet Yakovlev, but had not seen the train. Again suspicion arose, this time whether Yakovlev had not turned off at Bogdanovitch on to the branch line to Shadrinsk. Enquiries by telegraph, however, made it certain that the train had passed Bogdanovitch and was on its way to Ekaterinburg.

The morning of April 30 found the Romanovs in great anxiety.

P. M. Matveyev thus describes Nicholas' frame of mind before they reached Ekaterinburg.*

"When we began to approach Ekaterinburg, I ordered my boys to get ready, dressed and went out on to the platform of the car to instruct the sentries. Returning to the carriage, I met Nicholas coming out of the coupe which I and other comrades occupied. Romanov suddenly asked me:

" 'Tell me, is it definitely settled that we shall stay at Ekaterinburg?'

"Receiving my reply in the affirmative, he said:

" 'I would have gone anywhere but to the Urals.'

"When I asked what difference it made where he went, since the Soviet power extended all over Russia, he replied that he nevertheless would not care to stay in the Urals, as judging from the local papers the workers there were bitterly hostile to him."

When the train stopped at "Ekaterinburg I" station, it was learned that a vast crowd had assembled to meet it, and was demanding to be shown the Romanovs. By arrangement with the representative of the Regional Soviet, it was decided to move the train back to "Ekaterinburg II," on the other side of the town. Here they had to hand over the Romanovs.

* From Matveyev's unpublished M.S., *Tsarskoye Selo-Tobolsk-Ekaterinburg.*

* * *

CHAPTER XI

AT THE CAPITAL OF THE URALS

THE train was met at the station by Beloborodov and Didkovsky, on behalf of the Regional Soviet, to take over the Romanovs from Yakovlev. The Imperial family were accommodated in an automobile, Didkovsky taking the front seat with the driver. Beloborodov and Avdeyev went in a second car. Both cars passed through the city without any guard.

In anticipation of the Romanovs' arrival, the Soviet had had prepared for them the private house of an engineer, N. N. Ipatiev, at the corner of Voznesensky Prospekt (now Karl Liebknecht Street) and Voznesensky Lane. The house is situated at the top of a hill which dominates the city. Voznesensky Lane begins the descent to the large lake in the centre of the city, and thus the Ipatiev house is on an incline, so that the lower story is a semi-basement on one side and above the street level on the other. The upper story is entered from the square, a sloping drive leading down from the square to the main entrance. The house was well chosen, being in the centre of the city and convenient strategically.

The owner was given twenty-four hours to vacate the house. All the goods except the furniture were stored away, under receipt of the Soviet representatives, and sealed. A fence, shutting off the view of the house from the street was hastily erected. Subsequently a second high fence was put up along the facade down the hill, through the square, and also round the garden, which was situated below the house.

The same evening a meeting of the Regional Executive was held, and Yakovlev was invited. He attended the meeting in the company of some of his colleagues and the guardsmen from Tobolsk. Reports were made by Zaslavsky and Avdeyev. They exposed the "humble and loyal attitude of Yakovlev, both at Tobolsk and on the journey and demanded an immediate search in the train, the disarming of the guardsmen, and the arrest of Yakovlev.

In reply to these charges, Yakovlev said that, although it was true that he had received instructions in Moscow to deliver the Romanovs to Ekaterinburg, he also had verbal orders from J. M. Sverdlov to protect the Romanovs by every available means. In view of the attitude at Tobolsk of Zaslavsky and Avdeyev, who, he was convinced were preparing an attempt against the Romanovs' lives, he decided to inform the A.R.C.E.C of his apprehensions. The conversation with the A.R.C.E.C took place by direct wire, and Yakovlev produced the tape record. The latter showed that Yakovlev, distrusting the Ural Soviet and hoping to preserve the "person" of Nicholas Romanov, had asked the A.R.C.E.C. for permission to take the former Tsar to his home in the Ufa province, and for the time being to conceal him in a place known to himself, "in the hills." The A.R.C.E.C., of course, rejected this suggestion.

It was then that Yakovlev, according to his story, being afraid to proceed to Ekaterinburg direct from Tiumen, lest Zaslavsky should attack the train, took the Romanovs by the circuitous route through Omsk (Kulomzino) and Cheliabinsk.

Naturally, this explanation did not satisfy the Executive, but since the Romanovs were already under a reliable guard in the Ipatiev house, it was decided to let Yakovlev return to Moscow. He was given an official receipt, signed by Beloborodov, chairman of the Soviet, and the vice-chairman Didkovsky, certifying that the Ural Soviet had received from Tobolsk (1) the ex-Tsar Nicholas Alexandrovitch Romanov, (2) the ex-Tsaritsa Alexandra Feodorovna Romanov, (3) the ex-Grand Duchess Marie Nikolaevna Romanov, for detention under guard at Ekaterinburg.

Yakovlev and his detachment left, while the eight members of the former guard, under Lieutenant Matveyev, were disarmed and sent back to Tobolsk.

The appointment of Yakovlev as special commissary of the A.R.C.E.C. was undoubtedly a mistake. Later he betrayed the Revolution. After his return to Moscow he was given a command on the Samara front, and in October 1918 attempted to lead his whole army over to Kolchak. The army would not follow him, however, and he fled to the Whites with a few officers.

A letter soon appeared in the White papers of Ufa, in which Yakovlev made public recantation and repentance of his Bolshevik "sins." According to R. Wilton, Yakovlev later was appointed to one of the White armies on the southern front.

As soon as the river was clear for navigation, the remaining members of the Imperial family were also transferred to Ekaterinburg. On May 20 they were taken on board the same steamship *Rus* on which they had come to Tobolsk. They were accompanied by twenty-seven members of the "suite" and household.

Early on May 23 the Romanov children arrived at Ekaterinburg, and were taken by droschky from the station to the Ipatiev house. Of those who had accompanied them, General Tatischev, Hendrikova, Schneider and Volkov were at once sent to gaol. A few days later they were joined by Chemodurov, Nagorny, and Ivan Sednev, who had come with the ex-Tsar in April. Only five persons were given access to the Romanovs : Doctor Botkin, the cook Haritonov, the valet Trunp (sic), the kitchen-boy Leonid Sednev, and the chambermaid Demidova. All the others, with the exception of those in prison and Doctor Derevenko, were requested to leave the territory of the Urals. Derevenko was permitted to remain at liberty in Ekaterinburg.

Only now, after their transfer to the Urals, were the Romanovs really treated as persons under arrest. They were under the most careful vigilance of a guard composed of workers from the former Zlokazov Brothers' factory and the Sysertskoe Works. "A mere glance at the plans of the Ipatiev house," writes N. Sokolov, "is sufficient to show that, under such a guard, the Imperial family was in a trap with no way out."

The internal regime of the Romanov household was also much altered. There was no longer the abundance, the relatively wide tolerance, which they enjoyed at Tobolsk.

"The day passed usually as follows," writes the valet Chemodurov. "In the morning the whole family drank tea, with black bread left over from the day before. Dinner was at two, and was sent already prepared from the local Soviet" (dining-room P.B.). It consisted of meat soup and a roast, usually cutlets. As we had not brought table linen or silver with us, and here were given nothing, dinner was served on a bare table : the plates and generally the service were very poor. For supper the same dishes were served. Exercise in the garden was only permitted once a day, for fifteen or twenty minutes, and during this period the garden was entirely surrounded by guards. Sometimes His Majesty would address a remark of little consequence, with no bearing on the house regulations, to one of the guard : there was either no reply or a rude rebuff. . . . Day and night three Red soldiers were on guard in the upper story: one at the outer door, one in the vestibule, a third near the lavatory."*

It will be seen that the Romanovs' conditions at the Ipatiev house bore little resemblance to those at Tobolsk.†

* N. Sokolov, *op. cit.*, p. 128.
† However, the ex-Tsar's diary (*Krasny Arkhiv*, 1928, No. 27), shows that the regulations were not rigidly enforced. Thus, on June 9 the family spent one and a half hours out of doors, and from June 10 two hours. (Translator.)

* * *

CHAPTER XII

THE LAST DAYS OF THE ROMANOVS

HAVING placed the Romanovs under reliable guard, and after taking steps to prevent any attempt to carry them off from the "special house" (as at that time the Ipatiev mansion was called), the Regional Soviet took up the question of their ultimate fate.

At one of its sessions, the Soviet unanimously decided in favour of the execution of Nicholas Romanov. The majority, however, did not wish to take this responsibility upon itself without preliminary consultation with the centre. It was decided again to send Goloschekin to Moscow, in order to raise the question of the fate of the Romanovs with the Central Committee of the Party and the Presidium of the All-Russian Central Executive Committee.

In Moscow this question was also being discussed by the leaders. On his very first visit to the Presidium of the A.R.C.E.C., he met in Sverdlov's office Marie Spiridonova, who had come on behalf of the Central Committee of the Left Socialist-Revolutionaries to insist that the Romanovs be handed over to them to be dealt with.

The Presidium of the A.R.C.E.C. was inclined to the idea that it was necessary to hold a public trial of Nicholas Romanov. The Fifth All-Russian Congress of Soviets was to be held shortly. It was proposed to refer the whole matter to the Congress, and to move there that a public trial of the Romanovs be held at Ekaterinburg. L. Trotsky was to go to Ekaterinburg as principal Public Prosecutor of the ex-Tsar for his crimes against the people.

However, following Goloschekin's report on military operations in the Urals, where owing to the Czecho-Slovak rising the situation was not satisfactory, and the early fall of Ekaterinburg might be expected, the question was reviewed. It was decided not to refer the matter to the Congress, which might drag on for some time. Goloschekin was instructed to return to Ekaterinburg and arrange for a public trial of the Romanovs at the end of July, by which time Trotsky would be there.

In actual fact, civil war was spreading in the Urals. The Cossack bands of Dutov, which had risen at the beginning of the winter, were crushed by the guerrilla detachments of the Ural workers : but their place was taken by the Czecho-Slovaks. The Czecho-Slovak mutiny immediately transformed the whole region of the Urals into an arena of bloody fighting between semi-irregular workers' detachments and the regular Czecho-Slovak troops, supplemented by White officers and volunteers. Ekaterinburg, as the capital of the Red Urals, had at great speed to form companies, detachments and regiments of Ural workers, out of whom later were built the first units of the regular Red Army.

The peril of the conquest of the Urals by the White bands was only too obvious, and every ounce of energy was concentrated on the fight against them. Naturally, in these circumstances the broad masses of the workers were little concerned about the fate of the former Imperial family, confined as it was under reliable guard.

But from the first days of the Romanovs' transfer to Ekaterinburg there began to flock in monarchists in great number, beginning with half-crazy ladies, countesses and baronesses of every calibre and ending with nuns, clergy, and representatives of foreign Powers.

The correspondence addressed by them to Nicholas consisted mostly of greetings and condolences. Sometimes there were letters of obviously abnormal persons, describing their dreams, visions and similar nonsense. Requests for permission to visit either Nicholas or other members of the Romanov family were fairly frequent. The reasons given were extremely varied : "To see our relations" ; "To render any service necessary," etc. But access to Nicholas was limited to a very small circle of members of the Ural Regional Soviet, while permission for others to see him was given only by the A.R.C.E.C. Hence the constant attempts of various persons to penetrate to him always ended in failure.

Almost at the same time as the Romanov family were transferred from Tobolsk, others of their relatives were sent from Viatka to Ekaterinburg. Amongst these were the former Grand Dukes Sergei Michaelovitch, Igor Konstantinovitch, Konstantin Konstantinovitch, Ivan Konstantinovitch, and Prince Paul, son of the Grand Duke Paul Alexandrovitch. Here, too, was sent Elizabeth Feodorovna, widow of the Grand Duke Sergei executed by the revolutionaries years ago, who was expelled from Moscow. All these individuals lived at hotels under very indifferent observation, and moved freely through the city. Amongst the bourgeoisie of Ekaterinburg they had many well-wishers, who willingly invited these "noble guests" to their evening parties at which a secret organisation to carry off the

Romanovs was formed.

E. Semchevskaya, wife of an officer of the General Staff Academy recounts these facts in the pages of a monarchist journal. She states that at the "intimate parties" with the Grand Dukes there was rapidly set up an active group of thirty-seven officers, "ready for everything" to save the dynasty. However, they decided in the end to leave the city and join the Czecho-Slovaks, "in order to hasten the fall of Ekaterinburg and thereby set free the Imperial family."*

In the middle of June there came to Ekaterinburg from Odessa according to Dieterichs,† a well-known Monarchist—I. I. Sidorov, formerly aide-de-camp to the Emperor—with the express object of liberating the Romanovs.

At Ekaterinburg he established contact with Doctor Derevenko who was permitted to visit the sick Alexei. Through Derevenko he organised the supply of foodstuffs to the Romanovs and a regular exchange of letters.

The White organisers acted fairly openly. Enjoying the support of the bourgeoisie, which was growing bolder as the front drew nearer, they were preparing to raise an insurrection at a convenient moment in the city itself, with the object of setting free the Romanovs. The success of such an attempt was not out of the question. At this time there had been transferred from Moscow to Ekaterinburg the General Staff Academy, which consisted almost entirely of former officers who represented a ready-made organised force for anti-Soviet action.

Nevertheless the Regional Extraordinary Commission succeeded in finding the track of these organisations, and some of the most active Whites were arrested.

Amongst other persons, closely connected with the Romanov family, there were arrested a certain Serbian Major Michich, Sergeant-Major Bojechich and Smirnov (steward of Elena Petrovna, Queen of Serbia and wife of the Grand Duke Ivan Konstantinovitch, who had been expelled with her husband to Ekaterinburg). These individuals came to the Regional Soviet as delegates of the Serbian Minister Spalaikovitch, first to ascertain from Nicholas Romanov his opinion as to the termination of the war,

* E. Semchevskaya: *Recollections of the Grand Dukes*, in *Douglavy Orel*, Berlin, 192 No. 15.
† M. K. Dieterichs, op. cit., p. 376.

and then, when the Soviet emphatically refused this request, with a request that the ex-Princess Elena of Serbia be allowed to leave for Petrograd, for which they alleged permission of the central authorities had been obtained. Enquiries undertaken by the Regional Soviet in Moscow and Petrograd revealed that the Presidium of the A.R.C.E.C. had rejected the request of Spalaikovitch that Elena Romanov should be allowed to come to Petrograd. It was established that the so-called "Serbian mission" was in close contact with the monarchist organisations which had been formed at Ekaterinburg.

In order to free the city to some extent from the patrons of monarchist enterprise, the Regional Soviet had all members of the Romanov house living in lodgings and hotels transferred to the town of Alapayevsk. But this was not sufficient to eliminate the danger of counter-revolutionary outbursts.

With the approach of the front and the retreat of the Red Army, the monarchists became increasingly bolder in their efforts to establish communication with the prisoners in the "special house."

The "offerings" of the local nuns were often found to contain notes of a far from monastic origin. The well-wishers of the Romanovs were exceedingly ingenious in transmitting them. Apart from notes in loaves of bread, on parcels and wrapping-paper, one note was even discovered in the cork of a bottle of milk.

"The hour of liberation is approaching, and the days of the usurpers are numbered," wrote their friends in one letter. "The Slav armies are coming nearer and nearer to Ekaterinburg. They are a few miles from the city. The hour is becoming critical. The time has come for action." "Your friends sleep no longer," ran another message, "and trust that the hour so long awaited is nigh."

The Moscow papers printed some time ago several documents which confirmed the impression that a plan for carrying off the Romanovs existed. General Dieterichs quotes two characteristic letters, pointing to the existence of such a plan, in his book.*

An anonymous correspondent of the Romanovs writes : "With God's help and your prudence we hope to achieve our object without running any risk. It is necessary to unfasten one of your windows, so that you can open it : please let me know exactly which. If the little Tsarevitch cannot walk, matters will be very complicated;

* Dieterichs, *op. cit.*, p. 58.

but we have weighed this up too, and I do not consider it an insurmountable obstacle. Let us know definitely whether you need two men to carry him and whether any of you could undertake this work. Could not the little one be put to sleep for an hour or two with some drug ? Let the doctor decide, only you must know the time exactly beforehand. We will supply all that is necessary. Be sure that we shall undertake nothing unless we are absolutely certain of success beforehand. We give you our solemn pledge of this before God, history and our own conscience." The letter was signed: "Officer."

On their part the Romanovs passed over information concerning the state of affairs inside the house. Dieterichs prints the text of a letter sent out by Nicholas :

"The second window from the corner, looking out on to the square has been kept open for two days already, even at night. The seventh and eighth windows near the main entrance, also looking out on the square, are likewise kept open. The room is occupied by the commandant and his assistants, who constitute the inner guard at the present time; They number thirteen, armed with rifles, revolvers and grenades. No room but ours has keys. The commandant and their assistants can enter our quarters whenever they please. The orderly officer makes the round of the house twice an hour at night and we hear his arms clattering under our windows. One machine-gun stands on the balcony and one above it, for any emergency. Opposite our windows, on the other side of the street, is the guard in a little house. It consists of fifty men. All the keys, and key No. 9 are kept by the commandant, who treats us well. In any case, inform us when there is a chance, and let us know whether we can take our people. A car always stands before the entrance. From every post there is a bell to the commandant and a signal to the guard-room and other places. If our people stay behind, can we be certain that nothing will happen to them ? "

The Romanovs lived in hopes of early liberation. Nicholas himself attempted to send a letter in an envelope with a coloured lining. The envelope aroused suspicion, and when the lining was detached, there was found under it a plan of the upper story, with details of every room and of who lived in it.

In the corner room, farthest removed from the guard, consultations often took place. Usually in such cases the family sent

Marie or Tatiana out into the corridor, where they sat down on a trunk engaged in some handiwork. When any member of the guard appeared they rose and hastily went back into the room.

The prisoners were forbidden to stand at the windows, in order to prevent signalling. This regulation was frequently broken, however, and on one occasion Tatiana, the eldest daughter of the ex-Tsar even put her head out of the ventilating pane of the window looking on to the neighbouring street. The sentry of the outer guard, seeing this immediately fired. . . . After this incident the family began to carry out instructions more carefully.

Inside the house the prisoners did everything possible to win over the guard. For the most part the Romanovs' "advocate" was Doctor Botkin, who often went into the commandant's room and by skilful conversations attempted to ascertain the chances of the Romanovs and the attitude of the Regional Soviet and the Central Government to their fate. Of the Romanov family Marie showed great activity in this direction, coquetting with the soldiers at every available opportunity.

All this prompted the Regional Soviet, at the beginning of July, to appoint Y. M. Yurovsky, a member of the Presidium of the Regional Extraordinary Commission, commandant of the house, and G. P. Nikulin as his second-in-command. Changes were also made in the personnel of the guard, and a strict regime established which permitted of no communications whatsoever between the prisoners and the city. A superficial search was made in the Romanovs' quarters, and they were requested to surrender all their valuables. The Romanovs drew up an inventory of their property and handed it to the commandant, leaving the valuables in their rooms.

At the same time as it had to beat off the attempts of the White Guards, the Regional Soviet also had to defend the Romanovs against "attacks" of another kind. The Ekaterinburg organisations of the Left Socialist-Revolutionaries and the Anarchists were not certain that the Bolsheviks would shoot the ex-Tsar, and decided to take steps to do so with their own forces. A plan of attack on the house was worked out by the "fighting groups" of the S.R.'s and Anarchists, the aim being to shoot the Romanovs during the attack.

However, neither this attack nor the White rising took place, leaving out of the reckoning the counter-revolutionary demonstration of returned soldiers, which was speedily crushed and its leaders shot.

CHAPTER XIII

THE EXECUTION OF THE ROMANOV FAMILY

ON Goloschekin's return from Moscow, a meeting of the Regional Soviet was held on July 12, and a report made on the attitude of the central authorities to the execution of the Romanovs.

The Regional Soviet came to the conclusion that the trial proposed by Moscow could no longer be organised: the front was too close and any delay in dealing with the Romanovs might cause new complications. It was decided that the commander of the front be asked how long Ekaterinburg could be held, and what was the position at the front. The military command made a report to the Soviet from which it was clear that the situation was very bad. The Czechs had already outflanked Ekaterinburg from the South, and were attacking it on two sides. The Red forces were inadequate, and the fall of the city might be expected within three days. In consequence of this, the Regional Soviet decided to shoot the Romanovs without waiting for a trial. The execution and the destruction of the bodies was entrusted to the commanders of the guard, together with a few reliable Communist workers. At a preliminary conference in the Regional Soviet the procedure of execution and the method of disposing of the bodies were determined. The destruction of the bodies was important because of the anticipated fall of Ekaterinburg, in order not to afford the counter-revolutionaries the opportunity of playing on the ignorance of the mass of the people with the "relics" of the ex-Tsar. This decision, as will be seen, was very provident: after the occupation of Ekaterinburg, the Whites spent a long time in searching for the "holy bodies" of the members of the Imperial family.

On the evening of July 16, the persons appointed by the Regional Soviet to carry out the sentence on the Romanovs gathered in the commandant's room in the "special house." The rooms in the upper story, where the family lived, were recognised to be inconvenient for the execution. It was decided to take the family downstairs, to one of the semi-basement rooms, and there carry out the sentence. Until their execution the Romanovs knew nothing of the decision.

At twelve midnight on the same day they were requested to dress and go downstairs. In order not to arouse their suspicion, they were told that this was necessary because of a White attack on the house anticipated that night. For the same reason the other persons dwelling in the house were also told to go downstairs. The boy Leonid Sednev, eleven years old, had been transferred the night before to the house opposite, where the guard lived, as a precaution.

When they were all assembled on the lower floor, in the room appointed for the execution, they were read the decision of the Ural Regional Soviet. Thereupon all the eleven—Nicholas Romanov, his wife, son, four daughters and four of their household— were shot.

Thus on the night of July 16-17 the Romanov family ceased to exist. After the execution, the bodies were carried in blankets into the courtyard and put in a lorry. The lorry left the city along a route previously determined—through a suburb, the Verkh-Isetsky Works, on to the road leading to the village of Koptiaki. Half way along this road, about eight versts from the city, is a plot of land called the "Four Brothers," from four large pines which formerly grew there. To the left of the road in this area are old disused workings, formerly used in the production of iron ore. The area is called Gavina's Pit, from the name of a small pond in the centre of the workings. It was here, along a forest path off the Koptiaki road, that the bodies of the Romanovs were brought. They were temporarily laid in one of the diggings, and the next day their destruction was begun.

On the corpses of Alexandra and her daughters many valuables were found—gold and diamonds, sewn into their clothing (chiefly in the bodices of the Romanov daughters, in cloth buttons, etc). All the clothing was carefully examined and the valuables collected.

On July 18 the "funeral" was completed, and so thoroughly, that thereafter, the Whites, who for two years carried on special excavations in this area, could not find the graves of the Romanovs.

After the sentence had been carried out, the Regional Soviet sent Goloschekin and Yurovsky to Moscow. They took with them most of the valuables taken from the Romanovs, their correspondence, diaries and all the materials which gave the Soviet the necessary grounds for shooting the ex-Tsar and his family.

At the session of the Presidium of the All-Russian Central Executive Committee on July 18, J. M. Sverdlov, the chairman, read out the telegram received by direct wire about the execution of the former Tsar. After discussing the circumstances which had prompted the Ural Regional Soviet in its decision to execute Nicholas Romanov, the Presidium decided to approve of the decision and action of the Ural Soviet. The same evening a report was made at the Council of Peoples' Commissaries :

"During the discussion of the draft Public Health Law, in the middle of Semashko's report, Sverdlov came in and sat down on a chair behind Ilich (Lenin). Semashko concluded. Sverdlov came up, bent down over Ilich, and said something.

" 'Comrade Sverdlov wants to make a statement.'

" 'I have to say,' Sverdlov began in his customary even tones, 'that we have had a communication that at Ekaterinburg, by a decision of the Regional Soviet, Nicholas has been shot. Nicholas wanted to escape. The Czecho-Slovaks were approaching. The Presidium of the A.R.C.E.C. has resolved to approve.'

"Silence of everyone.

" 'Let us now go on to read the draft clause by clause,' suggested Ilich.

"The reading clause by clause began."*

On July 19 the Council of People's Commissaries published a decree confiscating the property of Nicholas Romanov and the members of the former Imperial House. The latter included all persons entered on the genealogical book of the former Imperial Court : the former Tsarevich, Heir-Apparent, the ex-Grand Dukes and Grand-Duchesses, the ex-Princes, Princesses, and Princesses of the Blood-Imperial. All their property was proclaimed the property of the Soviet Republic.

The news of the execution of the Romanovs was officially published at Ekaterinburg on July 22. The evening before, a statement was made to a workers' meeting in the City Theatre, and was met with a storm of enthusiasm. The meeting adopted a resolution declaring :

"The execution of Nicholas the Bloody is a reply and a stern warning to the bourgeois monarchist counter-revolution, which is trying to drown the workers' and peasants' revolution in blood.

"All the enemies of the working people have united around the watchword of the restoration of the capitalists' and landlords' autocracy.

"The whole working people is united under the banner of the

* V. Miliutin : *Pages from My Diary* (*Projektor*, 1924, No. 4).

Socialist Republic. The struggle between them is for life or death, and all who will not march to-day with the people, in its struggle for existence, are in the camp of the people's enemies. This meeting calls on all to whom the gains of the Revolution are dear to enter the ranks of those who are fighting for the social emancipation of the toilers.

"Long live the Soviet Power!

"Long live the international working-class revolution! "*

* The *Uralski Rabochi*, No. 144-241, July 23, 1918.

* * *

CHAPTER XIV

THE EXECUTION OF THE FORMER GRAND DUKES

It was in the Urals that the other members of the Romanov dynasty found their grave: at Perm Nicholas' brother, Michael Alexandrovitch Romanov.

Since March 1917 he had lived with his family at Gatchina. Only a year later, in February 1918, owing to the monarchist movement in his favour, he was arrested on the demand of the Petrograd Soviet and sent with his secretary, N. Johnson, to Perm. The accompanying letter to the Perm Soviet stated that Michael Romanov was being sent to Perm on the responsibility and under the observation of the Soviet, but it suggested that no special restrictions be imposed upon him. However, the Perm Soviet could not make up its mind to liberate him at once and detained him under domestic arrest in the former "Hall of the Nobility." Michael Romanov protested against his arrest and insisted on his release, referring to the Petrograd decision as a justification. However, at the sessions of the town Soviet and at workers' meetings, particularly at the Motovilikha Works, the workers themselves repeatedly raised the question of shooting Michael Romanov, in order thereby once for all to block the monarchists' inclination to hunt for a candidate to the Imperial throne.

In spite of the attempts of the leading committees to combat this tendency, numerous meetings passed resolutions demanding the extirpation of the Romanovs.

Reckoning with the danger of allowing Michael to live freely in Perm, and with the possibility of irresponsible acts, the Perm Soviet suggested to him that he should be transferred to a specially fitted-up section of the prison hospital. Romanov made a complaint to the Council of People's Commissaries and the All-Russian Extraordinary Commission. In reply to this complaint, the Perm Soviet received an instruction, over the signature of the chief of the secretariat of the Council of People's Commissaries, Bonch-Bruyevitch, to liberate Michael Romanov but retain him under observation, and another letter from the Extraordinary Commission, signed by Uritsky, granting Romanov the right of free sojourn in Perm. Romanov was then informed by representatives of the Soviet

Executive that he was being liberated without any guarantees, and the Soviet did not take responsibility for anything that might happen.

Romanov with his secretary Johnson, his valet Chelyshev and his chauffeur Borunov settled down in the Sibirskaya ulitsa—one of the busiest streets in Perm—in the King's Hotel, the best in town, near the river Kama.

At first watch was kept over him by the militia. Later, when the Executive had communicated with the centre, explained the situation, and repudiated all responsibility for Romanov's safety, observation was entrusted on the suggestion of Petrograd to the Provincial Extraordinary Commission, where Michael accordingly went to "sign on" on fixed days.

Living in freedom, Michael Romanov was in close contact with his friends and relations, and there was constant communication between Perm and Petrograd. Countess Brassova, Michael's wife, visited Perm in May and then proceeded to Moscow, where, according to R. Wilton, she had an interview with Lenin and asked permission for her husband to go abroad. This, of course, was refused. Later Brassova was arrested, but managed to escape abroad.

Meanwhile, influenced by the demands of the Perm and Motovilikha workers for the execution of Michael Romanov, a secret group was formed with the object of killing him. It was composed of the chairman of the Motovilikha Soviet, G. I. Miasnikov, with the following workmen: A. Markov, Ivanchenko, N. Zhuzhkov, and I. Kolpashnikov. The group had no connection with either Party or Soviet organisations, and acted in great secret at its own risk.

On the evening of June 12-13 this group came to the hotel with forged documents from the Provincial Extraordinary Commission. Michael Romanov was already asleep. He was awakened and presented with a document ordering him immediately to leave Perm. Romanov was incredulous, and refused to follow his visitors, demanding that they should call a doctor and Malkov, chairman of the Extraordinary Commission. They then said they would use force. The ex-Grand Duke's secretary, Johnson, said that he would follow his "master." Although Johnson did not enter into the plans of the group, they decided however to take him along in order not to delay in the hotel. Both the "arrested" men were put into carriages which were ready, and taken out of the town along the track to Motovilikha. After passing the Nobel kerosine dump, six versts from Motovilikha, they turned off into the forest to the right, and there shot Michael Romanov. After this, in order to cover up their tracks, one of those participating rang up the militia and the Provincial Extraordinary Commission, and informed them that some persons unknown had entered the King's Hotel the previous night and carried off Michael Romanov in the direction of Siberia.

This event was a complete surprise for all the organisations of Perm. A chase was organised immediately, which however set out on the false route and could find no traces. At the same time telegrams were sent to Petrograd and in every direction announcing the escape of Michael Romanov.

For some time the Perm organisations were in ignorance of the true course of events, and only after some time discovered the actual state of affairs from rumours which spread among the rank and file.

After the rumours had been checked and those whom reports indicated as having participated had been questioned, it became clear that Michael Romanov had been really shot, which was published in the Press.

The military situation in the Urals and the execution of the whole Imperial family at Ekaterinburg caused very little attention to be paid among the workers of the Urals to the death of this scion of the dynasty.

A month later the members of the Romanov family exiled in May to Alapayevsk also met with their deaths.

Alapayevsk is a small town on the Irbit-Nijni-Tagil Railway. Formerly a county town of the Perm province, now it is a district centre. As a place of exile for the Romanovs it was well chosen; it was out of the way, on the railway, and, as an industrial centre, entirely reliable. When the transfer of Nicholas Romanov to the Urals was being first discussed, Alapayevsk was suggested as the place of detention, and suitable premises had actually been found. Later, however, in consequence of nearness to the front, it was decided to leave the elder Romanovs at Ekaterinburg.

Later still, Alapayevsk was utilised by the Ural Soviet as the place of detention of the Grand Dukes. On May 20, 1918, there were brought to Alapayevsk the following ex-Grand Dukes and Duchesses: Elizabeth Feodorovna, Sergei, Michaelovitch, Elena (ex-

Queen of Serbia), Ivan, Igor and Konstantin (sons of Konstantin Konstantinovitch), and Vladimir Paley, son of the ex-Grand Duke Paul Alexandrovitch. They were all housed in a new stone building, the so-called "School in the Fields," situated on the outskirts, which was hastily fitted up as a dwelling-house.

At first the Romanovs lived fairly freely at Alapayevsk. They went about alone, without guards, visited church, took walks in the fields near the school, etc. But soon here, as in other places, there was soon grouped around them a close body of friends, who brought the pious Grand Duchesses and Dukes an abundance of voluntary offerings, flowers, foodstuffs, and their sympathy. On the other hand, the workers of Alapayevsk, alarmed by the threats of the counter-revolutionaries, expressed in a rising at the Neviansky Works, near Alapayevsk, and generally by the developing operations on the eastern front, were insisting either on the close confinement of the Romanovs under guard, or on their destruction. Just at this time, at Perm, took place the "escape" of Michael, and the Ural Regional Soviet requested the Alapayevsk Soviet to establish more strict control over the Romanovs, in order to preclude any possibility of escape.

As from June 21 the Alapayevsk executive, by agreement with the Ural Soviet, introduced prison conditions for the Romanovs : parcels from outside were forbidden, all excursions outside the school railings prohibited, and all outsiders sent away from the prisoners, only the nun Yakovleva being left with Elizabeth Feodorovna and the servant Remez with Sergei Michaelovitch.

This change greatly alarmed the prisoners, and they decided to appeal to the Ural Soviet. On June 21 the ex-Grand Duke Sergei Michaelovitch, in the name of all his relatives at Alapayevsk, sent the following telegram : "Chairman of Regional Soviet, Ekaterinburg. By a decision of the Soviet we are from to-day under prison conditions. Knowing of no fault on our part, we beg that the prison regime be removed."

In reply the following telegram was received by Soloviev, the Alapayevsk commissary for justice : "Inform Sergei Romanov that their imprisonment is a preventive measure against escape, in view of Michael's disappearance from Perm.—Beloborodov."*

---

* N. Sokolov, *op. cit.*, p. 259.

With the approach of the front, and in view of the necessity of despatching all available forces against the enemy, in view also of the demands of the workers, the leaders of the Alapayevsk Soviet decided to execute the Romanovs.

This was done on the night of July 17-18, 1918. The bodies were thrown into a deep pit eleven miles from Alapayevsk, near the Verkhni-Siniachikhinsky Works.

With the shooting of the Romanovs ended the first period of the Soviet power in the Urals.*

* *Translator's Note*: The Grand Duchess Elena of Serbia was allowed to leave the country unharmed, thanks to the efforts of the Serbian Minister, Spalaikovitch. (See his preface to *Autour de l'Assassinat des Grands Ducs*.

* * *

CHAPTER XV

SEARCHING FOR THE ROMANOVS

ON the morning of July 25, Ekaterinburg was occupied by the Whites. Immediately on their entry, the officers rushed to the Ipatiev house to seek the bodies of the ex-Tsar and his family.

The military authorities decided to organise an investigation "into the murder of the Tsar," for which purpose they set up a special commission of General Staff Academy officers, under the chairmanship of Colonel Sherekhovsky, with the aid of investigating judge Nametkin.

On July 30, i.e., within a fortnight of the execution, the judicial investigation began.

Not knowing who exactly had been shot, the Commission sought in the first place for the corpse of Nicholas Romanov. The most varied rumours about the end of the Romanovs spread through the city. Some said that the ex-Tsar had been buried in the garden of the Ipatiev house—and the Special Commission had the whole garden dug over. Someone stated that he had been shot in the forest beyond the Ekaterinburg II station—and they dug up the ground in the forest for a long time. The city and Verkh-Isetsky ponds, where another rumour had it the bodies had been thrown, were searched with nets and spears. Several graves were dug up in the churchyard; but all the searches were fruitless.

Only on the morning of August 27 Lieutenant Sheremetevsky, who had remained concealed under the Reds in the village of Koptiaki, came to the Intelligence Department and reported that before their retreat the Bolsheviks had been burning bodies, which judging from the half-burned clothes remaining were those of members of the ex-Imperial family, in the district of "Ganina's Pit" in the forest.

For two summers, 1918 and 1919—water was pumped out of the pits in this area and the neighbourhood dug up in the search for the sacred remains."

The remains of the Romanov family could not be found, and the Special Commission, on the foundation of rumours, accidental documents and the mental processes of the investigators, formed one theory after another of the possible "salvation" of the Romanovs.

Particularly grateful to the monarchist hearts was the version supported by Kirsta, the head of the Criminal Investigation Department at Ekaterinburg—that the whole family had escaped from Ekaterinburg disguised as aviators, and that the Bolsheviks had executed other persons in their place. When this ridiculous story had been exploded, they began seriously to "work" on the question of the possible removal of the Romanovs by the Bolsheviks themselves. This version particularly interested the investigators. They chanced to come across a telegram referring to the despatch of the specially-secret train in which bank valuables were withdrawn from Ekaterinburg. They decided that this train must have borne, not valuables, but the family of the ex-Tsar. Numerous witnesses were found who saw "with their own eyes" how Nicholas was taken to the station in irons, how he was pushed into the carriage, and so forth.

However, other data of the Commission pointed to the fact that the Romanovs had not gone away anywhere, but had been shot.

A great deal of discussion was caused by the absence of any bodies, in spite of the most careful searches. But, as has been mentioned earlier, what remained of the bodies after burning was taken a considerable distance from the pits and buried in a swamp, in an area where the volunteers and investigators made no excavations. There the bodies remained and by now have rotted away.

On January 17, 1919, new persons were appointed as an Investigating Committee, General M. K. Dieterichs being invested by Kolchak with responsibility for their work. N. Sokolov, a monarchist who had escaped from the Bolsheviks at Saratov, was appointed principal investigator.

On the charge of "the murder of His Majesty the Emperor Nicholas Alexandrovitch, who had abdicated the throne, and the members of his family," Sokolov considered it necessary to bring to trial 164 persons on the other side of the front. A special order was circulated along the whole front in respect of these persons, "that the life of all the persons indicated be preserved, and that they be removed to the rear immediately upon their arrest."

Koshnev, an engineer, was put in charge of work at the pits. With the help of a barge steam-engine, he pumped the water from the most "suspicious" pits. In all twenty-nine pits were examined, but only rubbish was found.

As a result of the investigation, and the examination of persons who fell into the hands of the White Guards and were in one way or another cognisant of the shooting of the ex-Imperial family, it was established beyond possibility of doubt that the whole Imperial family had been executed.

Having arrived at this conclusion, the monarchists collected all the articles and ashes found around the pits and in the Ipatiev house and took them away as an "heirloom" to the friend and relative of the Romanovs—the King of England.

The White Guards dealt out a severe penalty to the workers and peasants of the Urals. Thousands of them, who perished under ramrod and bullet at the hands of drunken officers in the prisons of Ekaterinburg, Perm and other towns of the Urals, paid with their lives for the execution of the Romanovs.

The White bandits dealt severely, after tortures, with those few who were involved in the execution. There perished Doctor Sakovitch, a Socialist-Revolutionary member of the Regional Soviet who remained in Ekaterinburg in the hope of protection from the Constituent Assembly, and the worker P. Medvediev, who took part in the execution. According to Dieterichs and Wilton, they died in the most "peaceful" way—Sakovitch in prison at Omsk, of galloping consumption, Medvediev in prison at Ekaterinburg, of typhus. But the prison torture-chambers, which witnessed the deaths of these victims of Kolchak, tell a different story.

The investigation into the execution of the other members of the Romanov family did not find the body of Michael Romanov either. There were found only the bodies of the Grand Dukes shot at Alapayevsk. The "martyrs" were ceremoniously buried in a mausoleum beneath Alapayevsk Church. When the Red Army was advancing, the precious bodies were in great secrecy carried away from Alapayevsk by a certain abbot Serafim, and transported to Pekin! Later the coffin of the Grand Duchess Elizabeth Feodorovna and her nun were again exhumed, and transported to Jerusalem, where they were solemnly reburied at the end of January 1921.*

The workers and peasants of Alapayevsk paid dearly for the execution of this group of the Romanov family. It is sufficient to say that one of the pits near the village of Alapayevsk was piled twenty-eight feet high with bodies of peasants who were shot by the Whites.

* *The Dvuglary Orel*, Berlin, 1921, No. 6.

A wave of White terror rolled far and wide over the Urals, and the work of the monarchists opened the eyes of many workers to the true aims of the Kolchak bands. Numerous risings in the rear of the Whites, mass desertions to the Red Army of the workers and peasants mobilised by Kolchak, assisted the Soviet Government in the summer of 1919 to deliver a decisive blow at the Whites and to finish them off in the forests of Siberia.

Admiral Kolchak, the "Supreme Ruler" who attempted to become a new Russian autocrat, abandoned both by the Allies and his "Imperial" officer-regiments, ended his days at Irkutsk by the will of the insurgent Siberian workers, going to his grave in the same way as the Romanovs in the Urals.

By her victory over the last champions of Monarchism, Workers' Russia drove the stake still deeper into the grave of the Romanov dynasty, and whatever the surviving tail-ends of that house abroad may undertake, they will never raise that corpse from its grave.

END OF BOOK THREE

AFTERWORD

THE time of the last Tsar of Russia could be associated with the transformation from autocracy to communism; or the brief existence of the republic; or crossing the threshold in to the 20th nouveau siècle; or as an example in world history when the peasants reclaimed control of the governing institutions, but in this case failed to prevent the ensuing disarray from being hi-jacked by the Bolshevik faction. However it's perceived, it was remarkable in its scale and effect, yet the most turbulent of times still lay ahead, with interior racial cleansing and a devastating Civil War.

One cannot say that it was the end of the Russian civilisation as could be said about ancient Egypt, but the Revolution was highly significant, marking a fundamental change in that culture and only time will reveal whether the Revolution was the beginning of the end for Russia or simply a page in their story as William Wallace is to Scottish history.

The history of Russia is extremely 'extensive', an adjective that could be applied to its physical geography and the cultures that define its identity. Everything about Russia is humungous. The development of that part of the world can also be described in simplistic terms; the main gene pool was Slavic; the major expansion occurred when Siberia was incorporated which also brought in the Asian, making up two thirds of the Russian territory. In the West, in many ways the loss of Ukraine cut off a large part of the Slavic roots in the same way that losing Schleswig-Holstein to Prussia left Denmark cut off from its territorial roots unsure of how to reclaim its identity.

Siberia takes months for a human to traverse. This hinterland that we perceive as largely inhospitable, is landlocked by ice which forces the navy to predominantly locate at Kaliningrad in the extreme West and Vladivostok in the extreme East, where ice is not the issue in winter. This stark geology, spanning two continents, is also the primary defence against invasion – only the Russian can appreciate the magnitude of this desolation.

Given the diversity of the population, it's unsurprising that Russia is formed from territories distinguished by their cultural differences, each having been acquired through expansionism. It was, for much of its past, a system designed for continual territorial growth of

AFTERWORD

which the same might be said about much of Germany's past. From the Slavic to the Mongolian the common border successfully kept the economy in perpetual isolation, which the outside world read as a people stuck in the past, culturally and industrially, and perhaps even regarded it as an extension of insular China.

The pangs of growth, unfortunately for its progression, have been caused by the political, and in the administrative and logistical arenas, exemplified by the incompetence and corruption pertinent to the system of governance employed – projecting a philosophical view that the reigns have been held by individuals devoid of compassion and empathy, who place no value on human life. The Pogroms and Russification are but two examples of this.

It is of course an overly simplified and wrongful assessment and to imply that the Russian psyche is geared towards inhumanity is to show ignorance of how social structures evolve and to deny the art of that civilisation and the brilliance of its statesmen, artists and expert artisans – think Peter the Great, Dostoevsky and Fabergé.

How did this innate flair for excellence come to be regarded as cultural latency. Perhaps Imperial Russia ruled for several centuries because it became the necessary next step and perhaps it ended when that system became unfit for purpose or came to have no purpose at all. The common denominator was always power, and the regime was the real cause for the dissent that ultimately toppled the institutions. It was the aristocracy, the innocent bystanders that was blamed for everything and paid the ultimate price with their lives or having to exile because in the fold of time their protector, the emperor, was remiss in his responsibility and duty to them.

There never existed, of course, a divine right to rule, despite the proclamations to keep this idea atop the monarchy, State and Church. The autocracy was held together by brutal force with the implementation of fear for a deterrent, the manifestation of which was responsible for millions of deaths. Yet, faced with certain death in opposition to the State, people still rebelled and fought back with a bloody campaign of terrorism and eventually took back control of their country. How unfortunate that the leaders from oppressed groups such as the Jews, were left unchecked to infiltrate the country and take over the Revolution which in turn saw them implement a new era of terror more devastating than anything before and taking away the fought for freedoms of the people.

AFTERWORD

Against this backdrop the abundance of natural resources was largely overlooked and the empire saw itself as a civilisation made up of peasants. Who knew that just below the frozen surface lay such plentiful manna. The natural resources soon became the substrate of Russia's riches, as one views the oil under the states of Texas and Oklahoma that have similarly given self sufficiency in oil to America. Although America might be seen as the only remaining effective world power, Russia's subterranean manna is the hidden world power. Just days following the Russian invasion of Ukraine in February 2022 America experienced record high fuel prices with the European countries left asking where their fuel would come from that coming winter.

As early as 1902, Vladimir Lenin published 'What Is to Be Done?' his user manual for a revolution, and by 1903, at the Second Social Democratic Party Congress, he effectively split the party in to the Bolsheviks and Mensheviks. In the confusion of it all the underlying agrarian problems of old, e.g. famine etc, remained on the back burner, while millions were killed or starved to death at the hands of the State. The tragedy was that the tsar sided with the nefarious element, the Black Hundred and the Far Right movement which became the heartbeat of the tsarist regime itself.

Peter the Great, although opposed at home was respected in Europe and had brought back their traditions to his Court beginning the first reforms. Over the ensuing two hundred years it was not built upon and they headed decade by decade towards the revolutions in 1918 when the State was outmatched by the people. A lot of the experiences from the Court, the Government and the Military, come from the many memoirs. Among the numerous accounts we have Pavel Bykov's book in this volume, which despite its criticisms agrees with Nikolai Sokolov's account of what happened; the chief investigator of the judicial inquiry in to the murders in Ekaterinburg and Perm.

The wealth of memoirs throws up much that is untrue, and one must weigh up the likeliness of events and sometimes prod the figurative pitchfork to find the facts. In *The Fall of the Russian Monarchy*, Sir Bernard Pares mentions the book of R. H. Bruce Lockhart, *Memoirs of a British Agent*, who as Deputy British Consul General in Moscow rendered brilliant service to the Allied cause in WWI, "*but it is heavily coloured by the requirements of a*

AFTERWORD

best seller." In this respect we tend to rely on the best depictions from the sources that have the most integrity, in which esteemable company we can include Alexander Mossolov, (book 1 of this volume), and Pierre Gilliard, Major-General Sir John Hanbury-Williams among others. The book *Out of My Past: The Memoirs of Count Kokovtsov,* was first published in Russian, in Paris, in 1933, when he was eighty. Kokovtsov succeeded Pyotr Stolypin as Chairman of the Council of Ministers after Stolypin's assassination in 1911 and then to 1914 served as Russia's fourth Prime Minister (*See a photograph of Kokovtzov on page 168*).

The soup of memoirs does offer another layer for understanding Nicholas II. His weakness, his uncaring undertone, all come from the testimony of others, analysing a man that left virtually nothing of his thoughts on paper aside from his diaries and the letters to his wife and mother. In *Nicholas II - Tsar to Saint,* I argue that he could not have been unaffected by the suffering he saw around him, but there is also an acceptance that by his hand a lot of suffering was allowed and even promoted by him. I refute that he was as weak as is generally attributed to him, and that he was solely responsible for everything that happened.

The Revolutionary movement grew from the great famine of 1891-92, and took the form of the Socialist Revolutionaries that formed in 1901, which was the root of the terrorism war against the tsarist regime and the Government. The other manifestation of socialism was the Marxist movement that Karl Marx himself described as the 'class struggle'. Indeed, Marx predicted that the lower class, which he described as the 'proletariat', inevitably would rise up and the revolution would replace the status quo with socialism which in due course would become communism, in which every citizen functions at their optimum efficiency for the benefit of the greater commune.

Had the authorities taken heed of the many signs, or even considered the Marxist rule book that the revolutionaries were following, then perhaps socialism in its guises could have been quashed before it became a greater threat. Instead, the Marxists organised outside of Russia until Russia became ripe for ambush.

* * *

LIST OF ILLUSTRATIONS

All the additional images used for this volume are rights free, in the public domain, and were sourced from either Wikimedia or Yandex LLC.

A. A. Mossolov
Head of the Court Chancellery

PAGE

Cover A. Mossolov; F. Youssoupoff; P. Bykov
4   Nicholas II portrait, courtesy from the book The Romance of the Romanoffs by Joseph McCabe, published in 1917
13   Newspaper clipping about the Youssoupoff libel action, 1934
19   A. Mossolov with Sir George Truscott
20   The Emperoro Nicholas II in the uniform of the Hussars
25   Count Adolf Freederiksz standing portrait
26   Nicholas II on horseback
47   Nicholas II reading to Tatiana, 1913

ILLUSTRATIONS

51	Tsarina (and Empress) Maria Feodorovna, 1894
59	Print of the Hodynka Field tragedy, 1896
64	Drawings of Gerard Encause and Philippe Nazier
66	Empress Alexandra Feodorovna
68	The four grand duchesses
69	The Cesarevitch Alexei rowing
85	Grand Duke Michael Nicolaevitch
106	Grand Duchess Marie Pavlovna
164	Alexander Protopopov
164	Alexander Trepov
168	Vladimir Kokovtzov, Prime Minister (1911-1914)
215	Count Nicholas Sumarokov-Elston, tennis champion
215	Nicholas II, playing tennis
228	Nicholas II with his hunting team at Beloviezha
231	Maurice Paléologue, French ambassador to Russia
235	Front pages of Rasputin by Prince Youssoupoff
236	Frontispiece of Prince Youssoupoff's book
236	Newspaper clipping of headline about youssoupoff book
260	Rasputin
278	Tseravich Alexis with his tutors
309	Triptych of Rasputin's assassins; Dmitri Pavlovich, Vladimir Purishkevich and Sergei Sukhotin
314	Grand Duke Nikolai Nikolaivich of Russia
322	Rasputin with arm across midriff
329	Print of Purishkevich shooting Rasputin in the back
337	Newspaper portrait of Dr Stanislaus Lazovert
342	Photo Portrait of alexander Mikhailovich
342	Photo portrait of Theodore Alexandrovich
349	Anna Vyrubova, c1905
356	Gand Duke Dmitri Pavlovich
357	Photo portrait of Oswald Rayner
383	Photo of Nicholas II, head and shoulders
386	Mr and Mrs Youssoupoff onboard HMS Marlborough
387	Front pages of Pavel Bykov's book, 1934
388	Pavel Bykov chair portrait
409	Photos of Andrew Rothstein
503	Alexander Mossolov, Head of the Court Chancellery

* * *

REFERENCING

The mostly Latin referencing terms used in this volume in text and footnotes are explained below.

— *Generalissimo* is a military rank of the highest degree that is superior to a British Field Marshal and an American Five-Star General.

— *Verst* (plural versts) is an obsolete Russian unit of distance measuring 3,500ft, which is just over 1 kilometre (i.e. 1.0668 km). Similar to the Old English, a West Germanic language, 'Velt', to mean a field. The Russian word was in use from the mid-16th Century originating from the East Slavic language, which had perhaps adopted the variation from the Dutch word 'veld', meaning a field (feld in the Old English) to describe open land; both English and Dutch being derivative languages from the proto-Germanic.

— *Née* originally meant 'born'. In academic notation it denotes the 'former' name of a married woman, the name she was 'born'

— Etc. (an abbreviation of et cetera : et=and ; cetera=the rest) to denote that further items are included in a given list of examples.

— . . . (ellipsis - plural ellipses) are punctuation used to mark the omission of words or to present a pause or imply that something has been left unsaid.

— *Ibid* (an abbreviation of ibidem) is used to save space when the same source was previously used and means 'from the same source' or 'in the same place'. If the source differs from the previous citation then Ibid is not appropriate and the original source is repeated in full.

— *Op. cit.* (an abbreviation of opere citato) is used to cite the work from which the item is taken, 'in the work cited.'

N.B. (nota bene). Ibid cites the source of something that has previously been mentioned, whereas op. cit. usually includes the name of an author and page number, that has not necessarily been previously cited or that is separate from the work previously cited.

FURTHER READING

Books that are in the public domain (PD) are copyright free, being that 70 years have expired since the death of the author, and can be downloaded from online archives.

Internet Archive: https://archive.org/
Project Gutenberg: https://gutenberg.org/

The Murder of the Romanovs
by Captain Paul Bulygin
Pub: New York 1935
Robert M. McBride & Company
Pages: 286, B&W

The Mad Monk of Russia
by Iliodor
Pub: 1918 / PD: Internet Archive

The Kaiser's Memoirs
by Wilhelm II
(Emperor of Germany 1888-1918)
English translation
Pub: 1922
PD: Internet Archive

The End of The Romanovs
by Victor Alexandrov
Publisher: Hutchinson & Co Ltd
Pub: 1966

Rasputin The Untold Story
by Joseph T. Fuhrmann
Pub: 2012

Memories from Moscow to the Black Sea
by Teffi
Translated Pub: 2016

From Autocracy to Bolshevism
by Baron P. Graevenitz
Pub: 1918 / PD: Internet Archive

The Last Days of the Romanovs
by George Gustav & Robert Wilton
Pub: 1920 / PD: Project Gutenberg

Once a Grand Duchess
Xenia Sister of Nicholas II
by John Van der Kiste and Coryne Hall
Pub: 2007

The Emperor Nicholas II
as I knew him
by Major-General Sir John Hanbury-Williams
Pub: 1922
PD: Internet Archive

Upheaval
by Olga Kleinmichel Woronoff (wife of Pavel Voronov)

An Ambassador's memoirs
Vol 1 (July 1914-June 2nd, 1915)
by Maurice Paléologue
(Last French ambassador to the Russian Court)
Pub: 1925 / PD: Internet Archive

LIST OF NAMES

NOBLES

Nikolai Alexandrovitch (Nicholas II Tsar of Russia)
Emperor Alexander III (Nicholas II's father)
Emperor Alexander II (Nicholas II's grandfather)
Empress Alexandra Feodorovna (Alix Victoria Helen Louise Beatrice of Hesse-Darmstadt)
Alexis Nicolayevitch (Son of Nicholas II and Cesarevitch)
Grand Duchess Irina Alexandrovna (Daughter of GD Xenia)
Grand Duchess Xenia Alexandrovna (Daughter of Alexander III)
Grand Duke George Alexandrovitch (Nicholas II's brother)
Grand Duke Michael Alexandrovitch (Nicholas II's brother)
Grand Duke Alexander Alexandrovitch (Nicholas II's brother)
Grand Duke Alexis Alexandrovitch (Son of Alexander II and uncle to Nicholas II)
Grand Duke Paul Alexandrovitch (Nicholas II's paternal uncle) Married to Princess Olga Paley
Grand Duke Sergei Alexandrovich (also Sergei) (Uncle to Nicholas II and husband to GD Elizabeth Feodorovna)
Grand Duke Vladimir Alexandrovitch (Son of Alexander II and an uncle to Nicholas II)
Grand Duke Dimitri Pavlovitch (Son of GD Paul of Russia and grandson on Alexander II – One of the Rasputin assassins)
Grand Duke Nicholas Nicolayevitch (The younger – Son of Nicholas Nicolayvitch the elder and grandson of Nicholas I – first cousin removed to Nicholas II) Commander of the Hussar Guards Regiment and head of the Caucasus, later commander of Russian forces in World War I. Although he was a military man for much of his life, his inexperience at commanding large numbers of troops in part was responsible for the massacre at the Battle of Tannenberg.
Kaiser Wilhelm II (German Emperor and the last king of Prussia)
Grand Duchess Elizabeth Feodorovna (Sister to the Empress)
Dowager Empress Marie Feodorovna (Nicholas II's mother) Princess of Denmark.
Grand Duchess Victoria Feodorovna (Sister to the Empress)
Grand Duchess Marie Pavlovna (Aunt to Nicholas II and sister of GD Dmitri Pavlovitch)
Sheremetyevskaya, Countess Natalia Sergeyevna (Married as her third husband, Grand Duke Michael Alexandrovich and became known as Countess Brasova)

LIST OF NAMES

Princess Olga Paley (The morganatic second wife of GD Paul Alexandrovich) Born Countess Olga Karnovitsch Paley of Hohenfelsen, then on her first marriage she was Olga von Pistohlkors. Her second marriage was to Paul Aleksandrovich of Russia

Grand Duke Peter Nicolayevitch (Son of Nicholas Nicolayvitch the elder and grandson of Nicholas I)

Queen Alexandra (Queen consort of England, wife of King Edward VII)

Prince Nicholas I of Montenegro (The nation's only King) He was a prince from 1860 to 1910 and king from 1910 to 1918.

Grand Duke Cyril Vladimirovich (aka Kirill) Son of GD Vladimir Alexandrovitch and grandson of Alexander II. A cousin to Nicholas II.

Princess Catherine Yurievskaya (Morganatic wife of alexander II) Before her marriage she was called Princess Dolgorukaya.

Grand Duke Michael Nicolayevitch (Son of Nicholas I and brother of Alexander II)

Grand Duke Konstantin Nikolayevich (Second son of Nicholas I)

Grand Duchess Alexandra Iossifovna (Wife to GD Konstantin Nikolayevich) Formerly Princess of Saxe-Altenburg.

Grand Duke Nicholas Constantinovitch (Son of Konstantin Nikolayevich)

Grand Duke Constantine Constantinovitch (Son of Konstantin Nikolayevich)

Grand Duke Dimitri Constantinovitch (Son of Konstantin Nikolayevich)

Princess Victoria Melita of Edingburgh (A granddaughter of Queen Victoria of Britain and Emperor Alexander II of Russia) Born a British Princess, she was ostracised after her first marriage to her first cousin Ernest Louis of Hesse and by Rhine, and exiled after her second marriage to GD Cyril Vladimirovich of Russia without first receiving royal approvals from Edward VII and Nicholas II.

Prince Vladimir Pavlovich Paley (A poet) He was killed by the Bolsheviks when he was just 21 years old.

Grand Duke Michael Michailovitch (Son of Nicholas I. Brother to Alexander II.)

Grand Duke Nicholas Michailovitch (Eldest son of GD Michael Nikolaevich.)

Grand Duke Alexander Michailovitch (Son of GD Michael Nikolaevich. Husband to GD Xenia Alexandrovna)

Grand Duke George Michailovitch (Son of Nicholas I. Brother to Alexander II.)

Baroness Sophie von Buxhoeveden (Lady in waiting)

Countess Anastasia Vasilyevna Hendrikova (Lady in waiting)

LIST OF NAMES

Grand Duke Serge Michailovitch (Son of Nicholas I. Brother to Alexander II.)
Grand Duchess Hélene Vladimirovna (Daughter of GD Vladimir Alexandrovitch)
Grand Duchess Alexandra Georgievna of Russia (Mother to GD Dmitri Pavlovitch) Formerly Princess Alexandra of Greece and Denmark.

COURT OFFICIALS
(N.B. A Maid of honour is a junior position of a Lady in waiting)

Count Vladimir Borisovich Freedericksz (aka Frederiks) (anglicised; Adolf Andreas Woldemar) (Minister of the Imperial Court) He was a Finno-Russian statesman serving Nicholas II from 1897 to 1917. At the outbreak of the February Revolution 1917, his estate was attacked but he managed to avoid execution based on his testament that he was neither for or against the Tsar, and was just performing a job. He stayed on in Petrograd until 1925 when he was permitted to move to Finland. He died in 1927.
Count Alexander Alexandrovitch Mossolov (Minister of the Court)
Count Rostovtzev (Private secretary to Empress Alexandra Feodorovna)
Mr Charles Heath English language and life tutor to Nicholas II
Mr Stcheglow Librarian to Nicholas II
Doctor Gustav Ivanovich Hirsch (Personal physician to Emperor Alexander III) A graduate the Imperial Medical-Surgical Academy, he was appointed to then Tsarevich in 1866 and looked after the Emperor throughout his reign. Uncle to German tutor Ekaterina Schreider.
Princess E Obolenskaya (Maid of honour)
Mlle A. Olenina (Maid of honour)
Princess Marie Victorovna Bariatinskaya (Maid of honour)
Mme Elizaveta Alekseevna Naryshkin (Mistress of the Robes from 1910 to 1917) She was the eldest daughter of Prince Kurakin and Princess Golitsyn, two princely Russian houses – The House of Kurakin descending from Lithuanian roots.
M. Crozier (Chief of Protocol)
Mme Anna Vyrubova (Lady in waiting)
Prince Alexey Vasilyevich Obolensky (Head of the private office and previously the General in charge of the Moscow Governorate from 1861 to 1866)
Count Pavel Benckendorff (Marshal of the Court)
Countess Maria Nirod (Maid of honour)

LIST OF NAMES

Princess Vera Guedroytz (Head physician at Tsarskoe Selo hospital) The first female surgeon in Russia
Princess Sonia Orbehani (Maid of honour)
Monsieur Pierre Gilliard (Swiss tutor for French to Tsarevich Alexei)
Catherine Adolfovna Schneider (aka Ekaterina) Tutor for German to the Court.
Professor Pyotr Vasilievich Petrov (Russian tutor to Tsarevich Alexei)
Mlle Sofya Ivanovna Tuytcheva (aka Tyutcheva) Granddaughter of the Russian poet and politician Fyodor Ivanovich Tyutchev. Maid of honour to the Empress from 1896 and governess to the Grand Duchesses from 1907, she was exiled to Siberia in 1912 for her opposition to Rasputin.
Mme Marie von Flotow (Confidante to Maria Feodorovna and Lady in waiting to Alexandra Feodorovna) She was very influential at court and her role was to look after the Empresses jewels, wardrobe, and financial matters.
Major-General Vladimir Nikolaevich Voyeikov (Palace Commandant at the residence of Nicholas II in Tsarskoe Selo following the death of General Dediulin)
General V. N. Dediulin A. D. C. (Governor-General of St Petersburg and Palace Commandant at the residence of Nicholas II in Tsarskoe Selo)
Count Illarion Ivanovich Vorontzov-Dashkov (Minister of Imperial Properties from 1881 to 1897 – Full General of Cavalry and in charge of the Russian Caucasus Army)
Countess Elizabeth Andreevna Shouvalova (Married to Count Illarion Ivanovich Vorontsov-Dashkov)
Prince Vassily Alexandrovich Dolgorukov (General A. A. Mossolov's son-in-law. Marshal of the Court 1914 to 1917)
Count Rostovtzev (The Empress's private secretary)
Princess Maria Mikhaylovna Galitzin, née Pashkova (Mistress of the Robes from 1894 until her death in 1910)
Mlle Mary Vasiltchikova (Maid of honour)
Baron Meyendorf (Director of the Court balls)
Evgeny Sergeevich Botkin (Eugene) (Court physician) Born in Tsarskoe Selo the fourth child of a large family.
General Laiming (Grand Duke Dmitri Pavlovich's former tutor)
Adjutant-General Ilya Leonidovich Tatischev (Adjutant to Nicholas II) He followed Nicholas II during house arrest and was also murdered by the Bolsheviks and canonised by the Russian Orthodix Church.
Mlle Evreinovaone (Lady in waiting to GD Xenia Alexandrovna)
Marie Vassilchikova (Lady-in- waiting)

LIST OF NAMES

Konstantin Petrovich Pobedonostsev (Advisor to Nicholas II and Chief advisor to Alexander III) During his service for Alexander II he oversaw the education of Nicholas II which predisposed him to a harsh political outlook.

Sydney Gibbs (aka Gibbes)(English tutor)

Mme Elizaveta Ersberg (chambermaid)

Terenty Chemadurov (Nicholas II' valet from 1908) He resided with the Tsar. Under house arrest with the ex-Imperial Family he was separated at Ekaterinburg and imprisoned nearby. Fortunately in the confusion he was forgotten about and survived the Bolsheviks. He remains a vital witness of those times, although noted this would be limited due to his incarceration.

Ivan Dmitrievich Sednev (A sailor in the Russian Imperial Navy) He served on the Imperial Yacht Standart as the personal aide of the Imperial children and went in to exile with the family, under house arrest in Siberia. He and another sailor, Klimenty Grigorievich Nagorny, were killed by the Bolsheviks just under three weeks before the murders of the Imperial Family.

Leonid Ivanovich Sednev (Kitchen boy) Son of Ivan Dmitrievich Sednev. His life was spared by the Bolsheviks.

Klimenty Grigorievich Nagorny (A sailor in the Russian Imperial Navy) He served on the Imperial Yacht Standart.

Ivan Mikhailovich Haritonov (The chief cook for the Imperial household) He was one of the aides that followed the ex-Imperial Family in to exile and was murdered by the Bolsheviks.

Alexei Trunp (aka Trupp) (Valet to Nicholas II) He was one of the aides that followed the ex-Imperial Family in to exile and was murdered by the Bolsheviks.

Doctor Vladimir Nikolaevich Derevenko (Court physician assigned as the personal physician to Tsarevich Alexei from 1912). His son Koyla was a friend of the Tsarevich visiting him during his house arrest. He was the only aide that followed the Imperial Family to Ekaterinburg that was permitted to continue his practice without being executed, however, the soviet Union did execute him in 1936 during the Great Purge; i.e. Stalin's terror campaign to solidify his power by eliminating his enemies.

POLITICAL

President Émile Loubet (French President from 1899 to 1906)

Count Sergei Yulyevich Witte (Prime Minister)

Count Vladimir Nikolayevich Lamsdorff (Foreign Minister)

LIST OF NAMES

Pierre Marie René Waldeck-Rousseau (French President from 1899 to 1902)

Count Alexander Petrovich Isvolsky (Foreign Minister May 1906 to October 1910) He was a noble in his own right and through his wife Countess Marguerite von Toll had connections with the Imperial Court which is how he came to be at the Foreign Office. Having a rather successful political career as a Russian ambassador ranging from the Vatican to Tokyo, he is, perhaps unfairly, remembered for inviting a Japanese delegation to St Petersburg leading up to the Russo-Japanese War, for which he fell on the wrong side of Nicholas II, and in 1907 he finalised the Russo-Japanese peace agreement, being another unpopular event. His handling of the Turkish Straits issue led to some political embarrassment personally and for Russia and for which he resigned his post.

Count Friedrich Pourtalés (German ambassador to Russia 1907 to 1914) He came from a family of Swiss bankers and whose family members also held prominent positions in the Prussian government, not least his cousin who was the German Chancellor between 1907 to 1917.

Ivan Goremykin (Two times Prime Minister; 1906 and 1914 to 1916)

Sergey Andreyevich Muromtsev (The first Chairman of the State Duma)

General Vaimovsky (Minister of Education and a former Minister of War)

General Dmitri Feodorovich Trepov (aka Trefoff) (Head of the Moscow police. Governor-General of St. Petersburg) General A. A. Mossolov's brother-in-law.

Alexander Fyodorovich Trepov (Prime Minister from November 1916 to January 1917)

Pyotr Arkadyevich Stolypin (Interior Minister and Prime Minister) Assassinated in 1911.

Mikhail Vladimirovich Rodzianko (Chairman of the State Duma) General A. A. Mossolov's uncle.

Prince Nikolai Dmitriyevich Golitzin (Last Prime Minister of Imperial Russia who succeeded Alexander Trepov and resigned before the establishment of the Provisional Government in February 1917)

Alexander Dmitrievich Protopopov (Minister of Interior)

General Vladimir Fyodorovich Dzhunkovski (Governor-General of Moscow from 1908 to 1913. Vice-Minister of the Interior 1913.)

LIST OF NAMES

Aleksandr Aleksandrovich Makarov (Interior Minister from 1911 to 1912 and Justice Minister in 1916)
M. Galkin (The Deputy Public Prosecutor)
Colonel Konstantin Ivanovich Globachev (Chief of the Okhrana secret police in Petrograd)
Captain Ignatiev (Assistant-Director of the Okhrana secret police)
Vyacheslav von Plehve (Minister of Interior from 1902 to 1904)
General Alexei Andreyvich Polivanov (Minister of War from 1915 to 1916) His memoirs are considered as important as A. A. Mossolov's.
Fyodor Aleksandrovich Golovin (President of the Second Duma)
Pavel Nikolayevich Miliukov (Historian. Foreign Minister in the Provisional Grovernment)
Alexander Ivanovich Guchkov (Octobrist/Liberal leader and Chairman of the Third Duma)
Vasily Vitalyevich Shulgin (Right Wing Duma member)
Aleksandr Aleksandrovich Bublikov (Duma member)
Maurice Paléologue (French ambassador to Russia from 1914 to 1917. Historian)
Prince Georgy Lvov (First Prime Minister of the Russian Republic from March to July 1917)
Alexander Feodorovitch Kerensky (Lawyer. Head of the Provisional Government during the Russian Republic from July to November 1917)
Alexander Krivoshein (Politican) Led the White movement government in Crimea during the Civil War)

MILITARY (A.D.C. : aide-de-camp)

General Vassilkovsky (A.D.C.)
General G. G. Danilovitch, a Jesuit and teacher to Nicholas II
General Radko Dimitriev, Head of the General Staff of the Bulgarian Army from 1 January 1904 to 28 March 1907
General Aleksey Nikolayevich Kuropatkin (Minister of War from January 1898 to February 1904) Respectfully referred to by the title Generalissimo, but considered by some historians to be largely responsible for the loss of the Battle of Mukden in Manchuria.
General Nikolai Yanushkevitch (Chief of Staff of the General Staff - August 1914 to September 1915)
Adjutant General Alexander Petrovich Strukov (A.D.C.)

LIST OF NAMES

General Mikhail Vasilyevich Alexeyev (Commander in Chief of the southwestern and northwestern fronts) When Nicholas II went to the front and relieved GD Nicolayevitch from overall command, General Alexeyev was placed in charge at the Stavka in charge of all operations from August 1915. He was suspended from command by Nicholas II in the Summer of 1916 and resumed in March 1917 after the tsar's abdication, and resigned in May 1917.

Count Mikhail Loris-Melikov (General of the Cavalry)

Admiral Konstantin Dmitrievich Nilov (Flag Captain for Nicholas II) He married in to a noble family, Mariamna Kotchoubei, the daughter of Prince Mikhail Kotchoubei and Maid of honour to Marie of Hesse and by Rhine – Alexander II's empress consort.

General Richter (A.D.C.)

Prince Dmitry Ivanovich Shakhovskoy (Minister of Commerce. Member of the First State Duma)

Count Vladimir Kokovtzov (Minister of Finance. Prime Minister of Russia from 1911 to 1914)

General Hesse (A.D.C.)

Captain Tchaguin (Commanding Officer of HIY Standard)

Rear-Admiral Lomen (Flag Captain for Nicholas II)

General Vladimir Aleksandrovich Sukhomlinov (Minister of War from 1909 to 1915)

Captain Sergei Mikhailovich Sukhotin (Preobrazhensky Regiment)

General Nikolai Vladimirovich Russki (Commander of the Third Army and the Northwestern Front during World War I)

General Nikolai Baratov (Commander of the Persian Division)

Doctor Stanislaus de Lazovert (Military physician)

General Nikolay Bobrikov (Governor of Finland) He was appointed in 1898. Given full powers for Russification to quell uprisings and was assassinated in 1904.

General Mikhail Konstantinovich Dieterichs (A Chief of Staff of the third Army who later became more prominent during the Civil War for the White Army.)

General Habalov (Commander of the Petrograd Military District)

General Larv Georgiyevich Kornilov (Remembered for the Kornilov Affair, an attempt to assert the Kerensky Government but which was interpreted by Kerensky as a coup d'état)

Colonel Eugene Kobylinsky (Commander of the guard at Tsarskoe Selo during Nicholas II's house arrest)

LIST OF NAMES

General Maximovich (A.D.C.)

Lieutenant Sheremetevsky (White Army officer working undercover behind Red Army lines) The inspection of the mines at Ganina Yama near the village of Koptyaki was given to Lieutenant Colonel Igor Baftalovsky; Sheremetevsky was assigned prisoners of war to pump the water out of the pits.

Admiral Alexander Kolchak (White Army leader and self appointed Admiral.) He ruled Serbia from 1918 to 1920 and was eventually handed over by the Czech legion to advancing Red Army troops, whereupon he was executed and his body dumped in a river.

REVOLUTIONARY

Doctor Alexander Ivanovich Dubrovin (Leader of the URP – Union of the Russian People's party) Dr. Dubrovin gave up being a doctor to pursue a political career representing the right wing element. He personally arranged the pogroms that were carried out by their military arm the Black Hundred.

Alexander Georgiyevich Beloborodov (Chairman of the Council of the Ural Soviet Army)

Leon Trotsky (A central revolutionary and Marxist writer) He was a leading figure at the Treaty of Brest-Litovsk, during the October Revolution and in the Civil War. By 1940 he had positioned himself on opposite poles with Lenin and was assassinated. His literary contribution is extensive and includes 'Trotskyism', a political ideology aligned with Marxism.

Marie Spiridonova (Soviet official from Sverlov's office) She arrived in Ekaterinburg on behalf of the Central Committee of the Left Socialist-Revolutionaries to arrange a trial for Nicholas II for crimes against humanity to be prosecuted by Leon Trotsky.

Yakov Mikhailovich Yurovsky (Bolshevik and Cheka official) A member of the Presidium of the Regional Extraordinary Commission and Commandant of Ipatiev House. He was the main organiser of the murder squad that killed the Romanovs.

G. P. Nikulin (Yakov Yurovsky's Second-in-Command)

Vladimir Dmitrievich Bonch-Bruyevitch (Chief of the Secretariat of the Council of People's Commissaries and personal Secretary to Vladimir Lenin)

Pavel Malkov (Chairman of the Extraordinary Commission, i.e. Cheka)

OTHER NOTABLES

Prince Vladimir Mestchersky (Editor of the weekly paper Grashdanin) The Grashdanin (The Citizen) was a conservative newspaper that Tsar Nicholas II read daily. Mestchersky also authored several novels as well as memoirs.

Sir John Collins Squire (British writer. Editor of the London Mercury)

Doctor Hagberg Wright (Writer and longest serving librarian of the British Library from 1893 to 1940)

Seargei Mstislavsky (In charge of the Semenovsky Regiment) Later writer, 'Five Days which Transformed Russia'.

Julia Alexandrovna Den (aka Lily Dehn) Friend of Elexandra Feodorovna.

Philipp Isayevich Goloshchekin (People's Commisar for Military Affairs on the Urals. Bolshevik in the Soviet responsible for overseeing Nicholas II's house arrest in Ekaterinburg) At the establishment of the Soviet Union in 1922, he was promoted to the Executive Committee of the Communist Party.

Vasily Vasilyevich Yakovlev (Bolshevik terrorist) Responsible for transferring Nicholas II under house arrest from Tobols to Ekaterinburg.

Brusiatsky (Vasily Yakovlev's second-in-command)

Dovid Iosifovich Zaslavsky (Journalist) At first he was opposed to the Bolsheviks but turned to their cause becoming an ardent supporter and prominent Bolshevik himself.

Yakov Mikhailovich Sverdlov (Bolshevik Chairman of the Soviet Executive Committee from 1917 to his death in 1919).

Robert Archibald Wilton (British journalist from Norfolk) He was a biased right-wing antisemite reporter for The 'London' Times, the New York Herald and the Paris Times, mostly through the later part of Nicholas II's reign. He escaped Russia and ended up in Paris with the Russian emigres that were settling there in the early 1920s. His main works were Russia's Agony (1918) and 'The Last Days of the Romanovs (1920).

Nikolai Alexandrovich Sokolov (Lawyer in Omsk) He was the lead investigator for the White Army following the murders of the ex-Imperial Family and their aides.

INDEX OF NAMES

A

Alexander II, (The Liberator), 23, 36, 81, 88-89, 183, 219, 398
Alexander III, Emperor, 23-27, 36, 57-58, 78, 81, 83, 86, 101, 106, 108, 142-143, 173, 198, 202, 209-210, 242, 245, 249, 398
Alexandrovitch, Alexander, 150
Alexandrovitch, Alexis, 89
Alexandrovitch, George, 27
Alexandrovitch, Michael, 80-81, 101, 103, 417, 419, 424, 437, 492
Alexandrovitch, Nicholas (aka Emperor Nicholas II), 27-28, 57-58, 136, 142, 442, 498
Alexandrovitch, Paul, 8, 90, 103, 427, 445, 479, 483, 495
Alexandrovich, GD Sergei, 356
Alexandrovitch, Vladimir, 86
Alexandrovna, Empress Marie, 23
Alexandrovna, Princess Irina, 266
Alexandrovna, GD Xenia, 9, 100, 353
Alexeyev, General Mikhail Vasilyevich, (aka Alexeiev) 43, 385, 427-428,
Alvensleben, Count von, 234
Andronnikov, Prince M. M., 142, 157-160

B

Balk, General, 347
Baratov, General Nikolai, 375
Bariatinskaya, Princess Marie Victorovna, 49
Beloborodov, Alexander Georgiyevich,
Benckendorff, Dmitry, 403
Benckendorff, Count Pavel Konstantinovich, 60, 122, 201, 203, 206, 208, 403, 430-431, 433
Bezobrazova, Princess, 118
Bobrikov, General Nikolay, 399
Bojechich, Seargent-Major, 484
Bonch-Bruyevitch, Vladimir Dmitrievich, 492
Borunov, M. (chauffeur), 493
Botkin, Doctor Evgeny Sergeevich, 125-126, 146, 300-301, 433, 438, 462-463, 472, 480, 487
Brainitsky, M., 476
Brassov, Count, (aka George Mikhailovich), 102
Brassova, Countess, 493
Brusiatsky, M., 469, 473, 475-476
Bublikov, Aleksandr Aleksandrovich, 422-423
Büllow, Prince Bernhard von, 188-189
Bulyguin, M., 134
Buxhoeveden, Baroness Sophie von, 433

C

Chelyshev, M. (valet), 493
Chemadurov, Terenty, (valet), 472
Chkheidze, M., 419, 426, 429
Crozier, M., 52-53
Cyril, GD (aka Kirill), 80, 67-88, 99, 102, 447
Constantinovitch, GD Nicholas, 92
Constantinovitch, GD Constantine, 92-93
Constantinovitch, GD Dimitri, 92, 94, 224

D

Danilovitch, General G. G., 27-29
Dediulin, General V. N., 123
Demidova, Princess Anna Lopukhina-Demidova, 174
Den, Julia Alexandrovna (aka Lily von Dehn and Mme Denn), 17, 127, 450
Derevenko, Dr. Vladimir nikolaevich, 67 126 223 388 480 484
Didkovsky, V. B., 465
Dieterichts, General, 388, 405, 461, 463-464, 484-486, 498-499
Dimitriev, General Radko, 36-37
Dolgorukaya, Princess Catherine, (see Yurievskaya)

INDEX

Dolgorukov, Prince Vassily Alexandrovich, 122-123, 431, 433, 438, 454-455, 472
Dratchevsky, General, 393
Dubrovin, Alexander, (doctor), 140-141, 394
Dutzman, V. A., 464, 467
Dzhunkovski, General Vladimir Fyodorovich, 267

E

Edward VII of England, 400
Encausse, Gérard (see Papus), 8, 63-64
Ersberg, Mme Elizaveta, 443
Evreinovaone, Mlle, 353

F

Freedericksz, Count Adolf Andreas, (also spelled Frederiks), 19, 25, 28-29, 34, 43-44, 48-53, 54-56, 60, 72-74, 78, 84, 87, 97, 103-105, 107-121, 123-124, 126-127, 134, 140-143, 150-151, 155-160, 170-174, 180, 188, 194, 206-208, 219, 224-226, 229-232, 420, 433
Francis II, Grand Duke Frederick, 106
Feodorovna, Alexandra (also Empress) 8, 48, 55-60, 65-66, 73, 106, 123, 175, 183, 187, 244-245, 247, 249, 265, 347, 359-360, 362, 413, 421, 426-427, 435, 452, 461, 471, 479
Feodorovna, Princess Elizabeth, 50, 53, 73, 90, 242, 265, 311, 320, 338, 356, 360, 483, 494-495, 499
Feodorovna, Maria (aka Marie), 51-52, 77-78, 82, 102, 245, 266, 395, 448, 461
Feodorovna, GD Victoria, 55, 102
Flotow, Mme Marie von, 78

G

Galitzin, Prince Leo Lvovich, 210
Galitzin, Princess Maria Mikhaylovna, 173-174
Galkin, M., 367

Georgievna, GD Alexandra, 356
General Vassilkovsky, A.D.C., 26, 27
Gibbs, Charles Stanley, 433, 455
Gilliard, M. (i.e. Pierre Gilliard), 67, 73, 278, 405, 433, 436-438, 444, 455, 459-460, 464, 470-471
Globachev, Colonel Konstantin Ivanovich, 364-365
Golitzin, Prince Nikolai Dmitriyevich (aka Galitzin), 164, 173, 417-418
Goloshchekin, Philip Isayevich (aka Filipp), 465, 467-468, 482, 488-489
Golovin, Fyodor Aleksandrovich, 486
Golovina, Mlle, 150
Goremykin, Ivan (Prime Minister), 137
Guchkov, Alexander Ivanovich, 420-426
Guedroytz, Princess Vera (aka Gedroits), 64

H

Habalov, General, 418
Haritonov, Ivan Mikhailovich, 480
Heath, Charles, 26, 143
Hendrikova, Countess Anastasia Vasilyevna, 433, 455, 480
Hermogenes, Bishop of Tobolsk, 17-18, 447-451, 460-461
Hesse, General, 122, 219
Heyden, Count, 110, 123
Hirsch, Doctor Gustav Ivanovich, 49, 62, 73, 125, 219
Hochriakov, N. (A sailor), 467-469
Homiakov, M., (3rd Duma President), 402

I

Ignatiev, Captain, 375
Iossifovna, GD Alexandra, 86
Isvolsky, Count Alexander Petrovich, 113-114, 188

J

Jaguelsky, (court photographer, 74-75
Johnson, N. (Secretary), 492-493

INDEX

K

Karageorgevitch, Prince, 118
Kerensky, Alexander Feodorovitch, 8, 404, 424, 426, 428, 433, 435-438, 442-443
Kobylinsky, Colonel Eugene, 437, 441, 444, 452, 454-456, 458, 470
Kolchak, Admiral Alexander, 479, 498-500
Kornilov, General Larv Georgiyevich, 429-430, 441
Kokovtzov, Count Vladimir, 166, 168
Korjenevsky, Stanislas, 452
Koshnev, M. (engineer), 498
Kotchubey, Prince, 114, 209, 227, 233
Kotchubey, Princess, 176
Krivoshein, Alexander, 460, 472
Kurlov, M., 299, 414-415
Kuropatkin, General Aleksey Nikolayevich, 41, 393, 402-403

L

Lamsdorff, Count Vladimir Nikolayevich, 30, 188-189, 403
Lazovert, Doctor Stanislaus de, 9, 12, 308, 318, 331, 336-338, 348
Laiming, General, 364, 369, 375
Lomen, Rear-Admiral, 221
Loris-Melikov, Count Mikhail, 84
Loubet, President Émile, 52-53
Ludwig, GD Ernst, 403
Lvov, Prince Georgy, 424, 426, 428, 435, 447

M

Makarov, Aleksandr Aleksandrovich, 168, 351-352, 438, 441
Maklakov, Vasily, 306-307, 309, 333, 413-414
Malkov, Pavel, 493
Markov II, 18 450-451 462
Matveyev, 2nd Lieutenant A., 454-455, 479
Matveyev, P. M., 443, 477

Maximovich, General, 359-360, 364, 375
Mdivani, Mme Elizabeth Victorovna, 150-153, 155
Medvediev, P., 499
Melita, Princess Victoria, 87, 102
Mestchersky, Prince Vladimir Petrovich, 142, 173
Meyendorf, Baron, 183, 212
Michailovitch, GD Michael, (Junior) 100, 104
Michailovitch, GD Nicholas, 44, 99-100, 104
Michailovitch, GD Alexander, 100
Michailovitch, GD George, 100
Michailovitch, GD Serge, 101
Michich, Major, 848
Miliukov, Pavel Nikolayevich, 414-415
Mstislavsky, Sergei, 429-430
Muromtsev, Sergey Andreyevich, 137, 400

N

Nagorny, Klimenty Grigorievich, 480
Naryshkin, Mme Elizaveta Alekseevna, 52-53, 75, 123-124, 126-127, 194-195
Nicolayevitch, GD Michael, 84-85, 92
Nicolayevitch, GD Nicholas
(aka Nikolai Nikolaevich), 42-45, 58, 92, 95, 99, 103, 227
Nametkin, Judge Alexander, 497
Nazier, Philippe (mystic), 8, 63-64, 246
Nemtzev, M., 474
Nicholas I, Prince (of Montenegro), 79
Nicolayevitch, GD Peter, 63, 99
Nikulin, G. P., 487
Nilov, Admiral Konstantin Dmitrievich, 123, 187, 208, 219, 223
Nirod, Countess Maria, 60

O

Obolenskaya, Princess E, 49, 62
Obolensky, Prince Alexey, 56
Olenina, Mlle A., 49, 62
Orbehani, Princess Sonia, 67, 71

521

INDEX

Orlov, Prince Vladimir Nikolayevich, 115, 124-125, 156, 225

P

Paleologue, Maurice, 25, 425, 434-435
Paley, Princess Olga, 64, 91
Paley, Prince Vladimir Pavlovich, 495
Pankratov, V. (Commissary), 441-446, 452-454, 456-458
Papkhadze, Lieutenant, 367
Papus, (French physician), 8, 63-64
Pavlovitch, GD Dimitri, 29, 80-81, 103-104,, 413
Pavlovna, Grand Duchess Marie, 44, 59-60, 79, 81, 86, 88-89, 91
Petrov, Professor Pyotr Vasilievich (tutur), 73
Petrovna, Elana (Queen of Serbia), 484
Plehve, Vyacheslav von, 393
Pobedonostsev, Konstantin Petrovich, 398
Polivanov, General Alexei Andreyevich, 396-397
Polovtzev, M., 451
Pourtalés, Count, 119, 230, 276
Protopopov, Alexander Dmitrievich, 161, 163-166, 283-284, 299, 320, 323, 357, 360-361, 367, 369, 375, 415
Purishkevich, Vladimir Mitrofanovich, 9, 14, 306-309, 313, 318, 326, 331, 333-336, 344-345, 347-349, 351, 412-413
Pushkin, Count Mussin, 75
Pushkin, Alexander Sergeyevich (poet), 7

Q

Queen Alexandra, (of England), 78, 192

R

Rasputin, (aka *starets* & *Grigori Efimovich*) 6, 8-15, 17-18, 55, 61-64, 66, 80, 84, 91. 100, 103-104, 121, 123-125. 144-155, 157, 160-167, 248, 254, 261-262, 264-265, 267-273, 277-279, 281, 283-285, 287-293, 295-296, 297, 299-302, 305-306, 311-312, 319-325, 328, 339, 341, 345-346, 355, 359-360, 363, 370, 373
Rasputin, Matriona, 451
Ratchhovsky, M. (detective), 64
Rayner, Oswald, 9-12, 14-16, 337, 354-357
Repnin, Prince, (Master of the Court), 180
Reuss, Princess Augusta (of Köstritz), 106
Richter, General, 143, 394
Rodzianko, Mikhail Vladimirovich, 6, 148, 242, 352, 417, 419, 424, 470
Rostovtzev, Count, 33, 142
Rubinstein, Mitka, 320
Russki, General Nikolai Vladimirovich, 303

S

Safarov, G. N., 465
Schneider, Catherine Adolovna (tutor), 62, 73, 433, 480
Sednev, Ivan Dmitrievich, 472, 480
Sednev, Leonid Ivanovich, 480, 489
Semchevskaya, Mme E., 404, 484
Shakhovskoy, Prince Dmitry Ivanovich, 153, 163
Sherekhovsky, Colonel, 497
Sheremetyevskaya, Countess Natalia Sergueevna, 102, 176
Sheremetevsky, Lieutenant, 497
Shingarev, M., 416,
Shouvalova, Countess Elizabeth Andreevna, 176
Shulgin, Vasily Vitalyevich, 416, 420-424
Skobelev, Matvey Ivanovich, 426
Sokolov, Nikolai Alexandrovich, 405, 418, 425, 427, 433, 443, 450-451, 460, 462, 470, 472, 480-481, 495, 498
Soloviev, Lieutenant, 18, 451-452, 461-463, 495
Spalaikovitch, Minister (Serbian) 484-485, 496
Spiridonova, Marie, 482

INDEX

Squire, John Collins, 392, 401
Sukhomlinov, General Vladimir Aleksandrovich, 30, 211
Sukhotin, Captain, 275, 277, 287, 306-307, 309, 318, 326, 331, 336, 338, 348-349
Shulgin, 416, 421-424
Stcheglov, 47-48
Stolypin, Pyotr Arkadyevich, (Prime Minister), 29, 138-139, 242, 393, 400, 404
Strukov, General Alexander Petrovich, 69, 95-96
Sumarokov-Elston, Count Nicholas, (tennis champion), 215
Sverdlov, Yakov Mikhailovich, 476, 478, 482, 489-490

T

Tatischev, General Ilya Leonidovich, 438, 444, 480
Tchaguin, Captain, 222
Theophan, Bishop, 255,
Tolmachev, N. G., 465
Tolstoi, Count Leo Nikolayevich, (writer), 101
Trepov, Alexander Feodorovich, 29, 160-164, 373, 394, 402
Trepov, Dmitri Feodorovich, 138
Trotsky, Leon, 8, 482
Troubetzkoy, Prince, a sculptor, 24, 208
Trunp, Alexei, (aka Trupp), 480
Tuytcheva, Mlle Sofya Ivanova, 74, 156-157

V

Vaimovsky, General, 135
Vasiltchikova, Mlle Mary, 184
Vassilchikova, Marie, 403
Vassiliev, Father Alexei, 449, 455, 461
Vladimirovna, GD Hélene, 184
Vorontzova, Countess, 174, 176

Vorontzov-Dashkov, Count Illarion Ivanovich, 124-125
Voyeikov, General Vladimir Nikolaevich (aka Voeikov), 115, 122-123, 277-278
Vyrubova, Mme Anna (aka Taneieva), 15, 18, 55-56, 62, 123, 127, 155, 246-248, 250, 269, 283, 289-290, 301, 323, 346, 349, 404, 444, 451, 458, 461-462

W

Wilhelm II, Kaiser, (aka William II) 7, 33, 40, 79, 113-114, 135, 186-192, 195, 226, 229-231, 234, 251, 266, 276, 339
Waldeck-Rousseau, M., 53, 195
Wilton, Robert, (writer), 437, 479, 493, 499, 506
Witte, Count Sergei Yulyevich, 43, 96-98, 101, 140, 142, 151, 396, 399-401
Wright, Doctor Hagberg, 391-392

Y

Yakovlev, Vasily Vasilyevich, 18, 468-69, 470-476, 478-479, 495
Yanushkevitch, General Nikolai, 43, 229
Yevdokimov, Deacon, 449
Youssoupoff, Prince Felix (aka Yussupov), 9, 14, 15, 17, 236, 337, 357, 386, 391, 404.413-414
Youssupova, Princess, 176
Yurievskaya, Princess Catherine, 81-83, 182
Yurovsky, Yakov Mikhailovich, 487, 489

Z

Zaslavsky, Dovid Iosifovich, 18, 468, 473, 465, 478-479
Zenchikov, Captain, 375
Zlobin, M., (Mossolov's deputy) 116

OTHER BOOKS BY THIS AUTHOR

NICHOLAS, II – TSAR TO SAINT
THE RULER THAT LOST A DYNASTY

ebook
ISBN: 978-1-80352-908-0

Paperback
B&W on Groundwood paper
ISBN: 978-1-80352-799-4

Paperback
B&W on Cream paper
ISBN: 979-8-85465-243-8

Hardback
B&W on Groundwood paper
with dust jacket
ISBN: 978-1-80352-911-0

Hardback
B&W on Cream paper
ISBN: 979-8-85221-513-0

From the back cover: 546 absorbing pages

Why was Russia's Imperial Family murdered? What part did they play in the revolution that gave rise to the Bolsheviks and transformed Russian Orthodoxy and State in to the Soviet Union? Tony Abbott takes us back to the pivotal moment in 1894 when Nicholas Alexandrovich Romanov became Tsar and there existed a real opportunity for Russia to modernise and become an industrial power and world leader. This is an incredible story of two rulers very much in love, who unwittingly created the circumstances that collapsed their dynasty.

Through first hand commentaries and with over 200 images, the events around the twenty-three year reign of Nicholas II are presented with clear and acute observations. What emerges is a fascinating insight of the man who made history by helping to bring about the revolution of an empire.

OTHER BOOKS BY THIS AUTHOR

THE MEMORIES OF A RUSSIAN YESTERYEAR VOLUME II
RADZIWILL - DEHN - VYRUBOVA

Coming Soon

Volume II will be available in Ebook, paperback and hardback Formats in a choice of cream or Groundwood paper.

Ebook

Volume II of this packed memoir series from contemporaries around Nicholas II, provides a more intimate perspective of the times. Whereas Volume I described the day to day workings of the Court, the murder of Rasputin and the revealing and widely debated Bolshevik account of the murders of the royal family and their aides, Volume II takes us deeper in to the day to day lives of the people that were in and around palace life.

THE SOCIALITE: Princess Catherine Radziwill wrote under the pen name Paul Vassily and it's clear she was no supporter of the Imperial couple, herself having a somewhat shady past. THE FRIEND: Lily Dehn was not a noble but was liked and respected by the Empress. THE CONFIDANTE: Anna Vyrubova was the trusted person that Alexandra kept close by in her daily affairs, almost like a family member. Yet this Lady-in-waiting was for a time a mole in the camp for Rasputin, in betrayal of the Empress's trust.

OTHER BOOKS BY THIS AUTHOR

SERIES INFORMATION

To complement the main title *Nicholas II - Tsar to Saint*, a selection of memoirs have been presented unabridged taking the form of a set of volumes. Volume I and Volume II will be released in 2023 with more following in 2024. Six total volumes are planned for this series.

All the memoirs in this series are public domain works and can be downloaded individually, free of charge, from online archives. Each work in its own right are a cracking good read and have been brought together to give them a new life; if not for this project perhaps they would never reach the eyes of most history enthusiasts.

VOLUME I : Contains the accounts of three prominent men : Alexander Mossolov, Felix Youssoupoff and Pavel Bykov.

VOLUME II : Contains the accounts of three prominent women : Princess Radziwill, Lily Dehn and Anna Vyrubova.

Ebook   ISBN: 978-1-80517-077-8
Paperback   ISBN: 978-1-80517-078-5 (cream paper, matt cover)
Hardback   ISBN: 978-1-80517-079-2 (groundwood paper with dust jacket)
Hardback   ISBN: 979-8-85917-452-3 (cream paper, gloss cover)

VOLUME I – BOOK INFORMATION

<u>Word Count</u>

Introduction:	5,396
Book I:	73,482
Book II:	48,935
Book III:	40,061
Afterword	1,585
List of names	3,112
Total word count:	172,571

Comparisons: Ulysses   (265, 222)
               Pride and Prejudice (122,685)

<u>Volume I editions</u>

Ebook   ISBN: 978-1-80517-048-8
Paperback ISBN: 978-1-80517-049-5 (cream paper, matt cover)
Hardback   ISBN: 978-1-80517-076-1 (groundwood paper with dust jacket)
Hardback   ISBN: 979-8-86152-292-8 (cream paper, gloss cover)

www.ingramcontent.com/pod-product-compliance
Lightning Source LLC
Chambersburg PA
CBHW031052080526
44587CB00011B/660